First World War

and Army of Occupation

War Diary

France, Belgium and Germany

17 DIVISION
50 Infantry Brigade
Prince of Wales's Own (West Yorkshire Regiment)
10th Battalion
1 August 1915 - 22 April 1919

WO95/2004/1

The Naval & Military Press Ltd
www.nmarchive.com
Published in association with The National Archives

Published by

The Naval & Military Press Ltd

Unit 10 Ridgewood Industrial Park,
Uckfield, East Sussex,
TN22 5QE England
Tel: +44 (0) 1825 749494

www.naval-military-press.com
www.nmarchive.com

Contents

Document type	Place/Title	Date From	Date To
Heading	WO95/2004 10 W Yorks Regt. Jul 1915-Apr 1919 17 Div-50 Inf Bde		
Heading	17th Division 50th Infy Bde 10th Bn West Yorks Regt Jly 1915-Apr 1919		
Miscellaneous	??		
Miscellaneous	10th Battalion The West Yorkshire Regiment	13/07/1915	13/07/1915
Heading	50th Inf. Bde. 17th Div. 10th Battn. The West Yorkshire Regiment. August 1915		
War Diary	10th Battalion The West Yorkshire Regiment	01/08/1915	31/08/1915
Heading	50th Inf. Bde. 17th Div. 10th Battn. The West Yorkshire Regiment. September 1915		
War Diary	10th Battn. The West Yorkshire Regiment	01/09/1915	30/09/1915
Heading	50th Inf. Bde. 17th Div. 10th Battn. The West Yorkshire Regiment. October 1915		
War Diary	10th Battalion The West Yorkshire Regiment	01/10/1915	31/10/1915
Heading	50th Inf. Bde. 17th Div. 10th Battn. The West Yorkshire Regiment. November 1915		
War Diary	10th Battalion The West Yorkshire Regiment	01/11/1915	30/11/1915
Heading	50th Inf. Bde. 17th Div. 10th Battn. The West Yorkshire Regiment. December 1915		
War Diary	10th Battalion The West Yorkshire Regiment	01/12/1915	31/12/1915
Heading	10th W Yorks Jan 1916 50 Inf Bde		
War Diary		01/01/1916	31/01/1916
War Diary		21/01/1916	29/01/1916
War Diary	Oosthoek	01/03/1916	05/03/1916
War Diary	H 27 b Central Reninghelst	06/03/1916	09/03/1916
War Diary	Scottish Wood	10/03/1916	11/03/1916
War Diary	J Camp	12/03/1916	13/03/1916
War Diary	Strazeele	14/03/1916	31/03/1916
War Diary	Trenches	01/04/1916	06/04/1916
War Diary	Armentieres	07/04/1916	30/04/1916
War Diary		01/05/1916	31/05/1916
War Diary	Bayenghem	01/06/1916	11/06/1916
War Diary	Bussy	12/06/1916	14/06/1916
War Diary	Bois De Tailles	15/06/1916	20/06/1916
War Diary	Mericourt	21/06/1916	22/06/1916
War Diary	Heilly	23/06/1916	27/06/1916
War Diary	Trenches	28/06/1918	30/06/1918
Heading	50th Inf. Bde. 17th Div. War Diary 10th Battn. The West Yorkshire Regiment. July 1916		
Heading	War Diary 10th West Yorks Regt. July 1916 Vol 7		
War Diary	O.A.S.	01/07/1916	31/07/1916
Miscellaneous	Attach Orders by Lt. Col D. Dickson Comdg 10th West Yorkshire Regt. Appendix A	27/06/1916	27/06/1916
Heading	50th Brigade. 17th Division.1/10th Battalion West Yorkshire Regiment August 1916		
Heading	10th West Yorks. R. Vol 8		
War Diary	On Service	01/08/1916	31/08/1916
Heading	10th West Yorks R. Sept-Nov. 1916 Vol XI		
Heading	10th West Yorks Regt. Dec 1916 Vol 9		

War Diary	Hebuterne	01/09/1916	05/09/1916
War Diary	Sailly	06/09/1916	08/09/1916
War Diary	Hebuterne	01/09/1916	05/09/1916
War Diary	Sailly	06/09/1916	11/09/1916
War Diary	Hebuterne	12/09/1916	14/09/1916
War Diary	Sailly	08/09/1916	11/09/1916
War Diary	Hebuterne	12/09/1916	15/09/1916
War Diary	Bayencourt	16/09/1916	19/09/1916
War Diary	Barley	20/09/1916	20/09/1916
War Diary	Maizicourt	21/09/1916	21/09/1916
War Diary	Caours	22/09/1916	22/09/1916
War Diary	Hebuterne	14/09/1916	15/09/1916
War Diary	Bayencourt	16/09/1916	19/09/1916
War Diary	Barley	20/09/1916	20/09/1916
War Diary	Maizicourt	21/09/1916	21/09/1916
War Diary	Caours	22/09/1916	30/09/1916
War Diary	Caours	23/09/1916	30/09/1916
Heading	War Diary of 101 West Yorkshire Regt. For October-1916 Vol 10		
War Diary	Caours	01/10/1916	06/10/1916
War Diary	Conteville	07/10/1916	07/10/1916
War Diary	Frohen Le Grand	08/10/1916	10/10/1916
War Diary	Halloy	11/10/1916	13/10/1916
War Diary	Caours	01/10/1916	06/10/1916
War Diary	Conteville	07/10/1916	07/10/1916
War Diary	Frohen Le Grand	08/10/1916	10/10/1916
War Diary	Halloy	11/10/1916	20/10/1916
War Diary	Halloy	13/10/1916	20/10/1916
War Diary	Talmas	21/10/1916	21/10/1916
War Diary	Franvillers	22/10/1916	22/10/1916
War Diary	Meaulte	23/10/1916	27/10/1916
War Diary	Mansel Camp	28/10/1916	29/10/1916
War Diary	Talmas	21/10/1916	21/10/1916
War Diary	Franvillers	22/10/1916	22/10/1916
War Diary	Meaulte	23/10/1916	27/10/1916
War Diary	Mansel Camp	28/10/1916	29/10/1916
War Diary	Trenches	29/10/1916	31/10/1916
Map	XIV Corps Situation Map		
Operation(al) Order(s)	10th West Yorkshire Regt. Operation Order No. 19	05/10/1916	05/10/1916
Operation(al) Order(s)	10th West Yorkshire Regt. Operation Order No. 20	06/10/1916	06/10/1916
Operation(al) Order(s)	10th West Yorkshire Regiment. Operation Order No. 21	07/10/1916	07/10/1916
Operation(al) Order(s)	10th West Yorkshire Regiment. Operation Order No. 24	19/10/1916	19/10/1916
Operation(al) Order(s)	10th West Yorkshire Regt. Operation Order No. 22	09/10/1916	09/10/1916
Operation(al) Order(s)	10th West Yorkshire Regiment. Operation Order No. 28	26/10/1916	26/10/1916
Miscellaneous Miscellaneous	10th West Yorkshire Regiment. After Order.	21/10/1916	21/10/1916
Operation(al) Order(s)	10th West Yorkshire Regiment Operation Order No. 26	21/10/1916	21/10/1916
Operation(al) Order(s)	10th West Yorkshire Regiment. Operation Order No. 25	20/10/1916	20/10/1916
Miscellaneous	10th West Yorkshire Regiment. After Order	19/10/1916	19/10/1916
War Diary	Les Boeufs. Trenches	01/11/1916	02/11/1916
War Diary	Mansel Camp	03/11/1916	05/11/1916
War Diary	Les Boeufs. Trenches	01/11/1916	02/11/1916
War Diary	Mansel Camp	03/11/1916	05/11/1916
War Diary	Montauban	06/11/1916	06/11/1916
War Diary	Les Boeufs. Trenches	07/11/1916	09/11/1916
War Diary	Montauban	06/11/1916	06/11/1916

War Diary	Les Boeufs Trenches	07/11/1916	10/11/1916
War Diary	Montauben	11/11/1916	11/11/1916
War Diary	Sand Pits Camp Nr Meaulte	12/11/1916	12/11/1916
War Diary	Lamps-En Amienois	13/11/1916	13/11/1916
War Diary	Montauben	11/11/1916	11/11/1916
War Diary	Sand Pits Camp Nr Meaulte	12/11/1916	12/11/1916
War Diary	Camps-En-Amienois	13/11/1916	24/11/1916
War Diary	Camps-En-Amienois	14/11/1916	30/11/1916
War Diary	Camps-En-Amienois	25/11/1916	30/11/1916
Operation(al) Order(s)	10th West Yorkshire Regiment Operation Order No. 29	05/11/1916	05/11/1916
Operation(al) Order(s)	10th West Yorkshire Regiment Operation Order No. 30	12/11/1916	12/11/1916
Operation(al) Order(s)	10th West Yorkshire Regiment Operation Order No. 31	13/11/1916	13/11/1916
Heading	War Diary For The Month of December 1916 For 10th West Yorkshire Regiment. Vol 12		
War Diary	Camps En Amienois	01/12/1916	12/12/1916
War Diary	Camps En Amienois And Longpre-Les Corps	13/12/1916	13/12/1916
War Diary	Longfre-Les Corps And Ville Ville	14/12/1916	21/12/1916
War Diary	Camps-En Amienois And Longpre-Les Corps	13/12/1916	13/12/1916
War Diary	Longfre-Les Corps And Ville Ville	14/12/1916	21/12/1916
War Diary	Ville And Guillemont	22/12/1916	22/12/1916
War Diary	Guillemont And Les Boeufs Trenches	23/12/1916	23/12/1916
War Diary	Les Boeufs Trenches	24/12/1916	25/12/1916
War Diary	Ville And Guillemont	22/12/1916	22/12/1916
War Diary	Guillemont And Les Boeufs Trenches	23/12/1916	23/12/1916
War Diary	Les Boeufs Trenches	24/12/1916	25/12/1916
War Diary	Camp N 22 Carnoy	26/12/1916	27/12/1916
War Diary	Carnoy And Guillemont	28/12/1916	28/12/1916
War Diary	Les Boeufs Trenches	29/12/1916	29/12/1916
War Diary	Les Boeufs Trenches	25/12/1916	25/12/1916
War Diary	Camp No 22 Carnoy	26/12/1916	27/12/1916
War Diary	Carnoy And Guillemont	28/12/1916	28/12/1916
War Diary	Les Boeufs Trenches	29/12/1916	31/12/1916
Miscellaneous	50 Infantry Brigade	03/12/1916	03/12/1916
Operation(al) Order(s)	10th West Yorkshire Regt. Operation Orders No. 32	12/12/1916	12/12/1916
Operation(al) Order(s)	Operation Orders No 33	13/12/1916	13/12/1916
Operation(al) Order(s)	10th West Yorkshire Regt. Operation Order No. 34	21/12/1916	21/12/1916
Operation(al) Order(s)	10th West Yorkshire Regt. Operation Order No. 35	27/12/1916	27/12/1916
Operation(al) Order(s)	10th West Yorkshire Regt. Operation Order No. 36	28/12/1916	28/12/1916
Heading	10th W. York Jan 1917		
Heading	War Diary For January 1917 of 10th West Yorkshire Regiment		
Miscellaneous	50th Inf. Brigade	01/02/1917	01/02/1917
War Diary	No 22 Carnoy	01/01/1917	03/01/1917
War Diary	Carnoy And Guillemont	04/01/1917	04/01/1917
War Diary	Guillemont And Trenches	05/01/1917	05/01/1917
War Diary	Trenches	05/01/1917	06/01/1917
War Diary	Trenches And Carnoy	07/01/1917	07/01/1917
War Diary	Carnoy	08/01/1917	09/01/1917
War Diary	Guillemont And Carnoy	10/01/1917	10/01/1917
War Diary	Guillemont	11/01/1917	11/01/1917
War Diary	Guillemont And Trenches	12/01/1917	12/01/1917
War Diary	Trenches	13/01/1917	14/01/1917
War Diary	Trenches And Carnoy	14/01/1917	14/01/1917
War Diary	Carnoy And Corbie	15/01/1917	15/01/1917
War Diary	Corbie	16/01/1917	26/01/1917
War Diary	Combles And Corbie	26/01/1917	26/01/1917

War Diary	Combles	27/01/1917	27/01/1917
War Diary	Combles And Trenches	28/01/1917	28/01/1917
War Diary	Trenches	29/01/1917	29/01/1917
War Diary	Trenches And Bronfay Farm Camp	30/01/1917	31/01/1917
Operation(al) Order(s)	10th West Yorkshire Regt. Operation Orders. No. 38	03/01/1917	03/01/1917
Operation(al) Order(s)	10th West Yorkshire Regt. Operation Orders. No. 39	05/01/1917	05/01/1917
Miscellaneous	Operation Order	06/01/1917	06/01/1917
Operation(al) Order(s)	10th West Yorkshire Regt. Operation Order No. 40	09/01/1917	09/01/1917
Operation(al) Order(s)	Operation Order No. 41 by Major P.R. Simner D.S.O. Commanding 10th Week Yorkshire Regt	12/01/1917	12/01/1917
Operation(al) Order(s)	Operation Order No 42 by Major P.R. Simner D.S.O. Commanding 10th Bn West Yorkshire Rgt	13/01/1917	13/01/1917
Operation(al) Order(s)	Operation Order No. 42 by Major P.R. Simner D.S.O. Commanding 10th West Yorkshire Regt	14/01/1917	14/01/1917
Operation(al) Order(s)	10th West Yorkshire Regt. Operation Order No. 43	25/01/1917	25/01/1917
Operation(al) Order(s)	10th West Yorkshire Regt. Operation Order No. 44	28/01/1917	28/01/1917
Operation(al) Order(s)	10th West Yorkshire Regt. Operation Order No. 45	30/01/1917	30/01/1917
Heading	War Diary For February 1917 10th (S) Bn West Yorkshire Regt. Vol 14		
Miscellaneous	10th West Yorks Vol II		
War Diary	Bronfay And Combles	01/02/1917	01/02/1917
War Diary	Combles	02/02/1917	02/02/1917
War Diary	Combles And Trenches	03/02/1917	03/02/1917
War Diary	Trenches	04/02/1917	04/02/1917
War Diary	Trenches And Bronfay	05/02/1917	05/02/1917
War Diary	Bronfay And Combles	06/02/1917	07/02/1917
War Diary	Bronfay And Combles	01/02/1917	01/02/1917
War Diary	Combles	02/02/1917	02/02/1917
War Diary	Combles And Trenches	03/02/1917	03/02/1917
War Diary	Trenches	04/02/1917	04/02/1917
War Diary	Trenches And Bronfay	05/02/1917	05/02/1917
War Diary	Bronfay And Combles	06/02/1917	10/02/1917
War Diary	Trenches	10/02/1917	10/02/1917
War Diary	Trenches And Combles	11/02/1917	11/02/1917
War Diary	Combles And Bronfay	12/02/1917	13/02/1917
War Diary	Bronfay And Combles	14/02/1917	17/02/1917
War Diary	Trenches And Combles	11/02/1917	11/02/1917
War Diary	Combles And Bronfay	12/02/1917	13/02/1917
War Diary	Bronfay And Combles	14/02/1917	17/02/1917
War Diary	Combles	17/02/1917	17/02/1917
War Diary	Combles And Bronfay	18/02/1917	18/02/1917
War Diary	Bronfay And Meaulte	19/02/1917	19/02/1917
War Diary	Meaulte	20/02/1917	28/02/1917
War Diary	Combles	17/02/1917	17/02/1917
War Diary	Combles And Bronfay	18/02/1917	18/02/1917
War Diary	Bronfay And Meaulte	19/02/1917	19/02/1917
War Diary	Meaulte	20/02/1917	28/02/1917
Operation(al) Order(s)	After Order to Operation Order No 47	05/02/1917	05/02/1917
Operation(al) Order(s)	Operation Order No 51 by Lt Col P.R. Simner D.S.O. Commanding 10th Bn West Yorkshire Rgt	18/02/1917	18/02/1917
Operation(al) Order(s)	10th West Yorkshire Regt. Operation Order No. 52	19/02/1917	19/02/1917
Miscellaneous	To		
Operation(al) Order(s)	10th West Yorkshire Regt Operation Orders No 45	31/01/1917	31/01/1917
Operation(al) Order(s)	Operation Order No 50 by Lt Col. P.R. Simner. D.S.O. Commanding 10th Bn West Yorkshire Regt	16/02/1917	16/02/1917
Operation(al) Order(s)	10th West Yorkshire Regt Operation Order No 49	11/02/1917	11/02/1917

Operation(al) Order(s)	Operation Order No 47. by Lt. Col P.R. Simner D S O Commanding 10th Bn West Yorkshire Rgt	14/02/1917	14/02/1917
Operation(al) Order(s)	10th West Yorkshire Regt. Operation Order No. 46	03/02/1917	03/02/1917
Heading	War Diary 10th West Yorkshire Regiment March 1917		
War Diary	Meaulte And Warlov	01/03/1917	01/03/1917
War Diary	Warloy	02/03/1917	13/03/1917
War Diary	Warloy And Beauval	14/03/1917	14/03/1917
War Diary	Beauval And Bouquemaison	15/03/1917	15/03/1917
War Diary	Bouquemaison And Linzeux	16/03/1917	16/03/1917
War Diary	Linzeux	17/03/1917	22/03/1917
War Diary	Linzeux And Ivergny	23/03/1917	23/03/1917
War Diary	Ivergny	24/03/1917	31/03/1917
Operation(al) Order(s)	10th West Yorkshire Regt. Operation Order No. 54	13/03/1917	13/03/1917
Operation(al) Order(s)	10th West Yorkshire Regt. Operation Order No. 55	14/03/1917	14/03/1917
Operation(al) Order(s)	10th West Yorkshire Regt. Operation Order No. 56	15/03/1917	15/03/1917
Operation(al) Order(s)	10th West Yorkshire Regt. Operation Order No. 57	23/03/1917	23/03/1917
Heading	War Diary For April 1917 10th West Yorkshire Regt. Vol 16		
War Diary	Ivergny	01/04/1917	04/04/1917
War Diary	Ivergny And Magnicourt Sur Canche	05/04/1917	06/04/1917
War Diary	Magnicourt Sur Canche And Manin	07/04/1917	07/04/1917
War Diary	Manin And Agnez	08/04/1917	08/04/1917
War Diary	Agnez	09/04/1917	09/04/1917
War Diary	Arras	10/04/1917	11/04/1917
War Diary	Ref Map 51 B.N.W.	11/04/1917	11/04/1917
War Diary	Ref Map Sheet 51 B. H.36 a. C.D. and N.b.	12/04/1917	12/04/1917
War Diary	H.36 A.C.D. And N.G.B.	12/04/1917	12/04/1917
War Diary	H.31 C 29 H 31 B 64	12/04/1917	14/04/1917
War Diary	Arras Caves	15/04/1917	18/04/1917
War Diary	Railway Triangle Brown Line	19/04/1917	19/04/1917
War Diary	Brown Line	19/04/1917	22/04/1917
War Diary	Arras	23/04/1917	23/04/1917
War Diary	H 36.29	23/04/1917	24/04/1917
War Diary	Arras	25/04/1917	25/04/1917
War Diary	Sombrin	26/04/1917	30/04/1917
Heading	War Diary May 1917 10th (S) Bn. P.W.O. (The West Yorkshire) Regiment Vol 17		
War Diary	Sombrin	01/05/1917	02/05/1917
War Diary	Arras	03/05/1917	04/05/1917
War Diary	Y Huts	05/05/1917	09/05/1917
War Diary	St Nicholas	10/05/1917	27/05/1917
War Diary	St Nicholas And Halloy	28/05/1917	28/05/1917
War Diary	Halloy	29/05/1917	31/05/1917
Heading	War Diary June 1917 10th West Yorkshire Regt. Vol 18		
War Diary	Halloy	01/06/1917	18/06/1917
War Diary	Halloy And Arras	19/06/1917	19/06/1917
War Diary	St Nicholas Camp And Trenches	20/06/1917	21/06/1917
War Diary	Trenches	22/06/1917	24/06/1917
War Diary	Black Line	24/06/1917	28/06/1917
War Diary	Black Line And St Nicholas Camp	29/06/1917	30/06/1917
Heading	War Diary July 1917 10th West Yorkshire Regt. Vol 19		
War Diary	St. Nicholas	01/07/1917	07/07/1917
War Diary	St Nicholas And Trenches	07/07/1917	07/07/1917
War Diary	Trenches	08/07/1917	19/07/1917
War Diary	Gavrelle Line	20/07/1917	23/07/1917
War Diary	Camp G. 10.c.y.9	23/07/1917	25/07/1917

War Diary	Lancaster Camp	25/07/1917	31/07/1917
Map	P.B. Wireless		
Miscellaneous	To Babe 6 Herewith War Diary For August 1918		
War Diary	Ref Map 51 N.W. 1/10,000	01/08/1917	04/08/1917
War Diary	Trench Map Attached ("A")	05/08/1917	15/08/1917
War Diary	Ref Map 51 BNW. 1/10,000	16/08/1917	25/08/1917
War Diary	Ref. Sketch Map Attached ("B")	25/08/1917	31/08/1917
Map	Map For War Diary		
Operation(al) Order(s)	West Yorkshire Regt. Operation Order No. 3	18/08/1918	18/08/1918
Operation(al) Order(s)	Operation Order No. 4 West Yorkshire Regt	20/08/1918	20/08/1918
War Diary	Ref Maps 51B.N.W. Trench Sketch Map Attached	01/09/1917	24/09/1917
War Diary	Ref. Map Lens. 11.	25/09/1917	12/10/1917
War Diary	Schaap Balie 1/10,000	13/10/1917	16/10/1917
War Diary	Hazebrouck 5A	17/10/1917	31/10/1917
Miscellaneous			
Map	B C H I		
War Diary	Recques	01/11/1917	07/11/1917
War Diary	Bridge Camp	08/11/1917	13/11/1917
War Diary	Line	14/11/1917	14/11/1917
War Diary	Huddlestone Camp	15/11/1917	16/11/1917
War Diary	Line	17/11/1917	20/11/1917
War Diary	Dublin Camp	20/11/1917	24/11/1917
War Diary	Bridge Camp	25/11/1917	30/11/1917
War Diary	Elverdinghe	01/12/1917	01/12/1917
War Diary	Langemark No 1 Area	01/12/1917	08/12/1917
War Diary	Recques	08/12/1917	10/12/1917
War Diary	Zudrove	11/12/1917	12/12/1917
War Diary	Beaulencourt	13/12/1917	13/12/1917
War Diary	Zudrove To Beaulencourt	13/12/1917	14/12/1917
War Diary	Beaulencourt	15/12/1917	21/12/1917
War Diary	Bertincourt	22/12/1917	23/12/1917
War Diary	Q.3. Central	24/12/1917	29/12/1917
War Diary	Line	29/12/1917	31/12/1917
War Diary	Line Relief	31/12/1917	31/12/1917
War Diary	Ref Map Moeuvres 1/20,000	01/01/1918	07/01/1918
War Diary	Ref Map 57c 1/40,000	07/01/1918	07/01/1918
War Diary	Ref Map Moeuvres 1/20,000	07/01/1918	07/01/1918
War Diary	Ref 57 1/40,000	08/01/1918	10/01/1918
War Diary	Ref Map Moeuvres 1/20,000	10/01/1918	31/01/1918
Map	K L		
Map	Sketch. Map. Showing Dispositions. of Hedge	21/01/1918	21/01/1918
Map	Left Bde. Dispositions.		
War Diary	Ref. Map Moeuvres 1/20,000	01/02/1918	12/02/1918
War Diary	Ref. Map. France Sheet 57c 1/4000	13/02/1918	18/02/1918
War Diary	Ref. Map Moeuvres 1/20000	18/02/1918	28/02/1918
Map	Sketch Map A		
Map	Right Bde. Dispositions.		
Map	AA Gun Positions		
Heading	50th Inf. Bde. 17th Div. 10th Battn. The West Yorkshire Regiment. March 1918		
Heading	10 West Yorks Vol 3 March 1918		
War Diary	K 21a London Trench	01/03/1918	01/03/1918
War Diary	Hebburn	02/03/1918	02/03/1918
War Diary	Alban Av. K15a4-8	09/03/1918	13/03/1918
War Diary	Lislochertr K 13d 8-3	14/03/1918	14/03/1918
War Diary	Alban Av K 15a 4-8	18/03/1918	22/03/1918

War Diary	Maxwell AU K 25 d 50-90	23/03/1918	23/03/1918
War Diary	O.20a	23/03/1918	23/03/1918
War Diary	Barastre	24/03/1918	24/03/1918
War Diary	Gueudecourt	24/03/1918	24/03/1918
War Diary	Eaucourt L'Abbaye	25/03/1918	26/03/1918
War Diary	Q 16a	26/03/1918	26/03/1918
War Diary	Senlis	27/03/1918	27/03/1918
War Diary	Hennencourt	26/03/1918	26/03/1918
War Diary	Senlis	26/03/1918	27/03/1918
War Diary	Bouzincourt	27/03/1918	28/03/1918
War Diary	W15d	29/03/1918	31/03/1918
War Diary	Hennencourt	31/03/1918	31/03/1918
Heading	17th Division, 50th Infantry Brigade. War Diary 10th Battalion The West Yorkshire Regiment April 1918		
War Diary	Hennencourt	01/04/1918	03/04/1918
War Diary	Pierregot	03/04/1918	03/04/1918
War Diary	Pernois	04/04/1918	05/04/1918
War Diary	Montrelet	06/04/1918	10/04/1918
War Diary	Raincheval	11/04/1918	12/04/1918
War Diary	Englebelmer	14/04/1918	17/04/1918
War Diary	Mesnil	19/04/1918	23/04/1918
War Diary	Forceville	23/04/1918	26/04/1918
War Diary	Englebelmer-Millencourt Line	26/04/1918	28/04/1918
War Diary	Mesnil	29/04/1918	04/05/1918
War Diary	Forceville	04/05/1918	07/05/1918
War Diary	Leal Villers	08/05/1918	08/05/1918
War Diary	Arqueves	09/05/1918	26/05/1918
War Diary	Acheux Wood	26/05/1918	26/05/1918
War Diary	Auchonvillers	26/05/1918	31/05/1918
Miscellaneous	Operation Order by Lt Col G.K. Butt. Commanding 'Hector' App. 1.	04/05/1918	04/05/1918
Miscellaneous			
Miscellaneous	Operation Order by Lt Col G.K. Butt, Comdg 10th West Yorkshire Regt. App. 2	07/05/1918	07/05/1918
Miscellaneous			
Operation(al) Order(s)	No. 10 Operation Order by Lt Col G.K. Butt. Commanding 10th West Yorkshire Regt. App.3	08/05/1918	08/05/1918
Miscellaneous	2/Lt L.W.S. Spencer I.O		
Operation(al) Order(s)	West Yorkshire Regt. Operation Order No. 14	24/06/1918	24/06/1918
Operation(al) Order(s)	West Yorkshire Regiment Operation Order No. 16 App 6		
Miscellaneous			
Operation(al) Order(s)	West Yorkshire Regiment No 17 Operation Order App. 7	31/05/1918	31/05/1918
Miscellaneous	2/Lt E Cotterill for War Diary		
Diagram etc	Dispositions-Hector	03/05/1918	03/05/1918
Miscellaneous	West Yorkshire Regiment No 17 Operation Order	31/05/1918	31/05/1918
War Diary	Mailly Maillet	01/06/1918	01/06/1918
War Diary	Purple System	02/06/1918	09/06/1918
War Diary	Advanced Forward Zone	10/06/1918	13/06/1918
War Diary	Purple System	14/06/1918	17/06/1918
War Diary	Advanced Forward Zone	18/06/1918	22/06/1918
War Diary	Acheux Wood	23/06/1918	24/06/1918
War Diary	Rubempre	25/06/1918	30/06/1918
Operation(al) Order(s)	Operation Order No. 23 West Yorkshire Regiment	24/06/1918	24/06/1918
Operation(al) Order(s)	Operation Order No. 18 West Yorkshire Regiment	09/06/1918	09/06/1918

Diagram etc	B Coy		
Operation(al) Order(s)	Operation Order No. 19 West Yorkshire Regiment	14/06/1918	14/06/1918
Operation(al) Order(s)	Operation Order No. 20 West Yorkshire Regiment	14/06/1918	14/06/1918
Operation(al) Order(s)	Operation Order No. 21 West Yorkshire Regiment	17/06/1918	17/06/1918
Operation(al) Order(s)	Operation Order No. 22 West Yorkshire Regt	22/06/1918	22/06/1918
Operation(al) Order(s)	Operation Order No. 34 West Yorkshire Regiment	27/06/1918	27/06/1918
Miscellaneous	2/Lt E Cotterill For War Diary		
War Diary	Rubempre	01/07/1918	10/07/1918
War Diary	H.Q. V 14 60.5 Ap. 57 D. S.E.	11/07/1918	13/07/1918
War Diary	Bn. H.Q. V14 B 0.5 (Ref Map 57. D.S.E)	14/07/1918	16/07/1918
War Diary	Bn. H.Q-V 12c 4.O (Ref. Map 57 D.S.E)	17/07/1918	20/07/1918
War Diary	Bn. H.Q. W 762.6 (Ref. Map 57 D.S.E)	21/07/1918	24/07/1918
War Diary	Bn. H.Q. W13a 3.6 (Ref. Map 57 D.S.E)	25/07/1918	27/07/1918
War Diary	Bn. H.Q. V12 C 4.0 (Ref. Map 57 D.S.E)	28/07/1916	31/07/1916
Operation(al) Order(s)	West Yorkshire Regt Operation Order No. 26	09/07/1918	09/07/1918
Operation(al) Order(s)	Gozu Operation Order No 27	16/07/1918	16/07/1918
Operation(al) Order(s)	Gozu Operation Order No. 28	20/07/1918	20/07/1918
Miscellaneous	2/Lt H.W. Ramsden		
Operation(al) Order(s)	Donu Operation Order No. 29	24/07/1918	24/07/1918
Operation(al) Order(s)	Donu Operation Order No. 30	27/07/1918	27/07/1918
Miscellaneous	War Diary		
Heading	50th Bde. 17th Div. 10th Battalion. West Yorkshire Regiment. August 1918		
War Diary	Bn. H.Q. V12 C 4.0 (Ref Map 57 D.S.E)	01/08/1918	06/08/1918
War Diary	Herissart	07/08/1918	08/08/1918
War Diary	Lois L'Abbaye Corbie	09/08/1918	12/08/1918
War Diary	Bn. H.Q. R 20 A 7.1 (Ref Map 62 DSE)	13/08/1918	15/08/1918
War Diary	Bn. H.Q. R20 a 1.7 (Ref Map 62 DSE)	16/08/1918	16/08/1918
War Diary	Aubigny	17/08/1918	18/08/1918
War Diary	Puchevillers	19/08/1918	20/08/1918
War Diary	Argoeuves	21/08/1918	21/08/1918
War Diary	Bn. H.Q. Q7d (Ref Map 57 D.S.E)	22/08/1918	22/08/1918
War Diary	Bn. H.Q. Q-76c (Ref Map 57 D.S.E)	23/08/1918	23/08/1918
War Diary	Bn. H.Q. Q16c (Ref Map 57 D.S.E)	23/08/1918	23/08/1918
War Diary	Bn. H.Q. R19c (Ref Map 57 D.S.E)	24/08/1918	24/08/1918
War Diary	Bn H.Q.-X 3 b.64 (Ref Map 57 D.S.E.)	25/08/1918	25/08/1918
War Diary	Bn. H.Q.-M 32d 1.2 (Ref Map 57 D.S.E)	26/08/1918	26/08/1918
War Diary	Bn. H.Q.-M 34a 5.6 (Ref Map 57 D.S.E)	27/08/1918	27/08/1918
War Diary	Bn. H.Q.-M 35d 9.8 (Ref Map 57 D.S.E)	28/08/1918	29/08/1918
War Diary	Martin Puich	30/08/1918	30/08/1918
War Diary	Bn. H.Q.-N 25 c 86 (Ref Map 57 D.S.E)	31/08/1918	31/08/1918
War Diary	Bn. H.Q.-N 25 c 8.6 (Ref Map 57 D.S.E)	01/09/1918	01/09/1918
War Diary	Bn. H.Q.-N 28 c 1.1 (Ref Map 57 D.S.E)	02/09/1918	02/09/1918
War Diary	Bn. H.Q.-O 203 N.W. (Ref Map 57 D.S.E)	03/09/1918	03/09/1918
War Diary	Bn. H.Q.-R 31c 8.8 (Ref Map 57 D.S.E)	04/09/1918	04/09/1918
War Diary	Bn. H.Q.-P2 6c 6.5 (Ref Map 57 D.S.E)	05/09/1918	05/09/1918
War Diary	Bn. H.Q.-O 29 65.3 (Ref Map 57 D.S.E)	06/09/1918	07/09/1918
War Diary	Bn. H.Q.-P34a (Ref Map 57 D.S.E)	08/09/1918	09/09/1918
War Diary	Bn. H.Q.-W 4a5.50 (Ref Map 57 D.S.E)	10/09/1918	11/09/1918
War Diary	Rocquigny	12/09/1918	16/09/1918
War Diary	Bn. H.Q.-W 30 6.0 (Ref Map 57 D.S.E)	17/09/1918	17/09/1918
War Diary	Bn. H.Q.-W10 64.7 (Ref Map 57 D.S.E)	18/09/1918	18/09/1918
War Diary	Bn. H.Q.-W 6d 6.2 (Ref Map 57 D.S.E)	19/09/1918	19/09/1918
War Diary	Bn. H.Q.-X 7 6.4.4 (Ref Map 57 D.S.E)	20/09/1918	21/09/1918
War Diary	Bn. H.Q. W9a 7.1 (Ref Map 57 D.S.E)	22/09/1918	23/09/1918
War Diary	Bn. H.Q.-W4a 6.7 (Ref Map 57 D.S.E)	24/09/1918	25/09/1918

War Diary	Le Mesnil-En Arrouaise	26/09/1918	30/09/1918
Operation(al) Order(s)	Operation Order No. 35 West Yorkshire Regt	25/09/1918	25/09/1918
Operation(al) Order(s)	Operation Order No. 34 West Yorkshire Regt	25/09/1918	25/09/1918
Heading	10th West Yorkshire Regt Vol 34		
War Diary	Le Mesnil-En-Arrouaise	01/10/1918	05/10/1918
War Diary	Gouzencourt	05/10/1918	12/10/1918
War Diary	Inchy Montigny	13/10/1918	13/10/1918
War Diary	Montigny	14/10/1918	15/10/1918
War Diary	Neuvilly Sector	16/10/1918	17/10/1918
War Diary	Inchy	17/10/1918	19/10/1918
War Diary	Neuvilly Sector	20/10/1918	20/10/1918
War Diary	Neuvilly	20/10/1918	22/10/1918
War Diary	Inchy	22/10/1918	23/10/1918
War Diary	Neuvilly	23/10/1918	26/10/1918
War Diary	Poix Du Nord	26/10/1918	29/10/1918
War Diary	Neuvilly	30/10/1918	31/10/1918
Miscellaneous	10th West Yorkshire R. Vol 35		
War Diary	Neuvilly	01/11/1918	02/11/1918
War Diary	Vendigies BHQ F7a 77 (57 B NE)	03/11/1918	04/11/1918
War Diary	BHQ S 22d 1.2	04/11/1918	04/11/1918
War Diary	BHQ S24a 00	04/11/1918	04/11/1918
War Diary	BHQ S24d 0.4	04/11/1918	04/11/1918
War Diary	BHQ Institot Forestier	04/11/1918	04/11/1918
War Diary	Institut Forestier	04/11/1918	05/11/1918
War Diary	Lociquignol BHQ S24d32	05/11/1918	07/11/1918
War Diary	Aymeries	07/11/1918	07/11/1918
War Diary	Bachant	08/11/1918	08/11/1918
War Diary	BHQ Y16d 20	08/11/1918	08/11/1918
War Diary	Limont Fontaine V26a 56	09/11/1918	10/11/1918
War Diary	Limont Fontaine	11/11/1918	11/11/1918
War Diary	Berlaimont	11/11/1918	12/11/1918
War Diary	Engle Fontaine	12/11/1918	13/11/1918
War Diary	Bertry BHQ P14b 37	13/11/1918	16/11/1918
War Diary	Bertry P14b 37 (57B)	17/11/1918	24/11/1918
War Diary	Bertry	25/11/1918	30/11/1918
War Diary		01/11/1918	26/11/1918
War Diary		11/11/1918	30/11/1918
War Diary		01/11/1918	24/11/1918
War Diary		11/11/1918	17/11/1918
War Diary	Bertry Sheet 57B	01/12/1918	06/12/1918
War Diary	Bertry 57B	07/12/1918	08/12/1918
War Diary	Masignieres Val 1/100,000	09/12/1918	09/12/1918
War Diary	Hermies Val 1/100,000	10/12/1918	10/12/1918
War Diary	Favrieul Lens 1/100,000	11/12/1918	11/12/1918
War Diary	Albert Lens 1/100,000	12/12/1918	12/12/1918
War Diary	Allonville Amiens 1/100,000	13/12/1918	13/12/1918
War Diary	Picquigny Amiens 1/100,000	14/12/1918	14/12/1918
War Diary	Merelessart And Citerne	14/12/1918	14/12/1918
War Diary	Dieppe 1/100,000	15/12/1918	15/12/1918
War Diary	BHQ At	16/12/1918	16/12/1918
War Diary	Merelessart	16/12/1918	23/12/1918
War Diary	Merelessarty Citerne	24/12/1918	31/12/1918
War Diary		04/12/1918	30/12/1918
War Diary	Merelessart And Citerne	01/01/1919	01/01/1919
War Diary	BHQ Ac Merelessart (Dieppe 1/100000)	02/01/1919	04/01/1919
War Diary	Merelessart And Citerne	04/01/1919	19/01/1919

War Diary	Merelessart	20/01/1919	26/02/1919
War Diary		17/02/1919	17/02/1919
War Diary	Merelessart Supply 1/100000	01/03/1919	07/03/1919
War Diary	Merelessart	08/03/1919	14/03/1919
War Diary	Merelessart	15/03/1919	29/03/1919
War Diary	Hangest (Amiens 17 1/100000)	29/03/1919	31/03/1919
War Diary		04/03/1919	31/03/1919
War Diary	Hangest-Sur-Somme (Amiens 18)	01/04/1919	03/04/1919
War Diary	Hangest	03/04/1919	18/04/1919
War Diary	Longpre	18/04/1919	18/04/1919
War Diary	Le Havre	19/04/1919	22/04/1919

WO95/2004

10 W Yorks Regt.

Jul 1915 - Apr 1919

WW 17 Div - 50 Inf Bde.

17TH DIVISION
50TH INFY BDE

10TH BN WEST YORKS REGT

JLY 1915 - APR 1919

10th Battalion The West Yorkshire Regiment.

July 1915. (13/31.7.15)

10th West Yorkshire Rgt

War Diary

July

13. 11.0pm arrived BOULOGNE
14 3.30pm left by Rly for LUMBRES - arr 10.0pm
15 4.0 am arr OUVE-WIRQUIN
18 7.30 a.m left for ARQUES - arr 12 noon
19 8.45 a.m left for STEENVOORDE arr 3.30 pm
22 8.0pm left for LA CLYTTE arr 3.0am 23/
24 8.0 am A Coy & MG left for trenches 6/ Sherwood Foresters
8.0pm (a) 2 platoon B Coy for J trenches
25 8.0pm (b) 2 " " " " " "
11.0pm 2 platoon B (a) returned
26. 8.0pm 9 & 10 Pl for J. trenches
11.0pm 5 & 6 " returned
1 casualty No 5 - Pte Hall.
27. 11.0pm 9 & 10 return
28 2.0am A Coy & MG returned
8.0pm 11 & 12 pl. to J. trenches
29. Pte Hall died of wounds.
There have been many complaints about leather equipment.
29/30 Heavy gun fire heard in direction of YPRES - rifle fire all along front

July

30 one man killed on working party.
<u>General note on Working parties</u>

(1) far more men than required
(2) no definite instructions from RE
(3) No warning as to dangerous spots.
(4) above casualty cd have been avoided if proper care had been taken by RE

31 nil.

S.H. Brokley Capt & adjt
for. Lt Col
Cmy 10 West York Rgt

50th Inf.Bde.
17th Div.

10th BATTN. THE WEST YORKSHIRE REGIMENT.

A U G U S T

1 9 1 5

10th Battalion The West Yorkshire Regiment.

August 1915

AUGUST

1 Bn moved to H16d11 preparatory to going to the trenches. 9.0pm, arr 1.0am 2/8.

2 2.30pm 8 off 8 sgts to HQ. HAC to look round trenches. (Q). 8.0pm march to relieve HAC.

AUGUST

3 2.0 am relief completed -
B - Q2
C - Q3
A } SCOTTISH WOOD.
D }
Lt Howe wounded in back.
4.30am situation calm wind SW mild
10.45 am Q2 shelled - RA replied shelling stopped
11.10 am mine exploded near Q2 by Bosches - Lt Maidlow wounded and 4 OR - parapet damaged - 2 Germans killed - sandbags 250 sent up to Q2 at once.
1.0pm All Bn Pioneers taken by Bde HQ
4.0pm All quiet ; fresh SW wind MB

4th 5.0am Situation quiet - Wind WSW.
5.15 pm Q2 & Q3 shelled aerial torpedoes and "whiz-bangs" - no casualties MB

5th Situation quiet all day long with gentle S.W wind. MB

6th Draft arrived at SCOTTISH WOOD. no smoke helmets - quiet all day long. wind WSW gentle.

7th Heavy firing by own guns about 2.0 am all quiet by 4.0 pm - having heard guns most of day. - wind SW gentle.

One officer withdrawn from trenches for bombing course - a practice which might well be discontinued JMB

8th All quiet during the day - wind WSW gentle. JMB

9th Heavy rifle fire for about 3 minutes from 2.30 am onwards - followed by heavy bombardment stopping 4.50 am - Germans replied about 3.20 am - no damage. - 1 casualty SCOTTISH WOOD - shrapnel knee. JMB

10th Situation very quiet - misty till 7.0 am - wind nil -
Tunnel under parapet of Q2 to listening post completed.
Very quiet all day long. JMB

11th Nothing to report all day - Situation very quiet - gentle W wind. JMB

12th Quiet all day - except for slight bombardment 11.0 am - in Q2 + Q3 no casualties JMB

13th Border Rgt relieved Q3 - Quiet all day - one casualty Q2 - Pte Godfrey killed by sniper JMB

14th 5.0 am relief Q3 completed
Quiet all day
10 pm Bn marched back to LA CLYTTE
all reliefs completed JMB

15th 2.30 am arr. LA CLYTTE
no casualties during relief
JMB

16th Bil - refitting & making up
deficiencies
JMB

17th Bombing - physical drill - route
march - snipers training
JMB

18th ditto

19th 1 off 30 OR told off for guard
at HQ of Div (17th) -
A Coy sent to SCOTTISH WOOD for
four days to give working parties
to RE
JMB

20th Ordered to move to RENINGHELST -
9.0 am order cancelled. -
JMB

21st Same as 18th
JMB

22nd Church parade - 2 off 129 OR
C Coy - working party for
RE at 8.0 am
JMB

23rd Bombing & sniping training – etc
Route marches
Arrival of draft 1 off 39 OR.

24th Bombing etc carried on –
Conference of C.O's at Bde HQ

25th Bombing training etc – German aeroplane over LA CLYTTE – apparent disinclination (or absence) of our air craft, which did not appear for ½ a hour or so.

26th O.C. Coys etc left for P trenches – Bn marched off by platoons to relieve 7 Border Regt. in P trenches and O5 & S8. – relief complete 11.20 a.m. – no hitch – HQ WILTSHIRE Fm – damnable place

27th L/Cpl Mainwaring. A – killed by sniper – visited trenches – in a good state generally – P3 a bad trench. v isolated & right in the air – discovered sap –, apparently

made by the Germans right up
to parapet of P3 - had it
blocked up.
2 men of "B" Coy hit -
Saw new Bn HQ - cd be made very
good - new roofs required and
2 more dug outs -
CO went to trenches 6.30 pm.
Very quiet most of day - BOIS CONFLUENT
Shelled about 11.30 am.

28th Very quiet all day - party
working on new Batt HQ.

29th Quiet all day - Lt Panir
rejoined - work on Bn HQ

30th Very quiet - disappearance of
two Bavarian & German flags -
probable relief of Germans night
29/30. -
Visits to trenches of Brigadier
(warning given) & DAG 5 Corps.
who went alone & without
escort - aroused some suspicion.
rumored visit of GOC 17 Div -
wash out -

Sniping post started in rear of
P4.
Allen starting defensive mining
scheme in P4's.

31st Quiet day and night

JH Berkley Capt

50th Inf.Bde.
17th Div.

10th BATTN. THE WEST YORKSHIRE REGIMENT.

S E P T E M B E R

1 9 1 5

10th Battalion The West Yorkshire Regiment.

September 1915

SEPTEMBER
1915

1st Very quiet morning but during the afternoon the Boche whizzbanged the BOIS CONFLUENT without causing any casualties

2nd Quiet day - relieved by the 7th YORK and Lancaster Rgt - marched back to ROSENHILL CAMP less C Coy who remained in SCOTTISH WOOD

3rd to 11th Batt in rest at ROSENHILL CAMP - inspected by G.O.C. II Army 8th ; same evening A Coy relieved C in SCOTTISH WOOD - C Coy coming to ROSENHILL camp. - A to Q3. on 9th.

11th (eve) C & D Coy firing line ; B Support A remaining [illegible] Q3. relieving 7th York & Lancaster Rgt.

12th Very quiet day - a great deal of work to be done in the trenches especially draining and repairing parapet.

13th BOIS CONFLUENT shelled in the morning and P2 whizzbanged during the afternoon - 2 casualties neither serious

14th very quiet all day long - no shelling or sniping

15th B Coy to SCOTTISH wood - relieved in support line by Coy of 52nd Bde. - very quiet day - A Coy from P3 to CONVENT SCHOOL at VOORMEZEELE.

16th HQ whizzbanged about 6.0pm - also RIDGE WOOD shelled; very quiet in front line -

17th P4b shelled with small HE during the morning - in reply our RA bombarded PICCADILLY FARM

18th during the evening about 5.30 pm about 10 trench mortars were fired into Pub and again at about 8.0 pm 8 more were sent over - no damage - replied with 8 rifle grenades after which all was quiet

19th very quiet - no shelling -

20th Artillery bombardment of enemy lines - reply about 4.0 pm on RIDGE WOOD and round GORDON FARM

21st very quiet - a machine gun turned onto P4 & P2a about 8.0 pm from MOUND - no casualties.

22nd nothing doing -.

23rd Our artillery bombarded the Boche support line - no

reply

24th vigorous shelling by our guns - straw etc taken up to trenches to set fire to, to bluff the 'Boche'.

25th rapid fire opened 4.30 am - straw not lit as wind was in the wrong direction - ; P1 shelled about 10.0 am - no damage done at all.

26th Quiet day - A relieved D - B, C, i/c to SCOTTISH WOOD and D to VOORMEZEELE -

27th Support trenches and the BOIS CONFLUENT shelled with small HE also GORDON FARM.

28th very quiet all day long.

29th P2 whizzbanged about noon; part of parapet blown in - repaired the same night; machine gun from MOUND again active about 7.0 pm.

30th very quiet day.

50th Inf.Bde.
17th Div.

10th BATTN. THE WEST YORKSHIRE REGIMENT.

O C T O B E R

1 9 1 5

10th Battalion The West Yorkshire Regiment.

October 1915

OCTOBER
1915

1st very quiet day. .. no shelling at all work done on new strip at DEAD DOG FARM

2nd another very quiet day.

3rd Pub heavily whizzbanged at about 5.15 pm - 120 odd shells over but no casualties

4th Relieved by the KOYLI. (14th Division) awful muddle and block in DICKEBUSCH - luckily no shelling - to ROZENHILL CAMP

5th Agr & one officer per coy to STEEN-VOORDE for billeting -
Batt left 6.0 pm via POPERINGHE arrived at 11.0 pm

6th — 10th — 21st Battalion in rest at STEENVOORDE bombing training and attack practices carried out, one Brigade fieldday and one Brigade route -

march – cy route marches daily

21st Batt marched to camp on OUDERDOM – VLAMERTINGHE road

22nd to 26th } To ramparts at YPRES – 2½ coys only D & ½ C left in camp – heavy shelling on 22nd Fatigues for Battalion nightly

26th (eve) to trenches A & B firing line D at HQ C at KRUISSTRAAT

27th Quiet day – four casualties from snipers – parapets very thin – and non existent in C.T.

28th C6 heavily crumped by 5·9's no casualties – C5 whizzbanged a lot of damage done to the parapets

29th Quiet day – a lot of work done on damaged parapet but all spoilt by violent rain

30th pouring rain all day; CT and CULVERT shelled; also HQ for about ½ an hour between 3 and 3.30 pm.

31st WING HOUSE bombarded – no casualties; raining again and very little work could be done. – FISH HOOK was repaired.

50th Inf.Bde.
17th Div.

10th BATTN. THE WEST YORKSHIRE REGIMENT.

N O V E M B E R

1 9 1 5

10th Battalion The West Yorkshire Regiment.

November 1915

WAR DIARY

NOVEMBER 1915

1st to 7th — Battalion to rest camp from trenches - relieved by the 6th Dorset Regt - remained in rest camp till evening of 7th inst -

7th (eve) — went up to YPRES RAMPARTS no shelling in town

8th (eve) — to HOOGE trenches - C & D in firing line. B at HQ and A at KRUISSTRAAT

9th — C4 & C6 whizzbanged in the morning - dump shelled at night - no casualties

10th — ½ B Coy removed from RS4 up to waist in water - sent to portions 1H & 1K

11th — C6 & C7 shelled with "MINNEWERFER" FISH HOOK entirely cut off and one man buried!

12th. Batt HQ very heavily shelled in morning
(eve) to YPRES RAMPARTS.

13th. }
to } YPRES Ramparts – fatigue parties of 400 men found for work.
16th. }

16th (eve) } to rest camp YORK HUTS – very muddy and dirty
to } 2 coys in tents, accommodation generally most
24th. (eve) } inadequate – daily fatigues of 300 – 50 men.

24th (eve) to trenches relieved the 9th Duke of Wellington's Regt 52nd Bde
A & B firing line C at HQ
D at KRUISSTRAAT

25th Quiet day – reports that the trenches were in a very bad state – fully confirmed on inspection.

26th very quiet day - heavy frost and consequent collapse of a part of C7

27th one "minnenwerfer" dropped near CRATER C5 and C4 & C4 whizzbanged during morning our trench mortars replied with effect

28th Our trench mortars again active "Boche" m.g. emplacement blown up - no retaliation

(eve) to camp DRAGON HUTS 5 motor busses went to meet the Batt at the
to ASYLUM for first time
30th since Batt joined the BEF

50th Inf.Bde.
17th Div.

10th BATTN. THE WEST YORKSHIRE REGIMENT.

D E C E M B E R

1 9 1 5

10th Battalion The West Yorkshire Regiment.

December 1915

WAR DIARY

DECEMBER

Dec 1st - 10th	Rest camp YORK HUTS - Camp in a filthy state knee deep in mud - 1 coy in tents.; QM stores and Transport about 1 mile away; daily fatigues of 200 - 300 men.
10th (evening)	To HOOGE Trenches - relieving 9th D of W Rgt 52nd Bde C. Coy. C4 - C5 D " C6 - FH - C7 A " C7S - CULVERT & HQ B " KRUISSTRAAT
11th	Very quiet all day long no shelling on our lines at all. - Fire trenches were in a very bad state - C5 - C6 especially -
12th	Violent shelling of ground between HQ and MENIN ROAD - no on front or support lines. -

ZILLEBEKE road also shelled –

13th Great artillery activity all day from 10.0 am to 3.0 pm. no casualties from shelling – Y WOOD heavily bombarded.

14th very quiet all day; relieved by 6th Dorset Regt this evening relief completed 7.45 pm – Breastwork – HALFWAY HOUSE to ZILLEBEKE RD – heavily "whizzbanged" 7-45 – 8.0 pm.

15th to 18th YPRES ramparts
night fatigues of 450 men working up on breastwork and front line – also carrying parties.

— | —

19th Left the Ramparts YPRES & marched by Companies to the YORK CAMP, BUSSEBOOM. Transport & Q.M. Stores about 1 mile away – very inconvenient.

20th Owing to a Gas Attack by Enemy on NE Sector of YPRES SALIENT we were ordered to "Stand to" at 6-10 A.M. "Standing to" all day.

21st Still standing to

22nd
23rd
24th } Still in the YORK CAMP for 2 nights furnished fatigues of 500 for work on Breastwork by BARDON FARM, first night severely shelled.

25th The Machine Gunners & Bombers relieved the 6th West Ridings in trenches.

26th Went back to the trenches & occupied C4. C5. C6. C7

& Fishhook, C7S, CULVERT.
HALFWAY HOUSE (HQ & ½ Coy)
& half Coy in FORTINS (IK & [illegible]H)
Casualties 1 killed 1 wounded.
Enemy quiet.

27th Casualties 2 Killed, 1 wounded

28th Vacated FORTINS & took over C3, C3S & F1.

29th Enemy bomb attack on C4 – greatly repulsed, Three Machine Guns returned to FORTINS & 4 machine guns & Battalion bombers to KRUISSTRAAT DUGOUTS.

30th C3 & C4 subjected to heavy bombardment by enemy artillery – Bomb bag & also blown in & a mine brought there but evacuated [illegible]. The Machine Gun of 7th YORK Rgt in C2 buried by shell & lost 2 killed & 2 wounded. Relieved by the 6th DORSETS. three Companies & HQ marched

to KRUISSTRAAT DUGOUTS & 1 Company to huts.

31st furnished 5 working parties in all 205 men

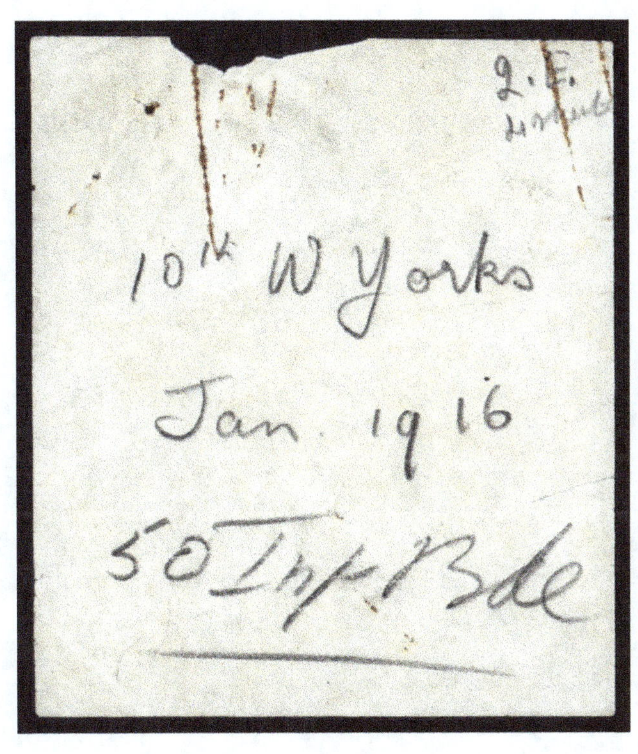
10th W Yorks
Jan 1916
50 Inf Bde

Jany 16

1916.

Jan 1st Still in the DUGOUTS at KRUISSTRAAT. Furnished another 5 working parties

2nd Furnished 1 working party

3rd Do Do

4th Do Do

5th Heavy shelling by enemy near DUGOUTS. The Battalion arranged for Night & relieved by the QUEENS of the 24th Division

6th Left Night at 7.15 am & entrained at B[illegible]ENTINY for AUDRUICQ - arrived at AUDRUICQ & marched to billeting area at RUMINGHEM 7 pm.

7th Rest in Billets

8th Light work.

9th Church Service

10th Training Commences. Bay drill, Handling of arms &c. Early morning physical parade

11th Do Do

Working on site for rifle range & bomb throwing trench

13th } Training Continues — work
14th } commenced on bomb
15th } throwing trench

16th Church Services

17th Preparatory for inspection by Army Commander

18th March past the Army Commander at NORDAUSQUES

19th

Jan[y] 19th Company training, construction of bombing practice trench.

20th General training. Completion of Bombing Practice Trench Construction of Rifle Range

21st General Training Construction of Rifle Range. Defeated R.E. 3-2 in Divnl Football.

22nd. General Training. Construction of Rifle Range

23rd Divine Service

24th. General Training. Inspection by G.O.C. 17th Divn.

25th. General Training

26th ——"——

27th General Training. Musketry Practices commenced

28th. Musketry.

29th. General Training. Lecture to Officers by G.S.O. 1 9th Division

30th Divine Service

31st. Divisional Field Day.

[illegible] Lt. Col.

Commdg 10th W. Yks Reg[t]

1.2.16

Instructions regarding War Diaries and Intelligence Summaries are contained in F. S. Regs., Part II. and the Staff Manual respectively. Title Pages will be prepared in manuscript.

WAR DIARY
or
~~INTELLIGENCE SUMMARY~~
(Erase heading not required.)

Army Form C. 2118

Place	Date	Hour	Summary of Events and Information	Remarks and references to Appendices
	21		Artillery played havoc with BLUFF 1 Coy 6th Dorsets attached for duty. Continued hard work by all ranks	
	22	5. 0 p.m.	False Gas alarm.	
	23	3 am / 8 am	Small parties reconnoitred ground to be covered in case of possible retirement.	
	24	11 am	Alarm given & all ranks quickly occupied alarm posts.	
	25		Quiet day	
	26		Quiet until 5 p.m.	
		5-8 p.m.	Enemy bombard heavily C.T. Supports and SPOIL BANK few casualties	
	27		Very Quiet Day	
	28		Quiet day. Spoil Bank and Kingsway whizzbanged in the evening for two hours.	
	29	2.30-4.	Heavy shelling round SPOIL BANK. and C.T.s	

[illegible] Edwards Lt Col.
Comndg 18th W. York. Regt.

1875 Wt. W593/826 1,000,000 4/15 J.B.C. & A. A.D.S.S./Forms/C. 2118.

10th. W. York. Regt

Instructions regarding War Diaries and Intelligence Summaries are contained in F. S. Regs., Part II. and the Staff Manual respectively. Title Pages will be prepared in manuscript.

WAR DIARY
~~or~~
~~INTELLIGENCE SUMMARY~~

(Erase heading not required.)

Army Form C. 2118

March 1916

Place	Date	Hour	Summary of Events and Information	Remarks and references to Appendices
OOSTHOEK	1	5.10pm	Preliminary bombardment of BLUFF by our artillery. Feint attack by troops in our sector	
"	2	4.30am	Attack on BLUFF. Lost trenches retaken and also enemy trenches captured.	
		All day	Heavy artillery retaliation by enemy. V28 demolished. SPOIL BANK practically demolished. About 120 casualties	
"	3		Quiet day snowing all night.	
"	4		~~Relieved~~ Quiet day. Damaged trenches being repaired.	
"	5	10.0pm	Relieved by 10th L.F. and proceeded to camp H27b. central	
H27b. central	6		Proceeded to J camp RENINGHELST.	
RENINGHELST	7. 8.		General cleaning up, bathing and re-equipping.	
	9.		Hdqrs and "B & D" Coys relieve 9th D. of Wellingtons in SCOTTISH WOOD	
			A Coy attd. 7th E. York at SPOIL BANK. C Coy attd. 6th Dorsets at VOURMEZEELE	
Scottish Wood	10		Quiet day.	
	11.	9.0pm	Battn relieved by 8th E York and proceeded to J camp.	
J Camp	12	9am.	Advance party proceed to STRAZEELE	
	13	8.0am	Battn with rest of 50th Bde march to STRAZEELE to rest camp	
Strazeele	14		General rest.	
"	15		Company training and general re-equipping	
"	16		General training and bathing	
"	17		General training	
"	18	11 am	Inspection and Speech by IInd Corps Commander.	
	19		Divine Service	

1875 Wt. W593/826 1,000,000 4/15 J.B.C. & A. A.D.S.S./Forms/C. 2118.

Page II

Instructions regarding War Diaries and Intelligence Summaries are contained in F. S. Regs., Part II. and the Staff Manual respectively. Title Pages will be prepared in manuscript.

WAR DIARY

~~or~~

~~INTELLIGENCE SUMMARY~~

(Erase heading not required.)

Army Form C. 2118

Place	Date	Hour	Summary of Events and Information	Remarks and references to Appendices
Strazeele	20.	9.30am	Presentation of Awards for Gallantry and inspection by C O	
	21.	8 am	Battn. moves to LA CRECHE	
	22	6 am.	Battn. moves to ARMENTIERES. In billets	
	23.	6am.	Battn. moves to HOUPLINES, takes over from 7th BORDER and remain as Brigade Reserve to 52nd Bde.	
	24		Guards + R E fatigues all day + night	
	25.		" Big draft. (90) joins Battn.	
	26.		Guards and fatigues Officers reconnoitre front trenches.	
	27		" "	
	28		"	
	29.		Advance parties proceed to take over from 10th. L.F. Battn. relieves 10th L.F. as Right Battn of Left Section. Draft of 50 + 1 offr. joins battn.	
	30.		Quiet Day. Very little shelling	
	31.		Quiet Day.	

[illegible]

Lt. Colonel

Comdg. 10th. W. York R.

1875 ... 26 1,000,000 4/15 J.B.C. & A. A.D.S.S./Forms/C. 2118.

10th W. York R

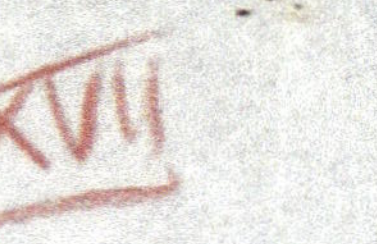

Instructions regarding War Diaries and Intelligence Summaries are contained in F. S. Regs., Part II. and the Staff Manual respectively. Title Pages will be prepared in manuscript.

WAR DIARY
or
INTELLIGENCE SUMMARY
(Erase heading not required.)

XVII

Army Form C. 2118

10 W Yorks Vol. 4

Place	Date April	Hour	Summary of Events and Information	Remarks and references to Appendices
Trenches	1		General Work and Repairs. Quiet Day	
	2.	morning	76 & 77 whizzbanged Slight Casualties	
	3	morning	Willow Walk shelled slightly Capt Henderson and few O R wounded.	
			76 & 77 Again shelled	
	4.	morning	76 & 77 Heavily Shelled. Our snipers very active	
	5.		Quiet Day	
	6	noon	74s shelled slightly Capt. Berkley 2nd Lt Rudd and one O.R. wounded.	
		evening	Relieved by 10th L F and proceeded to billets	
Armentieres	7		General Cleaning up	
	8		Capt. Berkley died. Bathing and General Training	
	9	morning	Divine Service	
	10.		General Training and Fatigues	
	11		General Training. Two companies Route Marching.	
	12		General Training. Fatigues. Two Companies Route Marching	
	13		General Training. Fatigues	
	14		Advance Parties proceed to trenches	
			Relieve 10th L F. in Left Sector 73 – 77	
	15		Quiet day. Desultory shelling.	
	16		Quiet Day.	
	17		———	
	18		Corps Commander Visits Front Line and finds fault	
	19.		Fairly Quiet Day. Lt. Buckmaster wounded by bullet.	5 E.

Page 2

Instructions regarding War Diaries and Intelligence Summaries are contained in F. S. Regs., Part II. and the Staff Manual respectively. Title Pages will be prepared in manuscript.

WAR DIARY
or
~~INTELLIGENCE SUMMARY~~
(Erase heading not required.)

Army Form C. 2118

Place	Date	Hour	Summary of Events and Information	Remarks and references to Appendices
	20	morning	Heavy bombardment of front line by enemy artillery & Minenwerfer. Good number of casualties. Retaliation nil	
		night	Enemy whizz bangs working parties & trenches all through the night at will	
	21.	4 pm	Slight retaliation by our artillery for previous day.	
	22.	noon.	Our 6 in. shell BRUNE RUE & trenches near. Fairly successful.	
		night	Relieved by 10th L7 & proceeded to permanent billets	
	23.	morning	Divine Service	
	24.		General Training & Fatigues	
	25		Fatigues. Two Coys bathing. General Training especially in wiring.	
	26	afternoon	Bombardment by both sides. 150 men inoculated	
		evening.	Working Parties cancelled. Battn stands by	
	27.	morning.	Normal arrangements. Quiet Day. General Training. Fatigues as usual,	
	28		Fatigues, General Training and Bathing.	
	29.		Fatigues for whole Battn owing to 7th York being inoculated	
	30.		Relieve 10th L.7. in the trenches	

[signature] Edwards Lt Col
Comdg 10th W. York R

1875 Wt. W593/826 1,000,000 4/15 J.B.C. & A. A.D.S.S./Forms/C. 2118.

10 W Yorks

Army Form C. 2118

Vol 5

Instructions regarding War Diaries and Intelligence Summaries are contained in F. S. Regs., Part II. and the Staff Manual respectively. Title Pages will be prepared in manuscript.

WAR DIARY
or
~~INTELLIGENCE SUMMARY~~

(Erase heading not required.)

Place	Date	Hour	Summary of Events and Information	Remarks and references to Appendices
	May 1st		Quiet day after relief. 3 casualties due to snipers	
	2nd		L'Epinette heavily shelled in the morning with 105 + 77s. Retaliation poor. Wiring parties out at night and good work done. One man of covering party hit + carried in by L/Cpl F Dean.	
	3rd		Very quiet day indeed.	
	4th		Fairly quiet day. Capt. V.E Reynolds killed.	
	5th		Heavy shelling from 6.0 a.m to 8 a.m. 6.0 pm to 8 30 p.m. intense bombardment of L'Epinette. Many casualties 2LT SHAW wounded. C.S.M Ovenden killed.	
	6th		Quiet day	
	7th		Quiet day. 2LT MARSDEN discovered 20 bombs 2 knobkerries and 2 canisters for the destruction of Sapheads laid out beyond HOUSE 6. Probably a trench raid frustrated by D Coys patrol which was out on night of 5th as soon as shelling ceased.	
	8th		Quiet day. Relieved by 10 L.F. Relief complete 11.15 p.m.	
	9th		Day of rest and general cleaning up.	
	10th		General Training and wiring drill.	
	11th		Preparations made for moving down for 'Intensive training'.	
	12th		Left ARMENTIERES at 10.15 p.m having handed over to 1st W.I.R. Arrived at Estaires 2.35 am Billet comfortable but scattered	
	13th		Left ESTAIRES at 12.30 p.m and marched to MORBECQUE and HAZEBROUCK. The day was very hot and not good for marching. Billets good.	
	14th		Marched from MORBECQUE to CAMPAGNE, left at 9.30 a.m and arrived at 12.30 p.m. Billets very good indeed. 32 men fell out. This is disgraceful.	
	15th		Marched from CAMPAGNE to BAYENGHEM-LES-EPERLECQUES 35 men sent on by train from ARQUES. The billets are very good indeed. Very compact and very comfortable.	6 E. 2 sheets

1875 Wt. W593/826 1,000,000 4/15 J.B.C. & A. A.D.S.S./Forms/C. 2118.

Instructions regarding War Diaries and Intelligence Summaries are contained in F. S. Regs., Part II. and the Staff Manual respectively. Title Pages will be prepared in manuscript.

WAR DIARY

or

~~INTELLIGENCE SUMMARY~~

(Erase heading not required.)

Army Form C. 2118

Place	Date	Hour	Summary of Events and Information	Remarks and references to Appendices
	16th		Complete rest and cleaning	
	17th		Company Training on Area. Two subalterns arrive.	
	18th		Coy Training. A + B Coys night operations. Capt RYAN + two subalterns arrive.	
	19th		Coy Training C + D Coys night operations	
	20th		Battn. Training in morning. Afterwards Coy training. 2LT H. MARSDEN awarded MILITARY CROSS + SGT P DUFFY MILITARY MEDAL	
	21st		Sunday a rest day. Arrival of very bad draft of 21 Bantams	
	22nd		Battn Training. Coys on range + bombing in afternoon.	
	23rd		Battn Training. Coys on range + bombing in afternoon.	
	24th		Brigade Training comprising of march to TILQUES and attack back on hill 90. Battn in reserve. On whole well done. 4 new subalterns arrive.	
	25th		Battn. Training and Bombing	
	26th		Battn Training and Bombing.	
	27th		Battn Inoculation.	
	28th		Rest after inoculation. Most of men really bad	
	29th		Company Training as far as possible. Men still suffering from inoculation.	
	30th		Kit inspection in morning. Afternoon Divnl Field Day from 2.30 p m until 10.15 p m. Medical Inspection of "Bantam" Draft.	
	31st		Lecture on 'Defensive Gas' by 17th Divnl Gas Officer + Coy training.	

J. Shaw [illegible] Adjt
for O.C. 10th W YORK R

1875 Wt. W593/826 1,000,000 4/15 J.B.C. & A. A.D.S.S./Forms/C. 2118.

10th W York R

Instructions regarding War Diaries and Intelligence Summaries are contained in F. S. Regs., Part II. and the Staff Manual respectively. Title Pages will be prepared in manuscript.

WAR DIARY

~~or~~

~~INTELLIGENCE SUMMARY~~

(Erase heading not required.)

Army Form C. 2118

Place	June Date	Hour	Summary of Events and Information	Remarks and references to Appendices
Bayenghem	1		Bde Route March 13 miles.	
"	2		Company Training. Intensive Digging	
"	3		Bn Operations (training)	
	4		Divine Service	
	5		Bde Field Operations	
	6		Training.	
	6	7.30am	Inspection by G.O.C. 17th Divn.	
	7		Bn Field Operations.	
	8		Bn Route March	
			Night Operations.	
	9		Coy Training. Intensive Digging.	
	10		"	
	11		Bn marches to St Omer & entrains.	
Bussy	12		Bn arrives from St Omer.	
"	13		Bn Resting.	
	14		Marched to Bois de Tailles.	
Bois de Tailles	15		Bn resting	
	16		General Fatigues	
	17		}	
"	18		} General Fatigues.	
	19		}	

1875 Wt. W593/826 1,000,000 4/15 J.B.C. & A. A.D.S.S./Forms/C. 2118.

2

Instructions regarding War Diaries and Intelligence Summaries are contained in F. S. Regs., Part II. and the Staff Manual respectively. Title Pages will be prepared in manuscript.

WAR DIARY
~~or~~
~~INTELLIGENCE SUMMARY~~
(Erase heading not required.)

XV4

Army Form C. 2118

10W Yorks
Vol 6
June

Place	Date	Hour	Summary of Events and Information	Remarks and references to Appendices
	20		Bn marched to Henencourt	
Henencourt	21		Bn General cleaning up	
	22		Bn marched to Heilly	
Heilly	23		General Fatigues & cleaning up	
"	24		"	
"	25		Inspection by G.O.C. 17th Divn.	
	26		Bn marched to Ville	
	27		moved to trenches. Bn Hdqrs at Happy Valley.	
Trenches	28		Two companies withdrawn to Bécordel.	
———	29			
———	30.		Bn moved to Battle Positions.	

A.A. Ross Lt. Colonel
Comdg 10th W. York R.

1875 Wt. W593/826 1,000,000 4/15 J.B.C. & A. A.D.S.S./Forms/C. 2118.

50th Inf.Bde.
17th Div.

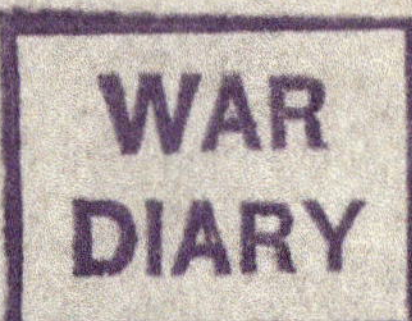

10th

16th BATTN. THE WEST YORKSHIRE REGIMENT.

J U L Y

1 9 1 6

Attached:

Appendix "A".

Confidential

50/17

July

Vol 7

WAR DIARY

10th WEST YORKS REGT

JULY 1916

Instructions regarding War Diaries and Intelligence Summaries are contained in F. S. Regs., Part II. and the Staff Manual respectively. Title Pages will be prepared in manuscript.

Army Form C. 2118

WAR DIARY
or
INTELLIGENCE SUMMARY
(Erase heading not required.)

Place	Date	Hour	Summary of Events and Information	Remarks and references to Appendices
O.A.S.	1st July		At 7 30 AM the Battn took part in the grand assault. The objective being as in the attached orders. On the right were the 7th Divn & on the left the 21st Divn. The Battn assaulted in 4 lines. 2 lines got through the German position to the 4th line & were cut-off, the attack on our left having failed. Casualties were very heavy chiefly ~~owing~~ caused by machine guns which enfiladed our left flank & were so deadly that the 3rd & 4th lines failed to get across "no-mans-land". 22 officer casualties including Lt Col Dixon Cmdg & Major J Knott 2nd in command (Both killed & approximately 750 O.R. The Battn was then withdrawn to ~~the~~ VILLE	attacked orders by Lt Col A Dixon appendix A
	2nd		The Battn marched to HEILLY Lt Col H A ROSS was appointed to command & assumed duty this day	

Instructions regarding War Diaries and Intelligence Summaries are contained in F. S. Regs., Part II. and the Staff Manual respectively. Title Pages will be prepared in manuscript.

WAR DIARY
or
INTELLIGENCE SUMMARY
(Erase heading not required.)

Army Form C. 2118

Place	Date	Hour	Summary of Events and Information	Remarks and references to Appendices
	8th		MEAULTE the Battn strength 211 all ranks marched to Fricourt & were employed on carrying duties under the orders of the 17th Div	
	9th		Fricourt The Battn was employed as on 8th casualties 1 officer 2Lt Bacon + 5 O R wounded	
	10th		Fricourt The Battn employed as on the 9th returning to MEAULTE to billets during the night-	
	11th		Battn marched to GROVETOWN & entrained to SALEUX thence by motor lorries to CAMPS-EN-AMENOIS for divisional rest & refit. Arrived in billets 1.15 AM on the 12th	
	12th		CAMPS-EN-AMENOIS. The Battn rested Lieut Osborne	

1875 Wt. W593/826 1,000,000 4/15 J.B.C. & A. A.D.S.S./Forms/C. 2118.

Instructions regarding War Diaries and Intelligence Summaries are contained in F. S. Regs., Part II. and the Staff Manual respectively. Title Pages will be prepared in manuscript.

WAR DIARY
or
INTELLIGENCE SUMMARY
(Erase heading not required.)

Army Form C. 2118

Place	Date	Hour	Summary of Events and Information	Remarks and references to Appendices
			arrived as Special transport officer to the Battn	
	13th		CAMPS-EN-AMENOIS. General refitting of the Battn Specialists concentrated training. Good billets & training area. General Pilcher CB payed the Battn farewell	
	14th		CAMPS-EN-AMENOIS General instruction & refitting	
	15th		Bde marched to BELLANCOURT 16½ miles to new billets. No man in Battn fell out on march	
	16th		BELLANCOURT. Devine service. Specialists at cocentrated training. Officers & N.C.Os at Special instruction	
	17th		BELLANCOURT. Battle training Capt RL WIND 2nd West Yorkshire Regmt posted as	

Instructions regarding War Diaries and Intelligence Summaries are contained in F. S. Regs., Part II. and the Staff Manual respectively. Title Pages will be prepared in manuscript.

WAR DIARY
or
INTELLIGENCE SUMMARY
(Erase heading not required.)

Army Form C. 2118

Place	Date	Hour	Summary of Events and Information	Remarks and references to Appendices
			2nd in Command arrived also 2 other officers.	
	18th		BELLANCOURT Battle training Draft of 206 OR arrived	
	19th		" " ~~Draft of 31 officers~~	
	20th		" " " Draft of 3 officers arrived	
	21st		" " " G.O.C. 50th Bde inspected the Battn at Battle training Draft of 5 officers arrived	
	22nd		The division ~~was~~ ordered to proceed to the Front. The Battn marched 12 miles to CONDE & went ~~goes~~ into billets there	
	23rd		Battn " 3½ " " HANGEST & entrained there with the Bde	
	24th		The Battn dis-entrained at MERICOURT & marched to a place NE of DERNANCOURT nr ALBERT 1 officer arrived.	

1875 Wt. W593/826 1,000,000 4/15 J.B.C. & A. A.D.S.S./Forms/C. 2118.

Army Form C. 2118

WAR DIARY
or
INTELLIGENCE SUMMARY
(Erase heading not required.)

Instructions regarding War Diaries and Intelligence Summaries are contained in F. S. Regs., Part II. and the Staff Manual respectively. Title Pages will be prepared in manuscript.

Place	Date	Hour	Summary of Events and Information	Remarks and references to Appendices
	25th		NR DERNANCOURT. Batt spent day in putting up fivonacs	
	26th		MAJOR ROSS handed over Bn to Major G.H. SOAMES 2/Lt W.J HARTNOLL took over adjutancy from Lt E J SMITH who was posted 2/in Command of B coy Bn was still Dernancourt	
	27th		Nr DERNANCOURT. Ceremonial parade + distribution of medals by the divisional commander for the corps Commander for deeds of bravery done during the attack ~~[illegible]~~ 2* officers arrived	*See app Sgt Taylor 11416 Sgt Lister Sgt Slyfield 11666 Pte Greaves 18576 awarded but not on parade Cpl Fallon [illegible] Olivey
	28th		Parades as usual 7-8, 10-12, 2,4 Battn still at DERNANCOURT 1 officer arrived	
	29th		DERNANCOURT. Same as yesterday	
	30th		DERNANCOURT Devine service for all demoninations	

1875 Wt. W593/826 1,000,000 4/15 J.B.C. & A. A.D.S.S./Forms/C. 2118.

Army Form C. 2118

Instructions regarding War Diaries and Intelligence Summaries are contained in F. S. Regs., Part II. and the Staff Manual respectively. Title Pages will be prepared in manuscript.

WAR DIARY
or
INTELLIGENCE SUMMARY
(Erase heading not required.)

Place	Date	Hour	Summary of Events and Information	Remarks and references to Appendices
	31st		DERNANCOURT. Same work as on 29th 1 officer arrived.	
			[signature] Lt Col Cmdg	
			10th WEST YORKSHIRE REGMT	

1875 Wt. W593/826 1,000,000 4/15 J.B.C. & A. A.D.S.S./Forms/C. 2118.

Attack Orders by

Lt. Col. A. Dickson

Comdg. 10th West Yorkshire Regt

Appendix A

GENERAL INSTRUCTIONS – 2nd PHASE

1. For the 2nd Phase of the Attack a new Zero hour will be fixed. This will be at least 3 hours after the original Zero. At the second Zero the 7th Yorkshire Regt. will assault on a front from the WING CORNER to South side of German Tambour, in conjunction with the 22nd. Brigade on the right, with the following objectives.–

(1) Of clearing up to the Eastern edge of FRICOURT Village from WELL LANE to COTTAGE Trench and COTTAGE Trench to WILLOW AVENUE, there joining with the 22nd Brigade.

On reaching this objective the Battalion will reorganize with the object of

(2) Clearing FRICOURT Wood as far as WILLOW Trench and the track leading N.E. to X 28. C. 8. 0. as soon as the Barrage on the West part of FRICOURT Wood lifts (i.e. <u>2nd Zero + 15 minutes</u> from S.W. edge of wood and <u>2nd Zero + 1 hour 45 minutes</u> from a parallel line 150 yds back from edge of wood)

2. The 10th West Yorkshire Regt. will co-operate with the 7th Yorkshire Regt. against both objectives.

3. The boundary between the two Battalions will be:

(1) Through FRICOURT Village:–

The line of trench running from the Junction of HARE LANE and RED TRENCH to WELL LANE at F. 3. 6. Central

(2) Through FRICOURT Wood:–

Roughly the line of clearing running N.E. through the middle of the Wood.

4. Assuming that the Battalion has gained its first objective with little difficulty the dispositions for co-operating with the 7th Yorkshire Regt. will be as follows:

at Zero

Battalion bombers will work down all trenches towards the German TAMBOUR & HARE LANE until in touch with clearing parties of the 7th Yorkshire Regt.

Bombing & Clearing parties already in trenches leading towards FRICOURT will similarly work up those trenches as the 7th Yorkshires advance progresses.

A Coy will concentrate on its right, leaving one Platoon in support of the Bombing parties at the German TAMBOUR and getting in touch with the 7th Yorkshire Regt, conform to their advance as far as junction of WELL LANE and Trench at F. 3. b. 5. 4 clearing all trenches and houses en route.

Here the Company will be reorganized with a view to forming the supporting Company for the attack on FRICOURT Wood.

D Coy. will move up to the line vacated by A Coy. and will dump stores there awaiting further orders, and relieving the platoon of A Coy. which will rejoin its own Company.

C Coy. as soon as A Coy. has cleared its front will reorganize behind A Coy. & will pass through it to form the right front Company of the attack on FRICOURT Wood.

Right flank in touch with 7th Yorkshire Regt., on roughly North edge of clearing in Wood centre of track running N.N.E. from WILLOW Trench. Frontage 100 yards, and to include BOSKY TRENCH running S.W. from WILLOW Trench.

B Coy. will close on C. Coy and prolong the line but Echeloned 50 yards back, & across the remainder of FRICOURT Wood with its left following the northern edge of the wood. On reaching objective one Platoon will hold N.E. edge of Wood, remainder in Support.

A Coy. will follow in Support to both of the leading Companies at 200 yards distance.

D Coy. will be moved up to the RED COTTAGE – Sunken Road position, leaving one platoon watching the approaches from the German TAMBOOR.

On arrival at objective B & C Coys. will consolidate the position. B Coy. occupying a Stong Point which should be in course of preparation on the N. edge of the wood

A. Coy. will prepare a second line 200 yards in rear and arrange for fire from Lewis guns along the track to WILLOW Trench and the clearing in the Wood.

(Sd) [illegible]
Lt & Adjt
1st West York Regt.

50th Brigade.

17th Division.

----- ----

1/10th BATTALION

WEST YORKSHIRE REGIMENT

AUGUST 1 9 1 6

10TH WEST YORKS. R.

Instructions regarding War Diaries and Intelligence Summaries are contained in F. S. Regs., Part II. and the Staff Manual respectively. Title pages will be prepared in manuscript.

WAR DIARY
or
~~INTELLIGENCE SUMMARY~~.
(Erase heading not required.)

Army Form C. 2118.

10/WEST YORKSHIRE REGT.

Place	Date	Hour	Summary of Events and Information	Remarks and references to Appendices
			BIVOUAC DERNANCOURT	
On Service	1/8/16		Training as usual. 14 reinforcements (OR) arrived from Etaples	
	2/8/16		We parade 6-35 AM & march about 3 miles to BELLE VUE farm (Nr Albert). We are given ground on the South side of the farm for camping on. We make bivouacs. During the afternoon we hear Albert (½ a mile away) being shelled. We are in Divisional Reserve.	
	3/8/16		The Coy Officers & 2nd in Command go off at 6:30 to visit the scene of the 1st of July battle at Fricourt they return about 8. The Battn parades at 2 p.m to march to the battle ground to make the attack again in the way that in the light of recent experiences would have been best. This was frustrated owing to men practicing bombing being on the ground between the trenches.	
	4/8/16		We receive orders to move into Div. Reserve. One Officer from each Coy, also Adjt and 1 N.C.O from each Coy, also one from Bombers & Signallers, parade at 10 to march to POMMIERS REDOUBT to take over from the Sherwood Foresters (51st Brigade). We arrived to find that the Sherwood Foresters are in POMMIERS trench. We leave the N.C.O's to take over & get back to the Battn. The Battn parades at 7 and marches via HALT to the new position leaving FRICOURT and MAMETZ to our left. We take over trenches. H.Q.R.S. is on the left of Battn then D.B.A with the Signallers and "C" Coy and Bombers behind. There was a good deal of shelling during the night and a few shells fell fairly close to the trenches in which we were situated.	
	5/8/16		We received orders to move and take up a position in close reserve. The first platoon paraded and moved off at 8.15 P.M, remainder following by platoons at 200 paces between platoons. Route roughly 750 yds up the POMMIERS REDOUBT – MONTAUBAN Road, then to the left across MONTAUBAN ALLEY to quarry at 22 C.o.5.	

T2134. Wt. W708—776. 500000. 4/15. Sir J. C. & S.

Instructions regarding War Diaries and Intelligence Summaries are contained in F. S. Regs., Part II. and the Staff Manual respectively. Title pages will be prepared in manuscript.

Army Form C. 2118.

WAR DIARY
or
~~INTELLIGENCE SUMMARY~~.
(*Erase heading not required.*)

Place	Date	Hour	Summary of Events and Information	Remarks and references to Appendices
On Service	5/8/16		There the Platoons picked up guides and marched to their destinations. H.Q was in an old German dugout, D Coy on the left, then 'A' Coy in front, 'C' Coy and behind 'B'. The position was on the right of BAZANTIN LE GRAND and on the left of LONGUEVAL. Battn H.Q. being roughly at S 16 b 1.4. Slight shelling of our trenches by the enemy occurred at about 8 p.m. but with no material damage.	
	6/8/16		Situation in trenches normal. Enemy Artillery fairly active all day, but shells mostly fell on dead ground in rear of trenches. Casualties 5	
	7/8/16		Fairly quiet day. Shelling & M.G. fire reported by C Coy. Received orders to move up to front line but these orders were cancelled in consideration of Artillery operations. It was published in D.R.Os of today's date that Capt D W Hunter R.A.M.C. was awarded the D.S.O. and Lieut Stower and C.S.M. Green had been awarded Military Crosses. Battn employed salvaging and improving communication trenches. Heavy bombardment by our Artillery started about 4 p.m. and continued for 2½ hours. After a lull it reopened again and reached it's zenith towards midnight. ~~[illegible]~~.	
	8/8/16		British bombardment from 4 AM to 6 AM. Fatigue parties provided for R.E. engaged in improving trenches. New communication trench dug to GREEN DUMP and trench for cable started. In the evening communication trench from right corner of 'C' Coys trench to PEAR ST. This communication trench is named WEST STREET in compliment to the Battns work complimented by G.O.C. DIV.	
	9/8/16		WEST ST completed by C & D Coy. The Battn was relieved at about 9 p.m. by the 7th Yorks Regt and marched to POMMIERS REDOUBT leaving D Coy behind to finish WEST STREET.	
	10/8/16		D Coy arrived at POMMIERS REDOUBT at 6.15 a.m. Brigade work at BEETLE ALLEY commenced under R.E.O	

Army Form C. 2118.

Instructions regarding War Diaries and Intelligence Summaries are contained in F. S. Regs., Part II. and the Staff Manual respectively. Title pages will be prepared in manuscript.

WAR DIARY
or
~~INTELLIGENCE SUMMARY~~.
(Erase heading not required.)

Place	Date	Hour	Summary of Events and Information	Remarks and references to Appendices
On Service	11/8/16		Work on BEETLE ALLEY continued until 5 pm. Battn was relieved at 8·30 p m by 7th K.R.Rs and proceeded to BELLE VUE FARM relief being complete by 11·40 p.m	
	12/8/16		The Battn marched to DERNANCOURT arriving about 8 p.m.	
	13/8/16		Sunday. Church Parade & Bathing Parades.	
	14/8/16		Transport move in advance of Battn. Morning Coy parades. Afternoon Coy Bathing Parades.	
	15/8/16.		Battn leaves DERNANCOURT at 1·30 a.m. and marches to MERICOURT, arriving at 3·50 A.M. Entrain at 5·55 a m arriving at CONDAS 11·15 A.M. March to LE MEILLARD arriving at 2·30 p.m.	
	16/8/16		March to BONNIERES arriving 5·45 p.m.	
	17/8/16		Leave BONNIERES and march to HALLOY (approx. 15 mls) arriving 3·20 pm. 23 fell out. Reinforcements one Officer & 89 other ranks arrived.	
	18/8/16		Battn left HALLOY at 12 noon and marched to SOUASTRE (8 miles) arriving 3 p.m. rested in huts until 7 pm 7·15 pm Battn marched by platoons at intervals of 100 yds to SAILLY-AU-BOIS. The last platoon reaching its billet by 9·50 pm. Reinforcements 53 OR arrive.	
	19/8/16		In Brigade reserve at SAILLY. Two other ranks wounded by shell fire toward mid-day. D Coy relieve one Coy of 1st London Scottish at the KEEP, HEBUTERNE, at 6·15 pm.	
	20/8/16		Battn relieved 1st London Scottish in trenches at HEBUTERNE. One Coy in billets in HEBUTERNE.	

T2134. Wt. W708—776. 500000. 4/15. Sir J. C. & S.

Instructions regarding War Diaries and Intelligence Summaries are contained in F. S. Regs., Part II. and the Staff Manual respectively. Title pages will be prepared in manuscript.

WAR DIARY
or
~~INTELLIGENCE SUMMARY.~~
(Erase heading not required.)

Army Form C. 2118.

Place	Date	Hour	Summary of Events and Information	Remarks and references to Appendices
On Service	21/8/16		Fairly quiet day, slight shelling of HEBUTERNE work commenced in Wood and Napier St. German Officer belonging to a Patrol captured at the head of Welcome St. K11 C23 in advance post, the remainder of patrol escaped	
	22/8/16		Fairly quiet day. Slight shelling of S4Y and HEBUTERNE continuation of trench improvements carried out.	
	23/8/16		Occasional shelling of trenches. Trench repairing continued, A new sap commenced at W.S.H8 Casualties one OR.	
	24/8/16		Patrols salvage a quantity of L.G ammunition working parties busy improving and repairing trenches. work on sap at NEW WELCOME STREET continued.	
	25/8/16		Sapping and trench repairing continued. Battn is relieved at 5 p.m by 6th Dorsets and march to Billets in BAYENCOURT.	
	26/8/16		General cleaning up throughout the Battn.	
	27/8/16		Sunday. Church Parades. Battn is in Div. reserve	
	28/8/16		Coy. training. Capt. S.B.E. CUTLER taken on strength from 17-8-16 and 2/Lt. W.A. MARSH taken on Strength from this date. Intelligence Section of One Officer and six men formed.	
	29/8/16		Battn Coy drill	
	30/8/16		Coy drill. CAPT. A.F.G. ANDERSON assumes the duties of Adjutant from 28/8/16. 2nd Lieut F.W. BANNER taken on Strength from 29/8/16	
	31/8/16		Battn relieved 6th Dorsets in trenches at HEBUTERNE relief being complete by 3 p.m.	

[signature] Lieut Col.
Commdg 10th West Yorkshire Regiment.

T2134. Wt. W708—776. 500000. 4/15. Sir J. C. & S.

12 E.
19 sheets

Vol XI

10th WEST YORKS R.

Sept – Nov. 1916

10.E.
10 sheets

Confidential

Vol 9

10th West Yorks Regt.

Dec 1916

Instructions regarding War Diaries and Intelligence Summaries are contained in F. S. Regs., Part II. and the Staff Manual respectively. Title pages will be prepared in manuscript.

WAR DIARY
or
INTELLIGENCE SUMMARY.
(*Erase heading not required.*)

Army Form C. 2118.

Place	Date	Hour	Summary of Events and Information	Remarks and references to Appendices
	1916.		Map ref. HEBUTERNE. 57D N.E. EDITION 2C $\frac{1}{10,000}$	
HEBUTERNE.	Sept 1		Situation very quiet. Nothing of importance to record.	
"	" 2		Situation remained quiet. Active patrolling of No man's land from midnight to dawn. Gas alert at night, but no gas reported on our front.	
"	3		Situation still quiet. Patrolling continued.	
"	4		Considerable shelling of HEBUTERNE with lachrymatory shells. Right Coy. front shelled in early part of night. Gas was reported to have been let off by the Division on our right, but was not noticed on our front. Casualties one O.R. killed two wounded. Patrolling continued.	
"	5		Very quiet during day, but considerable machine gun fire in HEBUTERNE at dusk. Gas was let off on Divisional front at 8-30 P.M, but was hardly noticeable on our front. The enemy did not retaliate very vigorously only a few shells falling near our lines. Two O.R. wounded.	
SAILLY	6		The Battalion were relieved in the trenches by the 6th Dorsets, relief being completed by 2-40 P.M and marched to SAILLY where they relieved the 7th East Yorkshire Regt in Brigade reserve.	
"	7		Quiet day in billets. Large working parties found at night for work in trenches under R.E. At 10 P.M the enemy shelled SAILLY fairly heavily for two or three minutes. Several shells falling round the Battalion billets. No casualties	
"	8.		Every available man in the Battalion employed on working parties during the night.	

T2134. Wt. W708—776. 500000. 4/15. Sir J. C. & S.

Instructions regarding War Diaries and Intelligence Summaries are contained in F. S. Regs., Part II. and the Staff Manual respectively. Title Pages will be prepared in manuscript.

WAR DIARY
or
INTELLIGENCE SUMMARY
(Erase heading not required.)

Army Form C. 2118

Place	Date	Hour	Summary of Events and Information	Remarks and references to Appendices
	1916.		Map ref. HEBUTERNE. 57D N.E. EDITION 2c $\frac{1}{10,000}$	
HEBUTERNE	Sept 1		Situation very quiet. Nothing of importance to record.	
"	" 2		Situation remained quiet. Active patrolling of No man's land from midnight to dawn. Gas alert at night, but	
"			no gas reported on our front.	
"	3		Situation still quiet. Patrolling continued.	
"	4		Considerable shelling of HEBUTERNE with lachrymatory shells. Right Coy. front shelled in early part	
"			of night. Gas was reported to have been let off by the Division on our right, but was not noticed on	
"			our front. Casualties one O.R. killed two wounded. Patrolling continued.	
"	5		Very quiet during day, but considerable machine gun fire in HEBUTERNE at dusk. Gas was let off	
			on Divisional front at 8-30 P.M, but was hardly noticeable on our front. The enemy did not retaliate very	
"			vigorously only a few shells falling near our lines. Two O.R wounded.	
SAILLY.	6		The Battalion were relieved in the trenches by the 6th Dorsets, relief being completed by 2-40 P.M and	
"			marched to SAILLY where they relieved the 7th East Yorkshire Regt in Brigade reserve.	
"	7		Quiet day in billets. Large working parties found at night for work in trenches under R.E. At 10 P.M	
"			the enemy shelled SAILLY fairly heavily for two or three minutes. Several shells falling round the	
"			Battalion billets. No casualties.	
"	8.		Every available man in the Battalion employed on working parties during the night.	

1875 Wt. W593/826 1,000,000 4/15 J.B.C. & A. A.D.S.S./Forms/C. 2118.

Instructions regarding War Diaries and Intelligence Summaries are contained in F. S. Regs., Part II. and the Staff Manual respectively. Title pages will be prepared in manuscript.

WAR DIARY
or
INTELLIGENCE SUMMARY.
(Erase heading not required.)

Army Form C. 2118.

Place	Date	Hour	Summary of Events and Information	Remarks and references to Appendices
SAILLY	Sept 8		Two parties of 75 men each employed in re-excavating NEW WOOD STREET and NEW WOMAN STREET under Battalion arrangements, the remainder under R.E	
"	9		325 men supplied for working parties under R.E. Re excavation of NEW WOOD STREET and NEW WOMAN STREET continued by parties of 75 men on each trench	
"	10		300 men supplied for working parties under RE. Re excavation of NEW WOOD STREET and NEW WOMAN STREET continued by same parties.	
"	11		265 men supplied for working parties under R.E. Re excavation of NEW WOOD STREET and NEW WOMAN STREET continued by the same parties.	
HEBUTERNE	12		Relieved Dorsets in right sector of Brigade Front in the HEBUTERNE trenches. Dispositions were as follows:- 'C' Coy Right front, 'A' Coy. left front, 'D' Coy. CROSS St. 'B' Coy Reserve in HEBUTERNE. Patrols encountered none of the enemy. They ascertained that the enemy wire on either side of the BUCQUOY ROAD was very thick and deep and that the barricade across the road consisted of two knife rests firmly fixed and too close together to allow a man to pass through.	
"	13		Situation in trenches normal. Some slight shelling of trenches and HEBUTERNE during the day. Three patrols were sent out but encountered none of the enemy.	
"	14		Situation normal. At 8-15 AM hostile aircraft dropped 3 bombs, their intended target being	

Instructions regarding War Diaries and Intelligence Summaries are contained in F. S. Regs., Part II. and the Staff Manual respectively. Title Pages will be prepared in manuscript.

WAR DIARY *or* INTELLIGENCE SUMMARY

(Erase heading not required.)

Army Form C. 2118

Place	Date	Hour	Summary of Events and Information	Remarks and references to Appendices
SAILLY	Sept 8		Two parties of 75 men each employed in re-excavating NEW WOOD STREET and NEW WOMAN STREET under Battalion arrangements, the remainder under R.E	
"	9		325 men supplied for working parties under R.E. Re excavation of NEW WOOD STREET and NEW WOMAN STREET continued by parties of 75 men on each trench	
"	10		300 men supplied for working parties under R.E. Re excavation of NEW WOOD STREET and NEW WOMAN STREET continued by same parties.	
"	11		265 men supplied for working parties under R.E. Re excavation of NEW WOOD STREET and NEW WOMAN STREET continued by the same parties.	
HEBUTERNE	12		Relieved Dorsets in right sector of Brigade Front in the HEBUTERNE trenches. Dispositions were as follows:- 'C' Coy Right front, 'A' Coy. left front, 'D' Coy. CROSS St. 'B' Coy Reserve in HEBUTERNE. Patrols encountered none of the enemy. They ascertained that the enemy wire on either side of the BUEGROY ROAD was very thick and deep and that the barricade across the road consisted of two knife rests firmly fixed and too close together to allow a man to pass through.	
"	13		Situation in trenches normal. Some slight shelling of trenches and HEBUTERNE during the day. Three patrols were sent out but encountered none of the enemy.	
"	14		Situation normal. At 8-15 A.M hostile aircraft dropped 3 bombs, their intended target being	

1875 Wt. W593/826 1,000,000 4/15 J.B.C. & A. -A.D.S.S./Forms/C. 2118.

Instructions regarding War Diaries and Intelligence Summaries are contained in F. S. Regs., Part II. and the Staff Manual respectively. Title pages will be prepared in manuscript.

WAR DIARY
or
INTELLIGENCE SUMMARY.
(Erase heading not required.)

Army Form C. 2118.

Place	Date	Hour	Summary of Events and Information	Remarks and references to Appendices
HEBUTERNE	Sept 14		HEBUTERNE. No damage or casualties. 2nd Lieut COUCHMAN and 2 OR went out on patrol, and were neither seen no heard of again.	
"	15		Considerable shelling of trenches and of HEBUTERNE. Gas was discharged from the 2nd + 17th Divisional fronts, but was not noticable in our lines. Further extensive patrolling. None of the enemy encountered and no trace of 2nd Lieut COUCHMAN'S party.	
BAYENCOURT	16		Battn were relieved by the 8th South Staffordshire Regt at 8 P.M but remained at work until 11-30 P.M when Coys marched back to billets at BAYENCOURT.	
"	17		Battn marched to billets in HALLOY via SOUASTRE, HENU, PAS, and GRENAS. Approximately 10 miles. No men fell out. Refce. map $\frac{1}{100000}$ LENS	
"	18		Rest and general cleaning up. Very heavy rain.	
"	19		Practical attack on an entrenched position.	
BARLEY	20		Marched to BARLEY via DOULLENS and OCCOCHES distance approximately 12 miles. No men fell out. Reference map $\frac{1}{100000}$ LENS	
MAIZICOURT	21		Marched to MAIZICOURT via REMAISNIL, FROHEN-LE-GRAND, BEAUVOIR approximately 10 miles No men fell out. Reference map $\frac{1}{100000}$ LENS	
CAOURS	22		Marched to CAOURS via BERNATRE, HEIRMONT, ST RIQUIER. Distance 13 miles. Only one man fell out. Reference map $\frac{1}{100000}$ LENS + ABBEVILLE.	

T2134. Wt. W708—776. 500000. 4/15. Sir J. C. & S.

Army Form C. 2118

Instructions regarding War Diaries and Intelligence Summaries are contained in F. S. Regs., Part II. and the Staff Manual respectively. Title Pages will be prepared in manuscript.

WAR DIARY
or
INTELLIGENCE SUMMARY
(Erase heading not required.)

Place	Date	Hour	Summary of Events and Information	Remarks and references to Appendices
HEBUTERNE	Sept 14		HEBUTERNE. No damage or casualties. 2nd Lieut COUCHMAN and 2 OR went out on patrol, and were neither seen nor heard of again.	
"	15		Considerable shelling of trenches and of HEBUTERNE. Gas was discharged from the 2nd & 17th Divisional fronts, but was not noticable in our lines. Further extensive patrolling. None of the enemy encountered and no trace of 2nd Lieut COUCHMAN'S party.	
BAYENCOURT	16		Battn were relieved by the 8th South Staffordshire Regt at 8 P.M but remained at work until 11-30 P.M when Coys marched back to billets at BAYENCOURT.	
"	17		Battn marched to billets in HALLOY via SOUASTRE, HENU, PAS, and GRENAS. Approximately 10 miles. No men fell out. Refce map $\frac{1}{100000}$ LENS	
"	18		Rest and general cleaning up. Very heavy rain.	
"	19		Practical attack on an entrenched position.	
BARLEY.	20		Marched to BARLEY via DOULLENS and OCCOCHES distance approximately 12 miles. No men fell out Reference map $\frac{1}{100000}$ LENS	
MAIZICOURT	21		Marched to MAIZICOURT via REMAISNIL, FROHEN-LE-GRAND, BEAUVOIR approximately 10 miles No men fell out. Reference map $\frac{1}{100000}$ LENS	
CAOURS	22		Marched to CAOURS via BERNATRE, HEIRMONT, ST RIQUIER. Distance 13 miles. Only one man fell out. Reference map $\frac{1}{100000}$ LENS & ABBEVILLE.	

1875 Wt. W593/826 1,000,000 4/15 J.B.C. & A. A.D.S.S./Forms/C. 2118.

Instructions regarding War Diaries and Intelligence Summaries are contained in F. S. Regs., Part II. and the Staff Manual respectively. Title pages will be prepared in manuscript.

WAR DIARY
or
INTELLIGENCE SUMMARY.
(Erase heading not required.)

Army Form C. 2118.

Place	Date	Hour	Summary of Events and Information	Remarks and references to Appendices
CAOURS	Sept 23		General Cleaning up.	
"	24		Church Services. RC and C of E	
"	25		Training under Coy. Commanders. Party of Officers & N.C.O's visited the Tank Park near S^T RIQUIER	
"			and witnessed a demonstration of Tanks manoeuvring	
"	26		In the morning Lecture to the whole of the 50th Brigade on the use of the bayonet by the Inspector,	
"			Army School of Physical Training. ~~Afternoon~~ Afternoon Coy. training continued	
"	27		Company training continued. The Commander of the 7th Corps SIR T D'OYLY SNOW visited the	
"			Battalion and inspected Coys in training.	
"	28		Company Training continued. Specialists under Specialist Officers	
"	29		Company Training continued. Specialists under Specialist Officers	
"	30		Company Training continued. Specialists under Specialist Officers	

[signature] Lieut. Col.
Commd^g 10th West Yorkshire Regiment.
2nd October 1916

T2134. Wt. W708–776. 500000. 4/15. Sir J. C. & S.

Army Form C. 2118

Instructions regarding War Diaries and Intelligence Summaries are contained in F. S. Regs., Part II. and the Staff Manual respectively. Title Pages will be prepared in manuscript.

WAR DIARY
or
INTELLIGENCE SUMMARY
(Erase heading not required.)

Place	Date	Hour	Summary of Events and Information	Remarks and references to Appendices
CAOURS	Sep 23		General Cleaning up.	
"	24		Church Services. RC and C of E	
"	25		Training under Coy. Commanders. Party of Officers + N.C.O's visited the Tank Park near S^T RIQUIER	
"			and witnessed a demonstration of Tanks manoeuvring	
"	26		In the morning Lecture to the whole of the 50th Brigade on the use of the bayonet by the Inspector,	
"			Army School of Physical Training. ~~Affechoon~~ Afternoon Coy. training continued	
"	27		Company training continued. The Commander of the 7th Corps SIR T D'OYLY SNOW visited the	
"			Battalion and inspected Coys in training.	
"	28		Company Training continued. Specialists under Specialist Officers	
"	29		Company Training continued. Specialists under Specialist Officers	
"	30		Company Training continued. Specialists under Specialist Officers	

[signature]
Lieut. Col.
Commd^g 10th West Yorkshire Regiment.
2nd October 1916.

1875 Wt. W593/826 1,000,000 4/15 J.B.C. & A. A.D.S.S./Forms/C. 2118.

11.E.
24 sheets

50
17

Vol 10

WAR DIARY
OF
10/ WEST LANCASHIRE REGT.
FOR
OCTOBER — 1916

Instructions regarding War Diaries and Intelligence Summaries are contained in F. S. Regs., Part II. and the Staff Manual respectively. Title pages will be prepared in manuscript.

WAR DIARY
or
INTELLIGENCE SUMMARY.
(Erase heading not required.)

Army Form C. 2118.

Place	Date	Hour	Summary of Events and Information	Remarks and references to Appendices
CAOURS	1-10-16		Divine Service in Billets	
do	2nd		Training in billets owing to inclement weather.	
do	3rd	Morning	Battalion Scheme for officers under Commanding Officer	
do		do Afternoon	Remainder Route March	
do		afternoon	Bayonet fighting under Brigade Instructor	
do	4th		Adjutant's Parade. Bayonet fighting instructions. Night operation	
do	5th		Adjutant's Parade. Bayonet fighting instructions. Company training.	
do	6th		Battalion marched to CONTEVILLE distance approximately 11 miles.	
CONTEVILLE	7th		Battalion marched to FROHEN-LE-GRAND distance approximately. 12 miles.	
FROHEN LE GRAND	8th		Battalion ordered to move to HALLOY but move cancelled.	
-do-	9th		Company training in Billets.	
do	10th		Battalion marched to billets in HALLOY distance approximately 12 miles only 1 other rank fell out on line of march	
HALLOY	11th		Company training at Billets.	
do	12th		Practising attack on enemy trenches on previously prepared flagged area.	
do	13th	Morning	Company training	

T2134. Wt. W708—776. 500000. 4/15. Sir J. C. & S.

Instructions regarding War Diaries and Intelligence Summaries are contained in F. S. Regs., Part II. and the Staff Manual respectively. Title Pages will be prepared in manuscript.

WAR DIARY
or
INTELLIGENCE SUMMARY
(Erase heading not required.)

Army Form C. 2118

Place	Date	Hour	Summary of Events and Information	Remarks and references to Appendices
CAOURS	1-10-16		Divine Service in Billets	
do	2nd		Training in billets owing to inclement weather.	
do	3rd	Morning	Battalion Scheme for officers under Commanding Officer	
do		do	Remainder Route March	
do		afternoon	Bayonet fighting under Brigade Instructor	
do	4th		Adjutants Parade. Bayonet fighting instructions. Night operation.	
do	5th		Adjutants Parade. Bayonet fighting instructions. Company Training.	
do.	6th		Battalion marched to CONTEVILLE distance approximately 11 miles.	
CONTEVILLE	7th		Battalion marched to FROHEN-LE-GRAND distance approximately 12 miles.	
FROHENLEGRAND	8th		Battalion ordered to move to HALLOY but move cancelled.	
-do-	9th		Company training in Billets.	
-do-	10th		Battalion marched to billets in HALLOY - distance approximately 12 miles only 1 other rank fell out on line of march	
HALLOY	11th		Company training at Billets.	
do	12th		Practising attack on enemy trenches on previously prepared flagged area.	
do	13th	Morning	Company training	

1875 Wt. W593/826 1,000,000 4/15 J.B.C. & A. A.D.S.S./Forms/C. 2118.

Instructions regarding War Diaries and Intelligence Summaries are contained in F. S. Regs., Part II. and the Staff Manual respectively. Title pages will be prepared in manuscript.

WAR DIARY
or
INTELLIGENCE SUMMARY.
(Erase heading not required.)

Army Form C. 2118.

Place	Date	Hour	Summary of Events and Information	Remarks and references to Appendices
HALLOY	13th	afternoon	Practising attack on enemy trenches	
do	14th		Practising attack on enemy trenches (1) By day (2) By night. Announced	
do	-		in London Gazette that: The King has been pleased to award the Military	
do	-		Medal for Bravery in the Field to No 12274 Sgt. W. DALTON B Coy	
do			No 6330 Sgt. J. A. FIELDING A Coy. No 10086 Sgt. W. H JUETT A Coy.	
do	15th		Church Parades. B Coy erecting wire entanglements for practice in wire	
do	-		cutting. Battalion attended a demonstration of trench making by means of the	
do	-		explosion of ammonal tubes given by the 93rd Field Coy. R.E.	
do	-			
do	16th	Morning	Practising attack on enemy trenches on flagged area in conjunction with 6th Dorsetshire Regt.	
do	-	afternoon	In afternoon practising wire cutting with live rounds. Capt W.A.L. BURNE resumes	
do	-		command of C Coy.	
do	17th		Company training. Practising attack on enemy trenches by night.	
do	18th		Company training.	
do	19th		Company training.	
do	20th		Battalion marched to TALMAS distance about 10 miles.	

T2134. Wt. W708—776. 500000. 4/15. Sir J. C. & S.

Instructions regarding War Diaries and Intelligence Summaries are contained in F. S. Regs., Part II. and the Staff Manual respectively. Title Pages will be prepared in manuscript.

WAR DIARY
or
INTELLIGENCE SUMMARY
(Erase heading not required.)

Army Form C. 2118

Place	Date	Hour	Summary of Events and Information	Remarks and references to Appendices
HALLOY	13th	afternoon	Practising attack on enemy trenches	
do	14th		Practising attack on enemy trenches (i) By day (ii) By night. Announced	
do	-		in "London Gazette" that "The King has been pleased to award the Military	
do	-		Medal for Bravery in the Field" to No 12274 Sgt. W. DALTON B. Coy.	
do	-		No 6330 Sgt. J. A. FIELDING A Coy. No 10086 Sgt. W. H JUETT. A Coy.	
do	15th		Church Parades. B. Coy erecting wire entanglements for practice in wire	
do	-		cutting. Battalion attended a demonstration of trench making by means of the	
do	-		explosion of Ammonal tubes given by the 93rd Field Coy. R.E.	
do	-			
do	16th	Morning	Practising attack on enemy trenches on flagged area in conjunction with 6th Dorsetshire Regt.	
do	-	afternoon	In afternoon practising wire cutting with live rounds. Capt W.A.L. BURNE resumes	
do	-	-	command of C. Coy.	
do	17th		Company training. Practising attack on enemy trenches by night.	
do	18th		Company training.	
do	19th		Company training.	
do	20th		Battalion marched to TALMAS distance about 10 miles	

Instructions regarding War Diaries and Intelligence Summaries are contained in F. S. Regs., Part II. and the Staff Manual respectively. Title pages will be prepared in manuscript.

WAR DIARY
or
INTELLIGENCE SUMMARY.
(Erase heading not required.)

Army Form C. 2118.

Place	Date	Hour	Summary of Events and Information	Remarks and references to Appendices
TALMAS	21st		Battalion marched to FRANVILLERS distance about 11 miles.	
FRANVILLERS	22nd		Battalion marched to MEAULTE distance about 9 miles	
MEAULTE	23rd		Company training. Medical officer lectured the Battalion on care of feet and	
do	.		precautions to be taken against "Trench Feet" during the winter.	
do	24th		Battalion ordered to march to the CITADEL Camp on the FRICOURT-BRAVE road,	
do	.		but move cancelled. Company training carried on.	
do	25th		Company training	
do	26th		Company training.	
do	27th		Battalion marched to A Camp, MANSEL Camp near MAMETZ taking over	
do	-		from the 1st Royal Dublin Fusiliers	
MANSEL CAMP	28th		Divine Service. Whole Battalion employed in draining camp and making	
do			chalk paths between the lines	
do	29th		Battalion marched at 8-25 AM to "A" Camp between BERNAFAY WOOD and	
	.		TRONES WOOD, resting there before proceeding to the trenches. At 5-0 p.m	
	.		the march was continued to the trenches N of LES BOEUFS where the	
	.		Battalion proceeded to relieve the 2nd West Yorkshire Regiment on the right	

T2134. Wt. W708–776. 500000. 4/15. Sir J. C. & S.

Army Form C. 2118

Instructions regarding War Diaries and Intelligence Summaries are contained in F. S. Regs., Part II. and the Staff Manual respectively. Title Pages will be prepared in manuscript.

WAR DIARY
or
INTELLIGENCE SUMMARY

(Erase heading not required.)

Place	Date	Hour	Summary of Events and Information	Remarks and references to Appendices
TALMAS	21st		Battalion marched to FRANVILLERS distance about 11 miles	
FRANVILLERS	22nd		Battalion marched to MEAULTE distance about 9 miles	
MEAULTE	23rd		Company training. Medical officer lectured the Battalion on care of feet and	
do	-		precautions to be taken against "Trench Feet" during the winter.	
do	24th		Battalion ordered to march to the CITADEL Camp on the FRICOURT-BRAVE road,	
do	-		but move cancelled. Company training carried on.	
do	25th		Company training	
do	26th		Company training.	
do	27th		Battalion marched to A Camp, MANSEL Camp near MAMETZ taking over	
do	-		from the 1st Royal Dublin Fusiliers	
MANSEL CAMP	28th		Divine Service. Whole Battalion employed in draining camp and making	
do.			chalk paths between the lines	
do	29th		Battalion marched at 8-25 A.M to "A" Camp between BERNAFAY WOOD and	
	.		TRONES WOOD, resting there before proceeding to the trenches. At 5-0 p.m	
	.		the march was continued to the trenches N of LES BOEUFS where the	
	.		Battalion proceeded to relieve the 2nd West Yorkshire Regiment on the right	

1875 Wt. W593/826 1,000,000 4/15 J.B.C. & A. A.D.S.S./Forms/C. 2118.

Instructions regarding War Diaries and Intelligence Summaries are contained in F. S. Regs., Part II. and the Staff Manual respectively. Title pages will be prepared in manuscript.

WAR DIARY
or
INTELLIGENCE SUMMARY.
(Erase heading not required.)

Army Form C. 2118.

Place	Date	Hour	Summary of Events and Information	Remarks and references to Appendices
TRENCHES	29th		of the sector allotted to the 17th Division in relief of the 8th Division. Considerable shelling was experienced en route, one man being killed and seven wounded. One unwounded prisoner of the 28th Reserve Infantry Regiment was captured by Sgt. Dickenson shortly after entering the trenches & was sent down under the charge of the 2nd Scottish Rifles who were being relieved at the same time by the 6th Dorsetshire Regt.	
	30th		Relief completed at 5/45 AM. Dispositions were as follows. 'B' Coy in ZENITH on left of sub-sector; 1/2 D Coy in right of ZENITH and 1/2 D Coy in support in SPECTRUM 'A' & 'C' Companies in reserve in WINDMILL trench. The 6th Dorsetshire Regt were on the left & the 2nd Argyll & Sutherland Highlanders of the 33rd Division on the immediate right. Weather conditions were deplorable, men in the front trenches having to stand at least two feet in mud water. Several men became stuck in the mud & were unable to move until they were dug out. Shelling was continuous and caused considerable casualties. D Company arranged with the 2nd Argyll & Sutherland Highlanders to commence a trench from the right of ZENITH to join up with the centre of the position occupied by that regiment. Great difficulty was experienced in getting up rations & water to the front line	

T2134. Wt. W708-776. 500000. 4/15. Sir J. C. & S.

Instructions regarding War Diaries and Intelligence Summaries are contained in F. S. Regs., Part II. and the Staff Manual respectively. Title Pages will be prepared in manuscript.

WAR DIARY
or
INTELLIGENCE SUMMARY
(Erase heading not required.)

Army Form C. 2118

Place	Date	Hour	Summary of Events and Information	Remarks and references to Appendices
TRENCHES	29th		of the sector allotted to the 17th Division in relief of the 8th Division. Considerable shelling was experienced en route, one man being killed and seven wounded. One unwounded prisoner of the 28th Reserve Infantry Regiment was captured by Sgt. Dickenson shortly after entering the trenches & was sent down under the charge of the 2nd Scottish Rifles who were being relieved at the same time by the 6th Dorsetshire Regt.	
	30th		Relief completed at 5/45 AM. Dispositions were as follows. 'B' Coy in ZENITH on left of sub-sector; 1/2 D Coy in right of ZENITH and 1/2 D Coy in support in SPECTRUM 'A' & 'C' Companies in reserve in WINDMILL trench. The 6th Dorsetshire Regt were on the left & the 2nd Argyll & Sutherland Highlanders of the 33rd Division on the immediate right. Weather conditions were deplorable, men in the front trenches having to stand at least two feet in mud water. Several men became stuck in the mud & were unable to move until they were dug out. Shelling was continuous and caused considerable casualties. D Company arranged with the 2nd Argyll & Sutherland Highlanders to commence a trench from the right of ZENITH to join up with the centre of the position occupied by that regiment. Great difficulty was experienced in getting up rations & water to the front line	

1875 Wt. W593/826 1,000,000 4/15 J.B.C. & A. A.D.S.S./Forms/C. 2118.

Army Form C. 2118

WAR DIARY
or
INTELLIGENCE SUMMARY
(Erase heading not required.)

Instructions regarding War Diaries and Intelligence Summaries are contained in F. S. Regs., Part II. and the Staff Manual respectively. Title Pages will be prepared in manuscript.

Place	Date	Hour	Summary of Events and Information	Remarks and references to Appendices
TRENCHES.	30th		trenches owing to the carrying party missing their way in the darkness	
			Rations were brought up by pack mules as far as the Battalion dump near	
			WIND MILL trench.	
do	31st		Shelling continuous throughout the night very little cessation during the day.	
			Casualties reported for the 24 hours ending noon – 3 killed, one died of wounds,	
			six wounded.	

W. Barnes Lieut. Col.
Comdg. 10th West Yorkshire Regiment.

1875 Wt. W593/826 1,000,000 4/15 J.B.C. & A. A.D.S.S./Forms/C. 2118.

Instructions regarding War Diaries and Intelligence Summaries are contained in F. S. Regs., Part II. and the Staff Manual respectively. Title Pages will be prepared in manuscript.

WAR DIARY
or
INTELLIGENCE SUMMARY
(Erase heading not required.)

Place	Date	Hour	Summary of Events and Information	Remarks and references to Appendices
TRENCHES.	30th		trenches owing to the carrying party missing their way in the darkness. These were brought up by packmules as far as the Battalion dump near WINDMILL trench.	
Do.	31st		Shelling continuous throughout the night very little cessation during the day. Casualties reported for the 24 hours ending noon – 3 killed, one died of wounds, six wounded.	

[signature] Lieut. Col.
Comdg. 10th West Yorkshire Regiment.

1875 Wt. W593/826 1,000,000 4/15 J.B.C. & A. A.D.S.S./Forms/C. 2118.

XIV CORPS SITUATION MAP SCALE - 1:20,000. No Y.17A

Apparent Situation - 9 AM. 24-10-16 British Front Line Blue

Bayonet Trench
Bacon Tr.
Barley Trench
Till Trench
Pumping Station
Reed Tr.
Stormy Tr.
Misty Tr.
Atom Trench
Grease Tr.
Cloudy Tr.
Sunray Tr.
Gueudecourt
Beaulencourt
Brimstone Tr.
Belt Alley
Sulphur Av.
Gleam Tr.
Eclipse Tr.
Shine Alley
Donald Tr.
Thistle Tr.
le Transloy
Sugar Factory
BAPAUME RD.
NORTH ST.
CHURCH ST.
H.Q. LANE
HOSPITAL LANE
SOUTH ST.
Cemetery Circle
Lesboeufs
FRENCH
Morval Mill
Moon Trench
Windmill
Morval
NOTU
SECRET
50th Bde

COPY No. 12.

12th West Yorkshire Regt.
Operation Order No. 19. 5-10-16.

REFERENCE MAPS. ABBEVILLE. [illegible] (Sheet 14.)
[illegible]NS. [illegible] (Sheet 11.)

1. The Battalion will march to billets at CONTEVILLE tomorrow 6th inst. Distance about 11 miles. [illegible] Marching Order.

2. ROUTE.

NEUF MOULIN ST. RIQUIER CONTEVILLE.

3. STARTING POINT

Cross Roads L.12 a 9 1. (Ref. Map ST. RIQUIER 20,000)

4. TIME

9-15 A.M.

5. ORDER OF MARCH. H.Q Cos. C. B. Band. A.D.

6. Advance Billeting [illegible] consisting of 2Lt J.E. ROSE, 1 Senior N.C.O. per Coy, and 1 from Batt. Headquarters will proceed ahead so as to be at CONTEVILLE at 8.0 A.M.

7. Transport will follow the Battalion.

8. All Officers' Kits, Mess Box and other Stores will be stacked outside the respective Coy [illegible] orderly by 9.30 A.M. The Transport Officer will arrange to collect same at that time.

9. Billets must be left scrupulously clean. An officer from each Coy will inspect his Coy billets prior to departure. A certificate to this effect will be rendered to the [illegible] 10 minutes before the Battalion moves off. Each Coy will leave behind a rear party consisting [illegible] 1 junior N.C.O. and 2 men, who will [illegible] billets [illegible] burn or. [illegible]

10. [illegible] ct [illegible] all billets and [illegible] [illegible] ect [illegible] and march [illegible]

SECRET

Copy No 14

10th West Yorkshire Regt

Operation Order No 20

6-10-16

REFERENCE MAP LENS 1/100,000 (Sheet 11)

1. The Battalion will move to MEZEROLLES area tomorrow 7th inst. Distance about 11 miles. Dress Marching Order.
2. ROUTE CONTEVILLE – BERNATRE – MAIZICOURT and thence under orders of 50th Brigade.
3. STARTING POINT CONTEVILLE Church facing N.E.
4. TIME 9.0 A.M.
5. ORDER of MARCH Hdqrs. B.A. Band [illegible] C. Signallers
6. BILLETING Advance Billeting Party consisting of 2/Lieut [illegible] Rose, 1 Junior [illegible] per Coy. and 1 from Battalion Headquarters will proceed ahead and report to Major COMYN at the Mairie, MEZEROLLES at 9.0 A.M.
7. TRANSPORT The whole of the Regimental Transport will leave CONTEVILLE at 8.[illegible] A.M. and proceed to Road Junction South of H in AUXI-LE-CHATEAU via HEIRMONT by the main road.
8. OFFICERS KITS. All Officers' Kits, Mess Boxes and other Stores will be stacked outside the respective Coy Headquarters by 7.0 A.M. The Transport Officer will arrange to collect same at that hour.
9. BILLETS Attention is called to paras 9 & 10 of Bn Operation Orders No 19 d/5-10-16. These orders will stand good and will be strictly adhered to.
10. Dinners will be cooked on the Line of March.
11. Parade States will be rendered to Orderly Room by 8.0 A.M.
12. Sick Parade. 3.0 P.M.

Issued at 7.40 P.M.

Edward Jomet [illegible]
Lt & Adjt
10th West York. Regt

Copy No 1. Cd. in C. [illegible]
2. O.C. A Coy.
3. O.C. B "
4. O.C. C "
5. O.C. D "
6. M.O.
7. T.O.
No 8. S.O.
9. Q.M.
10. L.G.O.
11. R.S.M.
12. S. Sgt.
13. Retained
14. War Diary.

Copy No 13

10th West Yorkshire Regiment [illegible]

OPERATION ORDER No. 21

[illegible] Map LENS [illegible] (Sheet 11)

1 The Battalion will move to HALLOY [illegible] tomorrow [illegible] inst. [illegible] about [illegible] miles. Dress Marching Order.

2 STARTING POINT. Battalion H.Q. [illegible] S.E.

3 TIME. 7.45 A.M.

4 ORDER OF MARCH. H.Q. A.D. BAND, C.B. Signallers.

5 BILLETING. Advance Billeting party consisting of [illegible] J.E. Ross [illegible] 1 N.C.O. [illegible] 1 from Battn. H.Q. will proceed ahead [illegible] the Staff Captain at L'ESPERANCE Cross Roads [illegible] of HALLOY [illegible]

6 TRANSPORT will follow in rear of the Battalion.

7 OFFICERS KITS. All Officers kits, mess boxes, and other Stores [illegible] outside the respective Coy H.Q. by 6.45 A.M. The Transport Officer will arrange to collect [illegible] at that time.

8 BILLETS. Attention is called to paras 9 & 10 of B.R. [illegible] [illegible] 19. d/ 5-10-16. These orders will [illegible] [illegible] strictly adhered to.

9 Dinners will be cooked on the line of march.

10 Parade states will be rendered to Orderly Room by 7 A.M.

11 Sick Parade tomorrow will be at 6 A.M.

Edward [illegible]

Lieut & A/Adjutant

10th West Yorkshire Regiment

Issued at 9.30 P.M.

Copy No 1. 2nd in C
" " 2. O.C. A Coy.
" " 3. " B "
" " 4. " C "
" " 5. " D "
" " 6. L.G.O
" " 7. T.O.

Copy No 8. I.O.
" " 9. C.M.
" " 10. M.O.
" " 11. R.S.M.
" " 12. [illegible]
" " 13. [illegible]
" " 14. [illegible]

SECRET. 10 West Yorkshire Regiment. Copy No. 14

Operation Order No. 24 19/10/16

Reference map LENS $\frac{1}{100000}$ (Sheet 11)

I. The Battalion will march to TALMAS tomorrow.
Distance about 10 miles.
Route ORVILLE BERNAVILLE BEAUQUESNE DOULLENS LE VAL DE MAISON
Starting point outside Battalion Orderly Room.
Time 9.15 A.M.
Order of March. H.Q., D.C., Drums, B.A., Lewis Guns, Transport.
The Battalion will form up two deep on the right of the road until the 7th East Yorkshire Regiment have passed through.
[illegible] will be carried strapped to the [illegible]

II BILLETING. An advance billeting party consisting of 2nd Lieut. J.E. R[illegible], and 1 Senior N.C.O. from H.Q. and each Company will leave for TALMAS at 6 A.M. They will report to the Staff Captain at the MAIRIE at 9 A.M.

III OFFICERS KITS, mess boxes and other Stores will be stacked at Battalion Orderly Room by [illegible] AM when the Transport Officer will arrange to collect them.

IV BILLETS. Billets must be left scrupulously clean. An Officer per each Company will inspect [illegible] billets prior to departure. A certificate to [illegible] will be [illegible] to the Orderly Room [illegible] before the Battalion [illegible]

V [illegible]

VI SICK PARADE. [illegible]

(Sd.) A.F.G. [illegible] Capt. & Adjutant.
[illegible] 10th West Yorkshire Regiment.

Copy No. 1	C.O.	No. 5	O.C. D. Coy	No. 9	I.O.
2	O.C. A Coy	6	L.G.O.	10	M.O.
3	B	7	T.O.	11	Q.M.
4	C	8	B.O.	12	R.S.M.
				13	[illegible]
				14	[illegible]

SECRET.

10th West Yorkshire Regt. — COPY NO 13

Operation Order No 22 — 9.10.16

Reference Map LENS 100,000 (Sheet 11)

1. The Battalion will march to HALLOY tomorrow 10th inst as ordered in Operation Order No 21 d/7-10-16

2. Operation Order No 21 will stand good with the following exception.

STARTING POINT Junction of FROHEN LE GRAND – REMAISNIL and FROHEN LE GRAND – MEZEROLLES Roads.

Edward Smith
Lt & A/Adjt.
10th West York. Regt.

Issued at 7.0 pm.

Copy No	
1	2nd in C
2	O.C. A Coy
3	" B "
4	" C "
5	" D "
6	L.G.O.
7	T.O.
8	I.O
9	Q.M
10	M.O.
11	R.S.M.
12	Sig. Sgt.
13	War Diary
14	Retained

SECRET   10th West Yorkshire Regiment.

OPERATION ORDER No. 28   26 [illegible]

Reference map   ALBERT 1/40000

1 The Battalion will march [illegible] to BRUSEL CAMP.

STARTING POINT CARCAILLOT CROSS ROADS

TIME The Battalion [illegible] form up [illegible] [illegible] a.m. in the following order – H.Q. B. A. D. C. Transport.

ROUTE [illegible] Destination

INTERVALS An interval of 100 yards [illegible] between companies. [illegible] will be no ten minutes halt on the way. The Transport will [illegible] distance [illegible] [illegible] yards [illegible]. The rear company [illegible] will [illegible] a distance of 200 yards between each unit.

DRESS. Marching order. [illegible] will be [illegible] [illegible] sheets and strapped to the back of the packs. Steel helmets will be worn.

2. BILLETING. An advance billeting party consisting of 2nd Lieut [illegible] and 1 [illegible] N.C.O. from H.Q., each company and the Transport, will leave Orderly Room at 5.45 a.m. They will report to the Camp Commandant of the Camp, and meet the Battalion on arrival to conduct units to their quarters.

3 OFFICERS KITS, mess boxes and other stores will be stacked at the Q.M. Stores by 5.15 a.m. where the Transport Officer will arrange to collect them.

4. BILLETS. The usual orders regarding billets being left clean must be strictly observed.

5 MARCH DISCIPLINE Companies will march in [illegible] care must therefore be taken to see that [illegible] and that the laid down intervals between Companies are observed. Owing to the bad state of the roads a slow pace will be set.

[illegible] A. F. G. [illegible] Capt + Adjutant.
10th West Yorkshire Regt.

21-10-16

10th West Yorkshire Regiment.

AFTER ORDER.

Reference Operation Orders No 26

BLANKETS will be packed in bundles of 10, & dumped at Billet No 175 next to Brigade Headquarters by 7.30 A.M. tomorrow. The Quartermaster will arrange to leave two reliable men in charge who will be supplied with rations for three days.

(sd) A. F. G. Anderson
Capt & Adjt
10 West York Regt

11. [illegible] will be cooked [illegible]

12. Parade States will be rendered [illegible] Orderly Room by 8.0 A.M.

13. Sick Parade tomorrow at 3.0 P.M.

[signature]

Lt. & A/Adjt.
10th. West Yorkshire Reg[illegible]

Issued at 8.45. P.M.

COPY. No. 1. 2nd in Command.
2. O.C. A. Coy.
3. O.C. B. "
4. O.C. C. "
5. O.C. D. "
6. Medical Officer
7. Transport Officer

COPY. No. 8. Qr. Mr.
9. L.G.O.
10. R.S.M.
11. Retained
12. War Diary
13. Signals Sergt.

SECRET. 10th West Yorkshire Regiment. Copy No.

Operation Order No. 26. 5/10/16.

Reference map AMIENS $\frac{1}{100000}$

1. The Battalion will march to MEAULTE tomorrow.

Distance about 9 miles.

Order of march. H.Q. C. D. Drums, A. B. Transport. Lewis Guns will march with their [illegible].

Route. HEILLY – RIBEMONT – BUIRE – VILLE

Starting point. Outside 50 Brigade Headquarters.

Time. 9.50 A.M.

An interval of 200 yards will be kept between the Headquarter Companies, and the Transport. [illegible] will be [illegible] synchronised with the Adjutant before starting.

2. Billeting. An advance billeting party consisting of [illegible] N.C.O. from H.Q. each Company and the Transport will meet the Staff Captain at the Town Major's Office in MEAULTE at 10.30 A.M. [illegible]

3. Officers Kits, mess boxes and other [illegible] will be [illegible] by 8.45 A.M. when the Transport Officer will [illegible]

4. Billets must be left scrupulously clean [illegible] each Company [illegible] before departure.

A certificate [illegible] will be rendered to the Adjutant ten minutes before the Battalion moves off.

5. Dinners will be cooked on the march.

6. Sick Parade. 1 hour after [illegible].

(Sd.) A. J. C. Anderson Capt. Adjutant

Issued at 10.15 P.M. 10th [illegible] Yorkshire Regiment.

Copy No. 1	C.O.	Copy No. 6	L.G.O.	Copy No. 11	Q.M.
2	O.C. A Coy.	7	T.O.	12	R.S.M.
3	" B "	8	B.O.	13	Sig. Off.
4	" C "	9	I.O.	14	War Diary
5	" D "	10	M.O.	15	Retained

SECRET. 10th West Yorkshire Regiment. COPY No. 14

Operation Order No. 25 20/10/16.

Reference map: LENS and AMIENS $\frac{1}{100000}$

I. The Battalion will march to the FRANVILLERS-LAHOUSSOYE area tomorrow. Distance about 11 miles.

Order of March H.Q., C.B. Drums A.D. Lewis Guns, Transport.

C.B and A Coy. will form up on the road in Column of Route facing W at 9.15 A.M., the head of the Column to be outside Orderly Room, clear of Cross roads.)

D Coy will form up two deep at the side of the road outside its billets and will join the column in its proper order. Transport will keep clear of leading Battalions and will follow the Lewis Guns, who will leave sufficient space for D Coy.

II. BILLETING. An advance billeting party consisting of 2nd Lieut. Rose and one senior N.C.O from H.Q and each Company, will parade at Battalion H.Q at 6.45 A.M. Further instructions will be issued later.

III. OFFICERS KITS, mess boxes and other stores will be stacked at Orderly Room by 8.45 A.M. where the Transport Officer will arrange to collect them.

IV. BILLETS must be left scrupulously clean. An Officer from each Company will inspect his Company billets prior to departure. A certificate to this effect will be rendered to the Adjutant ten minutes before the Battalion moves off.

V. DINNERS will be cooked on the march.

VI. SICK PARADE one hour after arrival.

(sd.) A. J. C. Anderson Capt. + Adjutant.

Issued at 11.30 P.M. 10th West Yorkshire Regiment.

Copy No. 1	C.O.		Copy No. 8.	B.O.
2	O.C. A Coy		9	I.O.
3	" B "		10	M.O.
4	" C "		11	Q.M.
5	" D "		12.	R.S.M.
6	L.G.O.		13	Sig Sgt
7	T.O.		14	War Diary
			15	Retained

10 West Yorkshire Regiment. 19/10/16

AFTER ORDER.

VII The order in respect to carrying blankets strapped to packs is cancelled. Blankets will be [illegible] in tens, marked with Company tallies, and stacked at billet No. Y11 by 8.0 A.M. One man per Company will be left in charge. The [illegible] will arrange for storage at [illegible] billet.

Any other surplus Kit may be left at the same place.

(sd.) A. F. C. Anderson Capt. Adjutant
10th West Yorkshire Regiment.

Instructions regarding War Diaries and Intelligence Summaries are contained in F. S. Regs., Part II. and the Staff Manual respectively. Title Pages will be prepared in manuscript.

WAR DIARY
or
~~INTELLIGENCE SUMMARY~~
(Erase heading not required.)

Army Form C. 2118

Place	Date	Hour	Summary of Events and Information	Remarks and references to Appendices
	1916			
LES BOEUFS. TRENCHES	Nov. 1st		The situation was fairly quiet during the morning but after NOON the Reserve Trenches were heavily shelled. The conditions in the FRONT and SUPPORT Trenches became worse owing to incessant rains. 2nd Lieut. J.H. CLOUGHLEY was sent down sick. The casualty return was 8. O.R. killed and 35 O.R. wounded – nearly all shell wounds.	
"	" 2nd		The situation was quiet in the morning but during the day the enemy shelled the whole of the sector occupied by the Battalion. The shelling was particularly intense whilst working parties were moving at dusk. A German prisoner, named LUDWIG HUBER of the 28th Ersatz Inf. Reserve was captured by Orderly No. 14717 Pte NEALE. H.	
			The Battalion was ordered to join ZENITH Trench to the left of the new trench made by the Unit on the right of the Battn. Sector. The work was commenced at dusk and continued by the relieving Battalion. The relief of the Battalion by the 7th EAST YORKSHIRE REGT. which was ordered to take place during the night 2nd/3rd was commenced.	
			The casualty return was:– 3. O.R. killed, 1. O.R. died of wounds and 27 O.R. wounded.	
MANSEL CAMP.	" 3rd.		The relief was completed at 5.0 A.M. The Battalion marched to 'C' Camp, MANSEL CAMP.	
			The men arrived in an exhausted state after the severe experiences in the trenches. Many were suffering from TRENCH FEET.	
"	" 4th.		The Battalion remained at the camp generally resting and cleaning up.	
"	" 5th		Divine Service.	

1875 Wt. W593/826 1,000,000 4/15 J.B.C. & A. A.D.S.S./Forms/C. 2118.

Army Form C. 2118

Instructions regarding War Diaries and Intelligence Summaries are contained in F. S. Regs., Part II. and the Staff Manual respectively. Title Pages will be prepared in manuscript.

WAR DIARY
or
~~INTELLIGENCE SUMMARY~~

(Erase heading not required.)

Place	Date	Hour	Summary of Events and Information	Remarks and references to Appendices
	1916			
LES BOEUFS. TRENCHES	Nov. 1st.		The situation was fairly quiet during the morning but after NOON the Reserve Trenches were heavily shelled. The conditions in the FRONT and SUPPORT Trenches became worse owing to incessant rains. 2nd Lieut. J.H. CLOUGHLEY was sent down sick. The casualty return was 8.O.R killed and 35 O.R. wounded – nearly all shell wounds.	
	" 2nd.		The situation was quiet in the morning but during the day the enemy shelled the whole of the sector occupied by the Battalion The shelling was particularly intense whilst working parties were moving at dusk. A German prisoner, named LUDWIG HUBER of the 28th Ersatz Inf. Reserve was captured by Orderly No. 14717 Pte NEALE. H.	
			The Battalion was ordered to join ZENITH Trench to the left of the new trench made by the Unit on the right of the Battn. Sector. The work was commenced at dusk and continued by the relieving Battalion. The relief of the Battalion by the 7th EAST YORKSHIRE REGT, which was ordered to take place during the night 2nd/3rd was commenced.	
			The casualty return was:– 3.O.R. killed, 1.O.R. died of wounds and 27 O.R. wounded.	
MANSEL CAMP.	" 3rd.		The relief was completed at 5.0 A.M. The Battalion marched to 'C' Camp, MANSEL CAMP. The men arrived in an exhausted state after the severe experiences in the trenches. Many were suffering from TRENCH FEET.	
	" 4th.		The Battalion remained at the camp generally resting and cleaning up.	
	" 5th.		Divine Service.	

1875 Wt. W593/826 1,000,000 4/15 J.B.C. & A. A.D.S.S./Forms/C. 2118.

Instructions regarding War Diaries and Intelligence Summaries are contained in F. S. Regs., Part II. and the Staff Manual respectively. Title Pages will be prepared in manuscript.

WAR DIARY
or
~~INTELLIGENCE SUMMARY~~
(Erase heading not required.)

Army Form C. 2118

Place	Date	Hour	Summary of Events and Information	Remarks and references to Appendices
MONTAUBAN	1916 Nov. 6th		The Battalion marched to 'F' CAMP, MONTAUBAN leaving MANSEL CAMP at 8.0 A.M and rested at 'F' CAMP until 5.0 P.M. when the Battalion proceeded to the Trenches N. of LES BOEUFS to relieve the 7th. EAST YORKSHIRE REGT. on the right of the sector allotted to the 17th Division. The Battalion was heavily shelled en route and a number of casualties resulted.	
LES BOEUFS TRENCHES	" 7th.		The relief was completed at 4.10 A.M. when the situation was reported normal. This state of affairs lasted during the morning but in the afternoon there was considerable shelling particularly on the support (SPECTRUM) line. Great difficulty was experienced in getting even water to the men in the front lines. Enemy snipers became very troublesome and hampered movement 'on the top' anywhere in the region of ZENITH or SPECTRUM Trenches. An attempt was made to post Stokes Guns in the front lines but owing to the water logged condition of the ground and the total inability to find a firm base it was abandoned. The casualties for the day were 1.O.R. killed (by shell) and 6.O.R. wounded.	
"	" 8th.		The situation was reported normal during most of the day but conditions in the trenches became appreciably worse, officers and men in most of the sector having to stand in two feet of water or liquid mud. Some important work for this reason remained unfinished. The casualties for the 24 hours up to 4.0 P.M. were 1.O.R. killed, 30.O.R. wounded (gun shot wounds) 2nd Lieut I.P. WATERHOUSE, D. Coy. was killed by a sniper when conducting a ration party to the front line.	
"	" 9th.		Our own artillery shelled ORION in front of left of ZENITH which portion of the trench was temporarily evacuated.	

1875 Wt. W593/826 1,000,000 4/15 J.B.C. & A. A.D.S.S./Forms/C. 2118.

Instructions regarding War Diaries and Intelligence Summaries are contained in F. S. Regs., Part II. and the Staff Manual respectively. Title Pages will be prepared in manuscript.

WAR DIARY
or
INTELLIGENCE ~~SUMMARY~~
(Erase heading not required.)

Army Form C. 2118

Place	Date	Hour	Summary of Events and Information	Remarks and references to Appendices
MONTAUBAN	1916 Nov. 6th.		The Battalion marched to 'F' CAMP, MONTAUBAN leaving MANSEL CAMP at 8.0 A.M and rested at 'F' CAMP until 5.0 P.M. when the Battalion proceeded to the Trenches N. of LES BOEUFS to relieve the 7th. EAST YORKSHIRE REGT. on the right of the sector allotted to the 17th Division. The Battalion was heavily shelled en route and a number of casualties resulted.	
LES BOEUFS TRENCHES	7th.		The relief was completed at 4.10 A.M. when the situation was reported normal. This state of affairs lasted during the morning but in the afternoon there was considerable shelling particularly on the support (SPECTRUM) line. Great difficulty was experienced in getting even water to the men in the front lines. Enemy snipers became very troublesome and hampered movement 'on the top' anywhere in the region of ZENITH or SPECTRUM Trenches. An attempt was made to post Stokes guns in the front lines but owing to the water logged condition of the ground and the total inability to find a firm base it was abandoned. The casualties for the day were 1.O.R. killed (by shell) and 6.O.R. wounded.	
"	8th.		The situation was reported normal during most of the day but conditions in the trenches became appreciably worse, officers and men in most of the sector having to stand in two feet of water or liquid mud. Some important work for this reason remained unfinished. The casualties for the 24 hours up to 4.0 P.M. were 1.O.R killed, 3.O.R. wounded (gun shot wounds) 2nd Lieut I.P. WATERHOUSE, D. Coy. was killed by a sniper when conducting a ration party to the front line.	
"	9th.		Our own artillery shelled ORION in front of left of ZENITH which portion of the trench was temporarily evacuated.	

1875 Wt. W593/826 1,000,000 4/15 J.B.C. & A. A.D.S.S./Forms/C. 2118.

Instructions regarding War Diaries and Intelligence Summaries are contained in F. S. Regs., Part II. and the Staff Manual respectively. Title Pages will be prepared in manuscript.

WAR DIARY
or
~~INTELLIGENCE SUMMARY~~
(Erase heading not required.)

Army Form C. 2118

Place	Date	Hour	Summary of Events and Information	Remarks and references to Appendices
LES BOEUFS TRENCHES	1916 Nov. 9th.	(contd.)	Owing to casualties and sickness from exposure the front line Coys. were so reduced in numbers that with permission from Brigade the Reserve Coy in WINDMILL was sent up to reinforce. The fourth Coy. previously employed on Brigade carrying parties came up into reserve. Casualties reported 5 O.R. wounded G.S and 1 O.R by shell. Bicycle lamps with the glass covered with red linen were fixed on stakes 3 feet out of the ground to guide relieving troops and others to the trenches. 2nd Lieut. H.A.C. NEVILLE went down sick	
"	10th		Enemy aeroplane was shot down by one of our planes, the disabled machine falling near Battalion Headquarters. Casualties reported 2 O.R wounded by shells. The area by the Battalion Headquarters was heavily shelled about midday but without causing any casualties. The Battalion was relieved by the 7th EAST YORKSHIRE REGT, the relief commencing at 8.0 PM. The relieved Battalion marched by Companies to 'A' Camp TRONES WOOD. The majority of the men were greatly exhausted.	

1875 Wt. W593/826 1,000,000 4/15 J.B.C. & A. A.D.S.S./Forms/C. 2118.

Army Form C. 2118

WAR DIARY
or
INTELLIGENCE SUMMARY
(Erase heading not required.)

Instructions regarding War Diaries and Intelligence Summaries are contained in F. S. Regs., Part II. and the Staff Manual respectively. Title Pages will be prepared in manuscript.

Place	Date	Hour	Summary of Events and Information	Remarks and references to Appendices
LES BOEUFS TRENCHES	1916 Nov. 9th.	contd.	Owing to casualties and sickness from exposure the front line Coys. were so reduced in numbers that with permission from Brigade the Reserve Coy in WINDMILL was sent up to reinforce. The Fourth Coy. previously employed on Brigade carrying parties came up into reserve. Casualties reported 5 O.R. wounded G.S. and 1 O.R. by shell. Bivouac lamps with the glass covered with red linen were fixed on stakes 3 feet out of the ground to guide relieving troops and others to the trenches. 2nd Lieut. H.A.G. NEVILLE went down sick	
"	10th		Enemy aeroplane was shot down by one of our planes, the disabled machine falling near Battalion Headquarters. Casualties reported 2 O.R. wounded by shells. The area by the Battalion Headquarters was heavily shelled about midday but without causing any casualties.	
			The Battalion was relieved by the 7th EAST YORKSHIRE REGT, the relief commencing at 8.0 PM.	
			The relieved Battalion marched by Companies to 'A' Camp TRONES WOOD. The majority of the men were greatly exhausted.	

1875 Wt. W593/826 1,000,000 4/15 J.B.C. & A. A.D.S.S./Forms/C. 2118.

*Instructions regarding War Diaries and Intelligence Summaries are contained in F. S. Regs., Part II. and the Staff Manual respectively. Title pages will be prepared in manuscript.

WAR DIARY
or
INTELLIGENCE SUMMARY.
(Erase heading not required.)

Army Form C. 2118.

Place	Date	Hour	Summary of Events and Information	Remarks and references to Appendices
	1916. Nov.			
MONTAUBEN	11th		The Relief was completed about 12-0 MIDNIGHT.	
			There were many cases of Trench Feet and CAPT. S.B.E. CUTLER and 39 sick men were evacuated to hospital direct from 'A' Camp.	
			The following is a copy of return of casualties in the 10th WEST YORKSHIRE REGT. from 29-10-16 to 11-11-16 (This includes both tours in the trenches N. of LES BOEUFS.)	

	KILLED	DIED OF WOUNDS	WOUNDED	MISSING	KILLED ? → Total
OFFICERS	1			1	2
OTHER RANKS	21	8	97	44	170

Place	Date	Hour	Summary of Events and Information	Remarks and references to Appendices
			The Battalion moved to 'H' Camp MONTAUBAN, and leaving 'A' CAMP at 4-0 PM and arriving at 'H' CAMP at 6-30 P.M	
SAND PITS CAMP	12th		The Battalion moved to SAND PITS CAMP leaving 'H' CAMP, MONTAUBAN at 4-0 P.M. Route	
Nr MEAULTE			CARNOY RD. - MANSEL CAMP - FRICOURT CEMETERY and CARCAILLOT FARM.	
CAMPS-EN AMIENOIS	13th		The Battalion entrained at EDGE HILL SIDING, DERNANCOURT, for the XIV Corps Rest area at 10.0 AM., marching from SAND PITS CAMP at 6.45 A.M. The Battalion detrained at HANGEST at 2.0 P.M and proceeded in motor buses and lorries to billets in CAMPS-EN AMIENOIS,	

T2134. Wt. W708–776. 500000. 4/15. Sir J. C. & S.

WAR DIARY
or
INTELLIGENCE SUMMARY.
(Erase heading not required.)

Army Form C. 2118.

Instructions regarding War Diaries and Intelligence Summaries are contained in F. S. Regs., Part II. and the Staff Manual respectively. Title pages will be prepared in manuscript.

Place	Date	Hour	Summary of Events and Information	Remarks and references to Appendices
	1916. NOV.			
MONTAUBEN	11th		The Relief was completed about 12-0 MIDNIGHT.	
			There were many cases of Trench Feet and CAPT. S.B.E. CUTLER and sick 30 men were evacuated to hospital direct from 'A' Camp.	
			The following is a copy of return of casualties in the 10th WEST YORKSHIRE REGT. from 29-10-16 to 11-11-16 (This includes both tours in the trenches N. of LES BOEUFS.	

	KILLED	DIED OF WOUNDS	WOUNDED	MISSING	KILLED
OFFICERS	1			1	2
OTHER RANKS	21	8	97	44	170

Place	Date	Hour	Summary of Events and Information	Remarks and references to Appendices
			The Battalion moved to 'H' Camp MONTAUBAN, and leaving 'A' CAMP at 4-0 P.M. and arriving at 'H' CAMP at 6-30 P.M.	
SAND PITS CAMP	12th		The Battalion moved to SAND PITS CAMP leaving 'H' CAMP, MONTAUBAN at 4-0 P.M. Route CARNOY RD. - MANSEL CAMP - FRICOURT CEMETERY and CARCAILLOT FARM.	
Nr MEAULTE				
CAMPS EN AMIENOIS	13th		The Battalion entrained at EDGE HILL SIDING, DERNANCOURT, in the XIV Corps Rest Area at 10-0 A.M., marching from SAND PITS CAMP at 6-45 A.M. The Battalion detrained at HANGEST at 2-0 P.M. and proceeded in motor lorries and lorries to billets in CAMPS-EN AMIENOIS,	

T2134. Wt. W708–776. 500000. 4/15. Sir J. C. & S.

Instructions regarding War Diaries and Intelligence Summaries are contained in F. S. Regs., Part II. and the Staff Manual respectively. Title pages will be prepared in manuscript.

WAR DIARY

or

~~INTELLIGENCE SUMMARY.~~

(Erase heading not required.)

Army Form C. 2118.

Place	Date	Hour	Summary of Events and Information	Remarks and references to Appendices
	1916.			
CAMPS-EN-AMIENOIS	Nov 14th		General cleaning up and rest.	
"	" 15 "		General cleaning up and rest.	
"	" 16 "		Refitting and Company Training	
"	" 17 "		- do. - -do. -	
"	" 18 "		- do - -do -	
"	" 19 "		Church Services – C of E, R.C. and Free Churches.	
"	" 20 "		General & Company Training including battle patrols.	
"	" 21st		General & Company Training. N.C.O's class under 2nd in Command (Major R.J.W.IND) commences.	
"	" 22nd		General & Company Training, and Bathing parade at the Baths at MOLLIENS VIDAMES. Under directions from Brigade Headquarters the early morning physical training parades were stopped. The Battn constructed shooting Butts on the training ground N. of the railway. [illegible]	
"	" 23rd		The Butts completed. A Company use the range all day for grouping practices. Other companies engaged in general & company training and also in a tactical scheme under the C.O. "C" Company is inspected by the G.O.C. at MOLLIENS VIDAMES.	
"	24th.		Grouping practice on the Range and general training. Brig. General GLASGOW visits the training ground.	

Instructions regarding War Diaries and Intelligence Summaries are contained in F. S. Regs., Part II. and the Staff Manual respectively. Title pages will be prepared in manuscript.

WAR DIARY
or
~~INTELLIGENCE SUMMARY.~~
(Erase heading not required.)

Army Form C. 2118.

Place	Date	Hour	Summary of Events and Information	Remarks and references to Appendices
	1916.			
CAMPS-EN-AMIENOIS	Nov 14th		General cleaning up and rest.	
"	" 15 "		General cleaning up and rest.	
"	" 16 "		Refitting and Company Training	
"	" 17 "		- do. - - do. -	
"	" 18 "		- do - - do -	
"	" 19 "		Church Services – C of E, R.C. and Free Churches.	
"	" 20 "		General + Company Training including battle patrols.	
"	" 21st		General + Company Training. N.C.O's class under 2nd in Command (Major R.J.W. IND) commences.	
"	" 22nd		General + Company Training, and Bathing parade at the Baths at MOLLIENS VIDAMES. Under directions from Brigade Headquarters the early morning physical training parades were stopped. The Battn constructed shooting Butts on the training ground N. of the railway. Fe	
"	" 23rd.		The Butts completed A Company use the range all day for grouping practices. Other companies engaged in general + company training and also in a tactical scheme under the C.O. "C" Company is inspected by the G.O.C at MOLLIENS VIDAMES.	
"	24th.		Grouping practice on the Range and general training. Brig. General GLASGOW visits the training ground.	

T2134. Wt. W708–776. 500000. 4/15. Sir J. C. & S.

Army Form C. 2118.

Instructions regarding War Diaries and Intelligence Summaries are contained in F. S. Regs., Part II. and the Staff Manual respectively. Title pages will be prepared in manuscript.

WAR DIARY
or
~~INTELLIGENCE SUMMARY.~~
(Erase heading not required.)

Place	Date	Hour	Summary of Events and Information	Remarks and references to Appendices
	1916. Nov.			
CAMPS-EN-AMIENOIS.	25th		Under Divisional Instructions FOOT FRICTION DRILL is commenced morning and afternoon. General Training on the training ground. Night Operations by all companies	
"	26th		Church Services.	
"	27th		General training. Short route march for A. B. + D companies in the morning and Night Operations "Marching to a point of Assembly".	
"	28th		General Training and Musketry	
"	29th		General Training with night operations. Bathing Parades at MOLLIENS VIDAMES	
"	30th		Battalion Drill and general training, with night operations.	

[signature] Lieut. Col.
Commdg. 10th. West Yorkshire Regt.

T2134. Wt. W708—776. 500000. 4/15. Sir J. C. & S.

Instructions regarding War Diaries and Intelligence Summaries are contained in F. S. Regs., Part II. and the Staff Manual respectively. Title pages will be prepared in manuscript.

WAR DIARY
or
~~INTELLIGENCE SUMMARY.~~
(Erase heading not required.)

Army Form C. 2118.

Place	Date	Hour	Summary of Events and Information	Remarks and references to Appendices
	1916. Nov.			
CAMPS-EN-AMIENOIS	25th		Under Divisional Instructions FOOT FRICTION DRILL is commenced morning and afternoon. General Training on the training ground. Night Operations by all companies.	
"	26th		Church Services.	
"	27th		General training. Short route march for A. B. + D companies in the morning and Night Operations "Marching to a point of Assembly".	
"	28th		General Training and Musketry	
"	29th		General Training with night operations. Bathing Parades at MOLLIENS VIDAMES.	
"	30th		Battalion Drill and general training, with night operations.	

[signature] Lieut. Col.
Commdg. 10th. West Yorkshire Regt.

T2134. Wt. W708–776. 500000. 4/15. Sir J. C. & S.

SECRET. 10th West Yorkshire Regiment. 5/7/16

OPERATION ORDER No. 29 Copy No 13

Reference Trench map 57.c. S.W $\frac{1}{20,000}$

1 The Battalion will relieve the 7th East Yorkshire Regiment in the trenches tomorrow.

The Battalion will march at 8-0 A.M to F Camp at S28.c.4.11.

ROUTE. MAMETZ – MONTAUBAN.

STARTING POINT. North West extremity of MANSEL COPSE

A ORDER OF MARCH. as per margin.

C Distance of 200 yds will be kept between Companies who will march in file

D TRANSPORT. Cookers & Lewis Gun limbers only will accompany the Battalion.

B DRESS. Battle order. Leather jerkins will be worn.

HQ An advance party consisting of 1 N.C.O per Company and H.Q under

Transport. 2nd Lieut. J. E. Rose will march at 6-45 A.M to take over F Camp.

The Sapping Platoon under 2nd Lieut. W. J. Hartnoll will report to O/C 78th Field Company R.E. at Brigade H.Q at 3-0 P.M

O/C B Company will detail a carrying party of 1 Officer and 50 O.R.

O/C C Company will detail 1 Officer for the same party.

This party will relieve a similar party of the 7th East Yorkshire Regt at T.8. Central at 12 noon

The Senior Officer will take over all Stores at T.8. Central and report contents of dump to Brigade.

OFFICERS KITS will be stacked at Q.M. Stores by 7-30 A.M.

Great coats and blankets will be stacked at Q.M. Stores by 7-0 A.M.

The usual procedure as to cleaning up the Camp will be adhered to.

2 The Battalion will march from F Camp at 5-0 P.M in the same order via S edge BERNAFAY WOOD – CORDUROY ROAD – DUCKBOARDS.

Guides will be met at T.2.d. Central (approx)

Two days preserved rations will be carried by each man.

Water will be carried at the rate of 1 tin per 4 men.

These will be issued at F Camp during the mid-day halt

Company Commanders will arrange to detail 1 N.C.Os or selected men to carry VERY lights and flares for contact in their pockets to keep these articles dry. They will also arrange that Platoon

Commanders take 1 quart of rum (2 water bottles full) and Platoon Sergeants 1 quart of Whale oil, each, to the trenches.
Taking over parties of 1 Officer and 4 NCOs per Company, Lewis Gun Officer and Intelligence Officer will proceed to the trenches. They will report to the Adjutant at F Camp on arrival.

H A g [illegible] Act. Adjutant.
10th West Yorkshire Regiment

Issued at 10.0 P.M.

Copy No. 1. 2nd in C.
2 O/C. A. Coy.
3 " B "
4 " C "
5 " D "
6 L.G.O.
7 Q.M.
8 I.O.

Copy No. 9. B.O.
10 M.O.
11 R.S.M.
12 Sig. Sgt.
13 War Diary
14 Retained.

2T

10th West Yorkshire Regiment
Operation Orders No. 30 12-11-16.

1. The Battalion will march to SAND PITS CAMP (about E 18 d 3 4) at 4-0 P.M to day.
ROUTE CARNOY ROAD – MANSEL CAMP – FRICOURT CEMETERY – CARCAILLOT FARM.
Companies will move off in file in the following order A.B.C.D. The usual intervals will be observed.

2. Details will march from MANSEL CAMP direct to SAND PITS under the orders of Major R. J.W. IND.

3. An advance party of 1 N.C.O. per company under Lt. C.A. Owen will proceed to SAND PITS at 2-0 P.M to take over the Camp.

4. All Wheeled Transport will report to O.C. Divisional Train at SAND PITS CAMP. to night. Two cookers and one Water Cart will be retained which will report to O.C. Divisional Train on the night of the 13th inst.

5. The march of the Wheeled transport to the new area will be under the O.C. Train. The column will halt at DAOURS for the night of the 13th and will rejoin the battalion on the night of the 14th.

6. Arrangements as to transport from here are uncertain But it is hoped that a Motor Lorry will bring on blankets and packs to SAND PITS during to day.

(Sd) A. Y. G. Anderson Capt adjt
10th West Yorkshire Regiment.

SECRET

10th West Yorkshire Regiment
Operation Orders No 31 13-11-16

1 The Battalion will entrain for the XIV Corp Rest Area this morning at EDGE HILL station DERNANCOURT

ROUTE - CARCAILLOT FARM - MEAULTE - DERNANCOURT - EDGE HILL siding.

Order of March. B.C.D.A. H.Qtrs. Lewis Guns.

Hour of Start 6-45 A.M. Lame men for whom it has been impossible to arrange transport will parade at 5-30 A.m. under Lieut. E. J. SMITH and will march by the same route joining the Battalion at EDGE HILL SIDING. Company Commanders will nominate men for this party and will keep the number as low as possible.

The march to the train will be by half Companies or equivilant parties in single file at intervals of not less than 50 yards.

DRESS. Full marching order with packs.

Steel Helmets will be worn strapped to the packs in the authorized manner.

II The Camp must be left scrupulously clean. The Orderly Officer, Lieut. C. A. Owens will inspect the lines at 6.30 A.M. and will see that this is done.

III The entrainment must be carried out quickly and in silence and there must be no talking or shouting whilst entering the carriage. Men must on no account leave the compartments without the permission of an Officer.

(Sd) A. F. G. Anderson Capt. Adjt.

10th West Yorkshire Regiment

13 E.
Yorkshire
315d
8B

Vol 12

WAR DIARY FOR
THE MONTH
OF
DECEMBER 1916.
FOR

10TH WEST YORKSHIRE
REGIMENT

Instructions regarding War Diaries and Intelligence Summaries are contained in F. S. Regs., Part II. and the Staff Manual respectively. Title pages will be prepared in manuscript.

WAR DIARY
or
INTELLIGENCE SUMMARY.
(Erase heading not required.)

Army Form C. 2118.

10th W. Yorks.

Place	Date	Hour	Summary of Events and Information	Remarks and references to Appendices
CAMPS EN AMIENOIS	1/12/16		Battalion in billets at CAMPS-EN-AMIENOIS (refce map DIEPPE 16 1:100000) Battalion training and Musketry.	
"	2nd		Battalion training and musketry.	
"	3rd		Sunday Divine Service.	
"	4th		Battalion training and musketry.	
"	5th		Battalion inspected at MOLLIENS VIDAME by Brigadier General YATMAN D.S.O on assuming Command of the 50th Brigade.	
"	6th		Baths at MOLLIENS VIDAME. Battalion training	
"	7th		Battalion training and musketry.	
"	8th		Musketry. Route march with tactical scheme, night operations	
"	9th		Musketry. Route march with tactical scheme, night operations	
"	10th		Sunday. Divine Service	
"	11th		Musketry. Route march with tactical scheme. Lieut. Col. G.H. SOAMES left the Battalion and Major P.R. SIMNER from the 9th Duke of Wellingtons West Riding Regiment assumed Command.	
	12th		Route march with tactical scheme. Night operations.	

T2134. Wt. W708—776. 500000. 4/15. Sir J. C. & S.

Army Form C. 2118

Instructions regarding War Diaries and Intelligence Summaries are contained in F. S. Regs., Part II. and the Staff Manual respectively. Title Pages will be prepared in manuscript.

Duplicate

WAR DIARY
or
INTELLIGENCE SUMMARY
(Erase heading not required.)

10th 10 Yorks

Place	Date	Hour	Summary of Events and Information	Remarks and references to Appendices
CAMPS EN AMIENOIS	1/12/16		Battalion in billets at CAMPS-EN-AMIENOIS (refce map DIEPPE 16 1:100000) Battalion training and Musketry.	
"	2nd		Battalion training and musketry.	
"	3rd		Sunday. Divine Service.	
"	4th		Battalion training and musketry.	
"	5th		Battalion inspected at MOLLIENS VIDAME by Brigadier General YATMAN D.S.O. on assuming Command of the 50th Brigade.	
"	6th		Baths at MOLLIENS VIDAME. Battalion training	
"	7th		Battalion training and musketry.	
"	8th		Musketry. Route march with tactical scheme, night operations	
"	9th		Musketry. Route march with tactical scheme, night operations	
"	10th		Sunday. Divine Service	
"	11th		Musketry. Route march with tactical scheme. Lieut. Col. G.H. SOAMES left the Battalion and Major P.R. SIMNER from the 9th Duke of Wellingtons West Riding Regiment assumed Command.	
	12th		Route march with tactical scheme. Night operations	A7GA

1875 Wt. W593/826 1,000,000 4/15 J.B.C. & A. A.D.S.S./Forms/C. 2118.

Instructions regarding War Diaries and Intelligence Summaries are contained in F. S. Regs., Part II. and the Staff Manual respectively. Title pages will be prepared in manuscript.

WAR DIARY
or
INTELLIGENCE SUMMARY.
(Erase heading not required.)

Army Form C. 2118.

Place	Date	Hour	Summary of Events and Information	Remarks and references to Appendices
CAMPS-EN AMIENOIS AND LONGPRE-LES CORPS	13th		Battalion marched to temporary billets at LONGPRE-LES-CORPS-SAINTS (Refce map ABBEVILLE 1:100000) distance about 11 miles preparatory to moving up into CORPS RESERVE XIV Corps.	O.O. attached
LONGPRE-LES CORPS AND VILLE	14th		Battalion entrained at LONGPRE and proceeded by rail to EDGE HILL siding (Refce map ALBERT 1:40000 E25a) and marched to billets in VILLE.	
VILLE	15th		Training under Company Commanders. In the afternoon the Medical Officer lectured Companies on Sanitation in the trenches	
"	16th		Training of Specialists and close order drill by the remainder.	
"	17th		Sunday Divine Service.	
"	18th		Training of Specialists. Remainder - Bayonet fighting and close order drill	
"			Capt. W. A. BOWMAN R.A.M.C. reported for duty vice Lieut. P.A. BENNET-CLARKE proceeding on leave	
"	19th		Training of Specialists. Remainder - Bayonet fighting and drill.	
"	20th		Training of Specialists. Remainder - Bayonet fighting and drill.	
"	21st		Companies at the disposal of Company Commanders. Special attention paid to cleaning of billets preparatory to move.	

T2134. Wt. W708—776. 500000. 4/15. Sir J. C. & S.

Army Form C. 2118

Instructions regarding War Diaries and Intelligence Summaries are contained in F. S. Regs., Part II. and the Staff Manual respectively. Title Pages will be prepared in manuscript.

WAR DIARY
or
INTELLIGENCE SUMMARY
(Erase heading not required.)

Place	Date	Hour	Summary of Events and Information	Remarks and references to Appendices
CAMPS-EN AMIENOIS AND LONGPRE-LES CORPS	13th		Battalion marched to temporary billets at LONGPRE-LES-CORPS-SAINTS (Refer map ABBEVILLE 1:100000) distance about 11 miles preparatory to moving up into CORPS RESERVE - XIV Corps.	O.O. Attached
LONGPRE-LES CORPS AND VILLE	14th		Battalion entrained at LONGPRE and proceeded by rail to EDGE HILL siding (Refer map ALBERT 1:40000 E.25.a.) and marched to billets in VILLE.	
VILLE	15th		Training under Company Commanders. In the afternoon the Medical Officer lectured Companies on Sanitation in the trenches	
"	16th		Training of Specialists and close order drill by the remainder.	
"	17th		Sunday Divine Service.	
"	18th		Training of Specialists. Remainder - Bayonet fighting and close order drill Capt. W. A. BOWMAN R.A.M.C. reported for duty vice Lieut. P.A. BENNET-CLARKE proceeding on leave	
"	19th		Training of Specialists. Remainder - Bayonet fighting and drill.	
"	20th		Training of Specialists. Remainder - Bayonet fighting and drill.	
"	21st		Companies at the disposal of Company Commanders. Special attention paid to cleaning of billets preparatory to move.	

A7022

1875 Wt. W593/826 1,000,000 4/15 J.B.C. & A. A.D.S.S./Forms/C. 2118.

Instructions regarding War Diaries and Intelligence Summaries are contained in F. S. Regs., Part II. and the Staff Manual respectively. Title pages will be prepared in manuscript.

WAR DIARY
or
INTELLIGENCE SUMMARY.
(*Erase heading not required.*)

Army Form C. 2118.

Place	Date	Hour	Summary of Events and Information	Remarks and references to Appendices
VILLE AND GUILLEMONT	22nd		Battalion marched to new camp at GUILLEMONT (Refce map ALBERT 1:40000 T19.c) Distance about 11 miles.	O.O. attached
GUILLEMONT AND LES BOEUFS Trenches	23rd		Battalion moved into front line trenches at LES BOEUFS relieving 12th Battalion Rifle Brigade. Dispositions as follows. D. Coy. BENNETT trench B Coy. FALL and AUTUMN C. Coy. FROSTY and WINTER (in support) A Coy COW trench and strong points (in reserve)	
LES BOEUFS Trenches	24th		Quiet day. Enemy became very nervous in the evening opening a heavy barrage on LES BOEUFS and the support line at 8.45 p.m. The firing was very wild and little damage was done although OZONE support trench was hit in several places. All quiet at 9-20 p.m	
"	25th		Our artillery bombarded the German lines sharply for quarter of an hour at 8-30AM and again at 11-30 A.M. The enemy replied with searching fire on the support line and sunken roads. Very little damage was done. Our Casualties - 2/Lieut W. J. HARTNOLL wounded by shell splinter in thigh but remained at duty. 1. O.R was Killed, 1. O.R Died of Wounds 1. O.R Wounded. The Battalion were relieved at night by the 7th East Yorkshire Regiment	316d

T2134. Wt. W708—776. 500000. 4/15. Sir J. C. & S.

Army Form C. 2118

Instructions regarding War Diaries and Intelligence Summaries are contained in F. S. Regs., Part II. and the Staff Manual respectively. Title Pages will be prepared in manuscript.

WAR DIARY
or
INTELLIGENCE SUMMARY
(Erase heading not required.)

Place	Date	Hour	Summary of Events and Information	Remarks and references to Appendices
VILLE AND GUILLEMONT	22nd		Battalion marched to new camp at GUILLEMONT (Refce map ALBERT 1:40000 T19.c) Distance about 11 miles.	O.O. attached.
GUILLEMONT AND LES BOEUFS Trenches	23rd		Battalion moved into front line trenches at LES BOEUFS relieving 12th Battalion Rifle Brigade. Dispositions as follows. D. Coy. BENNETT trench B Coy. FALL and AUTUMN C. Coy. FROSTY and WINTER (in support) A. Coy. COW trench and strong points (in reserve)	
LES BOEUFS Trenches	24th		Quiet day. Enemy became very nervous in the evening opening a heavy barrage on LES BOEUFS and the support line at 8.45 p.m. The firing was very wild and little damage was done although OZONE ~~support~~ C.T. trench was hit in several places. All quiet at 9-20 p.m	
"	25th		Our artillery bombarded the German lines sharply for quarter of an hour at 8.30 AM and again at 11-30 A.M. The enemy replied with searching fire on the support line and sunken roads. Very little damage was done. Our Casualties – 2/Lieut W. J. HARTNOLL wounded by shell splinter in thigh but remained at duty. 1. O.R was Killed, 1. O.R Died. .. O.R Wounded. The Battalion was relieved at night by the 7th East Yorkshire Regiment	

1875 Wt. W593/826 1,000,000 4/15 J.B.C. & A. A.D.S.S./Forms/C. 2118.

Instructions regarding War Diaries and Intelligence Summaries are contained in F. S. Regs., Part II. and the Staff Manual respectively. Title pages will be prepared in manuscript.

WAR DIARY
or
INTELLIGENCE SUMMARY.
(Erase heading not required.)

Army Form C. 2118.

Place	Date	Hour	Summary of Events and Information	Remarks and references to Appendices
LES BOEUFS Trenches	25th		proceeded to Camp No 22. CARNOY - MONTAUBAN road. (Refer map ALBERT 1:40000 A.8.)	
			Evacuations for trench feet during the tour of the trenches. NIL.	
CAMP No 22 CARNOY	26th		General cleaning up and improvement of the Camp.	
	27th		General cleaning up and improvement of the Camp.	
CARNOY AND GUILLEMONT	28th		Battalion less details marched to GUILLEMONT Camp arriving there at 3·30 pm.	
	"		Details remained at No 22 Camp under the Command of Major R.J.W. IND	
	"		D Coy moved forward and occupied the FLERS line trench to provide carrying parties to the front line.	
LES BOEUFS Trenches	29th		Battalion relieved the 7th Border Regiment in the LES BOEUFS trenches dispositions being as follows:- C. Coy BENNETT TRENCH. A. Coy. FALL and AUTUMN. B Coy. (in support) WINTER and FROSTY. D. Coy moved up from the FLERS line to Battalion reserve in COW trench and strong points.	317d

Instructions regarding War Diaries and Intelligence Summaries are contained in F. S. Regs., Part II. and the Staff Manual respectively. Title Pages will be prepared in manuscript.

WAR DIARY
or
INTELLIGENCE SUMMARY
(Erase heading not required.)

Army Form C. 2118

Place	Date	Hour	Summary of Events and Information	Remarks and references to Appendices
LES BOEUFS Trenches	25th		proceeded to Camp No. 22. CARNOY - MONTAUBAN road. (Refce map ALBERT 1:40000 A.8.)	
			Evacuations for trench feet during the tour of the trenches NIL.	
CAMP No. 22 CARNOY	26th		General cleaning up and improvement of the Camp.	
	27th		General cleaning up and improvement of the Camp.	
CARNOY AND GUILLEMONT	28th		Battalion less details marched to GUILLEMONT Camp arriving there at 3·30 pm.	
	"		Details remained at No. 22 Camp under the Command of Major R. J. W. IND	
	"		D Coy. moved forward and occupied the FLERS line trench to provide carrying parties to the front line.	
LES BOEUFS Trenches	29th		Battalion relieved the 7th Border Regiment in the LES BOEUFS trenches dispositions being as follows:- C. Coy BENNETT TRENCH.	
			A. Coy. FALL and AUTUMN.	
			B Coy. (in support) WINTER and FROSTY.	
			D. Coy. moved up from the FLERS line to Battalion reserve in COW trench and strong points.	

1875 Wt. W593/826 1,000,000 4/15 J.B.C. & A. A.D.S.S./Forms/C. 2118.

Army Form C. 2118.

Instructions regarding War Diaries and Intelligence Summaries are contained in F. S. Regs., Part II. and the Staff Manual respectively. Title pages will be prepared in manuscript.

WAR DIARY
or
INTELLIGENCE SUMMARY.
(Erase heading not required.)

Place	Date	Hour	Summary of Events and Information	Remarks and references to Appendices
[..]ES BOEUFS TRENCHES	30th		Considerable shell fire all through the night of the 30/31st. 2/LIEUTS. N. NEWTON. C.R INGHAM, and F.L. TODD Joined the Battalion.	
"	31st		Battalion were relieved by the 7th East Yorkshire Regt. and proceeded to Camp No 22 CARNOY. Total Casualties during the two days in the trenches a/R.S.M TOSE and 2. O.R Wounded.	318d

Army Form C. 2118

Instructions regarding War Diaries and Intelligence Summaries are contained in F. S. Regs., Part II. and the Staff Manual respectively. Title Pages will be prepared in manuscript.

WAR DIARY
or
INTELLIGENCE SUMMARY
(Erase heading not required.)

Place	Date	Hour	Summary of Events and Information	Remarks and references to Appendices
LES BOEUFS TRENCHES	30th		Considerable shell fire all through the night of the 30/31st. 2/LIEUTS. N. NEWTON. C.R INGHAM and F.L. TODD joined the Battalion.	
	31st		Battalion were relieved by the 7th East Yorkshire Regt and proceeded to Camp No 22 CARNOY. Total Casualties during the two days in the trenches of R.S.M TOSE and 2. O.R Wounded.	

1875 Wt. W593/826 1,000,000 4/15 J.B.C. & A. A.D.S.S./Forms/C. 2118.

W.Y.175

58 Infantry Brigade

Attached please find War Diary for the month of November, 1916. Please acknowledge receipt.

3.12.16.

[signature] Lt Col.
Comdg 10 West York Regt.

10TH WEST YORKSHIRE REGT. SECRET.

Operation Orders No. 32 12-12-16

REFERENCE MAPS. 1/100000 AMIENS + DIEPPE
and Administrative Map Sheet 3.

1. The Battalion will move into Corps Reserve at VILLE tomorrow 13th instant, billeting at LONGPRE on the night of the 13th/14th instant and entraining for EDGE HILL at 8.0 A.M on the 14th instant.
2. Advanced Billeting parties will be found as follows:
   1. A party of 5.N.C.Os (one from each company and one from Headquarters) under Lieut. C.A. OWENS will parade at Orderly Room at 6.0 A.M tomorrow. They will leave MOLLIENS VIDAME by train at 7.30 A.M. A representative of the 50th Infantry Brigade will have a movement order for the party. On arrival at the destination the party will at once proceed to VILLE and report to the Town Major to take over all billets and stores.
   2. A party of 5.N.C.Os (one from each Company and one from Headquarters) under 2nd. Lieut. H.A.C. NEVILLE will parade with bicycles at Orderly Room at 7.0 A.M. They will proceed to MONTAGNE when they will report at the Orderly Room of the 7th. East Yorkshire Regiment at 8.0 A.M. Afterwards they will report to the Town Major, LONGPRE, and will arrange billets for the Battalion for the night of the 13th/14th instant.
3. While in Corps Reserve the Battalion will find a standing working party of 1 sergeant and 50 other ranks for loading and unloading R.E. Stores. They will report daily to the Foremen of Works at M.M. dump MEAULTE at E.22. Central.
   They will parade at Orderly Room at 7.30 A.M tomorrow and will be marched to the Orderly Room of the

7th East Yorkshire Regt. where they will report at 9.0 A.M. They will march and billet with the 7th East Yorkshire Regt. on the 13th and on detraining at destination will proceed at once to where they have to report in order to relieve a corresponding working party of the 29th Division. They will carry rations for the 13th and 14th instant. Whilst at VILLE they will be billeted and rationed by the Battalion and will report daily at 9.0 A.M.

A. Company will supply 25 men and C Company will supply 1 sergeant and 25 men.

4. SICK PARADE. will be at 6.0 A.M. to-morrow.

5. BATTALION PARADE. The Battalion will parade in the streets outside billets ready to march away at 8.45 A.M., with the head of the column at the crossroads, opposite the Village Church in the following order Headquarters, A, B, Drums, C, D. Lewis Guns.

DRESS. Full marching order. Steel helmets to be strapped to the packs. If raining ground sheets will be worn.

6. MARCH DISCIPLINE. The strictest march discipline will be observed. No man will fall out on the line of march without written permission from an officer. This order must be read out to all ranks on parade before starting.

7. BAGGAGE. All officers kits, blankets, and stores will be stacked at the Quartermaster's Stores by 7.0 A.M.

(Sd) A. F. G. Anderson, Capt.,
Adjutant,
10th West Yorkshire Regt.

No. W.Y. 535 Operation Orders No 33.

1 The Battalion will proceed in the square by the Church ready to march to the train at 6-55 A.M.

2/Lieut Hay and one N.C.O from each Company will report to the Staff Captain at the R.T.Os office at 6-45 A.M to arrange the entrainment.

Lewis Gun Handcarts and bicycles will be paraded separately at Orderly Room (2 men with each cart and one signaller for two bicycles) at 6-30 A.M. 2/Lieut. ROSE will see that they are in the railway yard by 7-0 AM

2. BILLETS must be left scrupulously clean and all latrines filled in. A certificate to this effect will be handed to the Adjutant on parade.

13/12/16

(Sd) A. T. G. Anderson Capt
Adjutant
10th West Yorkshire Regiment

10th. West Yorkshire Regt. SECRET.

Operation Order No. 34. 21-12-16.

I The Battalion will march to GUILLEMONT to-morrow preparatory to moving into the front line trenches.

STARTING POINT.	Road junction E 25 d central.
ORDER OF MARCH.	Headquarters, D.C, Drums, A.B. Sapping Platoon, Transport.
TIME.	Head of the column to be ready to march off at 10.15 A.M.
ROUTE.	MEAULTE, MAMETZ, MONTAUBAN BERNAFAY corner. East of MEAULTE the Battalion will march in file with 200 yards distance between Companies.
DRESS.	Marching Order without packs. Steel helmets will be worn. Water bottles will be filled before starting. Rifles will be wrapped in sandbags as explained personally to Company Commanders this afternoon. Greatcoats will not be worn or taken to the trenches.
BLANKETS.	All blankets will be rolled in bundles of ten and stacked in the archway at Battalion Headquarters by 5.30 A.M. They will be conveyed to GUILLEMONT by motor lorry.
PACKS.	Greatcoats will be left in packs, which will be stacked at Q.M. stores by 8.0 A.M. Two G.S. waggons from Brigade Headquarters will convey these to CARNOY where they will be available when the Battalion comes out of the trenches.

II. ADVANCE PARTY.	2nd Lieut. MAY and 5 N.C.O's (one from each Company and one from Headquarters) will proceed to GUILLEMONT at 8.30 A.M. to take over the camp. They will meet the Battalion on arrival and guide Companies to their quarters.
III. BILLETS.	Billets must be left scrupulously clean and a certificate to that effect rendered to the Adjutant before leaving

(Sd) A. F. G. Anderson, Capt.,
Adjutant,
10th West Yorkshire Regt.

319d

10th West Yorkshire Regt.

Operation Order No. 35

SECRET.

27-12-16

1. The Battalion, ~~less~~ Details, will move to Camp at GUILLEMONT to-morrow. Probable hour of start 12-0 noon. Order of march A.B.C.D. Companies will march in file with an interval of 200 yds. between Companies. The Transport Officer will arrange transport for the Lewis Guns and Officers kits. Steel helmets will be worn. Water bottles will be filled before starting. Rifles will wrapped in sand-bags. Blankets will be stacked in the Q.M. stores by 9.0 A.M.

II ADVANCED PARTY.

2nd Lt. MAY and 5 N.C.Os. (one from each company and one from Headquarters) will proceed to GUILLEMONT at 11-0 A.M. to take over the camp. They will meet the Battalion on arrival and guide Companies to their quarters.

III HUTS, LINES, LATRINES. must be left scrupulously clean and a certificate to that effect rendered to the Adjutant, by Company Commanders before leaving.

IV FEET: Foot Friction drill will be carried out before 9.0 A.M. under Company arrangements. a certificate that the feet of all men have been rubbed and properly treated. will be rendered to Orderly Room by Company Commanders by 10-30 A.M.

V. GUILLEMONT CAMP Whilst at GUILLEMONT the Battalion will be responible for the cleanliness of the camp, and the following procedure will be carried out:-

(a) At 9.0 A.M. all huts in the northern row will be cleared of personnel, who will be fallen in outside and clear of the huts with all their kits and blankets.

(B) A party will be told off from the Southern row to clean up the huts in the northern row and collect any salvage left unclaimed.

(C) At 10-0 A.M. huts in the southern row will be cleared in a similar manner.

VI FLERS-LINE After a short rest D. COY. will proceed from GUILLEMONT to the FLERS-LINE taking over from a Company of the 8th South Staffords Regt., who will send two guides to GUILLEMONT by 2.0 P.M. Each Battalion in the line will keep two guides at Company Headquarters in the FLERS-LINE to guide carrying parties to Battalion dumps. On the 29th inst D Coy. will send two guides to reach GUILLEMONT by 2.0 P.M. to guide up the releiving Company of the 6th Dorsetshire Regt.

VII CARRYING PARTIES:- If material has to be sent up from Brigade Headquarters the Companies at GUILLEMONT will carry to the FLERS-LINE and the Company in FLERS-LINE to the Battalion dump.

(SD) A. F. G. Anderson. Capt.
Adjutant
10 West Yorkshire Regt.

321a

10th West Yorkshire Regt. SECRET.
Operation Orders. No 36. 28-12-16.

I The Battalion will relieve the 7th Border Regt in the front line trenches to-morrow afternoon.
Companies will relieve as follows:-
C. Coy will relieve A Coy. 7th Borders in BENNETT
2 Platoons of A. Coy. will relieve 2 Platoons of D. Coy. 7th Borders in FALL
2 Platoons of A Coy will relieve 2 Platoons of D. Coy. 7th Borders in AUTUMN
2 Platoons of B. Coy. will relieve 2 Platoons of C. Coy. 7th Borders in WINTER
2 Platoons of B. Coy will relieve 2 Platoons of C. Coy. 7th Borders in FROSTY
D. Coy. from (the FLERS. line) will relieve B Coy 7th Borders in COW.

II HOUR OF START. 3.30 P.M. in the following order C. A. B. HQrs.

GUIDES will meet A.B.C. Coys and Headquarters at the end of the duckwalks near GINCHY corner Headquarters will proceed direct to the Headquarters of the 7th Border Regt.. The three Coys with one guide each will proceed to Battalion Dump COW trench where they will be met by 6 guides (2 per Coy.) ~~lead~~ who will lead them to RUNNERS POST. At RUNNERS POST guides for each platoon will be ready to conduct them to their trenches.

B. Company of the 7th Border Regt. will send 2 guides to the FLERS-line by 3.30 P.M. to guide D. Coy to COW. trench.

All guides will be provided with slips giving their destination.

GUM. BOOTS. As many as possible will be drawn before starting and carried up to the trenches where they will be put on. Names of the men to whom these are issued will be taken and they will be held responisible for the return of the boots on coming out of the trenches.

(v) Company Commanders and the Intelligence Officer will reconnoitre their sectors on 26th instant. Instructions will be issued later.

Issued by messenger
at 11.30 pm

Copy No. 1 War Diary
2 C.O.
3 O/c A. Coy.
4 " B "
5 " C "
6 " D "
7 Q.M. & T.O.
8 R.S.M.
9. O.C. Essex Reg.
10. File.

(Sd) A.F.G. ANDERSON, Capt
Adjutant
West Yorkshire Regt.

14. E.
[illegible]

50/17

10th W. Yorks,
Jan. 1917

4718B

WAR DIARY

FOR

JANUARY 19

OF

10TH WEST YORKSHIRE

REGIMENT.

Vol 13

To

WY0408

472a

50th Inf. Brigade

Herewith War Diary for the month January 1917.

1-2-17. A.R. Simner Lieut. Col

Comdg. 10th West Yorkshire Regt

10th (S) Bn. WEST YORKSHIRE REGT.
No.........................
Date.......................

Instructions regarding War Diaries and Intelligence Summaries are contained in F. S. Regs., Part II. and the Staff Manual respectively. Title pages will be prepared in manuscript.

WAR DIARY

or

~~INTELLIGENCE SUMMARY~~.

(Erase heading not required.)

Army Form C. 2118.

Place	Date	Hour	Summary of Events and Information	Remarks and references to Appendices
No 22 CARNOY	1-1-17		Battalion in Divisional Reserve in Camp No 22 CARNOY (Refce map ALBERT 1/40000 A 8) the day was devoted to general cleaning up after the trenches. Baths were obtained at the Divisional Baths in MONTAUBAN	
"	2nd		Company training and Gas Helmet drill. Instruction of Junior officers in Personal Hygiene by Second in Command and Medical officer	
"	3rd		Company training	
CARNOY and GUILLEMONT	4th		The Battalion (less C Coy) moved to GUILLEMONT camp. A working party consisting of 3 officers and 210 O.R carried duckboards from GINCHY to DECAUVILLE railhead. C Coy proceeded direct to FLERS line for the night to act as Brigade carrying party for material required to be taken up from the intermediate dump east of GINCHY to the new BULL dump at about T9. b4. 2nd Lt. W. R. G. HOLLAND joined the Battalion.	
GUILLEMONT AND TRENCHES	5th		Battalion engaged in sand bagging the huts in GUILLEMONT camp. 1800 sandbags laid. Battalion relieved the 7th BORDER Regt. in the front line trenches, dispositions being as follows. D. Coy. BENNETT trench.	473a

T2134. Wt. W708—776. 500000. 4/15. Sir J. C. & S.

Instructions regarding War Diaries and Intelligence Summaries are contained in F. S. Regs., Part II. and the Staff Manual respectively. Title pages will be prepared in manuscript.

WAR DIARY

or

~~INTELLIGENCE SUMMARY.~~

(Erase heading not required.)

Army Form C. 2118.

Place	Date	Hour	Summary of Events and Information	Remarks and references to Appendices
	Contd			
TRENCHES	5th		B Coy FALL and AUTUMN. A Coy WINTER and FROSTY	
			C. Coy COW trench and strong points	
	6th		Quiet day in trenches. Every available man employed in draining and improving trenches and wiring front line.	
TRENCHES and CARNOY	7th		Battalion was relieved by the 7th EAST YORKSHIRE Regt and proceeded to Camp XXII CARNOY. Casualties during tour of 48 hrs in trenches. 1 O.R. killed and 16 O.R. wounded	
CARNOY	8th		General cleaning up.	
-	9th		Company training. A party consisting of 1 officer and 50 O.R. proceeded	
-	-		to the CITADEL for the one days GAS course at the XIV Corp school	
-	-		All available officers and 100 O.R attended a lecture on cooperations	
-	-		between Infantry and aeroplanes by an Officer of the Royal Flying Corps in	
CARNOY	-		the Y.M.C.A hut CARNOY. 2/Lt E. CLOUGH Joined the Battalion.	
GUILLEMONT and CARNOY	10th		Battalion (less B Coy) moved to GUILLEMONT camp. A party consisting of 3 officers and 210 O.R. carried duck-boards from GINCHY to DECAUVILLE	
-	-		railhead. B. Coy proceeded direct to the FLERS line. Lieut. C.A. OWENS	
-	-		Killed by a shell at GINCHY corner while on detached duty with sapping platoons.	

4740

T2134. Wt. W708—776. 500000. 4/15. Sir J. C. & S.

Army Form C. 2118.

Instructions regarding War Diaries and Intelligence Summaries are contained in F. S. Regs., Part II. and the Staff Manual respectively. Title pages will be prepared in manuscript.

WAR DIARY
or
~~INTELLIGENCE~~ SUMMARY.
(Erase heading not required.)

Place	Date	Hour	Summary of Events and Information	Remarks and references to Appendices
GUILLEMONT	11th		Morning spent in sand bagging huts in GUILLEMONT camp. Large carrying	
	-		parties - 360 men in all - employed in carrying up material for wiring the	
	-		reserve line.	
GUILLEMONT and TRENCHES.	12th		Battalion relieved the 7th BORDER Regt in the front line trenches dispositions	
	-		being as follows. C. Coy. Right and Centre of BENNETT.	
-	-		A. Coy. Left of BENNETT, FALL and AUTUMN. D Coy. FROSTY and WINTER.	
-	-		B Coy. 2 Platoons COW trench 2 Platoons in sunken road dug outs.	
-	-		All available men were employed in carrying up wiring material to the front line.	
TRENCHES	13th		Lieut. F. J. REYNOLDS rejoined from England. Wiring of front line carried on	
-	-		by all available men throughout the night.	
-	14th		Wiring of front line completed on the entire length. One German prisoner	
-	14th		captured belonging to 121st Regt. 2nd Batt. 26th Division.	
TRENCHES and CARNOY	14th		Battalion relieved by 1st Kings Own Scottish Borderers and marched to Camp	
	-		N° ~~XXII~~ CARNOY. Total casualties during 48 hours in trenches 2/Lt. INGHAM	
-	-		slightly wounded but remaining at duty. 2/Lt. M. PLOWMAN and 10. O.R. Wounded.	
CARNOY and CORBIE	- 15th		Battalion moved into Corps Reserve in billets in CORBIE, entraining at PLATEAU	4751

Instructions regarding War Diaries and Intelligence Summaries are contained in F. S. Regs., Part II. and the Staff Manual respectively. Title pages will be prepared in manuscript.

WAR DIARY
or
~~INTELLIGENCE SUMMARY~~.
(Erase heading not required.)

Army Form C. 2118.

Place	Date	Hour	Summary of Events and Information	Remarks and references to Appendices
CARNOY and CORBIE	15th		station at 2-0 p.m. and arriving at 7-15 p.m. Major R. J. W. IND assumed	
	.		command during the absence on leave of Major P.R. SIMNER	
CORBIE	16th		General cleaning up.	
-	17th		Company Parades - Running drill	
-	18th		Company Parades - Running drill. A party consisting of 1 officer and 132 O.R.	
-	.		proceeded to PONT REMY by train for Musketry course at the Fourth Army	
-	.		Musketry Camp. The following honours and rewards gained by the	
-	.		Battalion were notified in D.R.O. as having been published in the New	
-	.		Year Despatch. Lieut. Col. P.R. SIMNER D.S.O.	
.	.		" " G.H. SOAMES Mention	
.	.		Capt. W.A.L. BURNE Mention	
.	.		Hon. Lieut and Quartermaster J. J. GREEN New higher rate of pay	
.	.		No 6166 Sgt. HUBBARD B. Mention	
.	.		No 17294 Sgt. HACKWORTH W.D Mention	
-	19th		Company training - Running drill. Specialist training	
-	20th		A party consisting of 5 officers and 24 O.R attended a practical demonstration	

476d

T2134. Wt. W708-776. 500000. 4/15. Sir J. C. & S.

Instructions regarding War Diaries and Intelligence Summaries are contained in F. S. Regs., Part II. and the Staff Manual respectively. Title pages will be prepared in manuscript.

WAR DIARY
or
INTELLIGENCE SUMMARY.
(Erase heading not required.)

Army Form C. 2118.

Place	Date	Hour	Summary of Events and Information	Remarks and references to Appendices
CORBIE	20th		of the use of aeroplanes and their cooperation with Infantry at the H. Qrs	
"	"		of the 9th Squadron Royal Flying Corps. Company training - running drill -	
"	"		Specialist training. 2/Lt. A.G. TITLEY reported for duty from Base.	
"	21st		Sunday Divine Service.	
"	22nd		Baths, Company training, running drill, and specialist training	
"	"		2/Lt. C.T.E. HALL reported for duty from the 2nd Entrenching Battalion. The	
"	"		following officers reported for duty 2/Lt. A.E. DENT. 2/Lt. A.R. FRETWELL	
"	"		2/Lt. W.V.C. WATSON 2/Lt. S.H.B GILL.	
"	23rd		Company and Specialist training and Musketry.	
"	24th		Company and Specialist training. Lt. P. HOWE and Lt. H. PARSONS	
"	"		reported for duty from Base. Musketry party returned from 4th	
"	"		Army Musketry Camp.	
"	25th		Company and Specialist training and Musketry.	
"	26th		Battalion moved to COMBLES proceeding in Buses to BRONFAY FARM -	
			thence by march route. Dispositions of Companies as follows:-	
			A. Coy. HAIE WOOD B. Coy. "CEMETERY dugouts.	

T2134. Wt. W708-776. 500000. 4/15. Sir J. C. & S.

Instructions regarding War Diaries and Intelligence Summaries are contained in F. S. Regs., Part II. and the Staff Manual respectively. Title pages will be prepared in manuscript.

WAR DIARY
or
~~INTELLIGENCE SUMMARY.~~
(Erase heading not required.)

Army Form C. 2118.

Place	Date	Hour	Summary of Events and Information	Remarks and references to Appendices
COMBLES and CORBIE	26th		C & D Coys. Reserve trenches at COMBLES. Details remained at BRONFAY FARM	
	.		Transport lines at MARICOURT. Advanced transport at COMBLES.	
COMBLES	27th		Brigade Reserve in COMBLES.	
COMBLES and TRENCHES	28th		Battalion relieved 7th YORKSHIRE Regt in front line trenches at SAILLY SAILLISEL.	
	-		Dispositions of Companies as follows. / B. Coy Right front line. D. Coy Left front line	
	.		A Coy { 3 Platoons Support line C Coy { 2 Platoons Chateau S.P	
	.		{ 1 Platoon South Copse S.P . . { 2 Platoons CUSHY S.P.	
			H. Qrs in CHATEAU	
TRENCHES	29th		Very quiet in the line. Lieut. Col. P.R. SIMNER returned from leave and reassumed command.	
TRENCHES and BRONFAY FARM CAMP	30th		Battalion relieved by 7th YORKSHIRE Regt. and proceeded to rest camp at BRONFAY (Refer map ALBERT (combined sheet F29.b.) marching to GUILLEMONT thence by lorries to BRONFAY. Casualties during 48 hours in trenches - 2 O.R. wounded	
	31st		Battalion in Divisional reserve at BRONFAY.	

A5834 Wt. W4973/M687 750,000 8/16 D. D. & L. Ltd. Forms/C.2118/13.

B

488d

10th West Yorkshire Regt.
Operation Orders. No. 38

3-1-17

SECRET.

I The Battalion (less Details + C Company) will move to Camp at GUILLEMONT to-morrow.
Order of march H.Qrs. B. D. A
Hour of start 2-15 p.m.
200 yds will be observed between Companies.
The Transport Officer will arrange transport for the Lewis Guns, & Officers kits. Cookers will not be taken
Steel Helmets will be worn.
Water Bottles will be filled before starting.
Rifles will be wrapped in SANDBAGS which will be obtained from the Quartermaster.

II ADVANCE PARTY

2nd Lt. MAY and 5 N.C.Os. (one from each company and one from Headquarters) will proceed to GUILLEMONT at 11-0 A.M. to take over the camp. They will meet Battalion on arrival and guide Companies to their quarters.

GUILLEMONT CAMP:

Whilst at GUILLEMONT the Battalion will be responsiable for the cleanliness of the camp and the following procedure will be carried out:-

(A) At 9.0 A.M. all huts in the northern row will be cleared of personnel who will be fallen outside and clear of the huts with all kits and blankets.

(B) A party will be told off from the southern row to clean up the huts in the northern row and collect any salvage left unclaim

(C) At 10-0 A.M. huts in the southern row will be cleared in a similar manner.

Company Commanders will be responsible that this order is properly carried out. 489a

On arrival at GUILLEMONT the Regimental Sergeant Major will detail a party from the Company on duty to draw 1,000 sandbags from the R.E. dump. These will be filled and built round each hut to a height of 4 feet and a thickness of one header and one stretcher. This work will be carried out under the supervision of the Orderly Officer.

IV. FLERS LINE C Company will proceed direct to the FLERS LINE marching away from Camp XXII at 2.0 p.m. and relieving a Company of the 8th South Staffordshire Regt.

Two guides with a thorough knowledge of the line will be provided by D Company. On relief on the 5th C Company will proceed to the Battalion reserve line in COW trench and strong points, relieving a Company of the 7th Border Regt.

X. The Company will be stationed in the FLERS LINE to carry up any material from the intermediate dump East of GINCHY or from the railway, to the Battalion dump (BULL dump) in OX trench at about T9 b 4.1. On relief 4 orderlies will be left behind to remain with incoming Company (A Company of the 6th Dorsetshire Regt) until that Company can find -

(A) Intermediate Dump T.14 a 3.5

(b) HOGS BACK station - one station short of railhead.

(C) FLANK station - railhead.

(D) BULL dump T.9 b 4.1

these points must also be reconnoitred [illegible] with the help of orderlies left behind by [illegible] outgoing company as soon as possible after occupying the line. 490a

O.C. "C" Coy. will be responsible for seeing that all material taken up by rail for left Infantry group is moved to BULL dump immediately. Orders will come direct to him from the Brigade. Signal messages will be addressed FLERS COMPANY.

A Corporal of the 7th Border Regt. is stationed permanently at Company Headquarters to assist Company Commander and to keep a book in which will be entered all material taken over by the FLERS Company and all material handed over to the dump.

V DETAILS.- Will remain behind in Camp No. 22 CARNOY.

(Sd) A. J. G. Anderson Capt.
Adjutant
10th West Yorkshire Regt.

10th West Yorkshire Regt. 486a

Operation Orders No. 39 5-1-17

SECRET.

1. The Battalion will relieve the 7th Border Regt in the front line trenches this afternoon.

Companies will relieve as follows:-

D Company will relieve C Coy 7th Borders in BENNETT

B Coy. will relieve A Coy. 7th Borders in FALL + AUTUMN

A Coy will relieve B Coy. 7th Borders in WINTER + FROSTY.

C Coy from FLERS line will relieve D Coy 7th Borders in COW.

HOUR OF START 3-45 P.M. in the following order D, B, A H.Q.

II. GUIDES will meet A, B and D. Coys. and H. Qrs. at the end of the duckwalks near GINCHY corner.

H. Qrs. will proceed direct to the old H.Qrs.

The 3 Coys. will proceed direct to their trenches by the new duckwalk track.

III. The necessary certificates in regard to the cleanliness of the lines and rubbing of feet will be rendered to the Adjutant before leaving.

IV. Completion of relief will be notified by wire to Bn. H. Qrs. by the word. RUM. prefixed by the initial letter of the Company. e.g. ARUM, BRUM, CRUM + DRUM.

V. Trench stores will be taken over and receipts given. Duplicate copies of list will be forwarded to H. Qrs. by 4.0 A.M. Lewis Gun Drums and bombs will be treated as trench stores.

VI. GUM BOOTS. As many as possible will be drawn before starting and carried up to the trenches where they will be put on. Names of the men to whom they are issued will be taken and they be held responsible for the return of the boots on coming out of the trenches. Company Commanders will see that the men will change into a dry pair of socks before putting on their gum boots.

4872

2

VII. WATER BOTTLES will be filled before leaving.

VIII. ROLLS will be called before leaving camp and again on arriving at the trenches.

IX. WHALE OIL can be obtained from BULL dump when required. Indents must be signed by an officer.

X. PETROL-TINS must be returned to the dump when empty. This matter is most important.

XI. SALVAGE all grenades lying about the area are to be returned to BULL dump and quantities dumped reported to H.Qrs. In every case the detonator is to be removed before the grenades are moved from the site in which they lie.

XII. Three G.S. Waggons will be at the GUM BOOTS hut in GUILLEMONT at 9-0 p.m. on the night when the Battalion is relieved for conveying very tired men coming out of the trenches to CARNOY CAMP. The wagons will not wait after mid-night. 2 Lt. May will meet the waggons at 9-0 P.M. and will see that they are used only by men unable to walk to camp. There is no objection to equipment being placed on the waggon provided it is under the charge of a responsible person. On no account must men sit on or lean against Rifles in the waggons.

Sd. A.T.G. Anderson Capt.
Adjutant
10th West Yorkshire Rgt.

477d

OPERATION ORDER.

6.1.17

I The Battalion will be relieved by the 7th East Yorkshire Regt. to-morrow evening.

II. After relief Companies will march back independently to Camp No. 23, CARNOY. Hot drinks will be provided at GUILLEMONT. Two waggons will be waiting to convey very tired men to camp. 2/Lt. MAY will meet these waggons & will see that men who are able to walk do not crowd into them.

III GUIDES Four guides from H.Qrs. will meet the 7th East Yorkshire Regt. (less the Coy in the FLERS line) at the end of the Duckwalks at GINCHY Corner at 4-0 p.m.. H.Qrs will be conducted direct to Battn H.Qrs. The three Companies will be led by the duckwalk track to railhead of the DECAUVILLE rly. Here 4 guides per Coy (one per platoon) to be detailed by O.C. A. B. & D Coys. will meet them & conduct them direct to the trenches by the new duckwalk track. O.C. "C" Coy. will supervise the distribution of guides at this point. Guides will

4781

by in position at railhead by 4.30
should the 4 guides from D Coy. not
be able to arrive in time, owing to [illegible] the H.Qrs.
guides will carry on as far as A Coy.
where D Coy must take over.
A guide will be waiting on the duckboards
to conduct the Medical Officer of the
7th East Yorkshire Regt to the new
Aid Post near BULL dump.
O.C. "C" Coy. will send two guides to the
FLERS line at 3.30 pm to conduct
the Company of the 7th East Yorkshire
Regt. to COW trench.

IV. GUM BOOTS will be handed in at GUILLEMONT
O.C. Coys. will be responsible that none
are left behind.

V. Trench Stores will be handed over to
the incoming battalion & receipts obtained.
Lists will be handed into Orderly Room
~~[illegible]~~ on return to camp.

VI. Completion of relief will be advised to
Bn. H.Qrs by wiring the word RUM
with the Company letter prefixed. Should
the wire be broken ~~[illegible]~~
~~[illegible]~~
relief will be advised by messenger.

VII. All empty water cans will be carried down
& dumped at BULL dump.

VIII Rolls will be called before leaving

4794

the trenches + again on arrival at Camp, where O.C. Coys. will report their Coys. present or otherwise.

IX. Foot friction drill will be carried out + socks changed on arrival at camp before the men settle down for the night.

A. H. G. [illegible]
Capt + Adjt
10 West Yorkshire Regt.

483a

10th West Yorkshire Regt.

9-1-17.

SECRET.

Operation Order No. 40.

I The Battalion (less Details and B Coy.) will move to camp at GUILLEMONT to-morrow.

Hour of start 3-15 P.M.

The Transport Officer will arrange transport for Lewis Guns and Officers kits.

Coopers will not be taken!

Steel helmets will be worn.

Rifles will be wrapped in sandbags which will be obtained from the Quarter Master.

Head-quarters and all available men will move off from Camp XXII under the orders of Capt. A.J.A. POIGNANT.

II ADVANCE PARTY.

2nd Lt. May and 5 N.C.Os. (one from each Coy and one from Headquarters) will proceed to GUILLEMONT at 11.0 A.M. to take over the camp. They will meet Battalion on arrival and guide Companies to their quarters.

III GUILLEMONT CAMP.

Whilst at GUILLEMONT the Battalion will be responsible for the cleanliness of the camp and usual procedure of cleaning the lines will be carried out.

The usual guards will be posted on the camp and also on the new camp near TRONES-WOOD.

IV WORKING PARTIES.

1. A party consisting of CAPT. G.D. PENTY, 2nd LT. INGHAM and 2nd LT. CLOUGH and 210 O.R. with the requisite number of N.C.Os will parade at Orderly Room at 12-30 P.M. in order to carry

4844d

duckboards from GINCHY to DECAUVILLE RAILHEAD. They will proceed to R.E. dump GINCHY where they will report to CAPT. SMYLY. Kits will be left at GUILLEMONT camp en route. CAPT. PENTY will post a guard of 1 Sgt. and 3. O.R. over these, who will be responsible for their safe custody until the return of the party.
Haversack rations will be carried.
The C.Q.M.S. of D Coy. will proceed to GUILLEMONT with 2 Cooks and will supply hot tea on the return of the party, using the SOYER stoves at the camp for this purpose.
All available men in A.C.+D Coys. will be in readiness to proceed with this party, which will be detailed by the Regtl. Sergeant Major.

2) A party consisting of 1 Sgt and 20 men from D Coy will parade at Orderly Room at 12-15 P.M. for work on the new third camp at GUILLEMONT. Their place of work will be 300 yds. north of the present camp beside the light railway. They will report there at 2. P.M. and work until dismissed.

V. FLERS LINE - B. Company will proceed direct to the FLERS LINE marching away from Camp XXII at 3-15. P.M. and relieving a company of the 8th South Staffordshire Regt. B. Company will arrange to pass GUILLEMONT cross roads at 4-35 P.M. and must be careful to follow in rear of the Battalion proceeding to the front line trenches from GUILLEMONT camp. Two guides with a thorough knowledge of the FLERS LINE will be provided by C. Coy.

On relief on the 11th B Company will proceed to the Battalion reserve line in "cow" trench and the strong points relieving a Company of the 7th Borders Regt.

The Company will be stationed in the FLERS LINE to carry up any material from the intermediate dump East of GINCHY or from the railway to the Battalion dump (BULL DUMP) in OX trench at about T9. C.41.

On relief 4 orderlies will be left behind to remain with the incoming Company (A Coy. of the 6th Dorsetshire Regt.) until that Company can find:-

(A) Intermediate dump T.14. A3.5

(B) HOGS BACK station - one station short of railhead.

(C) FLANK STATION - railhead.

(D) BULL DUMP T.9. C.41.

These points must also be reconnoitered by B. Coy. with the help of orderlies left behind by the outgoing company as soon as possible after occupying the line.

O. C. B. Coy. will be responsible for the seeing that all material taken up by rail for left Infantry group is moved to BULL dump immediatly. Orders will come direct to him from the Brigade. Signal messages will be addressed FLERS COMPANY.

A. Corporal of the 7th Border Regt. is stationed permanently at Company Headquarters to assist Company Commanders and to keep a book in which will be entered all material handed over to the dump, and taken over by the FLERS COMPANY

VI DETAILS. will remain behind in Camp. No. 22.

(sd) A. F. G. Anderson Capt.
Adjutant.
10th West Yorkshire Regt.

Copy No.

12-1-17

Operation Order No. 41

by Major [illegible] Sumner D.S.O.
Commanding 10th West Yorkshire Regt.

SECRET

481a

1. [illegible] Battalion will relieve 7th Border Regt in [illegible] trenches this afternoon.

2. [illegible] OF START [illegible] P.M. in the following order:
C A D HQ.

3. ORDER OF RELIEF.

2 PLATS. of C Coy with 2 L.Gs will relieve 2 PLATS of [illegible] Coy 7th Border Regt [illegible] [illegible] L.Gs on the right of BENNETT TRENCH.

2 PLATS of C Coy with 2 L.Gs will relieve 2 PLATS of B Coy 7th Border Regt with [illegible] L.Gs in the centre of BENNETT TRENCH.

2 PLATS. of A Coy with 1 L.G. will relieve 2 PLATS. of C Coy 7th Border Regt with 1 L.G. on the left of BENNETT TRENCH.

1 PLAT of A Coy with 2 L.Gs will relieve 1 PLAT of C Coy 7th Border Regt with 2 L.Gs in FALL TRENCH.

1 PLAT of D Coy will relieve 1 PLAT of C Coy 7th Border Regt [illegible]

2 PLATS of D Coy with 1 L.G. will relieve 2 PLATS of D Coy 7th Border Regt [illegible] [illegible] in FROSTY TRENCH.

2 PLATS of [illegible] Coy with 1 L.G. will relieve 2 PLATS of [illegible] Coy 7th Border Regt [illegible] 1 L.G. in WINTER TRENCH.

2 [illegible] of B Coy with 3 L.Gs will relieve 2 PLATS of A Coy 7th Border Regt with 2 L.G. in COW TRENCH.

2 PLA[illegible] B Coy will relieve 2 PLATS of A Coy 7th [illegible] Regt as BATTALION [illegible]

Bn. H.Qrs. 10th West Yorkshire Regt will take over from Bn. H.Qrs 7th Border Regt at NEW H.Qrs at RAILHEAD.

The Regimental Aid Post is at Bn. H.Qrs. RAILHEAD.

GUIDES One guide from the 7th Border Regt will meet H.Qrs at [illegible] CLEVER.

One guide for each Platoon will meet C A & D Companies on arrival at RAILHEAD to conduct them to their post.

Two guides from the 7th Border Regt will report at B Coy H.Qrs FLERS LINE by [illegible] P.M.

5 REPORT Completion of relief will be notified to Bn. H.Q. by wire
ON prefixed by the initial letter of the Coy. SOIL 4821

6 GUM-BOOTS These will be drawn before starting and carried up to the trenches. Names of men to whom they are issued must be kept and they will be held responsible for the return of the boots on coming out of the trenches. When ankle boots are changed a dry pair of socks will be put on.

7 ROLLS. Will be called before leaving Camp and again on arrival at the trenches.

8 WATER BOTTLES will be filled before leaving.

9 FOOT POWDER will be issued in two sprinklers to Companies at the rate of 2 per platoon.

When socks are changed a little of the powder will be shaken inside each sock before putting them on.

As previously O.C. Companies will send in certificates to Orderly Room before leaving camp that all men's feet have been massaged.

ACKNOWLEDGE.

Issued at

Copy No 1 O/C A Coy
2 B Coy
3 C Coy
4 D Coy
5 L.G.O.
6 B.O.
7 R.S.M.
8 Signal Sgt.
9 Retained
10 War Diary

Sd/ H. A. C. [illegible]
2/Lt.
a/Adjutant
10th West Yorkshire Regt.

SECRET

OPERATION ORDER Nº 42 COPY Nº 6.

by Major P.R. SIMNER DSO 491a

Commanding 10th Bn West Yorkshire Rgt

HQ 13-1-17

The Battalion will be relieved in the trenches on the night 14/15 by the 1st Bn Kings Own Scottish Borderers (29 Division)

1 ORDER OF RELIEF.

'C' Coy BENNETT (RIGHT POST) will be relieved by 2 PLATS of 'C' Coy 1st KOSB with 2 LG's

'C' Coy BENNETT (CENTRE POST) will be relieved by 2 PLATS of 'C' Coy 1st KOSB with 2 LG's

'A' Coy BENNETT (LEFT POST) will be relieved by 2 PLATS of 'A' Coy 1st KOSB with 1 LG

'A' Coy FALL will be relieved by 1 PLAT of 'A' Coy 1st KOSB with 2 LG's

'A' Coy AUTUMN will be relieved by 1 PLAT of 'A' Coy 1st KOSB. LG NIL.

'D' Coy FROSTY will be relieved by 2 PLATS of 'D' Coy 1st KOSB with 1 LG

'D' Coy WINTER will be relieved by 2 PLATS 'D' Coy 1st KOSB with 1 LG.

'B' Coy COW will be relieved by 1 PLAT of 'B' Coy 1st KOSB with 2 LG's

'B' Coy SUNKEN ROAD will be relieved by 1 PLAT of 'B' Coy 1st KOSB.

2. 492A

'B' Coy OLD Bn HQ will be relieved by
2 PLATS of B Coy 1st KOSB. LGs NIL

2 GUIDES 5 guides detailed from
Bn HQ will meet the in-coming
Battalion at the beginning of
the duckboards GINCHY CORNER
(1 for HQ + 1 for each company)
They will bring their companies
to RAILHEAD and will there
hand them over to guides
supplied from the companies
in the line as follows —:
O.C. 'A' Company will send down
4 guides to BULL DUMP.
OC 'C' Company will send down
4 guides to BULL DUMP.
These guides will leave the
line before daylight on 14th inst
and will report at Bn HQrs
OC 'D' Coy will send down 4 guides
to report at Bn HQrs by 4 pm.
O.C. 'B' Coy will detail 2 guides
to report to OC FLERS LINE Coy
by 4 pm.

GUIDES (CONTD) These guides will be very carefully selected and in each case will be men who are thoroughly acquainted with the way.

3. TRENCH STORES Fullest Receipts must be taken for all Stores handed over.

4 LEWIS GUN DRUMS. These will not be handed over to in-coming Units. O.C. Companies will see that all drums are collected, and will assist the LG teams by distributing the excess loads among their Companies when leaving the line. A supply of sandbags is being issued to Companies for carrying those drums that are found without proper 'CARRIERS'.
Limbers for the L.G.'s will be at the usual place.

5. GUM BOOTS. All gum boots Thigh will be collected and carried out of the trenches when in excess of the numbers taken in. They will be handed in at GUM BOOTS HUTS, near GUILLEMONT, and receipts obtained from the N.C.O. in charge of Store.

WATER TINS All water tins must be collected and left at BULL DUMP on the way out. An N.C.O from the Bn will be detailed to assist the N.C.O. i/c Dump in checking tins left as the Companies pass and he will also be responsible for obtaining the receipts from NCO i/c Dump. 'B' Coy will return all tins during the morning of the 14th inst and will obtain their own receipts.

4950 5.

7 ROLLS Rolls will be called before leaving the trenches and again on arrival at Camp 22. CARNOY.

8 Reporting Relief when the relief is complete O.C. Coys will assure themselves that the relief is promptly reported through to Btn HQrs using the "CODE WORD" — REST.

prefixing the initial letter of B REST.

9 AFTER RELIEF Companies will march off independently to Camp 22, stopping for tea etc: at the same place as before

Arrival at Camp 22 will be reported by O.C. Coys to Major IND

10 FOOT MASSAGE on arrival at Camp. All men will rub their feet & change their socks.

496d 6.
EB

(contd)

O.C. Companies will render the usual certificate.

11 WET SOCKS All pairs of wet or dirty socks must be brought out of the trenches and in view of the last issue of socks, they must also be checked before handing them in and the equivalent of the last issue returned.

12 Acknowledge

Hagluville 2/Lt
a/Adj
16th Bn West Yorkshire Rgt.

Issued at 8.50 pm

Copy No 1	O.C. 'A' Coy	Copy No 5 RSM
Copy No 2	OC 'B' Coy	" " 6 War Diary
Copy No 3	O.C. C Coy	" " 7 Retained
Copy No 4	OC D Coy	" " 8 1st K.O.S.B.

H.Q.

Operation Order No. 42

by Major P.R. Simner D.S.O.

Commanding 10th West Yorkshire Regt.

Cop. No. [illegible]

14-1-17

SECRET

480d

The Battalion will proceed to-morrow by rail to billets at CORBIE entraining at 2-10. P.M. at PLATEAU Station.

Hour of leaving camp 1-0 P.M.

Order of march D. C. B. A. H.Q.

Starting point entrance to XXII Camp.

Companies will march in file and the usual distance of 200yds. will be maintained.

DRESS. Marching Order. Steel helmets will be worn. One blanket per man will be carried folded on the pack.

DINNERS will be served at 12-0 noon.

An advance party consisting of 1 N.C.O. per Coy. and 1 from H.Q. under command of Lieut C.E. JARVIS will reach PLATEAU Station at 1-0 P.M.

Lieut C.E. JARVIS will report to the Adjutant at 10-0 A.M. for instructions.

III - The Transport under the Transport Officer will proceed by road to CORBIE at 11-0 A.M.

All Officers kits and other gear will be outside the Q.M. stores by 10-15 A.M.

IV The usual certificates as to the cleanliness of the camp will be rendered to the Adjutant prior to leaving.

(sd) A. F. G. Anderson Capt.
Adjutant
10th West Yorkshire Regt.

10th WEST YORKSHIRE REGT. 25-1-17

OPERATION ORDER No. 43. SECRET.

1. The Battalion will move to-morrow by bus to MALTZHORN and thence by march route to COMBLES.

Parade 8-15 A.M.

LA NOUVELLE – CORBIE RD. head of the column at S.E. extremity of billeting area and facing S.E.

H.Q Order of march as per margin.

A Dress marching order

B Leather jerkins and Greatcoats, the equipment

C being outside the latter.

D 1 Blanket to be carried in the pack.

Sapping Platoon Water bottles to be full and havercack rations carried.

Companies will be told off in parties of 30 inclusive of Officers and N.C.Os.

On arrival at MALTZHORN a party consisting of 2nd Lt S.T. MAY and 1 N.C.O. per Company and 1 from H.Qrs. will proceed to COMBLES to take over accomodation.

2. The Transport under orders of the Transport Officer will proceed by road to A16.a.3.3.

He will arrange for the Lewis Gun limbers, Cookers, Officers kits and Mess cart to join the Battalion at COMBLES.

Hour of start 7-30 A.M.

Officers kits and other gear will be stacked outside the Q.M. Stores not later than 7.0 A.M.

Blankets (1 per man) will be rolled in bundles of ten and stacked outside the Q.M. Stores by 7.0 A.M.

3. The usual certificate re cleanliness of billets will be handed to the Adjutant on parade.

A rear party consisting of 2nd LT. H.A.G. NEVILLE and 1 N.C.O. per Company and 1 from H.Qrs. will remain in CORBIE and proceed independantly to COMBLES.

4. DETAILS. The following under 2nd LT. N. NEWTON will proceed from MALTZHORN to BRONFAY Camp.

Q.M. Stores
Drill Instructors
Brigade Bombing class
Hutting section.

sd. A.Y.G. Anderson Capt.
Adjutant
10th West Yorkshire Regt.

10th WEST YORKSHIRE REGT 28-1-17.

OPERATION ORDER No. 44 SECRET.

(REF. T.M. COMBLES)

The Battalion will relieve the 7th Yorkshire Regt. in the left sub-section to-day as under

RIGHT FRONT

B Coy. will march via QUARRY to U.4.9.9 point 1493 timing their arrival at 5.45 P.M. where guides will meet.

The Battalion less B Coy will proceed by the day duck board N.E. of HAIE WOOD to a point immediately N of SOUTH CORSE where guides will meet them.

D Coy.
A
Hd Qrs
C Coy.

Order of march as per margin.

The O.C. D. Coy will time his arrival at the point for 6. P.M.

Distances of 500 yds will be maintained.

LEWIS GUNS. will proceed as follows.

3 Lewis Guns will accompany B Coy.

A special guide will meet two of these guns and guide them to their position.

3 Lewis Guns with D Coy

A special guide will meet one of these guns

3 Lewis Guns with A Coy.

A special guide will meet two of these guns.

3 Lewis Guns with C Coy.

Those teams for which special guides are allotted will march in front of their respective Companies.

11 Drums per gun will be carried.

The R.S.M. will proceed to the CHATEAU arriving there not later than 3.0.P.M. to take over stores.

2. DRESS. Battle order.

Jerkins and greatcoats will be worn.

Water bottles filled.

2 days rations will be carried.

O.C. Coys will make the usual arrangements to ensure a supply of rum and whale oil.

All blankets rolled in bundles of ten and packs will be sent to Bn. H.Q. not later than 2 p.m.

3. The completion of relief will be notified to Bn. H.Q. by the word UN preceded by the letter of the Coy.

sd. A. H. G. Anderson Capt.
Adjutant.
10th West Yorkshire Regt.

SECRET. 10th West Yorkshire Regt. SECRET.

Operation Order No. 45. 30/1/17.

1 The Battalion will be relieved tonight by the 9th Yorkshire Regt. and will proceed on relief to Camp No 15a. BRONFAY FARM. Details as to route will be issued later.

2 GUIDES will be provided by Companies as follows:-

A. Coy. 4 guides - one for each Platoon.

B. Coy. 5 guides - one for each Platoon + one for Lewis Guns

C. Coy. 4 guides - one for each Platoon

D. Coy. 5 guides - one for each Platoon + one for Lewis Guns

B. Coys guides will be sent to Battalion Headquarters before daybreak. Guides of A. C & D. Companies will report at Battalion Headquarters not later than 5 pm.

3 LEWIS GUNS. Drums will be handed over to the incoming Battalion + receipts obtained except the four dirtiest of each gun which will be brought out by the relieved team.

4 GUM BOOTS (Thigh) will be handed over & receipts obtained

5 WATER CANS. All water cans will be brought out and handed in at CHATEAU dump. B. Coy will take their cans to D. Coy. Hd. Qrs & D Coy will supply a party to carry them to the dump

6 RELIEF. Will be advised to Headquarters by the word U.S. prefixed by the Company letter. On relief Companies will proceed independently to the soup kitchen at COMBLES. A guide will be stationed near the entrance to the CATACOMBS to direct companies to the kitchen. After obtaining the soup Companies will at once proceed independently to a rendezvous to be notified later.

7 ROLLS will be called before leaving the trenches and again on arrival at Camp.

(Sd) A. F. G. Anderson Capt
Adjutant
10th West Yorkshire Regt

50/17

15E.
28 sheets

Vol 14

War Diary
for
February 1917

10th (S) Bn West Yorkshire Regt

10th West Yorks
Vol VI

Instructions regarding War Diaries and Intelligence Summaries are contained in F. S. Regs., Part II. and the Staff Manual respectively. Title pages will be prepared in manuscript.

WAR DIARY
or
~~INTELLIGENCE SUMMARY.~~

(Erase heading not required.)

Army Form C. 2118.

Place	Date	Hour	Summary of Events and Information	Remarks and references to Appendices
BRONFAY and COMBLES.	1-2-17		Battalion moved up to Brigade Reserve in COMBLES, details remaining at Camp No 15 BRONFAY	
COMBLES	2nd		Brigade Reserve in COMBLES. Large carrying parties to front line.	
COMBLES and TRENCHES	3rd		Relieved 12th MANCHESTERS in front line trenches, dispositions being as follows:-	
	"		C. Coy Right of front line	
	"		A Coy Left of front line	
	"		D Coy in Support 3 Platoons in CANE ALLEY & 1 Platoon in Smith Copse strong point	
	"		B Coy CHATEAU & CUSHY strong points	
	"		Capt L G PETERS rejoined the Battalion from the Second Army School.	
TRENCHES	4th		Some enemy shelling of our front & support points & CHATEAU strong point, but very little damage caused. Every available man employed in improving the line	
TRENCHES and BRONFAY	5th		Battalion relieved by the 12th MANCHESTERS & proceeded to No 15 camp, BRONFAY, travelling by train from GUILLEMONT to CARNOY & marching the rest of the way.	
"	"		Total Casualties during the tour 50 O.R. Wounded. A large amount of work was done by the Battalion whilst in the line - notably on joining up posts 1 to 9 so as to form a continuous front line and in improving CUSHY and CHATEAU strong points. A large quantity of material and S.A.A was carried up by Special parties to CANE ALLEY and SAILLY strong points. All salvage that could be found was collected and handed in at CHATEAU dump	
BRONFAY	6th		Divisional Reserve at BRONFAY. General cleaning up.	
" and COMBLES	7th		B & D Coys proceeded to COMBLES coming under the orders of O.C. 12th MANCHESTER REGT	

A5834 Wt. W4973/M687 750,000 8/16 D. D. & L. Ltd. Forms/C.2118/13.

Instructions regarding War Diaries and Intelligence Summaries are contained in F. S. Regs., Part II. and the Staff Manual respectively. Title pages will be prepared in manuscript.

WAR DIARY
or
~~INTELLIGENCE SUMMARY.~~
(*Erase heading not required.*)

Army Form C. 2118.

Place	Date	Hour	Summary of Events and Information	Remarks and references to Appendices
BRONFAY and COMBLES	1-3-17		Battalion moved up to Brigade Reserve in COMBLES, details remained at Camp No 15 BRONFAY.	
COMBLES	2nd		Brigade Reserve in COMBLES. Large carrying parties to front line.	
COMBLES and TRENCHES	3rd		Relieved 12th MANCHESTERS in front line trenches, dispositions being as follows:- C. Coy Right of front line A Coy Left of front line D Coy in Support 3 Platoons in CANE ALLEY & 1 Platoon in Smith Copse strong point B Coy CHATEAU & CUSHY strong points Capt L G PETERS rejoined the Battalion from the Second Army School.	
TRENCHES	4th		Some enemy shelling of our front & support lines & CHATEAU strong point but very little damage caused. Every available man employed in improving the line.	
TRENCHES and BRONFAY	5th		Battalion relieved by the 12th MANCHESTERS & proceeded to No 15 camp BRONFAY travelling by train from GUILLEMONT to CARNOY marching the rest of the way. Total Casualties during the tour 50 O.R. Wounded. A large amount of work was done by the Battalion whilst in the line - notably on joining up posts 1 to 9 so as to form a continuous front line and in improving CUSHY and CHATEAU strong points. A large quantity of material and S A A was carried up by special parties to CANE ALLEY and SAILLY strong points. All salvage that could be found was collected and handed in at CHATEAU dump.	
BRONFAY	6th		Divisional Reserve at BRONFAY. General cleaning up.	
and COMBLES	7th		"B" & D Coys proceeded to COMBLES coming under the orders of O.C. 12th MANCHESTER REGT	

A5834 Wt. W4973/M687 750,000 8/16 D. D. & L. Ltd. Forms/C.2118/13.

Army Form C. 2118.

Instructions regarding War Diaries and Intelligence Summaries are contained in F. S. Regs., Part II. and the Staff Manual respectively. Title pages will be prepared in manuscript.

WAR DIARY
or
~~INTELLIGENCE~~ SUMMARY.
(*Erase heading not required.*)

Place	Date	Hour	Summary of Events and Information	Remarks and references to Appendices
BRONFAY AND COMBLES	7th		"A" & "C" Coys physical training under the Brigade Gymnastic Instructor.	
	8th		Company training - also bayonet fighting under special instructor furnished by 51st Brigade.	
	9th		Early on the morning of this day the 7th YORKSHIRE Regt. attacked and captured the German front line trench from U14 b 85.35 to U15 c 05.40 a frontage of approximately 300yds taking 71 prisoners including 2 officers. The captured trench was consolidated and re-named GREEN HOWARD trench. "B" & "D" Coys were in reserve in this attack and did very good work carrying up stores and ammunition to the front line.	
			The Battalion moved up to COMBLES in lorries and then relieved the 7th YORKSHIRE Regt and 4 Companies of the 12th Manchester Regt in the front line trenches dispositions being as follows:	
			C. Coy. GREEN HOWARD trench	
			A. Coy. Old front line	
			D. Coy. CANE ALLEY (3 Platoons)	
			B. Coy. CHATEAU ECUSHY strong point	
			One Company of the 6th Dorsetshire Regt was held in reserve at MOUCHOIR COPSE	
	10th		At 1-5 AM the enemy opened a very heavy barrage on front & support lines strong-points and the back area which lasted until 1-50 AM. At the same time bombing attacks were launched against both flanks of our new position in GREEN HOWARD trench, to which we replied vigorously with bombs, rifle grenades, rifle - machine guns & Lewis Gun fire, frustrating all attempts to reach trench. At 1-30 AM bombs were thrown opposite the centre of GREEN HOWARD & it was reported that the enemy advanced from his trenches at this point.	

A7834 Wt. W4973/M687 750,000 8/16 D. D. & L., Ltd. Forms/C.2118/13.

Instructions regarding War Diaries and Intelligence Summaries are contained in F. S. Regs., Part II. and the Staff Manual respectively. Title pages will be prepared in manuscript.

WAR DIARY
or
~~INTELLIGENCE SUMMARY.~~
(Erase heading not required.)

Army Form C. 2118.

Place	Date	Hour	Summary of Events and Information	Remarks and references to Appendices
BRONFAY AND COMBLES	7th 8th 9th		A & C Coys physical training under the Brigade Gymnastic Instructor. Company training – also bayonet fighting under special instructor furnished by 51st Brigade. Early on the morning of this day the 7th YORKSHIRE Regt attacked and captured the German front line trench from U14 b 85.25 to U15 c 05.70 a frontage of approximately 300 yds taking 71 prisoners including 2 officers. The captured trench was consolidated and re-named GREEN HOWARD trench. B & D Coys were in reserve in this attack and did very good work carrying up stores and ammunition to the front line.	
			The Battalion moved up to COMBLES in lorries and then relieved the 7th YORKSHIRE Regt and 4 Companies of the 12th Manchester Regt in the front line trenches dispositions being as follows: C. Coy. GREEN HOWARD trench; A Coy. Old front line; D. Coy. CANE ALLEY (3 Platoons); B Coy. CHATEAU & CUSHY strong point.	
			One Company of the 6th Dorsetshire Regt was held in reserve at MOUCHOIR COPSE	
	10th		At 1-5 AM the enemy opened a very heavy barrage on front & support lines, strong points and the back area which lasted until 1-50 AM. At the same time bombing attacks were launched against both flanks of our new position in GREEN HOWARD trench, to which we replied vigorously with bombs, rifle grenades, rifle, machine gun & Lewis Gun fire, frustrating all attempts to reach trench. At 1-30 AM bombs were thrown opposite the centre of GREEN HOWARD and it was reported that ~~[illegible]~~ the enemy advanced from his trenches at this point.	

A5834 Wt. W4973/M687 750,000 8/16 D. D. & L. Ltd. Forms/C.2118/13.

WAR DIARY
or
INTELLIGENCE SUMMARY.
(*Erase heading not required.*)

Army Form C. 2118.

Instructions regarding War Diaries and Intelligence Summaries are contained in F. S. Regs., Part II. and the Staff Manual respectively. Title pages will be prepared in manuscript.

Place	Date	Hour	Summary of Events and Information	Remarks and references to Appendices
TRENCHES	10th		A heavy rifle & Lewis Gun fire was however immediately opened by us & nothing more	
-	-		was seen. At about 1-45 AM one of our rifle grenades blew up a very light store	
-	-		in the enemy's front line causing a very fine display of fireworks. Almost immediately	
-	-		after the opening of the enemy barrage all our signal wires were cut and we were	
-	-		left without any means of communicating either with the Brigade or the Artillery, our	
-	-		attempts at lamp signalling apparently not being observed. It was not considered	
-	-		necessary to send up the S.O.S. signal and our Artillery did not open fire. Fortunately	
-	-		their assistance was not required. G. H. Q report on the above events read as follows:-	
-	-		"After a heavy preliminary bombardment, the enemy attacked our new position	
-	-		East of SAILLY - SAILLISEL, but were repulsed at all points".	
-	-		Towards morning the enemy endeavoured to shell our right bombing stop, but	
-	-		several of his shells fell into his own trench. It was then observed that whenever	
-	-		this occurred single red lights were sent up from the trench, causing the fire to cease.	
-	-		As our men had found several of these lights in one of the old German dugouts	
-	-		they were able to send them up from the flanks whenever enemy shells fell unpleasantly	
-	-		close, and the fire invariably ceased. The enemy seemed very nervous and kept up	
			considerable artillery fire on our lines and approaches all through the 10th and 11th	
			causing a few casualties among carrying and working parties of other regiments.	

A5834 Wt. W4973/M687 750,000 8/16 D. D. & L. Ltd. Forms/C.2118/13.

Instructions regarding War Diaries and Intelligence Summaries are contained in F. S. Regs., Part II. and the Staff Manual respectively. Title pages will be prepared in manuscript.

WAR DIARY
or
INTELLIGENCE SUMMARY.
(Erase heading not required.)

Army Form C. 2118.

Place	Date	Hour	Summary of Events and Information	Remarks and references to Appendices
TRENCHES	10th		A heavy rifle & Lewis Gun fire was however immediately opened by us & nothing more was seen. At about 1-45 AM one of our rifle Grenadiers blew up a Very Light store in the enemy's front line causing a very fine display of fireworks. Almost immediately after the opening of the enemy barrage all our signal wires were cut and we were left without any means of communicating either with the Brigade or the Artillery, our attempts at lamp signalling apparently not being observed. It was not considered necessary to send up the S.O.S. Signal and our Artillery did not open fire. Fortunately their assistance was not required. G. H. Q report on the above events read as follows:– "After a heavy preliminary bombardment, the enemy attacked our new position East of SAILLY - SAILLISEL, but were repulsed at all points". Towards morning the enemy endeavoured to shell our right bombing stop, but several of his shells fell into his own trench. It was then observed that whenever this occurred single red lights were sent up from the trench, causing the fire to cease. As our men had found several of these lights in one of the old German dugouts they were able to send them up from the flanks whenever enemy shells fell [illegible] close and the fire invariably ceased. The enemy seemed very nervous and kept up considerable Artillery fire on our lines and approaches all through the 10th and 11th causing a few casualties among carrying and working parties of other regiments.	

A5834 Wt. W4973/M687 750,000 8/16 D. D. & L. Ltd. Forms/C.2118/13.

Instructions regarding War Diaries and Intelligence Summaries are contained in F. S. Regs., Part II. and the Staff Manual respectively. Title pages will be prepared in manuscript.

WAR DIARY
or
INTELLIGENCE SUMMARY.
(Erase heading not required.)

Army Form C. 2118.

Place	Date	Hour	Summary of Events and Information	Remarks and references to Appendices
TRENCHES AND ~~BRONFAY~~ COMBLES	11th		The Battalion was relieved by the 12th Manchester Regt plus one Company of the 6th Dorsetshire Regt and proceeded into Brigade Reserve in COMBLES. Total casualties during the tour - 6 Killed 4 Died of Wounds and 24 Wounded - all O.R	
COMBLES and BRONFAY	12th		Brigade Reserve in COMBLES. D Coy moved up to CHATEAU, CUSHY and SOUTH COPSE strong points coming under the command of O.C. 12th Manchester Regt.	
	13th		D Coy relieved by a Company of the 7th East Yorkshire Regt. Battalion moved back to Divisional Reserve at BRONFAY	
BRONFAY AND COMBLES	14th		General cleaning up. Baths - Foot treatment. Battalion fitted with new box respirators.	
	15th		Battalion relieved the 7th Yorkshire Regt in the trenches. Lorries were provided to take the Battalion to COMBLES, but owing to the road being shelled these were stopped half way between GUILLEMONT and COMBLES. From this point Companies proceeded independently to the Reserve trenches in COMBLES. After a rest of about half an hour the march was resumed to the trenches. Owing to continuous heavy shelling Battalion Headquarters in the remains of the CHATEAU at SAILLY SAILLISEL had been abandoned & new headquarters were established in the HEBULE at U.13.a.6.3 (Refer. map COMBLES)	
	16/17th		Heavy and incessant shelling of all parts of the sector - both front and back areas	
	17th		Battalion were relieved by the 6th Dorsetshire Regt and proceeded to COMBLES	
			Total casualties during the 48 hours in the trenches - 8 Killed, 3 Died of Wounds and 21 Wounded	
			During the period that the Battalion were at SAILLY-SAILLISEL the signal lines were continuously	

Instructions regarding War Diaries and Intelligence Summaries are contained in F. S. Regs., Part II. and the Staff Manual respectively. Title pages will be prepared in manuscript.

WAR DIARY
or
INTELLIGENCE SUMMARY.
(Erase heading not required.)

Army Form C. 2118.

Place	Date	Hour	Summary of Events and Information	Remarks and references to Appendices
TRENCHES AND ~~BRONFAY~~ COMBLES	11th		The Battalion was relieved by the 12th Manchester Regt plus one Company of the 6th Dorsetshire Regt and proceeded into Brigade Reserve in COMBLES. Total casualties during the tour - 6 Killed 4 Died of Wounds and 24 Wounded - all O.R.	
COMBLES and BRONFAY	12th		Brigade Reserve in COMBLES. D Coy moved up to CHATEAU CUSHY and SOUTH COPSE strong points coming under the command of O.C. 12th Manchester Regt	
	13th		D Coy relieved by a Company of the 7th East Yorkshire Regt. Battalion moved back to Divisional Reserve at BRONFAY	
BRONFAY AND COMBLES	14th		General cleaning up. Baths - Foot treatment. Battalion fitted with new box respirators.	
	15th		Battalion relieved the 7th Yorkshire Regt in the trenches. Lorries were provided to take the Battalion to COMBLES, but owing to the road being shelled these were stopped half way between GUILLEMONT and COMBLES. From this point Companies proceeded independently to the Reserve trenches in COMBLES. After a rest of about half an hour the march was resumed to the trenches. Owing to continuous heavy shelling Battalion Headquarters in the remains of the CHATEAU at SAILLY SAILLISEL had been abandoned & new headquarters were established in the HEBULE at U.13.a.6.3 (Refer map COMBLES)	
	16/17th		Heavy and incessant shelling of all parts of the sector - both front and back areas.	
	17th		Battalion were relieved by the 6th Dorsetshire Regt and proceeded to COMBLES. Total casualties during the 48 hours in the trenches 9 Killed 3 Died of Wounds and 21 Wounded. During the period that the Battalion was at SAILLY-SAILLISEL the signal lines were continuously	

Instructions regarding War Diaries and Intelligence Summaries are contained in F. S. Regs., Part II. and the Staff Manual respectively. Title pages will be prepared in manuscript.

WAR DIARY
or
~~INTELLIGENCE SUMMARY.~~

(Erase heading not required.)

Army Form C. 2118.

Place	Date	Hour	Summary of Events and Information	Remarks and references to Appendices
COMBLES	17th		being cut by shell fire, and the linesmen of the Battalion behaved admirably - always going out immediately the breaks occurred to repair the lines - often under very heavy fire.	
COMBLES AND BRONFAY	18th		Battalion marched to BRONFAY Camp, being relieved by the 1st Border Regt of the 29th Division.	
BRONFAY AND MEAULTE	19th		Battalion marched to MEAULTE taking over billets from 2nd Royal Fusiliers	
MEAULTE	20th		General cleaning up. Kit inspection	
"	21st		Running Drill and Company training	
"	22nd		do - - do -	
"	23rd		do - - do -	
"	24th		do - - do - Battalion Concert in the Y.M.C.A hut.	
"	25th		Sunday Divine Service	
"	26th		Running Drill and Company training	
"	27th		do - - - do	
"	28th		Running Drill, Company training and preparation for the move to the new area at WARLOY	

P.R. Simner Lieut. Col.
Commdg. 10th West Yorkshire Regt.

A5834 Wt. W4973/M687 750,000 8/16 D. D. & L. Ltd. Forms/C.2118/12.

Army Form C. 2118.

Instructions regarding War Diaries and Intelligence Summaries are contained in F. S. Regs., Part II. and the Staff Manual respectively. Title pages will be prepared in manuscript.

WAR DIARY
or
INTELLIGENCE SUMMARY.
(Erase heading not required.)

Place	Date	Hour	Summary of Events and Information	Remarks and references to Appendices
COMBLES	17th		being cut by shell fire and the linesmen of the Battalion behaved admirably always going out immediately the breaks occurred to repair the lines often under very heavy fire	
COMBLES AND BRONFAY	18th		Battalion marched to BRONFAY Camp being relieved by the 1st Border Regt of the 29th Division	
BRONFAY AND MEAULTE	19th		Battalion marched to MEAULTE taking over billets from 2nd Royal Fusiliers	
MEAULTE	20th		General cleaning up - kit inspection	
-	21st		Running drill and Company training	
-	22nd		do - do	
-	23rd		do - do	
-	24th		do - do - Battalion Concert in the Y.M.C.A. hut	
	25th		Sunday Divine Service	
	26th		Running Drill and Company training	
	27th		do - do	
	28th		Running Drill Company training & preparation for the move to the new area at WARLOY	

P. R. Simner Lieut Col.
Comdg. 10th West Yorkshire Regt

A5834 Wt. W4973/M687 750,000 8/16 D. D. & L. Ltd. Forms/C.2118/13.

SECRET COPY No 7.

AFTER ORDER to OPERATION ORDER No 47.

by Lt COL. P.R. SIMNER. D.S.O.
Commanding 10th Bn West Yorkshire Regt

HQ. 5-2-17.

Ref para 8.

After stopping at the SOUP KITCHEN, COMBLES. Companies will march with 500 yards intervals to GUILLEMONT STATION Ref 57 C. SW. 1/20,000. S. 24. D. 9. 9½.

(Turn left where lines cross GUILLEMONT-LONGUEVAL ROAD).

LT. C.E. JARVIS with 4. H.Q. guides will proceed ahead to allot carriages to the Companies when this is done, guides will return to the Junction of the GUILLEMONT-COMBLES ROAD. and will lead the Companies

2

in the train.

The first Company will entrain at 10pm

H. A. Smith ? Lt
a/Adj
[illegible] Bn West Yorkshire Rgt

Issued at 5.30pm

COPY No 1 OC 'A'
" " 2 OC 'B'
" " 3 OC 'C'
" " 4 OC 'D'
" " 5 Lt C E JARVIS
" " 6 WAR DIARY
" " 7 RETAINED.

Operation Order No 51 Copy No 2

by Lt Col P.R. Simner DSO

Commanding 10th Bn West Yorkshire Rgt

HQ 18-2-17

1 The Battalion will march from the COMBLES AREA to BRONFAY CAMP 15-A this afternoon. Companies will march independently after handing over their billets to a Company of the 1st Bn BORDER Rgt.

2 <u>BLANKETS + OFFICERS VALISES</u> + LG's must be ready for loading on to the West Yorkshire limbers as soon as they call for them

NB limbers for LG's.

3 <u>SICK</u>. The Medical officer will arrange for any sick men to be conveyed to BRONFAY

4. All billets & [illegible] must be left clean and the [illegible] certificate will be sent to [illegible] Room on arrival at Camp [illegible]

5. Reporting all present [illegible] Companies have taken steps [illegible] given [illegible] at [illegible]. OC Coys must report of their men [illegible] present or absent. This is not being done in all cases.

6. ACKNOWLEDGE

Issued at 2 30 pm [illegible]

Copy 1 to OC A
" 2 " B
3 C
4 D
5 WAR DIARY Returned
6

10th West Yorkshire Regt.

OPERATION ORDER No. 52. SECRET 19-2-17

I The Battalion will move to billets in MEAULTE to-day.

Companies will march away independently at the following times.

D Coy.	11-30 a.m.
C "	11-35 am.
B	11-40 am.
A	11-45 am.
H.Qrs.	11-50 am.

A distance of 500 yds. will be kept between Companies.

II ROUTE. BRONFAY FARM - Road junction F.15. c. 3.8. - BRAYE to ALBERT road - CARCAILLOT CORNER - MEAULTE.

Guides will be waiting at CARCAILLOT corner to conduct Companies to billets.

III TRANSPORT. The Transport Officer will arrange to move Stores and kits as follows:-

1. Packs and Company stores and Blankets 7-30 A.M.
2. Lewis Guns + Drums at 8.30 a.m.
3. Officer's valices and mess boxes at 10-0 a.m.
4. Orderly Room and Signal stores at 10.0 a.m.

All the above must be at the Q.M. stores by the times stated. Blankets will be rolled in bundles of ten, which must be tied neatly at each end.

IV Huts, lines and latrines will be left scrupulously clean. A certificate to the effect will be rendered to the Adjutant by Company Commanders before leaving camp

(sd.) A. H. G. Anderson Capt
Adjutant
10th West Yorkshire Regt.

10th West Yorkshire Regt 31-7-17
Operation Orders No 45 SECRET.

I The Battalion will march to COMBLES to-morrow. Companies will occupy the same quarters as on the last occasion.
Order of March A.B.C.D H. Qtrs
Hour of Start 1-30 PM
An interval of 500 yds will be observed between Companies.
Water bottles will be filled before starting.

2. An advance party consisting of 2/Lt. DENT and 1 N.C.O. from each Company and 1 from Headquarters will proceed to COMBLES at 10-0AM to take over quarters from the outgoing Battalion.

3. The usual certificates as to the cleanliness of huts and lines will be rendered to the Adjutant before leaving.

(Sd) A.F.G Anderson Capt.
Adjutant
10th West Yorkshire Regt.

JE. CERTIFIE QUE LA TROUPE CANTONNÉE CHEZ MOI DU.

AU

N'A COMMIS AUCUN DEGAT

A. COMMIS LES DEGATS SUIVANTS

JE N'AI RIEN
RIEN D'AUTRE } A RECLAMER CONTRE CETTE UNITE.

SIGNATURE DU PROPRIETAIRE.

ADDRESSE DU PROPRIETAIRE.

(No ET. RUE.)

DATE

SIGNATURE OF OFFICER

RANK AND UNIT.

DATE.

SECRET

COPY No 5.

OPERATION ORDER No 50

by Lt Col. P.R.SIMNER.D.S.O. commanding
10th Bn West Yorkshire Regt.

HQ 16 - 2 - 17.

The Battalion will be relieved by the 6th Bn DORSET Regt 17/18th, in the trenches

1 ORDER OF RELIEF

FRONT LINE.

Left. Half 'B' Coy will be relieved by half 'C' Coy 6th Dorsets with same No of LG's & Bombing Post.

Right Half 'D' Coy will be relieved by half 'A' Coy 6th Dorsets Same No of LG's & Bombing Post.

OLD FRONT LINE

Left. Posts 3–1 inclusive, and A.B.C.
Half 'B' Coy will be relieved by half "C" Coy 6th Dorset Regt

Right Posts 4–9 inclusive. Half 'D' Coy will be relieved by half 'A' Coy 6th Dorset Regt

LG's take over gun for gun

CANE ALLEY "C' Company will be relieved by 'D' Coy 6th Dorset Regt.

STRONG POINTS.

'A' Company will be relieved by "B' Coy 6th DORSET Regt in the Strong Points —:

1 PLTN SAILLY SP. 1 LG
1 PLTN CUSHY SP. 1 LG
1 PLTN CHATEAU SP. 1 LG
1 PLTN SOUTH.COPSE. —

2 GUIDES. OC 'D' Company will furnish
(1) 5 guides { 1 for Bombing Stop on right
2 Platoon Guides Front Line
2 Platoon guides Old Front line

OC 'B' Company will furnish
5 guides { 1 for Bombing Stop on Left
2 platoon guides for Front Line
2 platoon guides for Old Front Line

These guides will leave the front line before daylight, and will proceed via BULLET CROSS ROADS to Battⁿ HQ. The place of meeting the in-coming Unit will be at BULLET CROSS ROADS.

(2) OC 'C' Company will furnish
4 guides 1 per platoon

OC 'A' Company will furnish
4 guides. 1 per platoon.

These guides will report at Bⁿ HQ at 4 pm The place of meeting the in coming Unit for these guides will be at HAIE WOOD.

3 REPORTING RELIEF:
Great care must be taken that relief is correctly and promptly reported through to Bⁿ HQ^{rs}. If there is any doubt O.C. Coy's should report by runner as well. RELIEF COMPLETE will be sent through by the word — AT — prefixing the initial letter of the Company.
eg BAT.

4. AFTER RELIEF. Companies will proceed independently to the dugouts in COMBLES AREA, and will occupy the same dugouts as last time

'A' COMBLES RESERVE TRENCHES
'B' CEMETRY DUGOUT
'C' COMBLES RESERVE. TRS
'D' HAIE WOOD. DUGOUT.

OC Companies will send report to Bn HQ in COMBLES VILLAGE as soon as their companies are present in the BRIGADE RESERVE AREA allotted. Whilst in the BRIGADE RESERVE Companies are at half-an-hours notice to move into any part of the Sector.

5 TRENCH STORES. Special attention must be given to the correct handing over of Stores and receipts for all obtained.
Especially Lewis Gun Drums. and WATER TINS.

6 ACKNOWLEDGE.

H. A. [illegible] 2/Lt
a/adj

10th Bn West Yorkshire Regt

Issued at 10.30 pm

COPY No 1 OC 'A'
No 2 OC 'B'
No 3 OC 'C'
No 4 OC D
No 5 War Diary
No 6 Retained.

10th West Yorkshire Regt.

Operation Order No 49.

I The Battalion will be relieved to night by the 6th Dorsetshire Regt & will proceed to COMBLES, where Companies will be located as follows:-

D. Company HAIE WOOD
B " CEMETERY
A & C Companies Reserve trenches

Companies will send down advance parties of 1 NCO & 2 men to take over quarters

II Companies will be relieved as follows:-

C. Company by D Company 6th Dorsetshire
A " " B " " "
D " " A " " "
B " " C " " "

III Guides will be furnished by Companies to the relieving Battalion as follows:-

"C" Coy 6 guides at BULLET CORNER U 20. a 1. 9½ at 6.45 PM - i e one per platoon & two for Lewis Guns (Right & Left)
"A" Coy 4 guides at BULLET CORNER at 6.50 PM one per platoon
"D" Coy 3 guides on Duckboards near South Copse at 6-45 pm for Platoons in Support Line. Platoon for South Copse will be directed on the spot.
"B" Coy 1 Guide on duckboards near South Copse at 6-45 pm

IV Completion of relief will be notified to H.Qrs by the word **ONE** preceded by the initial letter of the Company

V All Trench Stores & Lewis Gun Drums will be handed over and receipts taken.

VI Water cans must be brought out by all Companies without fail and taken to CHATEAU dump, where receipts will be obtained. The whole of each Company need not be taken past the dump. A & C Companies will detail special parties to carry their own water cans

VII All rifle grenade cap attachments will be brought out of the line without fail.

VIII Rolls will be called before leaving the trenches and again on ~~exit~~ reaching COMBLES and all absentees reported immediately

IX The mens feet will be attended to directly after arriving at COMBLES

X ACKNOWLEDGE

(Sd) H. F. G. Anderson Capt.
Adjutant
10 West Yorkshire Regt

11-2-17

SECRET

COPY. No 6.

OPERATION ORDER No 47.

by Lt COL P.R. SIMNER D.S.O.

Commanding 10th Bn West Yorkshire Rgt.

H Q. 14 - 2 - 17.

The Battalion will be relieved by the 12th Manchester Regt tomorrow night 5/6th.

1 ORDER OF RELIEF Companies will be relieved as follows:—
'C' Company will be relieved by 'C' Company 12 Manchester in Right Front
'A' Coy will be relieved by 'B' Company 12 Manchester Rgt in Left Front
'D' Company will be relieved by 'D' Company 12th Manchester in Support
'B' Coy will be relieved by 'A' Company 12th Manchester Rgt in Reserve. Their dispositions will be the same as ours.

2 GUIDES O.C. 'C' Company will detail 7 guides to leave the line before daylight. One guide for each platoon, and one for the Lewis Guns. O.C. 'A' Company will detail seven guides; one for each platoon and one for each Lewis Gun. O.C.'s D & B Coy will each detail 4 guides one for each platoon.
Guides of 'A' 'D' & 'B' Companies will report at Battalion H.Q.rs at 4 pm.
Lt C.E. JARVIS will superintend the distribution of guides at Battalion H.Q.rs at 5.30 pm

3 TRENCH STORES Fullest Receipt must be taken for all stores handed over. Receipts will be sent to Orderly Room on arrival at BRONFAY CAMP, as soon as possible on the following morning.

4/ GUM BOOTS will be treated as trench stores and handed over accordingly.

5/ WATER TINS All empty Petrol Cans will be either sent or brought out, and delivered at CHATEAU DUMP where an N.C.O. of the battalion will be posted to check the number and help the NCO i/c: O.C. 'C' Coy will send all his empty tins to 'D' Coy for carriage to Dump.

6/ REPORTING RELIEF. When the relief is complete OC Companies will assure themselves that the relief is promptly reported through to Bn HQrs using the Code Word:—

PORT

prefixing the initial letter of their Company

eg DPORT.

7/ AFTER RELIEF Companies will proceed independently to the RIGHT GROUP SOUP KITCHEN at T.28. a 9.6.

Lt TITLEY will leave the line at 6pm with two men, who will act as GUIDES to the Companies on their reaching COMBLES. His duties will be to superintend the issue of Soup and tea as at present there is too much congestion and delay.

Men must be warned not to leave any Sandbags which they have taken off their feet around or near the SOUP KITCHEN. SANDBAGS if worn will be left at HAIEWOOD DUMP.

8/ ORDERS relating to mode of conveyance to BRONFAY will be issued later.

9 <u>LEWIS GUN DRUMS</u> All the drums will be handed over, and receipts obtained. OC Companies will hand over the three carriers brought in last time.

10. Rolls will be called before leaving & on arrival at Camp

11 <u>Acknowledge</u>

[illegible] 2/Lt
a/Adjt
SAME.
10th Battalion West Yorkshire Regt

Issued at 2 am.

Copy No 1 OC 'A' Coy
" " 2 OC 'B' Coy
" " 3 OC 'C' Coy
" " 4 OC 'D' Coy
" " 5 WAR DIARY
" " 6 RETAINED.

10th WEST YORKSHIRE REGT. 3-2-17.

Operation Order No. 46. SECRET.

The Battalion will relieve the 12th Manchester Regt. in the trenches to-day.

1. HOUR of START Companies will proceed to destinations in the following order. C. A. D. B. H.Qrs.

O.C. "C" Coy. will proceed via the FREGICOURT ROAD, and will time his departure to arrive at BULLET Cross Roads about 6.45 P.M.

A.D+B. Coys will time their departure so that the leading Company reaches the duckboards (T. 24. a. 1.7.) at 6.0.P.M. remaining two so that there is 500 yds intervals between Companies. From the time of moving off an interval of 200 yds. between half companies will be observed.

2. ORDER of RELEIF

"C" Coy. will relieve "A" Coy. 12th Manchester Regt. on the right front
"A" " " " "D" " " " " on the left front
"D" " " " "B" " " " " in supports

as follows:- 3 Platoons in CAIN ALLEY
1 " " SOUTH COPSE. S.P.

"B" Coy will relieve "C" Coy. 12th Manchester Regt. in the strong points as reserve.

Lewis Guns will be taken over as follows:-

1 Lewis Gun in Post 9		RIGHT-FRONT.
1 " " " " 7		
1 " " in BEAN SUPPORT		

1 Lewis Gun in Post A		LEFT-FRONT
1 " " " " B		
1 " " " " C		

3 Lewis Guns in CAIN ALLEY SUPPORT.
2 " " " CHATEAU S.P. } RESERVE.
1 " " " CUSHY S.P. }

3. GUIDES:- One guide for each platoon and one for each L.G. will meet the right Coy. at BOLLET cross Roads at U.20, a.1.9.

Guides for the remaining Companies one for each platoon and one for each Lewis Gun for Left Company.

One guide for each platoon of the support Company, and one for each platoon of reserve Company will meet the Battalion at SOUTH COPSE.

4. ADVANCE PARTY. The Provost Sgt. with the Rgth. Police will leave at 3-0 P.M. to take over the CHATEAU DUMP, and all Stores at Battalion Headquarters. Report to 12th Manchesters Regt. on arrival.

SIGNALLERS - Batt. H.Qrs. and O.Cs Support and Reserve Companies will send their Signallers in advance to take over their Stations. They will leave their respective quarters at 3-0 P.M. One Company signaller will remain behind for rations.

5. LEWIS GUN DRUMS - O.C. "B" Coy. + O.C. "D" Coy. will each send down a party to Batt. H.Qrs. at 3-0 P.M. to take up 12 Lewis Gun Carriers, which will be left at the CHATEAU DUMP. "B" Coy. party will carry up 8 Carriers, and "D" Coy. party taken from the platoon occupying SOUTH COPSE will carry up 4 Carriers.

6. Companies will send in their morning reports, List of Trench Stores taken over during relief.

sd. H. A. G. Neville 2nd Lt.
a/Adjt.
10th West Yorkshire Regt.

16 E. 11 sheets

WAR DIARY

10th West Yorkshire Regiment

MARCH. 1914.

Instructions regarding War Diaries and Intelligence Summaries are contained in F. S. Regs., Part II. and the Staff Manual respectively. Title pages will be prepared in manuscript.

WAR DIARY
or
~~INTELLIGENCE~~ SUMMARY.
(Erase heading not required.)

Army Form C. 2118.

Vol 15

Place	Date	Hour	Summary of Events and Information	Remarks and references to Appendices
MEAULTE AND WARLOY	MARCH 1st 1917		Battalion marched from MEAULTE to WARLOY via ALBERT, the division being transferred to	
	"		Fifth Army II Corps. a.t.g.a.	
WARLOY	2nd		Company Training a.t.g.a.	
"	3rd		Company and Specialist Training a.t.g.a.	
"	4th		Sunday Divine Service a.t.g.a.	
"	5th		Company and Specialist Training. 2/Lieuts J. D. LE GROVE and G. A. TWIGG Joined	
"	"		the Battalion a.t.g.a.	
"	6th		Specialist Training and practising Platoons in attack formations a.t.g.a.	
"	7th		Specialist Training and Battalion Training a.t.g.a.	
"	8th		Specialist Training and practising contact and reconnaissance patrols a.t.g.a.	
"	"		2/Lts. G. I. LARKINS and R. N. P. WILSON Joined the Battalion a.t.g.a.	
"	9th		Practising attacks on Strong Points. a.t.g.a.	
"	10th		Battalion practising attack on an Enemy position a.t.g.a.	
"	11th		Sunday Divine Service 2/Lts. S. W. AGAR and A. T. BROWN Joined the Battalion a.t.g.a.	

A5834 Wt. W4973/M687 750,000 8/16 D. D. & L. Ltd. Forms/C.2118/13.

Army Form C. 2118.

Instructions regarding War Diaries and Intelligence Summaries are contained in F. S. Regs., Part II. and the Staff Manual respectively. Title pages will be prepared in manuscript.

WAR DIARY

or

~~INTELLIGENCE SUMMARY.~~

(Erase heading not required.)

Place	Date	Hour	Summary of Events and Information	Remarks and references to Appendices
WARLOY	MARCH 12-1917		Practising advance and attack in Cooperation with a Contact aeroplane.	
"	13th		Specialist and Company Training.	
WARLOY and BEAUVAL	14th		Battalion marched to BEAUVAL distance 13 miles.	
BEAUVAL and BOUQUEMAISON	15th		Battalion marched to BOUQUEMAISON distance 8½ miles.	
BOUQUEMAISON and LINZEUX	16th		Battalion marched to LINZEUX. Only two men fell out during the three days	
"	16th		march. The Division was now transferred to Third Army.	
LINZEUX	17th		General cleaning up and inspection of Kit, Arms, and Equipment.	
"	18th		Sunday Divine Service	
"	19th		Battalion Training 2/Lieut H.M. CARMICHAEL Joined the Battalion.	
"	20th		-do- -do-	
"	21st		-do- -do-	
"	22nd		Company Training	
LINZEUX and IVERGNY	23rd		Battalion moved to IVERGNY by bus and march route.	
IVERGNY	24th		Company Training	
"	25th		Sunday Divine Service.	
"	26th		Company and Specialist Training. Instruction of Junior Officers. Capt A. N. L	
"	26th		CLARK Joined the Battalion.	

A5834 Wt. W4973/M687 750,000 8/16 D. D. & L. Ltd. Forms/C.2118/13.

Instructions regarding War Diaries and Intelligence Summaries are contained in F. S. Regs., Part II. and the Staff Manual respectively. Title pages will be prepared in manuscript.

WAR DIARY
or
~~INTELLIGENCE SUMMARY.~~
(Erase heading not required.)

Army Form C. 2118.

Place	Date	Hour	Summary of Events and Information	Remarks and references to Appendices
IVERGNY	March 27/1917		Musketry and Company Training.	
"	28th		Tactical Scheme Company Training.	
"	29th		Brigade Route March Company Training.	
"	30th		Tactical Scheme under G.O.C. 50th Infantry Brigade.	
"	31st		Company Training and Musketry.	
			31-3-17.	
			P.R. Simner Lieut Col. Comdg. 50th Infantry Brigade.	

A5834 Wt. W4973/M687 750,000 8/16 D. D. & L. Ltd. Forms/C.2118/13.

SECRET.

No.......

10th West Yorkshire Regt.

Operation Order No. 54

13.3.17.

Ref. Map LENS 11.

I. The Battalion will march to billets at BEAUVAL to-morrow – distance approximately 13 miles.

(i) ROUTE. CONTAY – HERISSART – VAL DE MAISON

(ii) ORDER of MARCH Headquarters B, C, Drums, D & A Coys. Transport Echelon A.

(iii) HOUR of START. 7-0 a.m.

(iv) RENDEZVOUS. Head of the column to be in the street outside Battalion Headquarters facing north at time above stated.

(v) DRESS. Marching order. Steel helmets will be worn. Jerkins & greatcoats will be carried in the pack. Caps will be ~~strapped~~ carried in a manner detailed by C.S.Ms. ~~to the back of the pack.~~ Box respirators will be carried on the top of the pack. Water bottles will be filled before starting. Haversack rations will be carried.

II TRANSPORT. Echelon A will march in rear of the Battalion.

Echelon B will be brigaded under the order of the Brigade Transport Officer.

III. BILLETING PARTY. A billeting party consisting of one N.C.O from each Company & from Headquarters, Q.M. stores and Transport will parade at Orderly Room at 5-30 a.m. under the command of Lieut. C.E. JARVIS. They will proceed to BEAUVAL, & will meet the Staff Captain at the Town Major's Office at 10-0 a.m.

IV. REAR PARTY. A straggler party of 10 reliable men (to be detailed by the Regtl. Sergt. Major) under the command of Lieut. A.C. TITLEY will march in rear of the Transport (Echelon A) and will bring on all men who are not in possession of a chit authorising them to go to the Ambulance.

Sd. A.F.G. Anderson Capt.
Adjutant
10th West Yorkshire Regt.

SECRET

10th West Yorkshire Regt.

Operation Order No. 55 14-3-17.

Ref. map: LENS 11.

I. The Battalion will march to billets in the BONNIERES area to-morrow morning. Actual destination will be notified later.

(i) ROUTE. DOULLENS - HTE. VISEE - BOUQUE MAISON

(ii) ORDER of MARCH Headquarters, C.D. DRUMS, A.B. Coys. Transport ECHELON A.

(iii) HOUR of START. 8-0 a.m.

(iv) RENDEZVOUS. Head of the column to be in the street outside Orderly Room facing north at the time above stated.

(v) DRESS. The same as for to-day march. Water bottles will be filled before starting. Haversack rations will be carried.

II TRANSPORT. Echelon "A" will march in rear of the Battalion. Echelon "B" will be brigaded under the order of the Brigade Transport Officer. This Echelon is due to pass BEAUVAL railway station at the north end of the Town at 9-15 a.m. Ammunition mules will draw the Lewis Gun handcarts, which will accompany Echelon A.

III BILLETING PARTY. A billeting party consisting of one N.C.O. from each Coy, from Headquarters, Q.M. Stores, and from the Transport, will parade at Orderly Room, at 6-0 a.m. under the command of LIEUT. C.E. JARVIS. They will proceed to BOUQUEMAISON on bicycles & will meet the Staff Captain at the Church at 9-0 a.m.

IV) REAR PARTY. A straggler party of 10 reliable men (to be detailed by the Regtl. Sergt. Major) under the command of LIEUT. A.G. TITLEY will march in rear of the Transport (ECHELON A) and will bring on all men who are not in possession of a chit authorising them to go to the Ambulance.

(V) LEWIS GUNNERS will all wear their packs & equipment. Nothing whatsoever will be allowed on the hand carts. Men will on no account sit on the carts when halted.

(Sd) A. Y. G. Anderson Capt.
Adjutant
10th West Yorkshire Rgt.

under the command of 2nd Lt. CLOUGH in rear of the rear transport, and will bring on all men who are not in possession of a chit authorising them to go to the Ambul.

II. DISCIPLINE. The strictest march discipline will be maintained throughout. Particular attention wi be paid to covering and dressing. Ranks must be kept well closed up. No man will be allowed to fall out without the written permission of an Officer. All water bottles will be filled before starting. No man will drink from his water bottle before the second halt and then only by permission.

The Transport Officer will ride up and down the column and will see that no unauthorised loads or men get on the transport.

The Medical Officer will not send men with chits to ride on the transport wagons except in case of dire necessity.

It must be firmly impressed on all ranks that falling out & straggling bring great discredit on the Battalion.

III. BILLETS. All Billets must be left scrupulously clean & the usual certificates rendered to the Adjutant before leaving.

2nd Lt. NEWTON and a party of 2. O.R. from each Company will remain behind to inspect billets, and to obtain signed certificates from the owners that they have no claims against the Battalion. 2nd Lt. NEWTON will report to Orderly Room for forms & instructions at 9.0. P.M.

(Sd.) A. F. G. Anderson Capt.
Adjutant
15th [illegible] Yorkshire Regt.

SECRET

10th West Yorkshire Regt.

15/3/17

Operation Order No. 56.

Ref. map LENS II

1. The Battalion will march to LINZEUX to-morrow - distance approximately 13 miles.

(i) ROUTE FREVENT. - FILLIEVRES

(ii) ORDER of MARCH. H. Qrs, D. A, DRUMS, B+C Coys, Transport

(iii) RENDEZVOUS. The Battalion will parade in the main street facing north - the head of the column to be outside Headquarters Mess.

(iv) HOUR of START. 8-10 a.m.

II DRESS.

Marching Order as detailed for to-days march

Water-bottles will be filled before starting. Haversack rations will be carried.

III BILLETING PARTY The advanced Billeting party (as previously detailed) under Lieut. C.E. JARVIS and 2/Lt. H. MARSHALL will proceed to LINZEUX on bicycles & will report to the Staff Captain at 10-30 a.m.

IV. 2nd Lt. N. Newton and the Interpreter will remain behind to assist the Quartermaster in rendering billeting returns + obtaining certificates from the inhabitants in regard to claims &c.

V. REAR PARTY. A Straggler party of 10 reliable men (to be detailed by the Regtl. Sergt. Major) under the command of Lieut. A. G. Titley will march in rear of the Transport and will bring on all men who are not in possession of a chit authorising them to go to the Ambulance.

VI TRANSPORT. The whole of the Transport to-gether with the Lewis Gun handcarts, will march in rear of the Battalion.

(Sd) A. J. G. Anderson. Capt.
Adjutant.
10th West Yorkshire Regt.

SECRET.

10th West Yorkshire Regt. 23-3-17

Operation Order No. 57.

Ref. Map. LENS 11.

1. The Battalion will move to-day to the IVERGNY area by bus and march route.

(i) Route. PETIT FILLIEVRES - FREVANT - REBREUVIETTE

(ii) Order of March A. B. C. D. Coys. All Signallers, Police, & other details will march with their Companies.

(iii) Rendezvous. The Battalion will parade in the village ready to march in the direction of FILLIEVRES, the head of the column to be immediately clear, (i.e N.E.) of the cross roads LINZEUX to WILLEMAN and LINZEUX to FILLIEVRES.

(iv) Hour of Start. 9-15 a.m.

(v) Dress. Marching Order. Greatcoats will be worn. One blanket will be carried in the pack. Water bottles will be filled. Haversack rations will be carried.

(vi) Drums. The Drums will play the Battalion until the lorries are reached, & will march between B & C Companies. They will then rejoin their Companies.

2. BILLETING:- The advanced billeting party (as previously detailed) under Lieut. C.E. JARVIS & 2nd Lt. H. MARSHALL will parade at Orderly Room at 7.30 a.m. and will proceed to IVERGNY on bicycles as rapidly as possible. Lieut. JARVIS will report to the Staff Captain at IVERGNY church at 10-30 a.m.

(2) 2nd Lt. H. NEWTON and 1 N.C.O. & 2 men from the Company on duty will remain behind & complete billeting returns & certificates. If possible a certificate should be obtained from the MAIRE that there are no outstanding claims against the Battalion and that the area has been left clean.

3. REAR PARTY. A straggler party of 10 reliable men to be detailed by the Regt. Sergt. Major under the command of Lieut. A.G. TITLEY will march in rear of the Battalion and will bring on all stragglers to the lorries so that no delay will be caused in moving off.

4. MARKERS A party consisting of one N.C.O. from each Coy. will march away at 8.45am. under the Regtl. Sergt. Major and will be posted by him to mark the rear of the eight lorries allotted to each Coy. There will be 33 lorries, the 33rd lorry will be the Headquarters lorry.

5. TRANSPORT will proceed by march route. Starting point LINZEUX church 10-8 am. Lewis Gun carts will march with the Transport, and will be under the orders of the Transport Officer. Four Lewis Gunners will accompany each cart, O.C. A, B & C Coys will detail 4 each and O.C. D Coy. will detail 6 for this party. The party will be under the immediate charge of Sgt. FINNEY who will report to the Transport Officer with his party at 9.15am.

6. BILLETS and all Officers quarters must be left scrupulously clean. Company Commanders will be held personally responsible that this is done. A written certificate to this effect will be rendered to Orderly Room before leaving.

Issued at 1.0 P.M.

(Sd) [illegible] Capt.
Adjutant
10th West Yorkshire Regt.

17.E
10 sheets 1917

CONFIDENTIAL.

Vol 16

WAR DIARY

FOR

APRIL 1917

10th

WEST YORKSHIRE REGT.

Instructions regarding War Diaries and Intelligence Summaries are contained in F. S. Regs., Part II. and the Staff Manual respectively. Title pages will be prepared in manuscript.

WAR DIARY

or

~~INTELLIGENCE~~ SUMMARY.

(*Erase heading not required.*)

SECRET

Army Form C. 2118.

Place	Date	Hour	Summary of Events and Information	Remarks and references to Appendices
IVERGNY	APRIL 1st		Battalion in billets at IVERGNY (Refce map LENS 11). Sunday Divine Service.	AJBh
"	2nd		Musketry Tactical Scheme under G.O.C. 50th Infantry Brigade.	AJBh
"	3rd		Musketry - Tactical Scheme.	AJBh
"	4th		Musketry Company Training	AJBh
IVERGNY and MAGNICOURT-SUR-CANCHE	5th		Battalion marched to Billets at MAGNICOURT-SUR-CANCHE	AJBh
"	6th		Company training	AJBh
MAGNICOURT-SUR-CANCHE to MANIN	7th		Battalion marched to billets at MANIN.	AJBh
MANIN and AGNEZ	8th		Battalion marched to TALAVERA CAMP at AGNEZ.	AJBh
AGNEZ	9th		Information was received that the Division was attached to the Cavalry Corps and would advance behind the Cavalry. In the afternoon orders were received to move. Greatcoats and blankets were collected and stored in the huts and the Battalion marched with the Brigade through AGNEZ and DUISANS to the main ARRAS road. Here the traffic was greatly congested with CAVALRY, Guns, Lorries and Ambulances. Long halts were frequent and progress became very difficult. At dusk orders were received to bivouac for the night in a field to the south of the road at approximately L.18 d (Refce. map FRANCE sheet 51c). Snow fell heavily throughout the night and no	

T2134. Wt. W708—776. 500000. 4/15. Sir J. C. & S.

Instructions regarding War Diaries and Intelligence Summaries are contained in F. S. Regs., Part II. and the Staff Manual respectively. Title pages will be prepared in manuscript.

WAR DIARY

~~or~~

~~INTELLIGENCE SUMMARY.~~

(Erase heading not required.)

Army Form C. 2118.

Place	Date	Hour	Summary of Events and Information	Remarks and references to Appendices
AGNEZ	APRIL			
	9th		cover was available. After midnight the Cavalry commenced to return and were streaming back along the road until morning.	[illegible]
ARRAS	10th		Shortly after daybreak the Brigade marched into ARRAS and the Battalion found quarters in cellars in the GRANDE PLACE. Here news was received that the Infantry attack to the east of ARRAS had been successful and that cavalry were advancing in the direction of MONCHY-LE-PREUX.	[illegible]
	11th		Information was received that all plans had been altered and that the Division now formed part of the VI Corps. In the afternoon the Brigade marched out of ARRAS along the ARRAS-CAMBRAI road. Progress was again slow, traffic in both direction being most congested. At a point in H.32.c (Refer map FRANCE sheet 51 B.N.W.) the Brigade left the road and proceeded by cross country tracks to the Broken Mill at H.34.b.3.3. Here there was a halt of about 4 hours to await orders. Brigade Headquarters were established near FEUCHY at H.28.a.4.9. Snow fell heavily and the weather was bitterly cold. Orders were then received that the Brigade were to relieve units of the 15th Division between the boundary line of map squares H.I. N and O.	

Instructions regarding War Diaries and Intelligence Summaries are contained in F. S. Regs., Part II. and the Staff Manual respectively. Title pages will be prepared in manuscript.

WAR DIARY
or
INTELLIGENCE SUMMARY.
(Erase heading not required.)

Army Form C. 2118.

Place	Date	Hour	Summary of Events and Information	Remarks and references to Appendices
Ref map 51 B.N.W	11th		(Refer. map FRANCE sheet 51 B. N.W) and the river SCARPE, the 10th West Yorkshire Regiment on the right and 6th Dorsetshire Regiment on the left of the front line with 7th East Yorkshire Regt in support and 7th Yorkshire Regt in reserve. The Battalion accordingly moved forward and proceeded to relieve the 7/8 K.O.S.B and small detachments of 8 other units.	[illegible]
Ref. map sheet 51 B. H.36. a.c.d and N.b.	12th		Ref map FRANCE sheet 51 B) Relief completed and touch gained with 6th Dorsetshire Regt. on the left, and with detachments of 10th Hussars and Essex Yeomanry in MONCHY WOOD and the Royal West Kent Regt in MONCHY on the right. The line taken over in H36. a.c.d and N6.b. was found to consist of small lengths of shallow trench facing in all directions where the advancing troops had dug themselves in. The best possible line was chosen through these and the Battalion dug itself in with the right resting on MONCHY and the left meeting the 6th Dorsetshire Regt at H36 a. 2.6. Information was received that the 9th Division was relieving the 4th Division on the North bank of the SCARPE and would advance against the ROEUX-GAVRELLE road with ROEUX as the second objective. The 10th West Yorkshire Regiment.	

Army Form C. 2118.

Instructions regarding War Diaries and Intelligence Summaries are contained in F. S. Regs., Part II. and the Staff Manual respectively. Title pages will be prepared in manuscript.

WAR DIARY
or
INTELLIGENCE SUMMARY.
(Erase heading not required.)

Place	Date	Hour	Summary of Events and Information	Remarks and references to Appendices
H.36.a.c.0 and H.6.b.	12th		and 6th Dorsetshire Regt were ordered to advance in conjunction with them and to attack and capture a line following the road from MONCHY to I.25.d.Y.9 and push strong patrols thence to the RIVER SCARPE: objective of this Battalion MONCHY to H.31 central. The Battalion got into position to conform with the 6th Dorsetshire Regt, strong patrols were sent forward and established themselves on the MONCHY - PELVES road at H.31.d.2.9 and H.31.c.6.4. Owing to a change of plan the attack was cancelled and orders received to reoccupy the original line.	
? H31 c 29				
d H31 b 64				
			There was very heavy shelling along the Battalion front throughout the day and considerable damage was done to our trenches. This was however immediately repaired.	
			After nightfall the 6th Dorsetshire Regt was relieved by the 7th EAST Yorkshire Regt. The Cavalry on the right were withdrawn and direct touch was gained with the 6th Royal West Kent Regt.	
			During the night patrols sent out reported LONE COPSE clear and a patrol sent ~~out reported~~ [illegible] eastward reported meeting no enemy until a few were encountered at H.31.d.5.6. these hastily retired.	
	13th		Throughout the day the enemy assisted by his aeroplanes heavily shelled our positions. Lt. A. G. TITLEY. Lt. H. PARSONS 2/Lt. H. MARSHALL and 2/Lt. C. W. ANDREWS were killed by shell fire. Orders were received to cooperate with	

A5834 Wt. W4973/M687 750,000 8/16 D. D. & L. Ltd. Forms/C.2118/13.

Instructions regarding War Diaries and Intelligence Summaries are contained in F. S. Regs., Part II. and the Staff Manual respectively. Title pages will be prepared in manuscript.

WAR DIARY
or
INTELLIGENCE SUMMARY.
(Erase heading not required.)

Army Form C. 2118.

Place	Date	Hour	Summary of Events and Information	Remarks and references to Appendices
	APRIL 13th		the 88th Brigade in an attack to be made by them eastwards on the line O.2 d 5.0 to O.2 b 5.2 and to cover their flank by pushing forward northward of MONCHY during the night and occupying the 15 pursatts spurs in I.31 c & d. with a series of strong points. Strong patrols were sent out along the MONCHY PELVES roads and over the country between encountering the enemy at I.26.c.2.3 and about 1000 yards NORTH of MONCHY. AGR	
	14th		Under cover of a screen a series of posts were dug with the left on the PELVES road at I 31.c.4.5 and the right on the other road at O.1 b 8.8. a support trench was dug inside N. edge of MONCHY wood: the posts contained a garrison of 100 men with six Lewis Guns and one Machine Gun. The attack of the 88th Brigade apparently coincided with a counter attack on MONCHY from the EAST and NORTH by the 3rd BAVARIAN Division with orders to retake the village at all ~~cost~~ costs. Throughout the day our posts were heavily engaged but succeeded in beating off the attack from the NORTH and inflicted heavy losses on the enemy.	

T2134. Wt. W708—776. 500000. 4/15. Sir J. C. & S.

Instructions regarding War Diaries and Intelligence Summaries are contained in F. S. Regs., Part II. and the Staff Manual respectively. Title pages will be prepared in manuscript.

WAR DIARY
or
INTELLIGENCE SUMMARY.
(*Erase heading not required.*)

Army Form C. 2118.

Place	Date	Hour	Summary of Events and Information	Remarks and references to Appendices
	14th		Considerable execution was also done to bodies of the enemy advancing to attack from the N. E. By 3-30 pm the attack was broken, and the enemy opened an intensely heavy fire with 5.9 shells on MONCHY and our position near it. This was maintained without cessation for four hours. A7Gh	
ARRAS.	15th		Battalion was relieved by 9th Northumberland Fusiliers and proceeded	
CAVES.			to CAVES in ARRAS. A7Gh	
-	16th		Resting in CAVES A7Gh	
-	17th		do do A7Gh	
-	18th		Moved to dugouts in RAILWAY TRIANGLE. A7Gh	
RAILWAY TRIANGLE. BROWN LINE.	19th		Moved up to BROWN LINE H28 with Battalion Headquarters in railway	
BROWN LINE			cutting FEUCHY. A7Gh	
-	20th		In BROWN LINE (H28) Carrying parties to front line. A7Gh	
-	21st		In BROWN LINE (H28) Relieved by 7th LINCOLN Regt and proceeded to MUSEUM cellars in ARRAS. A7Gh	
-	22nd		Resting in ARRAS. A7Gh	
ARRAS.	23rd		At midnight 22nd/23rd the Battalion moved up to WHITE (or ORANGE) LINE behind the east of ORANGE HILL. At daybreak the 51st Brigade attacked BAYONET TRENCH and at 8.0 A.M. the Battalion moved up to the right sector of the original front line (H.36 129) with the 6th Dorsetshire	

A5834 Wt. W4973/M687 750,000 8/16 D. D. & L. Ltd. Forms/C.2118/13.

Instructions regarding War Diaries and Intelligence Summaries are contained in F. S. Regs., Part II. and the Staff Manual respectively. Title pages will be prepared in manuscript.

WAR DIARY
or
INTELLIGENCE SUMMARY.
(Erase heading not required.)

Army Form C. 2118.

Place	Date	Hour	Summary of Events and Information	Remarks and references to Appendices
H36·29.	23rd		Regt. in the left sector. During the day 100 men were continuously employed in carrying bombs and ammunition to BAYONET trench through constant shell fire and Machine Gun fire. Orders were received to attack RIFLE trench at 6.0 p.m. in conjunction with an attack by the 6th Dorsetshire Regt on the northern half of BAYONET trench. The launching of this attack was at once perceived by the enemy who met it as it advanced down the slopes with a hurricane barrage consisting mainly of 5.9 and 8 inch shells and concentrated Machine Gun fire from the NORTH of the RIVER SCARPE. In spite of heavy losses the men struggled on and finally dug themselves in about 200 yards in advance of and to the EAST of LONE COPSE in touch with the 6th Dorsetshire Regt and hung on until relieved by the 7th East Yorkshire Regt. Capt. P.K. ALLEN killed. A7Bh	
–	24th		On relief the Battalion withdrew to the original front line. Carrying parties for 7th East Yorkshire Regt. A7Bh	

A5834 Wt. W4973/M687 750,000 8/16 D. D. & L. Ltd. Forms/C.2118/13.

Instructions regarding War Diaries and Intelligence Summaries are contained in F. S. Regs., Part II. and the Staff Manual respectively. Title pages will be prepared in manuscript.

WAR DIARY
or
INTELLIGENCE SUMMARY.
(Erase heading not required.)

Army Form C. 2118.

Place	Date	Hour	Summary of Events and Information	Remarks and references to Appendices
ARRAS	APRIL 25th		Battalion was relieved by 7th Suffolk Regt of the 12th Division and proceeded to billets in ARRAS.	
SOMBRIN	26th		Battalion entrained for SAULTY and marched thence to rest billets in SOMBRIN. Total casualties from 10th to 25th 5 officers Killed 8 officers Wounded. 38 O.R. Killed. 264 Wounded and 11 missing.	
	27th		Rest billets in SOMBRIN - General cleaning up.	
SOMBRIN	28th		Company Training.	
	29th		Sunday Divine Service	
	30th		Specialist Training.	

1-5-17.

P.R. Simner Lieut. Col

Comdg. 10th West Yorkshire Regt.

18.E. 11 sheets

WAR DIARY MAY · 1917.

Vol 17

10th

(S) Bn. P.W.O.

(THE WEST YORKSHIRE)

REGIMENT

Instructions regarding War Diaries and Intelligence Summaries are contained in F. S. Regs., Part II. and the Staff Manual respectively. Title pages will be prepared in manuscript.

WAR DIARY

or

~~INTELLIGENCE~~ SUMMARY.

(Erase heading not required.)

Army Form C. 2118.

Place	Date	Hour	Summary of Events and Information	Remarks and references to Appendices
SOMBRIN	1-5-17		Battalion in Rest billets in SOMBRIN. Specialist training and preparations for move to the forward area.	
	2nd		Battalion proceeded in lorries to billets in ARRAS. G.22 a.4.2	Ref map FRANCE Sheet 51 b
ARRAS	3rd		Billet in ARRAS. Considerable shelling in neighbourhood of billets and adjacent Ammunition Dump. (G.22.a.7.8)	
–	4th		Billets in ARRAS.	
–			At 7-45 p.m. a fire was observed in the Ammunition dump. This was followed by frequent explosions of shells and S.A.A.	
–			At 8.30 p.m. a warning order was received to be prepared to move to Y huts on the ARRAS – ST POL road (L.1 b) at 6-0 AM.	Sheet 51 C
–			At about 9-15 p.m. orders were received to proceed to Y huts immediately and the Battalion moved off at 10-30 p.m.	
Y. HUTS.	5th		Arrived at Y huts at 1-0 AM.	
	6th		Sunday – Divine Service. Two Companies. Musketry on Rifle Range in the afternoon.	
	7th		Musketry – Tactical Scheme.	

2353 Wt. W2544/1454 700,000 5/15 D. D. & L. A.D.S.S./Forms/C. 2118.

Instructions regarding War Diaries and Intelligence Summaries are contained in F. S. Regs., Part II. and the Staff Manual respectively. Title pages will be prepared in manuscript.

WAR DIARY
or
~~INTELLIGENCE~~ SUMMARY.
(Erase heading not required.)

Army Form C. 2118.

Place	Date	Hour	Summary of Events and Information	Remarks and references to Appendices
Y HUTS	8th		Tactical Scheme - Company Training	Sheet 51c
	9th		Tactical Scheme Company Training	
ST NICHOLAS	10th		Battalion marched to ST NICHOLAS and rested in a field opposite the Candle Factory - Ref. G.16.b 5.5. At 2.30 pm C.D. Coys moved forward and relieved two Companies 7th Cameron Highlanders of the 9th Division in the FAMPOUX - GAVRELLE line. At 8.15 pm H. Qrs + A+B Coys proceeded to the POINT DE JOUR line with H. Qrs at H10 d 5.4 - relieving the 10th Argyll and Sutherland Highlanders of the 9th Division.	Sheet 51b. N.W.
	11th		The 4th Division on the right of the 17th Divisional front attacked and captured ROEUX CHEMICAL WORKS and the STATION BUILDINGS up to and inclusive of the Junction of CROOK and CROW trenches with CAM trench. The 6th Dorsetshire Regt was attached to the 11th Brigade, 4th Division for this operation, their objective being the Junction of CAM, CROW, and CROOK trenches with orders to establish a defensive flank for the 4th Division. It was reported that all objectives were gained and had been consolidated. A and B Companies moved forward from the POINT DE JOUR line to the FAMPOUX - GAVRELLE line.	Ref map PLOUVAIN 1:10.000 (attached).

2353 Wt. W2544/1454 700,000 5/15 D. D. & L. A.D.S.S./Forms/C. 2118.

Instructions regarding War Diaries and Intelligence Summaries are contained in F. S. Regs., Part II. and the Staff Manual respectively. Title pages will be prepared in manuscript.

WAR DIARY
or
INTELLIGENCE SUMMARY.
(Erase heading not required.)

Army Form C. 2118.

Place	Date	Hour	Summary of Events and Information	Remarks and references to Appendices
	12th		In consequence of the success of the attack by the 4th Division further operations were ordered, the objectives being CORONA - railway cutting at the point where CUPID meets it - CURLIE - CHARLIE to its junction with Cuthbert - thence back to front line at I 1 b 4.0, the attack to take place at 6-30 AM. The 50th Brigade attack was between a line joining the junction of CLOVER and CAM to the point where CUPID joins the railway and an East and West line just North of cross roads in I 4 a (inclusive) the 4th Division attacking on the right, and the 51st Brigade on the left of the Brigade. The attack was ordered to be delivered by the 7th Yorkshire Regt on the right and the 7th East Yorkshire Regt on the left, the 10th West Yorkshire Regt to remain in the FAMPOUX - GAVRELLE line with two Companies ready to move forward to COPPER trench. The operation was reported to have been successful, the Division on the right having reached its objective and the 7th Yorkshire Regt having captured CUPID trench.	
			At 9.0 AM C and D Companies were ordered to proceed to COPPER trench coming under the orders of O.C. 7th East Yorkshire Regt, who then moved them forward to the position of CUBA trench North of CUT.	
	13th		It was reported by 50th Brigade that the 7th Yorkshire Regt had rushed the enemy post at the junction of CUPID and CURLY and had established a stop 40 yards up CURLY. Shortly after 11-0 pm the Battalion relieved the two	

2353 Wt. W2544/1454 700,000 5/15 D. D. & L. A.D.S.S./Forms/C. 2118.

Instructions regarding War Diaries and Intelligence Summaries are contained in F. S. Regs., Part II. and the Staff Manual respectively. Title pages will be prepared in manuscript.

WAR DIARY
or
INTELLIGENCE SUMMARY.
(Erase heading not required.)

Army Form C. 2118.

Place	Date	Hour	Summary of Events and Information	Remarks and references to Appendices
	13th		Companies of the 7th East Yorkshire Regt in CUBA, the command of the front line passing to O.C. 10th West Yorkshire Regt. Dispositions were then as follows:– 4 Companies 10th West Yorkshire Regt in CUBA and two Companies 7th East Yorkshire Regt (attached) in CASH and CUBA. Battalion H. Qrs. were established in CUBA.	
			Shell fire continued to be very heavy throughout the day.	
	14th		Hostile artillery was very active throughout the day, all communications being very heavily shelled with H.E., shrapnel, and gas shells. ROEUX was also bombarded.	
			After nightfall the Brigade front was rearranged. The two Companies of the 7th East Yorkshire Regt rejoined their Battalion. The 10th Sherwood Foresters took over CUBA (north of CUT) and the 10th West Yorkshire Regt occupied CUBA (south of CUT) CASH and CHAPLIN with H Qrs in CLARK.	
	15th		Battalion came under the orders of G.O.C. 51st Brigade.	
			The enemy bombardment continued with increasing severity. Battalion H. Qrs were shelled out of CLARK and reestablished in CHILI. Orders were received for the relief of the Battalion by a unit of 51st Division, each Company to be relieved by a platoon.	

2353 Wt. W2544/1454 700,000 5/15 D. D. & L. A.D.S.S./Forms/C. 2118.

Army Form C. 2118.

WAR DIARY
or
INTELLIGENCE SUMMARY.
(*Erase heading not required.*)

Instructions regarding War Diaries and Intelligence Summaries are contained in F. S. Regs., Part II. and the Staff Manual respectively. Title pages will be prepared in manuscript.

Place	Date	Hour	Summary of Events and Information	Remarks and references to Appendices
	16th		Relief commenced at about 2-30 A.M. A and B Companies had already moved out when at about 4-0 A.M news was received that the Germans had broken through along the railway. These two Companies were immediately brought back and placed in CASH & CUTE trenches. It being ascertained that the enemy had gained possession of the STATION BUILDINGS as well as the CHEMICAL WORKS defensive flanks were formed from the centre of CUTE to CUSHION and from CUBA along CUT to west of the ROEUX-GAVRELLE road. Patrols ascertained that CROOK and CROW were still occupied by men of the 6th Dorsetshire Regt and some details of the relieving Division. The sector held by this Battalion was and remained intact. Rifle and Lewis Gun fire was brought to bear on the enemy in the STATION BUILDINGS and along the railway while preparations were being made for a counter attack. At 9-30 A.M a counter attack was delivered by regiments of the 51st Division and 51st Brigade. The enemy were driven out of the STATION BUILDINGS and the CHEMICAL WORKS and streamed in full flight along both sides of the railway and over GREENLAND HILL. Every available rifle and Lewis Gun in the Battalion was brought to	

2353 Wt. W2544/1454 700,000 5/15 D. D. & L. A.D.S.S./Forms/C. 2118.

Instructions regarding War Diaries and Intelligence Summaries are contained in F. S. Regs., Part II. and the Staff Manual respectively. Title pages will be prepared in manuscript.

WAR DIARY
or
INTELLIGENCE SUMMARY.

(Erase heading not required.)

Army Form C. 2118.

Place	Date	Hour	Summary of Events and Information	Remarks and references to Appendices
	16th		fire upon them as they fled and heavy casualties were inflicted. During the rest of the day the enemy shelled the whole of our lines very heavily but made no further attack. Owing to the relief not being carried out the men were for 24 hours without food or water, emergency rations having been eaten by order the previous day. The Battalion was relieved after dark & marched back to Camp at ST NICHOLAS where the men arrived in a very exhausted condition.	
ST NICHOLAS	17		Resting in camp. Total casualties during tour in the trenches - 9 killed & 35 wounded.	
"	18		General cleaning up & inspection of kit & equipment.	
"	19		Baths - Specialist training - Musketry.	
	20		Battn. moved up to FAMPOUX-GAVRELLE line, coming under the orders of G.O.C. 51st Brigade.	
	21		Battalion relieved part of the 7th Border Regt in the front line. Dispositions were as follows: 'C' Coy in CHAPLIN, 'A' Coy in CASH, 'B' Coy in CUBA (continuation of CASH), 'D' Coy in CUTE.	
	22		Battalion Headquarters moved forward to western end of CADIZ. Active patrolling carried out all night. CURLY trench found to be strongly held by the enemy.	

Instructions regarding War Diaries and Intelligence Summaries are contained in F. S. Regs., Part II. and the Staff Manual respectively. Title pages will be prepared in manuscript.

WAR DIARY
or
INTELLIGENCE SUMMARY.
(Erase heading not required.)

Army Form C. 2118.

Place	Date	Hour	Summary of Events and Information	Remarks and references to Appendices
	23rd		Considerable shelling of CHEMICAL WORKS and communication trenches in our area all through the day. Battalion reinforced by one Company 8th South Staffordshire Regt in CADIZ (south of CLYDE) [initials]	
	24th		Active patrolling all through the night of 23rd/24th. Enemy found to be hard at work in CURLY. Enemy artillery again very active on front line and communications, the fire increasing in violence during the day. During the tour all available men were kept hard at work deepening the trenches. The small number of casualties in spite of the heavy shell fire was clearly due to the depth to which the trenches were dug. Fire steps were also completed in all trenches occupied by the Battalion. The Battalion was relieved by the 8th South Staffordshire Regt and proceeded to the FAMPOUX - GAVRELLE line. [initials]	
	25th		Battalion relieved by 7th Border Regt. and proceeded to camp in ST. NICHOLAS rejoining 50th Brigade. Total casualties during tour 1 killed & 7 wounded. [initials]	
	26th		General cleaning up inspection of kit.	
	27th		Sunday Divine Service. [initials]	

2353 Wt. W2544/1454 700,000 5/15 D. D. & L. A.D.S.S./Forms/C. 2118.

Army Form C. 2118.

Instructions regarding War Diaries and Intelligence Summaries are contained in F. S. Regs., Part II. and the Staff Manual respectively. Title pages will be prepared in manuscript.

WAR DIARY
or
INTELLIGENCE SUMMARY.
(Erase heading not required.)

Place	Date	Hour	Summary of Events and Information	Remarks and references to Appendices
ST NICHOLAS to HALLOY	28th		Battalion moved by train from ARRAS to billets in HALLOY detraining at MONDICOURT station	ref map LENS 11
HALLOY	29th		Running drill. Physical training - Musketry - general cleaning up.	-
-	30th		Inoculation of all men who had not been inoculated since Nov 1916.	-
-	31st		Working parties on rifle range by all men who had not been inoculated the previous day.	-
			31/5/17	

P. R. Simner Lieut. Col.
Comdg. 10th West Yorkshire Regt.

2353 Wt. W2544/1454 700,000 5/15 D. D. & L. A.D.S.S./Forms/C. 2118.

19 E.
10 Infantry

Vol 18

WAR DIARY

JUNE 1917

10th

West Yorkshire

Regt.

Instructions regarding War Diaries and Intelligence Summaries are contained in F. S. Regs., Part II. and the Staff Manual respectively. Title pages will be prepared in manuscript.

WAR DIARY
or
INTELLIGENCE SUMMARY.
(*Erase heading not required.*)

Army Form C. 2118.

Place	Date	Hour	Summary of Events and Information	Remarks and references to Appendices
HALLOY	JUNE 1-1917		Battalion in billets at HALLOY. Company parades It was announced that the following Honours and Rewards had been obtained by Officers and men of the Battalion MILITARY CROSS 2/Lieut. H.A.G. NEVILLE DISTINGUISHED CONDUCT MEDAL No 12946 Coy S.M. DICKINSON W.H. CROIX DE GUERRE No 9214 Coy S.M. EVERARD R.J. MILITARY MEDAL No 2145 L/Cpl. Mc. MAHON T No 12589 Sgt. TAYLOR A. No 43245 Pte. RUTTER C. No 43248 " FISHER G.R. No 22134 " GALES J. No 24830 " STONE S. No 15483 L/Cpl. BAKER S.	Refer map France Sheet LENS 11.

2353 Wt. W2544/1454 700,000 5/15 D. D. & L. A.D.S.S./Forms/C. 2118.

Instructions regarding War Diaries and Intelligence Summaries are contained in F. S. Regs., Part II. and the Staff Manual respectively. Title pages will be prepared in manuscript.

WAR DIARY
or
INTELLIGENCE SUMMARY.
(Erase heading not required.)

Army Form C. 2118.

Place	Date	Hour	Summary of Events and Information	Remarks and references to Appendices
HALLOY	JUNE 1-1917	(Contd)	MENTIONED IN DESPATCHES	Refer map France Sheet LENS II
			Captain A.F.G. ANDERSON	
			Captain E.J. SMITH	
			Nº 18404 Cpl. HARDING N	
			Nº 21415 L/Cpl. Mc MAHON T	AFGA
HALLOY	2nd		Musketry on rifle range - Battalion drill - Specialist training - Baths.	AFGA
"	3rd		Sunday Divine Service	AFGA
"	4th		Musketry on rifle range - Bayonet fighting - Specialist training	AFGA
"	5th		Musketry on rifle range - Platoon and Company training - Specialist training	AFGA
"	6th		- do - - do - - do -	AFGA
	7th		Musketry on rifle range - Platoon and Company training - Specialist training	AFGA
			Divisional Horse Show at MONDICOURT. The Battalion obtained second prize for limbers (1st class) Driver Nº 13413 Pte. DOBSON A.	AFGA
"	8th		Musketry on rifle range - Platoon and Company training - Specialist training	
			Brigade Sports - Mile race won by Nº 21014 Pte SANDERSON of B Company.	AFGA
"	9th		Musketry on rifle range - Platoon and Company training - Specialist training.	AFGA

2353 Wt. W2544/1454 700,000 5/15 D. D. & L. A.D.S.S./Forms/C. 2118.

Instructions regarding War Diaries and Intelligence Summaries are contained in F. S. Regs., Part II. and the Staff Manual respectively. Title pages will be prepared in manuscript.

WAR DIARY
or
INTELLIGENCE SUMMARY.
(Erase heading not required.)

Army Form C. 2118.

Place	Date	Hour	Summary of Events and Information	Remarks and references to Appendices
	JUNE			Ref. map, France Sheet LENS 11
HALLOY	10th		Sunday Divine Service.	
			Brigade Cross Country Race. The Battalion on the result of the heats was represented by two teams in the final viz – 'B' and 'D' Companys, of these 'B' Coy won the final and supplied the first man home. No 21017 Pte SANDERSON of 'B' Coy. The 'D' Company team finished third	[initials]
	11th		Musketry on rifle range – Battalion drill. Platoon & specialist training	[initials]
	12th		Musketry on rifle range. Battalion drill – Platoon and specialist training	
			Tactical scheme for Officers (without troops).	[initials]
	13th		Musketry on rifle range – Battalion drill – Platoon and specialist training – Baths –. The following officers were authorised by the Divisional Commander to wear the appropriate badges of rank pending official notification in the London Gazette	
			To be Temporary Captain Lieut (Acting Captain) E. J. REYNOLDS	
			To be Acting Captain Lieut P. HOWE M.C.	
			To be Temporary Lieutenant 2/Lt H. A. G. NEVILLE M.C.	
			" H. MARSDEN M.C.	
			" H. NEWTON	
			" G. T. R. HALL	[initials]

2353 Wt. W2544/1454 700,000 5/15 D. D. & L. A.D.S.S./Forms/C. 2118.

Instructions regarding War Diaries and Intelligence Summaries are contained in F. S. Regs., Part II. and the Staff Manual respectively. Title pages will be prepared in manuscript.

WAR DIARY
or
INTELLIGENCE SUMMARY.
(Erase heading not required.)

Army Form C. 2118.

Place	Date	Hour	Summary of Events and Information	Remarks and references to Appendices
HALLOY	JUNE 14th		Musketry on rifle range - Battalion drill - Platoon and Specialist training. Lieut Col. P.R. SIMNER D.S.O. proceeded on leave and Major R.J.W. INO assumed command of the Battalion [illegible]	Ref. map France Sheet LENS 11
	15th		An "EVELYN WOOD" competition was held by 50th Infantry Brigade. RESULTS	
			1. 10th West Yorkshire Regt No 13 Platoon 56	
			2. 6th Dorsetshire Regt No 2 Platoon 38.	
			3. 7th East Yorkshire Regt No 5 Platoon 37.	
			4 10th West Yorkshire Regt No 7. Platoon 31.	
			Relative scores of Battalions	
			10th West Yorkshire Regt 6½	
			6th Dorsetshire Regt 5½	
			7th Yorkshire Regt. 3½	
			7th East Yorkshire Regt ZERO. [illegible]	
	16th		Tactical scheme - Company and specialist training [illegible]	
	17th		Sunday - Divine Service - Battalion Boxing competition [illegible]	
	18th		Tactical scheme - musketry - specialist training [illegible]	

Instructions regarding War Diaries and Intelligence Summaries are contained in F. S. Regs., Part II. and the Staff Manual respectively. Title pages will be prepared in manuscript.

WAR DIARY
or
INTELLIGENCE SUMMARY.
(*Erase heading not required.*)

Army Form C. 2118.

Place	Date	Hour	Summary of Events and Information	Remarks and references to Appendices
	JUNE			
HALLOY AND ARRAS	19th		Battalion moved by bus (Transport by road) to ST NICHOLAS Camp ARRAS refce map G.14 a	Ref map France 51 B.N.W.
(ST NICHOLAS Camp) AND TRENCHES	20th		Battalion proceeded to relieve the 21st Battn. NORTHUMBERLAND FUSILIERS (2nd TYNESIDE SCOTTISH) in the front line system south of GAVRELLE Dispositions were as follows:– 'A' Coy. CONRAD & COLIN with right where COLIN cuts the wire. 'B' Coy. CONRAD with left on its junction with CIVIL (inclusive). 'D' Coy. in support in CORK. 'C' Coy. in reserve in HELFORD. (GAVRELLE line) Battalion H. Qtrs in HELFORD. The 18th Battn. West Yorkshire Regt. of the 31st Division were on the left and the 4th East Yorkshire Regt. on the right.	France 51 B.N.W. and French map attached
	21st		Relief completed at 2-20 A.M. Very quiet during the day – practically no enemy activity on our front. 15th West Yorkshire Regt. relieved the 18th West Yorkshire Regt on the left.	

Instructions regarding War Diaries and Intelligence Summaries are contained in F. S. Regs., Part II. and the Staff Manual respectively. Title pages will be prepared in manuscript.

WAR DIARY
or
INTELLIGENCE SUMMARY.
(Erase heading not required.)

Army Form C. 2118.

Place	Date	Hour	Summary of Events and Information	Remarks and references to Appendices
TRENCHES	JUNE 22nd		Active patrolling carried on throughout the night of the 21st/22nd. The pits or shell holes marked on the map in front of CONRAD were found to be occupied by the enemy. Every available man in the front and support lines were kept at work improving the trenches. The reserve Company carried R.E. material to the front line.	FRANCE 57 B. N.W. and Trench map attached.
			At 10.20 p.m. our Artillery shelled the enemy's front line system. The Enemy replied almost immediately with H.E. trench mortar and machine gun fire.	
			His Artillery fire was wild on our front line, but more accurate on the support line and the communication trenches. The situation quietened down about 11-15 p.m.	atw
	23rd		Patrolling continued throughout the night. A working party in front of WIT which had been observed by one of our patrols was dispersed by Lewis Gun fire. Enemy Artillery activity increased slightly during the day. C Coy were sent forward to occupy CORK trench on the right of D Coy. A Coy was ordered to withdraw to HELFORD trench and B Coy. to extend to the right in order to occupy the whole of the front line.	atw
	24th		At 1-30 A.M a small enemy party crept up through the long grass and attempted to raid CONRAD trench. None of our men were missing.	atw

2353 Wt. W2544/1454 700,000 5/15 D. D. & L. A.D.S.S./Forms/C. 2118.

Army Form C. 2118.

Instructions regarding War Diaries and Intelligence Summaries are contained in F. S. Regs., Part II. and the Staff Manual respectively. Title pages will be prepared in manuscript.

WAR DIARY
or
INTELLIGENCE SUMMARY.
(Erase heading not required.)

Place	Date	Hour	Summary of Events and Information	Remarks and references to Appendices
TRENCHES	JUNE 24th	(Contd).	"A" Coy. remained in the front line until after daylight when all was quiet and then proceeded to HELFORD trench.	Trenches 51.B. N.W and Trench map attached.
BLACK LINE			The Battalion was relieved by the 6th Dorsetshire Regt. and proceeded to the BLACK LINE at H I C, less "A" Coy which remained in HELFORD trench.	AND 51.b. N.W
-	25th		General cleaning up. Large carrying parties were found on which every available man was employed. "A" Coy. was withdrawn from HELFORD trench to the BLACK line.	
-	26th		"A" Company with 20 men of "B" Company practised an attack on the pits or shell holes in front of CONRAD trench on a previously prepared area - both by day and by night. Every available man again employed on carrying parties to the front line. "D" Coy. proceeded to HELFORD trench on the redistribution of the Brigade system.	
-	27th		Attack again practised by "A" Company, but information was received that [illegible] attack had been cancelled. "A" Coy. proceeded to HELFORD trench. Carrying parties as usual.	

2353 Wt. W2544/1454 700,000 5/15 D. D. & L. A.D.S.S./Forms/C. 2118.

Army Form C. 2118.

Instructions regarding War Diaries and Intelligence Summaries are contained in F. S. Regs., Part II. and the Staff Manual respectively. Title pages will be prepared in manuscript.

WAR DIARY
or
INTELLIGENCE SUMMARY.
(Erase heading not required.)

Place	Date	Hour	Summary of Events and Information	Remarks and references to Appendices
BLACK LINE	28th		All available men employed in cleaning the BLACK LINE	
			Carrying parties as usual.	ATM
	29th		Battalion relieved and proceeded to ST NICHOLAS Camp "A and D Coys	
in ST NICHOLAS Camp			in HELFORD trench were relieved by 2 Coys. of the 3rd/4th ROYAL WEST KENT Regt.	
			and "B" and "C" Coys. in the BLACK line by the 4th BORDER Regt.	ATM
"	30th		Baths and general cleaning up.	ATM
			1-4-16. P.R. Simner Lieut Col.	
			Comdg 10th West Yorkshire Regt.	

WAR

DIARY

JULY

1917

10th

WEST YORKSHIRE

REGT

20 Div
10 W Yorks

Instructions regarding War Diaries and Intelligence Summaries are contained in F. S. Regs., Part II. and the Staff Manual respectively. Title pages will be prepared in manuscript.

WAR DIARY

~~or~~

~~INTELLIGENCE SUMMARY.~~

(Erase heading not required.)

Army Form C. 2118.

Place	Date	Hour	Summary of Events and Information	Remarks and references to Appendices
	JULY			Ref. map FRANCE Sheet 51 B NW
ST. NICHOLAS	1-1914		Battalion in Camp at ST NICHOLAS. Sunday - Divine Service	
"	2nd		Battalion training - Musketry and care of arms. Specialist training - Lecture on Trench warfare by the Commanding Officer. Large working party at night burying cable between the railway & MONCHY.	Hagu
"	3rd		Battalion training, Physical drill - Specialist training - Sandbagging and wiring under R.E. instructors. 2/Lt J. C. BRAITHWAITE and 2/Lt C. D. SYMES Joined Battalion. The same working party supplied for burying cable.	Hagu
"	4th		Battalion training. Physical drill. Specialist training. Sandbagging and wiring under R.E. instructors. The same working party supplied for burying cable. 2/Lt J. D. LE GROVE transferred to R.F.C.	Hagu
"	5th		Battalion training - Physical drill - Specialist training - wiring - sandbagging. A practice trench to trench attack was carried out. The same working party was supplied.	Hagu
"	6th		Battalion training - Physical training. Sandbagging and wiring. Patrolling and Patrol reports - same party for burying cable.	Hagu
	7th		Battalion training continued during the morning - Physical drill - Bayonet fighting. 2/Lt F. H. R. LAW transferred to R.F.C.	Hagu

2353 Wt. W2544/1454 700,000 5/15 D. D. & L. A.D.S.S./Forms/C. 2118.

Instructions regarding War Diaries and Intelligence Summaries are contained in F. S. Regs., Part II. and the Staff Manual respectively. Title pages will be prepared in manuscript.

WAR DIARY
or
INTELLIGENCE SUMMARY.
(Erase heading not required.)

Army Form C. 2118.

Place	Date	Hour	Summary of Events and Information	Remarks and references to Appendices
ST NICHOLAS and TRENCHES	JULY 7th 1917		The Battalion relieved the 10th Bn. LANCASHIRE FUSILIERS in the RIGHT FRONT Battalion sector of the CHEMICAL Sub sector marching away from the TENT CAMP ST NICHOLAS through ATHIES thence along CANAL south bank to the RAILWAY ARCH H.24.a.4.7. thence along the Railway. The GAVRELLE line was passed at 10.55 p.m. Relief Complete was reported at 1.58 AM and active patrolling was carried out till dawn. Work on 5 T. head saps from the front line was commenced. The 4th Division held the line on our right and the 7th YORKSHIRE Regt on our left.	Ref. map FRANCE sheet 51 B N.W. Haye
TRENCHES	8th		Work in CROFT + CARBUNCLE trench CORONA SUPPORT + STRONG POSTS "A" and "B" and COLUMBO TRENCH between our sector and the 4th Division on our right was carried out. During the night the 5 T. head saps were pushed forward for a further 10 yds. Patrols were out during the hours of darkness. All available men of "C" Company were employed on work in the front trenches and Strong Posts. The artillery carried out a creeping Barrage in which our Stokes Mortars, Machine Guns and the Lewis Guns of the Battalion took part. This necessitated the discontinuance of work between 12 midnight and 12-30 A.M.	Ref. Map attached. Haye
-	9th		Work on Strong Posts "A" + "B" continued CROFT. CORUNA, and CARBUNCLE C.T.	

2353 Wt. W2544/1454 700,000 5/15 D. D. & L. A.D.S.S./Forms/C. 2118.

Instructions regarding War Diaries and Intelligence Summaries are contained in F. S. Regs., Part II. and the Staff Manual respectively. Title pages will be prepared in manuscript.

WAR DIARY

or

~~INTELLIGENCE SUMMARY.~~

(Erase heading not required.)

Army Form C. 2118.

Place	Date	Hour	Summary of Events and Information	Remarks and references to Appendices
				Ref. map FRANCE Sheet 51 B. N.W. Ref. trench sketch attached. [initials]
TRENCHES	9th		deepened and improved with fire bays in CROFT and CORONA, sandbagged and revetted. Work on the T. head saps was continued and another 10' pushed forward from each sap. 6 Company furnished the same parties for work on front line. Patrols again active during the hours of darkness.	
	10th		Work on STRONG Point "A" and CARBUNCLE C.T. continued. 5 T. head saps completed and a distance of 40 yds from front line. Wire apron put out in front of left sector. Sanitary arrangements improved generally. 7th Bn YORKSHIRE Regt on our left were relieved by the 7th EAST YORKSHIRE Regt.	[initials]
	11th		Work of deepening and revetting all trenches carried on and widening and deepening of the 5 T. head saps where necessary. The Battalion was relieved by the 6th DORSETSHIRE Regt. On relief companies proceeded as follows "A" & "D" Companies to the RAILWAY CUTTING. B. & C. to the right of the GAVRELLE LINE in PUDDING and LEMON TRENCH. Headquarters in the CUTTING. The casualties for the tour were 8 O.R. Wounded.	[initials]
	12th		First day in CUTTING & GAVRELLE LINE. Day was spent in resting and	

2353 Wt. W2544/1454 700,000 5/15 D. D. & L. A.D.S.S./Forms/C. 2118.

Instructions regarding War Diaries and Intelligence Summaries are contained in F. S. Regs., Part II. and the Staff Manual respectively. Title pages will be prepared in manuscript.

WAR DIARY

or

~~INTELLIGENCE SUMMARY.~~

(*Erase heading not required.*)

Army Form C. 2118.

Place	Date	Hour	Summary of Events and Information	Remarks and references to Appendices
				Ref. map FRANCE 51 B. N.W
TRENCHES	12th		General cleaning up. Large working parties and carrying parties found. 8 Officers and 281 O.R. being employed. 2/Lt. M.F. SMITH joined the Battalion. 2/Lt. C. ARGILE joined the Battalion.	[illegible]
–	13th		Party employed collecting Salvage. Working parties and carrying parties supplied. 7. Officers and 260 O.R. Employed	[illegible]
–	14th		Owing to a minor operation carried out by the 7th BORDER Regt. no carrying parties were furnished on this night and the relief of the left Battalion which should have taken place on the night 14/15 inst. was postponed till the following night.	[illegible]
	15th		Salvage collected during the day. The Battalion relieved the 6th DORSETSHIRE Regt. in the right of the CHEMICAL SUB-SECTOR. Companies occupied the same positions as before. RIGHT SECTOR 'B' Company with 1 Platoon in the front line. 1 Platoon in COLUMBA CORONA and Strong Post A. CENTRE SECTOR 'A' Company with 1 Platoon in front line and one in CORONA. LEFT SECTOR D Company with 1 Platoon in front line CROFT. 1/2 Platoon in CORINA. 1/2 Platoon in STRONG Post B. For this tour 2 Platoons of 'A' Company 3/10th MIDDLESEX Regt were attached	[illegible]

2353 Wt. W2544/1454 700,000 5/15 D. D. & L. A.D.S.S./Forms/C. 2118.

Instructions regarding War Diaries and Intelligence Summaries are contained in F. S. Regs., Part II. and the Staff Manual respectively. Title pages will be prepared in manuscript.

WAR DIARY
or
INTELLIGENCE SUMMARY.
(Erase heading not required.)

Army Form C. 2118.

Place	Date	Hour	Summary of Events and Information	Remarks and references to Appendices
TRENCHES	15		to the Battalion for training. Each of our companies being allotted 2 sections. Battalion strength for this tour was 16 Officers 414 O.R. 2 Platoons of 3/10th MIDDLESEX REGT. 1 officer and 80 O.R.	Ref. map Sheet FRANCE 51.B.NW. [illegible]
–	16.		Work of deepening and widening the trenches where necessary and wiring was carried on. Active Patrolling during the hours of darkness. Enemy trench Mortars from the RAILWAY and the QUARRY were very active. The part of CORONA from the Junction with CABBAGE to its Junction with COLOMBO was cleared of all obstacles and deepened. CHEMICAL TRENCH was deepened by a party from 'C' Company	[illegible]
–	17		Work done, wiring front line and deepened trenches viz COCOA & CORONA trenches also CROFT to its Junction with CARBUNCLE. Saps deepened, Belts of grass were cut down where the view was obstructed.	[illegible]
–	18		Whilst superintending the wiring of his Company Lt. C. E. JARVIS was severely wounded by a M.G Bullet and Died of Wounds. Work of wiring T. heads and weak places in the front and support system continued. CAPT. B.W. RYAN rejoined the Battalion	

2353 Wt. W2544/1454 700,000 5/15 D. D. & L. A.D.S.S./Forms/C. 2118.

Instructions regarding War Diaries and Intelligence Summaries are contained in F. S. Regs., Part II. and the Staff Manual respectively. Title pages will be prepared in manuscript.

WAR DIARY
or
~~INTELLIGENCE SUMMARY.~~
(Erase heading not required.)

Army Form C. 2118.

Place	Date	Hour	Summary of Events and Information	Remarks and references to Appendices
				Ref. map 51-B.N.W FRANCE
TRENCHES	19		Work on saps continued under cover of camouflage. Deepening and widening of strong points, support and front lines. The Battalion were relieved by the 6th Dorsetshire Regt. After relief the Companies took up the following positions:- Headquarters in Sunken Road H.11.a.6.2. Three Companies 'D' 'A' & 'C' in GAVRELLE LINE in PUDDING - LEMON & LUCID trenches, with two Coys of the 7th YORKSHIRE Regt. on our left. 'B' Company in RAILWAY CUTTING H.8.c.1.2. The two platoons of the 2/10th MIDDLESEX Regt were withdrawn with the Battalion and proceeded to their Camp at ST. NICHOLAS. The Casualties for this tour were, 1 Officer Killed 3.O.R. Wounded 1.O.R. 2/10th MIDDLESEX Regt Wounded.	H.11.a.6.2
GAVRELLE LINE	20		General cleaning up and work on the GAVRELLE LINE. Large carrying parties and working parties furnished. 8. Officers and 206 O.R. One O.R. Wounded. 'B' Company moved up from the Railway Cutting (H.8.c.1.2) to the GAVRELLE line on the right of 'D' Company.	[initials]
-	21st		Work on the GAVRELLE line continued. Carrying & working parties supplied. 9. Officers and 284 O.R. being Employed.	[initials]

2353 Wt. W2544/1454 700,000 5/15 D. D. & L. A.D.S.S./Forms/C. 2118.

Instructions regarding War Diaries and Intelligence Summaries are contained in F. S. Regs., Part II. and the Staff Manual respectively. Title pages will be prepared in manuscript.

WAR DIARY
or
INTELLIGENCE SUMMARY.
(*Erase heading not required.*)

Army Form C. 2118.

Place	Date	Hour	Summary of Events and Information	Remarks and references to Appendices
GAVRELLE LINE	JULY 22nd 1917		Work on GAVRELLE LINE Sandbagging Revetting and deepening continued Carrying parties and working parties furnished. 6 officers and 210 O.R. 1 O.R. Wounded	FRANCE Sheet 51 B.N.W [initials]
"	23rd		Work on GAVRELLE LINE continued. Party of 10 O.R detailed to carry dead horses and mules on TANK DUMP which was heavily shelled on night of 22nd inst. 50th Infantry Brigade Relieved by 51st Infantry Brigade.	
[illegible] Camp. G.10.c.4.9.			The Battalion was relieved by the 10th B. SHERWOOD FORESTERS. On relief the Battalion moved to a new camp G.10.c.4.9. The old camp occupied by the 7th Border Regt having been moved back owing to enemy shelling. One O.R. Wounded on the way back from the trenches.	Ref map 51.B/1/20000 G.10.c.4.9. [initials]
Camp G.10.c.4.9.	24		Battalion in Camp. Day spent in cleaning up generally. Baths for Battalion at ST. NICHOLAS from 8.0 A.M. till 11.0 A.M. Musketry on the small MOAT Range ARRAS. (G.21.a) from 12.0 NOON till 4.0 p.m 52 O.R. Employed on Working parties during the day.	[initials]
	25th		The Battalion moved from Camp to another Camp about G11 Central now known as LANCASTER Camp. Old Camp was cleared by 9.0 A.M. Battalion training during the day. Musketry on the BUTTE DE TIR Range (G.20. a.) from 8.0 A.M. to 12.0 NOON Physical drill. Bayonet fighting. Wiring. Close Order drill as per Battalion training	

2353 Wt. W2544/1454 700,000 5/15 D. D. & L. A.D.S.S./Forms/C. 2118.

Instructions regarding War Diaries and Intelligence Summaries are contained in F. S. Regs., Part II. and the Staff Manual respectively. Title pages will be prepared in manuscript.

WAR DIARY
or
~~INTELLIGENCE SUMMARY.~~
(Erase heading not required.)

Army Form C. 2118.

Place	Date	Hour	Summary of Events and Information	Remarks and references to Appendices
LANCASTER CAMP	1917 JULY 25.		Programme. 2/Lt. A. OUTHWAITE and 2/Lt. D. LYNCH Joined the Battalion	HRGH
	26		Battalion training - Physical drill. Specialist training. Wiring - sandbagging. A. B. Coys. night operations. Work on New Camp continued.	HRGH
	27th		Battalion training. Physical drill - sandbagging - wiring. Musketry - C. D Coys. Night operations. The Battalion was taken to the 17th Divisional CINEMA Performance.	HRGH
	28th		Battalion training. Running & Jumping. Specialist training digging and wiring.	HRGH
	29th		Sunday. Divine Service for all Denominations.	HRGH
	30th		Battalion training. Physical drill. Bayonet fighting. A + B. Practice attack C. + D. on BUTTE de TIR Rifle range. Musketry. The Battalion was taken to the performance of the "DUDS" 17th Divisional Concert Party at ST NICHOLAS.	HRGH
	31st		Battalion training during the morning, Physical training, Box respirator drill, and instruction in trench discipline. Remainder of the day spent in preparing for move to support trenches. Battalion relieved the 9th Bn. NORTHUMBERLAND Fusiliers in the GAVRELLE Switch. Location of Companies as follows from North to South from the Junction of HONEY & HUDSON Trenches. D.C.B.A. Headquarters H.11.b.65.85. Battalion marched away from LANCASTER CAMP at 9.15. pm.	Ref FRANCE 1/10000 Sheet 51b NW. HRGH

Aug 1st 1917.

H. A. Glenville Lt. & Adjt. for Lieut. Col.
Comdg. 10th West Yorkshire Regt.

2353 Wt. W2544/1454 700,000 5/15 D. D. & L. A.D.S.S./Forms/C. 2118.

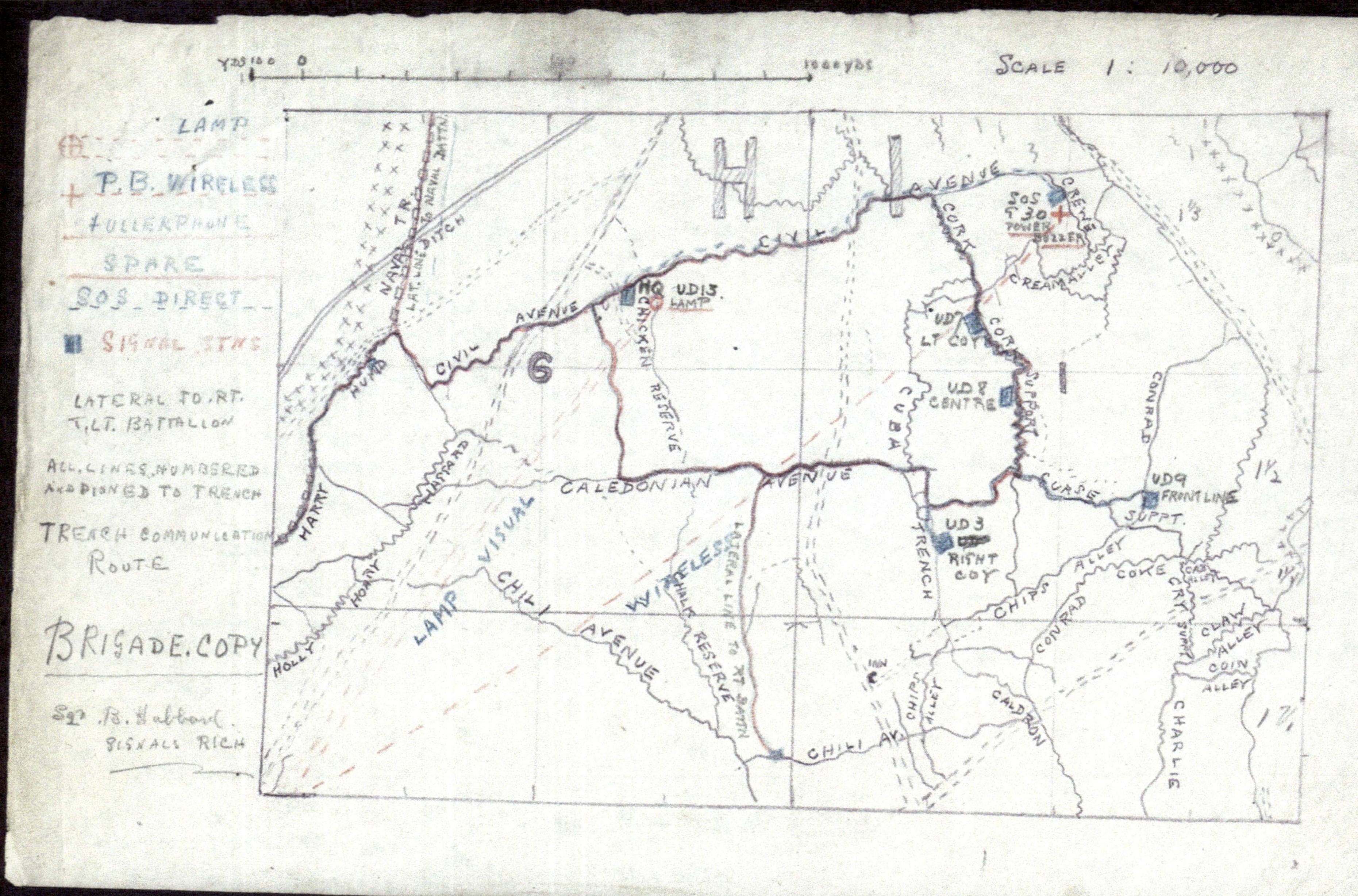SCALE 1 : 10,000
YDS 100 0 1000 YDS
LAMP
P.B. WIRELESS
FULLERPHONE
SPARE
SOS DIRECT
SIGNAL STNS
LATERAL TO RT. T. LT. BATTALION
ALL LINES NUMBERED AND PINNED TO TRENCH
TRENCH COMMUNICATION ROUTE
BRIGADE. COPY
Sgt. B. Hubbard
SIGNALS RICH
H
I
G
CIVIL AVENUE
CORK
CREWE
SOS T 30 POWER BUZZER
CREAM ALLEY
HQ UD13. LAMP
CHICKEN RESERVE
UD7 LT COY
UD8 CENTRE
SUPPORT
CUBA
CONRAD
UD9 FRONT LINE
CURSE
SUPPT.
UD3 RIGHT COY
TRENCH
CALEDONIAN AVENUE
HUMP
NAVAL TR.
LAT. LINE TO NAVAL BATTN
DITCH
HARRY
HAZARD
HORNY
HOLLY
LAMP VISUAL
WIRELESS
CHILI AVENUE
CHALK RESERVE
LATERAL LINE TO RT BATTN
CHILI AV.
INN
CHIPS ALLEY
CALDRON
COKE
CRY SUPPT
CLAW ALLEY
COIN ALLEY
CHARLIE

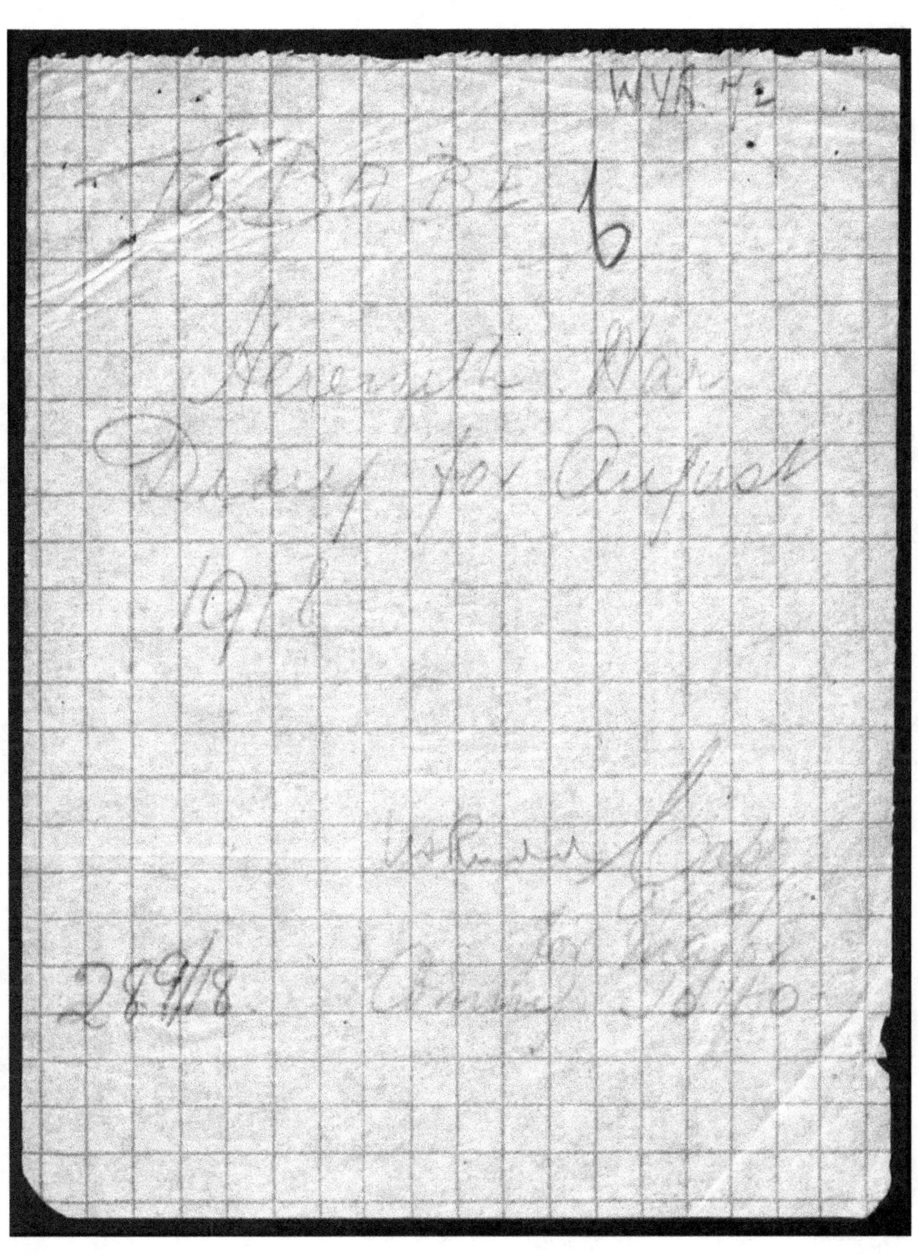
6
War
Diary for August
1918
28/9/18

10th (Bn.) West Yorkshire Regt.

Instructions regarding War Diaries and Intelligence Summaries are contained in F. S. Regs., Part II. and the Staff Manual respectively. Title pages will be prepared in manuscript.

WAR DIARY
or
~~INTELLIGENCE SUMMARY.~~
(Erase heading not required.)

Army Form C. 2118.

Vol 20

Place	Date	Hour	Summary of Events and Information	Remarks and references to Appendices
Ref Map. 51B N.W. 1/10,000	August 1st		Battalion in Brigade Reserve in the GAVRELLE SWITCH. All ranks employed in improving the trench by day & in carrying to the front by night	
	2nd		ditto ditto	
	3rd		ditto ditto 2Lt. J. MAGERISON, 2Lt. F.E. BARKER & 2Lt. W.F.W. BIGGER joined	
	4th		ditto ditto	
Trench Map attached ("A")	5th		Battalion moved to the front line trenches relieving the 6th Bn. DORSETSHIRE Regt. in the right of GREENLAND HILL sub. sector. Dispositions were as follows:- 'D' Coy. on the right 'C' " in the centre 'B' " on the left 'A' " in support The following work was done by the Battalion between 1st & 5th August in the GAVRELLE SWITCH:- 103 New duckboards laid Drains cut beneath duckboarding for 327 yards. 2 new latrines constructed & 7 reconstructed and deepened.	

2353 Wt. W2544/1454 700,000 5/15 D. D. & L. A.D.S.S./Forms/C. 2118.

Army Form C. 2118.

Instructions regarding War Diaries and Intelligence Summaries are contained in F. S. Regs., Part II. and the Staff Manual respectively. Title pages will be prepared in manuscript.

WAR DIARY
or
~~INTELLIGENCE~~ ~~SUMMARY~~.

(*Erase heading not required.*)

Place	Date	Hour	Summary of Events and Information	Remarks and references to Appendices
	August 5th (Contd)		Ten English Trench Shelters (each consisting of three pieces of metal roofing) completed and three commenced. N.B. The construction of these shelters entailed (a) in each case the making of two timber frames (b) the excavation of the site 9ft x 5ft (c) the revetting of the fronts with corrugated iron or expanded metal and angle irons (d) sandbagging of the sides & roof.	[illegible]
			Two Cookhouses rebuilt and enlarged + 3 SOYER stoves installed. 810 superficial feet of sandbag revetting - mostly to a depth of two sandbags - including the filling of the sandbags. 190 feet of revetting with expanded metal + angle irons. Six trench shelters constructed with corrugated iron + sandbags - One O.P. constructed and duckboarded - One Ammunition shelter constructed - four sump holes cleaned out and revetted with expanded metal - One new sump hole dug + revetted.	[illegible]
	6th		Quiet day - Very little shelling - All ranks employed improving the trenches. Each Company sent out two patrols in the course of the night 6th/7th.	[illegible]
	7th		Work + patrolling continued.	
			At 8-0am the sentry in our Bombing Post at I.1.d.8.2. saw three or four of the enemy	

2353 Wt. W2544/1454 700,000 5/15 D. D. & L. A.D.S.S./Forms/C. 2118.

Instructions regarding War Diaries and Intelligence Summaries are contained in F. S. Regs., Part II. and the Staff Manual respectively. Title pages will be prepared in manuscript.

WAR DIARY
or
~~INTELLIGENCE SUMMARY~~.

(*Erase heading not required.*)

Army Form C. 2118.

Place	Date	Hour	Summary of Events and Information	Remarks and references to Appendices
	August 7th (Contd)		creeping along a disused communication trench about 30 yards east of the bombing post. He fired and gave the alarm. They threw five bombs, only two of which reached our post, the others falling very short. They then vanished. Our rifle-bombers immediately searched the communication trench, the long grass, & all visible shell holes with rodded Mills bombs, & rifle fire was opened at the spot where the enemy was seen. The enemy made no reply. No damage was caused by the bombs which were thrown hurriedly & wildly. Barbed wire gooseberries were prepared & the communication trench was filled up by us after dark.	APhe
	8th		At about 3.30am the enemy opened an extremely heavy bombardment on the whole Brigade front & on the front of the 51st Brigade on our right. Dust & smoke made observation very difficult. Specially reliable men were posted to look for S.O.S. signals, but although none were observed our Artillery were very quick in replying to the enemy's fire. The enemy's bombardment continued on our sector until 4.15 am. Touch was kept with Battalion on the right & left but no definate news was received until O.C. "D" Coy. (our right Coy) reported that he had been through to the 7th LINCOLNSHIRE Regt. on our right, that their centre Company had been raided,	

2353 Wt. W2544/1454 700,000 5/15 D. D. & L. A.D.S.S./Forms/C. 2118.

Instructions regarding War Diaries and Intelligence Summaries are contained in F. S. Regs., Part II. and the Staff Manual respectively. Title pages will be prepared in manuscript.

WAR DIARY
or
INTELLIGENCE SUMMARY.
(Erase heading not required.)

Army Form C. 2118.

Place	Date	Hour	Summary of Events and Information	Remarks and references to Appendices
	Aug 8th (Cont.)		that the enemy had been bombed out, the line re-established, & that all was quiet.	
			The casualties in our Battalion were very slight - one O.R. wounded in the head, & two O.R. buried & bruised, but remained at duty.	[illegible]
			A daylight patrol consisting of No. 10981 Sgt. PICKARD. J. No: 13581 Cpl. McLELLAND. E. and 18083 Pte LAMB J. went out at 3.0 pm. to reconnoitre the ground over which they would have to pass at night to examine the enemys wire. They went out at I.7.6.74:68 and proceeded for 70 or 80 yards before getting sight of the German lines. As the enemy did not take any notice of them they crawled on, reached the German wire & proceeded to examine it. Sgt. PICKARD endeavoured to cut off a piece with a jack knife, but as it was not possible the patrol decided to return for some wire cutters. These were obtained & the patrol again reached the wire without being observed and brought a piece of the wire.	
			The wire was found to be very strong - about 4'-6" high & in two rows about 5 yards in depth. The patrol crawled along the wire for some distance but could not find any way through nor could they crawl under it.	[illegible]

2353 Wt. W2544/1454 700,000 5/15 D. D. & L. A.D.S.S./Forms/C. 2118.

Instructions regarding War Diaries and Intelligence Summaries are contained in F. S. Regs., Part II. and the Staff Manual respectively. Title pages will be prepared in manuscript.

WAR DIARY
or
INTELLIGENCE SUMMARY.
(*Erase heading not required.*)

Army Form C. 2118.

Place	Date	Hour	Summary of Events and Information	Remarks and references to Appendices
	Aug 9th		Work & Patrolling continued	AThr
	10th		ditto 2/Lt W.H. JAMIESON joined.	AThr
	11th		ditto	AThr
	12th		Battalion was relieved by the by the 6th DORSETSHIRE Regt. & proceeded to its previous quarters in the GAVRELLE SWITCH	AThr
	13th		All ranks employed in improving the trenches by day & in carrying parties to the front line by night.	AThr
	14th		ditto.	AThr
	15th		ditto 2/Lt H. DEAN joined.	AThr
Ref. MAP 51B N.W. 1/10,000	16th		Battalion was relieved by the 7th LINCOLNSHIRE Regt. and proceeded to LANCASTER camp St NICHOLAS, 50th Brigade going into Divisional Reserve.	AThr
			The following work was done by the Battalion in the GAVRELLE SWITCH between the 12th & 16th August:-	
			New Kitchen constructed - dimensions 6' x 3' x 6"	
			Anti-Aircraft Lewis Gun emplacement 10' x 6" x 9" dug & completed.	
			Latrine trench dug 6' x 9" x 9".	

2353 Wt. W2544/1454 700,000 5/15 D. D. & L. A.D.S.S./Forms/C. 2118.

Instructions regarding War Diaries and Intelligence Summaries are contained in F. S. Regs., Part II. and the Staff Manual respectively. Title pages will be prepared in manuscript.

WAR DIARY
or
INTELLIGENCE SUMMARY.
(*Erase heading not required.*)

Army Form C. 2118.

Place	Date	Hour	Summary of Events and Information	Remarks and references to Appendices
	Aug 16th (Contd)		Two new Fire Bays constructed.	
			Ten "Elephant" shelters constructed (one double) - all the wooden frames for these were also made by the Battalion.	
			One sump made 6' x 4' x 4'.	
			One ablution place dug, revetted, & finished with sump.	
			148x duckboarding lifted & relaid - drains cleaned beneath to the depth of one foot.	
			New latrine constructed 2' x 2". - 37 square yards sandbag revetment.	
			57 yards revetment with XPM and corrugated iron & angle irons.	
			26 new duckboards laid on stakes - Trench beneath drained & dug to a depth of one foot.	[initials]
	17th		Lieut Col P.R. SIMNER D.S.O. proceed to the XVII Corps Rest Station at WARLUS	
			Capt. A.K.O. HALL [illegible] joined the Battalion & assumed command.	
			The day was devoted to Baths and general cleaning up.	[initials]
	18th		Musketry on the MOAT RANGE ARRAS - Physical Training - Bayonet Fighting - Wiring - Sandbags [illegible]	[initials]
	19th		Sunday - Divine Service	[initials]
	20th		Training continued - Physical training - Close Order Drill - Bayonet fighting - Fire Control - Two Companies practising patrols by night.	[initials]

2353 Wt. W2544/1454 700,000 5/15 D. D. & L. A.D.S.S./Forms/C. 2118.

Instructions regarding War Diaries and Intelligence Summaries are contained in F. S. Regs., Part II. and the Staff Manual respectively. Title pages will be prepared in manuscript.

WAR DIARY
or
INTELLIGENCE SUMMARY.
(Erase heading not required.)

Army Form C. 2118.

Place	Date	Hour	Summary of Events and Information	Remarks and references to Appendices
Aug,	21st		Ditto.	[initials]
	22nd		Battalion Route March - distance approximately 7 miles - no men fell out. In the afternoon Musketry Instruction.	[initials]
	23rd		Physical Training & Special Classes - Musketry on Moat Range ARRAS The following extracts from the London Gazette were published in Battalion Orders for Information:- Temp. Lt. P. HOWE M.C to be Acting Captain whilst commanding a Company (Apl. 9) Temp. 2Lt. R.N.P. WILSON to be Temp Lieut (June 15). In addition to the above the Divisional Commander authorised the u/m Officers to wear the badges of the rank of Captain pending notification in the London Gazette of their appointment as A/Captains additional to the establishment in accordance with General Routine Order No. 2494 d 5/8/17. Temp. Lieut. H. MARSDEN M.C. G.T.B. HALL	[initials]
	24th		Physical training - rapid loading - Gas lecture. Capt. A.K.O. HALL authorised by Divisional Commander to wear the badges	[initials]

Army Form C. 2118.

Instructions regarding War Diaries and Intelligence Summaries are contained in F. S. Regs., Part II. and the Staff Manual respectively. Title pages will be prepared in manuscript.

WAR DIARY
or
INTELLIGENCE SUMMARY.

(Erase heading not required.)

Place	Date	Hour	Summary of Events and Information	Remarks and references to Appendices
	Aug 24th (Cont.)		of rank of Major pending official notification in the London Gazette.	
			The Battalion proceeded to the front line to relieve the 3/4th Bn Royal West Kent Regt.	
			in the CHEMICAL SECTOR	[illegible]
	25th		Relief complete 12-47 am.	
Ref. Sketch map attached ("B")			Dispositions:-	
			Front line "D" Coy. on the right	
			"A" " in the centre	
			"C" " on the left	
			Support "B" in CADIZ	
			Trench Strength 22 Officers, 4 W.Os 20 Sergeants, 16 Corporals + 380 Privates	[illegible]
	26th		Vigilant patrolling carried on throughout the night.	
			Enemy Trench Mortars active on front of our centre & right companies.	[illegible]
	27th		Patrolling and work continued. – Enemy Trench Mortars still active.	[illegible]
	28th		Patrolling and work continued – Enemy Trench Mortars flattened out our post	
			in COAL SOUTH killing 3 + wounding 1 ORs.	[illegible]
	29th		Patrolling & work continued.	[illegible]

2353 Wt. W2544/1454 700,000 5/15 D. D. & L. A.D.S.S./Forms/C. 2118.

Instructions regarding War Diaries and Intelligence Summaries are contained in F. S. Regs., Part II. and the Staff Manual respectively. Title pages will be prepared in manuscript.

WAR DIARY
or
INTELLIGENCE SUMMARY.
(Erase heading not required.)

Army Form C. 2118.

Place	Date	Hour	Summary of Events and Information	Remarks and references to Appendices
	Aug. 30th		Battalion relieved by the 6th Dorsetshire Regt. moved back into Brigade Reserve. "C" + "D" Coys. in the CADIZ + COLT RESERVE line and "A" + "B" Coys in the GAVRELLE SWITCH	
	31st		Battalion in Brigade Reserve as above.	[illegible]

A.H.D. Hall. Major
Commdg 1st West Yorkshire Regt.

2353 Wt. W2544/1454 700,000 5/15 D. D. & L. A.D.S.S./Forms/C. 2118.

-A-

MAP FOR WAR DIARY FOR 5th AUG - 12th AUG 1917.

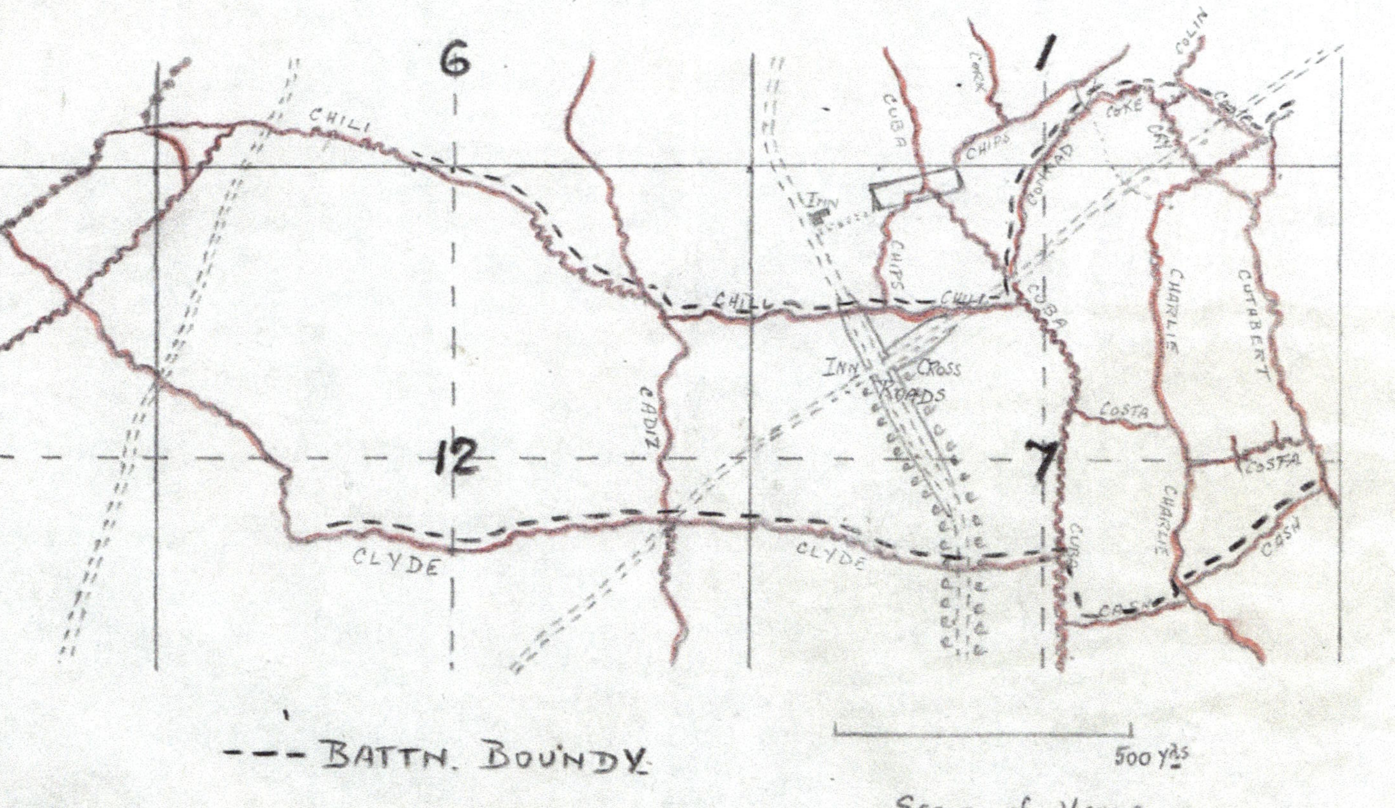

This map should be read in conjunction with 51 B. N.W. & S.W.

— B —

MAP · FOR · WAR · DIARY · FOR · 24th AUG. — 30th AUG. 1917.

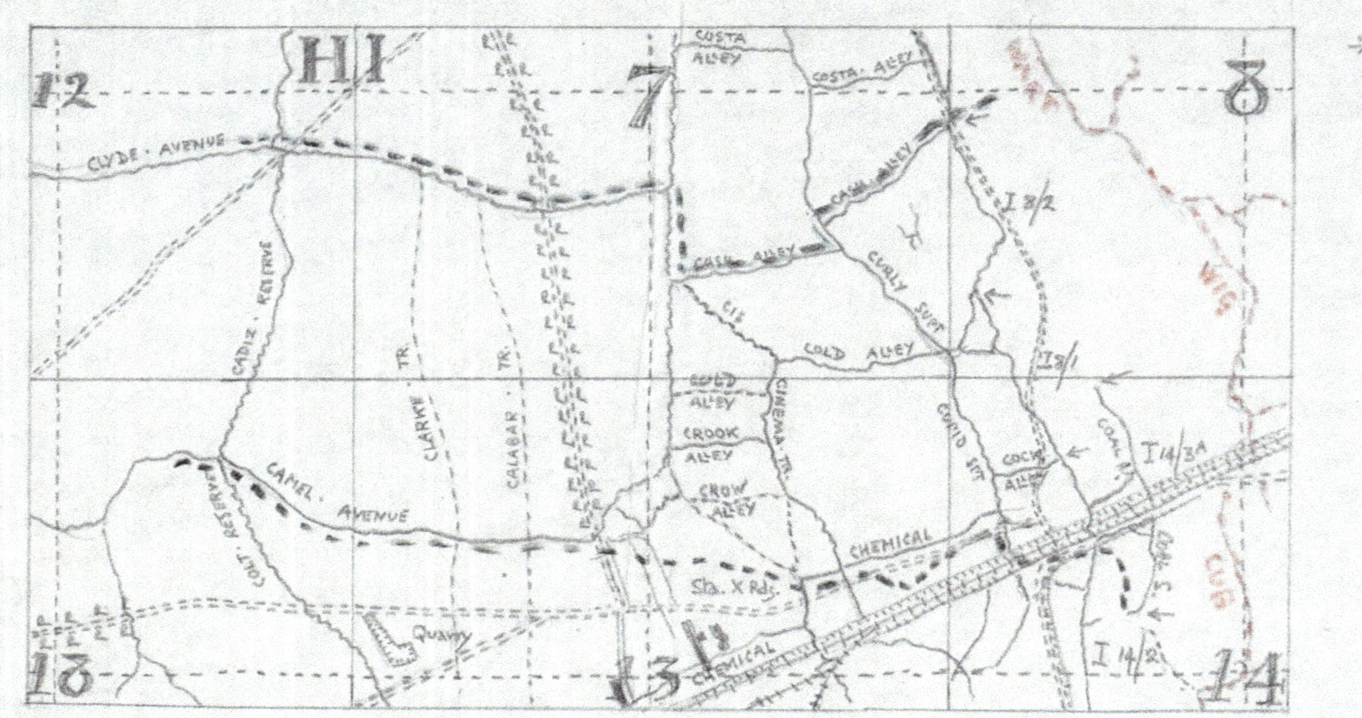

--- BATTN. BOUNDY.

N. B. German line marked in red.
This sketch map should be read in conjunction with 51 B. N.W. & S.W.

10th West Yorkshire Regt
Operation Order No 3 18.8.18

Ref Maps.
62D
57D } 1/40,000

1. The 50th Infantry Brigade Group will move by march Route from AUBIGNY to PUCHEVILLERS to-night the 18/19 instant.

2. STARTING POINT Road Fork O8 b5.6

3. ROUTE. VECQUEMONT – PONT NOYELLES BEHENCOURT – MONTIGNY BEAUCOURT SUR L'HALLUE – RUBEMPRE.

4. TIME. The 10th West Yorkshire Regiment will pass starting point ROAD FORK O8 b5.6 at 10.35 pm

5. ORDER OF MARCH.
Band, HQrs B.C.D & A Coys

6. INTERVALS
The following intervals will be observed –
between Companies 100x

(2)

between Battn & transport 100^x
" each section of 12 vehicles 50^x

7 DISCIPLINE.

Strict discipline will be maintained throughout the march.

Platoon Commanders in particular will look to the covering off from front to rear. Marching by the right and keeping ranks closed up.

8/ PACKS

These will be dumped at Bde HQ as for previous order.

Sd J.C. BRAITHWAITE 2Lt
for Capt & Adjt
West Yorkshire Regt

Copy No 1 C.O.
" " 2 War Diary
" " 3-6 O/C Coys.
" " 7 QM & T.O.
" " 8 File
" " 9 50 Inf. Bde

7. DRESS. Full marching order. Steel helmets to be worn.

8 TRANSPORT. Will move in rear of the Battalion.

9. BILLETS. All billets are to be left scrupulously clean and certificates to this effect to be rendered to Orderly Room by 9.30pm to-night by Company Commanders. The Orderly Officer will obtain a certificate from the Town Major that all Billets have been left in a clean condition, and free from Salvage.

10. BATTLE SURPLUS. will report to the QM at the stores at 6pm.

11. OFFICERS' KITS. and cooking utensils will be dumped at the QM Stores by 8pm.

12 ACKNOWLEDGE.

(Sd) K. S. RUDD Capt
Adjt
West Yorkshire Regt

Copy No 1. C.O.
" " 2 War Diary
" " 3-6 O/C Coys
" " 7 QM & T.O.
" " 8 Brigade
" " 9 File

SECRET

Ref. Map 57D SW 1/20000

Operation Order No 4 — 20.8.18

West Yorkshire Regt.

INFORMATION.

The 50th Inf. Bde will move to ARQUEVES tonight and on arrival will go into Billets.

INSTRUCTIONS.

1. PARADE. The Battalion will parade on the PUCHEVILLERS-RAINCHEVAL road; head of the column to be opposite PUCHEVILLERS CHURCH, ready to move off at 10.10 pm.
   Order of March. HQRS Band 'C' Coy 'D' Coy, 'A' Coy, 'B' Coy
2. INTERVALS. 100 yards between Companies
   100 " " B Coy & Transport
   Transport 50x between every 12 Vehicles.
3. STARTING POINT Junction of track 'A' and PUCHEVILLERS-RAINCHEVAL road at N 22 d 0.4.
4. TIME. The Battalion will pass the starting point at 10.20 pm.
5. ROUTE. Track 'A' – SOUTH of RAINCHEVAL – through O 19 c to ARQUEVES.
6. ADVANCE PARTY. Already detailed

Secret

Instructions regarding War Diaries and Intelligence Summaries are contained in F. S. Regs., Part II. and the Staff Manual respectively. Title pages will be prepared in manuscript.

WAR DIARY
or
~~INTELLIGENCE SUMMARY~~.
(Erase heading not required.)

Army Form C. 2118.

10th W Yorks

Vol 21

Place	Date	Hour	Summary of Events and Information	Remarks and references to Appendices
Ref maps 51B N.W + Trench sketch map attached	Sept 1st 1917		Battalion in Brigade Reserve. "C" + "D" in the CADIZ-COLT RESERVE line and Bn H. Qrs. with "A+B" Coys in the GAVRELLE SWITCH. Large carrying parties found at night.	
	2nd		ditto	
	3rd		ditto	
	4th		ditto	
	5th		The Battalion proceeded to relieve the 6th Dorsetshire Regt. in the front line of the CHEMICAL sector. Relief complete 12 midnight. Dispositions were as follows:- "B" Coy on the right. "A" " in the centre. "C" " on the left. "D" " in support in the two strong points + CADIZ reserve.	
	6th		Quiet day with very little shelling. Some slight enemy Trench Mortar activity in the vicinity of COAL NORTH. Every available man employed in improving the trenches. Active patrolling carried on all night.	
	7th		Enemy artillery quiet during the day, but shelled our front + support lines	

22 E. 5 sheets

2353 Wt. W2544/1454 700,000 5/15 D. D. & L. A.D.S.S./Forms/C. 2118.

Army Form C. 2118.

Instructions regarding War Diaries and Intelligence Summaries are contained in F. S. Regs., Part II. and the Staff Manual respectively. Title pages will be prepared in manuscript.

WAR DIARY
or
~~INTELLIGENCE SUMMARY~~.
(Erase heading not required.)

Place	Date	Hour	Summary of Events and Information	Remarks and references to Appendices
	7th (Cont)		fairly heavily between 9.45 + 10.5 pm at which time their Trench Mortars were also very active. Work + patrolling continued. A7HW	
	8th		Some slight shelling of CINEMA and CUPID SUPPORT during the day. In reply to a bombardment by our Artillery the enemy shelled the Support lines + the ROEUX GAVRELLE Road very heavily at 10.0pm. Enemy Trench Mortars again active. Work + patrolling continued. A7HW	
	9th		Considerable shelling of the CHEMICAL WORKS throughout the day. The Battalion was relieved by the 8th South Staffordshire Regt. and proceeded into Divisional Reserve at LANCASTER CAMP ST. NICHOLAS. Total Casualties during the tour 3 Killed 7 Wounded. A7HW	
	10th		Baths + general cleaning up. A7HW	
	11th		General training including, Close Order Drill + Communicating Drill, Fire Control + Bayonet Fighting. Inspection of Gas Helmets. A7HW	
	12th		Physical Training - Specialist classes - Fire Control - Gas Drill - Patrolling. Communicating Drill A7HW	
	13th		Physical Training - Communicating drill. Gas drill - Bayonet fighting - Patrolling A7HW	
	14th		In the morning Battalion Route March - distance approximately 7 miles - in the afternoon foll...	

2353 Wt. W2544/1454 700,000 5/15 D. D. & L. A.D.S.S./Forms/C. 2118.

Instructions regarding War Diaries and Intelligence Summaries are contained in F. S. Regs., Part II. and the Staff Manual respectively. Title pages will be prepared in manuscript.

WAR DIARY
or
~~INTELLIGENCE SUMMARY.~~
(Erase heading not required.)

Army Form C. 2118.

Place	Date	Hour	Summary of Events and Information	Remarks and references to Appendices
	14th (Cont.)		In the afternoon a free performance was given to the men at the Divisional Cinema. ATH	
	15th		Physical Training - specialist classes - communicating drill - Fire control - Gas drill. ATH	
	16th		Sunday - Divine Service - ATH	
	17th		Musketry on MOAT RANGE ARRAS. ATH	
			No: 36929 Pte. J. PADGETT was awarded the Military Medal for gallant conduct in rescuing wounded men from an advanced post in COAL SOUTH which had been flattened out by Trench Mortar fire. ATH	
			The Battalion relieved the 12th Battn. Manchester Regt. in the left support (in the GAVRELLE SWITCH) to the GREENLAND HILL sector. Relief complete 10.5 p.m. ATH	
	18th		All available men employed in improving the trench by day and in carrying parties at night. ATH	
	19th		Ditto. ATH	
	20th		Ditto. ATH	
	21st		Battalion relieved the 6th Dorsetshire Regt in left sub-sector of the GREENLAND HILL sector. Relief complete 9.50 p.m. ATH	
	22nd		Unusually quiet in the trenches. Very little shelling or M.G. fire. ATH	

2353 Wt. W2544/1454 700,000 5/15 D. D. & L. A.D.S.S./Forms/C. 2118.

Instructions regarding War Diaries and Intelligence Summaries are contained in F. S. Regs., Part II. and the Staff Manual respectively. Title pages will be prepared in manuscript.

WAR DIARY
or
~~INTELLIGENCE SUMMARY~~.

(Erase heading not required.)

Army Form C. 2118.

Place	Date	Hour	Summary of Events and Information	Remarks and references to Appendices
	Sept 22nd (Cont)		Some slight enemy Trench Mortar activity.	
			Active patrolling carried out and every available man employed, in improving the trenches & wire.	
			Lieut. Col. P.R. SIMNER D.S.O re-assumed Command of the Battalion.	
	23rd		~~ditto~~ Patrolling work continued.	
	24th		~~ditto~~	
			Battalion was relieved by the 2nd/4th Gloucester Regt. of the 61st Division and proceeded to billets in ARRAS.	
Ref. Map LENS. 11	25th		Battalion marched to billets in MANIN - approximately 13 miles. Great heat was experienced, which made the march very arduous.	
	26th		Battalion marched to billets in - AMBRINES - about 2½ miles.	
	27th		Baths and general cleaning up. - Attack practice by Platoons.	
	28th		Battalion training - Attack practice.	
	29th		ditto ditto	
	30th		Sunday - Divine Service.	

P.R. Simner Lieut. Col.
Commanding 10th West Yorkshire Regt.

2353 Wt. W2544/1454 700,000 5/15 D. D. & L. A.D.S.S./Forms/C. 2118.

50/17 10 W York Rgt

SECRET

Army Form C. 2118.

Instructions regarding War Diaries and Intelligence Summaries are contained in F. S. Regs., Part II. and the Staff Manual respectively. Title pages will be prepared in manuscript.

WAR DIARY
or
INTELLIGENCE SUMMARY.
(Erase heading not required.)

Vol 22

Place	Date	Hour	Summary of Events and Information 10th W Yorks	Remarks and references to Appendices
Ref Map Lens - 11	1917 Oct. 1st		Battalion in billets at AMBRINES - Attack practise by all Companies in the morning - by 50th Brigade in the afternoon	[illegible]
	2nd		Physical training - Attack practise by Companies in the morning and by 50th Brigade in the afternoon.	[illegible]
	3rd		Attack practise by 50th Brigade	[illegible]
	4th		Companies practising the attack - Preparations for move to BELGIUM	[illegible]
	5th		At midnight the Battalion marched to SAULTY station and entrained for PEZELHOEK near POPERINGHE at 6-0 am - The train proceeded via DOULLENS, FREVENT, ST POL, LILLERS & HAZEBROUCK arriving at PEZELHOEK at 6-20 pm. The Battalion then marched to PITCHCOTT CAMP, PROVEN which was reached about 8-30 pm. The 17th Division was now transferred to XIV Corps - Fifth Army -	[illegible]
	6th		General cleaning up - Care of feet -	[illegible]
	7th		Sunday - Divine Service -	[illegible]
	8th		Battalion attack practise	[illegible]
	9th		Preparations for move to forward area - Care of feet Battalion moved by rail from PROVEN to ELVERDINGHE (trains leaving	

23 E
6 sheets

2353 Wt. W2544/1454 700,000 5/15 D. D. & L. A.D.S.S./Forms/C. 2118.

Instructions regarding War Diaries and Intelligence Summaries are contained in F. S. Regs., Part II. and the Staff Manual respectively. Title pages will be prepared in manuscript.

WAR DIARY
or
~~INTELLIGENCE SUMMARY~~.
(Erase heading not required.)

Army Form C. 2118.

Place	Date	Hour	Summary of Events and Information	Remarks and references to Appendices
	Oct 9th (Cont)		at 7.30 pm and 11.0 pm) and proceeded to CARDOEN CAMP – map Ref. A.18-6-1.8.	
			This operation formed part of the relief of the 29th Division the 50th Brigade coming temporarily under the tactical Command of the G.O.C. 29th Division	[illegible]
	10th		The neighbourhood of the Camp was bombed heavily by hostile aeroplanes between 2-0 am and 5-0 am. CARDOEN CAMP was not hit.	
			Battalion again came under 17th Division –	[illegible]
	11th		Orders were received from the XIV Corps to renew the attack on the enemy's positions between HOUTHULST FOREST & POELCAPELLE – the attack to be carried out by the 4th Division on the right, the 17th Division in the centre, the Guards Division on the left. The attack of the 17th Division was ordered to be carried out by the 51st Brigade with the 50th Brigade in support & the 52nd Brigade in Divisional reserve. In consequence of these orders the Battalion moved forward to the neighbourhood of PILCKEM and bivouacked in shell holes & pill boxes with Headquarters at C2.6.8.4.	[illegible]
	12th		Battalion engaged in erecting bivouacs and improving shell holes	

2353 Wt. W2544/1454 700,000 5/15 D. D. & L. A.D.S.S./Forms/C. 2118.

Instructions regarding War Diaries and Intelligence Summaries are contained in F. S. Regs., Part II. and the Staff Manual respectively. Title pages will be prepared in manuscript.

WAR DIARY
or
INTELLIGENCE ~~SUMMARY~~.

(Erase heading not required.)

Army Form C. 2118.

Place	Date	Hour	Summary of Events and Information	Remarks and references to Appendices
	Oct. 12th	(Cont)	The area was subject to frequent bursts of artillery fire resulting in 12 casualties. It was reported that the 51st Brigade had attacked at 5.25 am. and that all objectives had been gained except in the extreme left.	[illegible]
SCHAAP BALIE 1/10,000	13th		The Battalion moved forward to relieve the 8th South Staffordshire Regt. and 2 Coys. of the 7th Lincolnshire Regt. of the 51st Brigade in the front line. The Battalion was heavily shelled during the relief especially on the YPRES-STADEN railway - casualties 2Lt. F.E. BARKER and 4 O.R.	[illegible]
	14th		Relief was complete at 5.20 am - Battalion H. Qrs. established at U.12-c.60-85 Dispositions as follows:- 2 Coys. on right of YPRES-STADEN railway and 2 Coys. on the left of it arranged in depth. The line ran (from the left) V.1.c.5.3 to TURENNE CROSSING thence S.E. to COLIBRI FARM. It was found that a gap of 300 yards existed between the left of the Battalion and the right of the 2nd Grenadier Guards on its left. Their right post was located by a patrol + touch was also gained with their support Company. ADEN HOUSE (V.1.c35-35) was reported by the relieved Battalion to be in the enemy's hands. Throughout the day the enemy's artillery actively searched the area and	

Instructions regarding War Diaries and Intelligence Summaries are contained in F. S. Regs., Part II. and the Staff Manual respectively. Title pages will be prepared in manuscript.

WAR DIARY
or
INTELLIGENCE SUMMARY.
(Erase heading not required.)

Army Form C. 2118.

Place	Date	Hour	Summary of Events and Information	Remarks and references to Appendices
	Oct 14th (Cont)		registered with the assistance of numerous aeroplanes. Shell fire was at times very heavy. Our front and support posts were bombed by German aircraft which were vigorously fired at with our Machine Guns and Lewis Rifles. At 11-30 pm a patrol of 1 officer (2Lt D. LYNCH) and 25 O.R. of "B" Coy. reconnoitred ADEN HOUSE, which was found to be unoccupied + established 2 posts 50 yards to the N & N.E of it and posts E + W. of it establishing connection with the 2nd Grenadier Guards on the left: this advanced the line 150 yds on a front of 400 yds. The line now ran from V.1.c.2.4 to V.1.c.7.3, to TURENNE CROSSING thence S.E. to COLIBRI FARM.	Hagh.
	15th		From mid-night to 5-30 am. the enemy directed an exceptionally heavy fire from guns of every calibre onto the whole Battalion Sector. Bursts of heavy gun fire occurred throughout the day. The Battalion was relieved by the 7th East Yorkshire Regt. and took up position in support with 2 Coys. at OLGA HOUSES, one Coy. near EGYPT HOUSE and one Coy. E of the Railway triangle in U 18.b. Hd. Qrs at U.18.c.4-5. There was heavy	

2353 Wt. W2544/1454 700,000 5/15 D. D. & L. A.D.S.S./Forms/C. 2118.

Army Form C. 2118.

Instructions regarding War Diaries and Intelligence Summaries are contained in F. S. Regs., Part II. and the Staff Manual respectively. Title pages will be prepared in manuscript.

WAR DIARY
or
INTELLIGENCE SUMMARY.
(*Erase heading not required.*)

Place	Date	Hour	Summary of Events and Information	Remarks and references to Appendices
	15th (Cont.)		shell fire during relief - 2LT. W.V.C. WATSON killed -	[illegible]
HAZEBROUCK 5A	16th		Battalion was relieved partly by the 23rd Northumberland Fusiliers of the 102nd Brigade and (partly by) the 23rd Manchester Regt. of the 104th Brigade and marched to BOESINGHE station	[illegible]
	17th		Battalion entrained for PROVEN and proceeded to PATALIA CAMP in PROVEN - P 5 area.	[illegible]
	18th		Baths and general cleaning up - games - Total Casualties 2 Officers killed 2 officers wounded 11 O.R killed 103 Wounded 4 missing -	[illegible]
	19th		Physical Training - Route march - The Divisional Commander expressed his keen satisfaction with the conduct of the Battalion in the recent fighting and his admiration of the pluck and endurance displayed by all ranks under very trying circumstances	[illegible]
	20th		Battalion marched to WEMAERS-CAPELLE near CASSEL.	[illegible]
	21st		Battalion marched to ARNEKE, entraining thence to billets at RECQUES	[illegible]
	22nd		Company training	[illegible]
	23rd		Practice attack (a) by Companies (b) by Battalion -	[illegible]

2353 Wt. W2544/1454 700,000 5/15 D. D. & L. A.D.S.S./Forms/C. 2118.

Army Form C. 2118.

Instructions regarding War Diaries and Intelligence Summaries are contained in F. S. Regs., Part II. and the Staff Manual respectively. Title pages will be prepared in manuscript.

WAR DIARY
or
~~INTELLIGENCE SUMMARY.~~
(Erase heading not required.)

Place	Date	Hour	Summary of Events and Information	Remarks and references to Appendices
	24th		Musketry on Rifle Range - Specialist training	[illegible]
	25th		Practice attack (a) by Companies (b) by Battalion	[illegible]
	26th		Practise in dealing with Counter Attacks - Specialist Training	[illegible]
	27th		Specialist Training - Brigade Tactical exercise	[illegible]
	28th		Sunday - Divine Service	[illegible]
	29th		Divisional operations	[illegible]
	30th		Divisional operations	
			Announced in Divisional Orders that the following had been awarded the Military Medal:- No: 1217 Pte. BUTTON S.V. No 306327 Pte BLACKBURN J.W. and No: 11325 Pte. SMITH. F.	[illegible]
	31st		Company Training -	[illegible]

P.R. Simner Lieut. Col.
Commanding 10th West Yorkshire Regt.

2353 Wt. W2544/1454 700,000 5/15 D. D. & L. A.D.S.S./Forms/C. 2118.

322
CB

Company Commanders will see that the men will change into a dry pair of socks before putting on their gum boots.

V WATER BOTTLES will be filled before starting.

VI HUTS, LINES & LATRINES must be left scrupulously clean and a certificate to this effect rendered to Orderly Room by Company Commanders before leaving.

VII ROLLS will be called before leaving camp and again on arriving at the trenches.

VIII FOOT FRICTION It is of the utmost importance that the mens feet should be rubbed at least twice before going into the line.

I. The Lewis Gun Officer will arrange for 4 guns to accompany C. Coy. to BENNETT, 3 guns to accompany A. Coy. to FALL and AUTUMN, 2 guns for B. Coy. in WINTER and FROSTY and 1 gun for D. Coy. in COW.

I. Companies will report relief to H. Qrs by wire if possible if not, by messenger using the code word OXO prefixed by the letter of the company e.g. B Coy will report BOXO.

(sd) A. T. G. Anderson Capt.
Adjutant
10th West Yorkshire Regt.

30
25
B
C
H
I
WIDOW
HOOD
CIVIL
CORK
CONRAD
WIT
WISH
WHIP CROSS RDS
WHIP
6
1
CUBA
CALEDONIAN
COLIN
CURSE
COKE
CRY
HELFORD
HAWTHORNE
HURRUM
HALDVAN
CADIZ
CHILI
CHIPS
Inn
INN CROSS ROADS
CLARKE
CUTE
CHARLIE
CUTHBERT
COSTA
CHAPLIN
CASH
HOLLY
HARROW
HYDERABAD WORK
12
7
CLYDE

Instructions regarding War Diaries and Intelligence Summaries are contained in F. S. Regs., Part II. and the Staff Manual respectively. Title pages will be prepared in manuscript.

WAR DIARY
or
INTELLIGENCE SUMMARY.
(Erase heading not required.)

Army Form C. 2118.

10th WEST YORKSHIRE REGT.
NOV. 1917.

Vol 23

Place	Date	Hour	Summary of Events and Information	Remarks and references to Appendices
			10th WEST YORKSHIRE REGT.	
RECQUES	1st Nov		[illegible]	[illegible]
	2nd		[illegible]	[illegible]
	3rd		[illegible]	[illegible]
	4th		[illegible]	[illegible]
	5th		[illegible]	[illegible]
	6th		[illegible]	[illegible]
	7th		[illegible]	[illegible]
	8th		[illegible]	[illegible]
	9th		[illegible]	[illegible]

2353 Wt. W2544/1454 700,000 5/15 D. D. & L. A.D.S.S./Forms/C. 2118.

245

10th West Yorkshire Regt.

Instructions regarding War Diaries and Intelligence Summaries are contained in F. S. Regs., Part II. and the Staff Manual respectively. Title pages will be prepared in manuscript.

WAR DIARY
or
INTELLIGENCE SUMMARY.
(Erase heading not required.)

Army Form C. 2118.

Place	Date	Hour	Summary of Events and Information	Remarks and references to Appendices
[illegible] Camp	Nov 10/11		[illegible] weather continued.	[illegible]
	11th		[illegible]	[illegible]
	12th		Coys at the disposal of Company Commanders.	[illegible]
	13th		[illegible] the 10th Bn. The Battalion marched away from [illegible] CAMP at [illegible] BARDS CAUSEWAY [illegible]	Sheet 28 [illegible]
LINE			After dinner the Battalion moved off [illegible] to [illegible] the [illegible]	
			[illegible]	
			C Coy [illegible] 10th LANCS FUS. [illegible]	
			D [illegible]	
			B [illegible]	
			A [illegible]	
			[illegible] 12th MANCHESTER [illegible]	
			[illegible]	
			[illegible]	
	14th		Battalion in the line.	[illegible]
	15th		The Battalion was relieved by the [illegible] EAST YORKSHIRE [illegible]	

2353 Wt. W2544/1454 700,000 5/15 D. D. & L. A.D.S.S./Forms/C. 2118.

Instructions regarding War Diaries and Intelligence Summaries are contained in F. S. Regs., Part II. and the Staff Manual respectively. Title pages will be prepared in manuscript.

WAR DIARY
or
INTELLIGENCE SUMMARY.

(*Erase heading not required.*)

Army Form C. 2118.

Place	Date	Hour	Summary of Events and Information	Remarks and references to Appendices
[illegible]	[illegible]		[illegible]	[illegible]
	8		[illegible]	[illegible]
[illegible]	14th		The Battalion [illegible] the [illegible] on the [illegible] of [illegible] The Battalion left [illegible] [illegible] by [illegible] [illegible] [illegible]	
			[illegible]	[illegible]
[illegible]	18		Battalion in [illegible] accommodation [illegible] LANGEMARK [illegible] [illegible]	
			[illegible]	[illegible]
	19th 20th		The [illegible] [illegible]	[illegible]

2353 Wt. W2544/1454 700,000 5/15 D. D. & L. A.D.S.S./Forms/C. 2118.

Instructions regarding War Diaries and Intelligence Summaries are contained in F. S. Regs., Part II. and the Staff Manual respectively. Title pages will be prepared in manuscript.

Army Form C. 2118.

WAR DIARY
or
~~INTELLIGENCE SUMMARY~~.
(Erase heading not required.)

[illegible]

Place	Date	Hour	Summary of Events and Information	Remarks and references to Appendices
	Nov			
[illegible] CAMP	20th		[illegible] HALL [illegible]	
			[illegible]	[illegible]
	21st		[illegible]	[illegible]
	22nd		[illegible]	
			[illegible]	
			[illegible] J H GIBSON [illegible] 133 O.R. [illegible]	[illegible]
	23rd		[illegible]	[illegible]
	24th		[illegible]	[illegible]
BRIDGE [illegible]	25th		Battalion marched from [illegible] CAMP [illegible]	[illegible]
[illegible]	26th		[illegible]	
			[illegible]	
			[illegible]	
			[illegible] TRENCH	[illegible]
	27th		[illegible]	[illegible]
	28th		[illegible]	[illegible]

2353 Wt. W2544/1454 700,000 5/15 D. D. & L. A.D.S.S./Forms/C. 2118.

Instructions regarding War Diaries and Intelligence Summaries are contained in F. S. Regs., Part II. and the Staff Manual respectively. Title pages will be prepared in manuscript.

WAR DIARY

or

INTELLIGENCE SUMMARY.

(Erase heading not required.)

Army Form C. 2118.

Place	Date	Hour	Summary of Events and Information	Remarks and references to Appendices
	24th		[illegible]	
	30th		[illegible]	
			A.D. Hall [illegible]	

(1)

Army Form C. 2118.

Instructions regarding War Diaries and Intelligence Summaries are contained in F. S. Regs., Part II. and the Staff Manual respectively. Title pages will be prepared in manuscript.

WAR DIARY
or
~~INTELLIGENCE SUMMARY.~~
(Erase heading not required.)

Vol 24

Place	Date	Hour	Summary of Events and Information	Remarks and references to Appendices
DECEMBER. 1917.			OF THE 10th (S.) Battalion West Yorkshire Regt	
ELVERDINGHE.	1		Battalion in RESERVE (Div) at BRIDGE CAMP.	Ref Map FRANCE 28. NW.
			Companies at the disposal of Company Commanders for Gen Drill Musketry etc.	
			2/Lt. W.J. HARTNOLL gazetted T/Lieut 1/7/17	[initials]
			No 22488 Pte COOPER. D. and No 22488 Pte FAIRHAM. W. were awarded the Divisional Certificate for Gallantry and devotion to duty.	
LANGEMARK No 1 AREA			The Battalion relieved the 3/4th ROYAL WEST KENT REGT — HQrs C + D.	
			Moving by train from ELVERDINGHE to BOESINGHE at 2.30pm — A + B Coys by Route March via BARDS CAUSEWAY and 'B' Track,	
			HQrs C + D Coys after detraining proceeded by road + 'B' Track	Ref Maps SCHAAP-BALIE 1/20000 + BROEMBEEK 1/20000
			Companies were located as follows:—	
			A + B Coys in CANDLE TRENCH —— 'C' + 'D' Coy in EAGLE TRENCH. HQrs at DOUBLECOTTS.	[initials]
"	2		Slight redistribution of Companies — 'C' + 'D' side-slipping to the Right to make room in EAGLE TRENCH for 'A' Company of the 6th Bn DORSETSHIRE Regt.	[initials]
"	3		Orders received to relieve the 7th Bn EAST YORKSHIRE Regt in the RIGHT SECTOR of the Brigade Front on the next day. These orders were soon after cancelled	[initials]

25E 9 sheets

2353 Wt. W2544/1454 700,000 5/15 D. D. & L. A.D.S.S./Forms/C. 2118.

(2)

Army Form C. 2118.

Instructions regarding War Diaries and Intelligence Summaries are contained in F. S. Regs., Part II. and the Staff Manual respectively. Title pages will be prepared in manuscript.

WAR DIARY
or
INTELLIGENCE SUMMARY.
(Erase heading not required.)

Place	Date	Hour	Summary of Events and Information	Remarks and references to Appendices
LANGEMARK No 1 AREA.	4. Dec		Orders were received that the Battalion would be relieved by the 15th Bn SHERWOOD FORESTERS of the 105th Infantry Brigade 35th Division on our RIGHT.	[signature]
	5		The Battalion was relieved by the 15th SHERWOOD FORESTERS and on completion of relief companies marched to SOULT. CAMP. near DAWSON'S CORNER. Prior to Companies arriving at SOULT CAMP Enemy Aeroplanes dropped a number of bombs on an adjacent Camp and in close proximity to SOULT. CAMP. Casualties. 1.O.R. of the taking over party wounded. Several casualties occurred in REDAN CAMP just opposite.	[signature] Ref map Sheet 28 1/40,000 + HAZEBROUCK 5a
	6		Battalion in SOULT. CAMP. General Cleaning up.	[signature]
	7		The Brigade moved to the Back area. The Battalion entrained ELVERDINGHE Stn and detrained AUDRUICQ thence by route march to billets in RECQUES	[signature]
	8		Day spent in further cleaning up, inspections etc. and in view of	

2353 Wt. W2544/1454 700,000 5/15 D. D. & L. A.D.S.S./Forms/C. 2118.

(3)

Army Form C. 2118.

Instructions regarding War Diaries and Intelligence Summaries are contained in F. S. Regs., Part II. and the Staff Manual respectively. Title pages will be prepared in manuscript.

WAR DIARY
or
INTELLIGENCE SUMMARY.

(Erase heading not required.)

Place	Date	Hour	Summary of Events and Information	Remarks and references to Appendices
	Dec			
RECQUES	8 (contd)		the prospect of a long rest a meeting was held to organise the Sports and Recreational Amusements. Lt G.T.E. HALL was appointed "Amusements Officer"	[illegible]
"	9		Sunday — Voluntary Services — In the afternoon the Battalion played the R.O.D. at Rugby Football at AUDURICQ	[illegible]
	10		The BRIGADE moved from the RECQUES AREA to the WATTEN AREA by route march. The Battalion was billeted in ZUDROVE.	[illegible]
ZUDROVE	11		Readjusting and improvement of Billets — Platoon training — Inter Platoon "Soccer" matches preliminary to a "Soccer" league scheme were played	[illegible]
"	12		Specialist training — Lectures to N.C.O's by Company Commanders — Games —	[illegible]
BEAULENCOURT	13		Preparation for move in accordance with sudden orders received Coy's at disposal of OC Coys Games	Ref Map 27 [illegible]

2353 Wt. W2544/1454 700,000 5/15 D. D. & L. A.D.S.S./Forms/C. 2118.

(4)

Army Form C. 2118.

WAR DIARY
or
INTELLIGENCE SUMMARY.
(Erase heading not required.)

Instructions regarding War Diaries and Intelligence Summaries are contained in F. S. Regs., Part II. and the Staff Manual respectively. Title pages will be prepared in manuscript.

Place	Date	Hour	Summary of Events and Information	Remarks and references to Appendices
ZUDROVE to BEAULENCOURT	13 (Cont.)		The Battalion marched to St. OMER at midnight and entrained for BAPAUME	Haze
"	14		The Train left at 4.40 am and arrived at BAPAUME at 1 pm. After detraining the Battalion marched to "A" Camp (NISSEN HUTS) at BEAULENCOURT	Haze
BEAULENCOURT	15		Platoon Drill — Improvement of the Camp — Games	Haze
"	16		Divine Service (Sunday) and Games. The Bullet & Bayonet Course was completed	Haze
"	17		Parades Gas Helmet Inspections Coys at practice on the Bullet & Bayonet Course — Fire Control — Games —.	Haze
	18.		Baths for the Battalion — Platoon Drill — Musketry — Games — There was a Battalion Concert in the evening.	Haze
	19		Baths & washing & ironing clothes under Battalion arrangements Musketry — Physical Training — Games — Another Battalion Concert was held.	Haze
	20		Washing Clothes — Extended Order Drill etc — A Five Mile Paper chase was	Haze

2353 Wt. W2544/1454 700,000 5/15 D. D. & L. A.D.S.S./Forms/C. 2118.

(5)

Army Form C. 2118.

Instructions regarding War Diaries and Intelligence Summaries are contained in F. S. Regs., Part II. and the Staff Manual respectively. Title pages will be prepared in manuscript.

WAR DIARY
or
INTELLIGENCE SUMMARY.
(Erase heading not required.)

Place	Date	Hour	Summary of Events and Information	Remarks and references to Appendices
BEAULENCOURT.				
	20 (contd)		Organised open to the Brigade but was made compulsory to all men in the Battalion under 32 yrs	Hayn
	21		Practice in the Company in attack – Musketry on Range – Games etc. A further Battalion Concert was held. The Forward Areas were reconnoitred up to HERMIES & HAVRINCOURT.	Hayn
BERTINCOURT	22		The Battalion moved forward by road into billets in BERTINCOURT arriving at 5 pm. Enemy Aircraft very active. Casualties 2.OR. from hostile Bombing Raid.	Hayn
	23		The Battalion moved up into Brigade Support in relief of the 8th Bn LEICESTER Regt of the 177th Brigade. Companies were accomodated in Shelters and Trenches in the old British Front Line about Q.3. central	Hayn

2353 Wt. W2544/1454 700,000 5/15 D. D. & L. A.D.S.S./Forms/C. 2118.

(6)

Army Form C. 2118.

Instructions regarding War Diaries and Intelligence Summaries are contained in F. S. Regs., Part II. and the Staff Manual respectively. Title pages will be prepared in manuscript.

WAR DIARY
or
INTELLIGENCE SUMMARY.
(Erase heading not required.)

Place	Date	Hour	Summary of Events and Information	Remarks and references to Appendices
Q.3. central	24		Improvement of Shelters + Trenches generally. A great deal of Salvage was collected in HAVRINCOURT. WOOD. Gas Helmet Inspections etc: Sanitation improved	Hayes
"	25th		Christmas Festivities. In spite of the severity of the weather which had been prevailing for some days all ranks exhibited great cheerfulness after a dinner of Pork Plum puddings and rum.	Hayes
	26		Further reconnaissance of the forward areas and the Divisional Front — work on the Accomodation etc: carried on.	Hayes
	27.		50th Inf Brigade relieved 52nd Infantry Brigade in the Right DIVISIONAL Sector on the night 27/28th December. The Battalion relieved the 9th Bn DUKE OF WELLINGTON'S Regt leaving Q.3 central at 3.30pm, and took over the RIGHT Sector of the Brigade Front with HQrs in FLESQUIERES K.24.b.2.4. A + B Coys in the Front line C + D Coys in the Support.	Ref MOEUVRES Special Sheet 1/20,000 Ed. 5F. + 57 C. Hayes

2353 Wt. W2544/1454 700,000 5/15 D. D. & L. A.D.S.S./Forms/C. 2118.

(7)

Instructions regarding War Diaries and Intelligence Summaries are contained in F. S. Regs., Part II. and the Staff Manual respectively. Title pages will be prepared in manuscript.

WAR DIARY
or
INTELLIGENCE SUMMARY.
(Erase heading not required.)

Army Form C. 2118.

Place	Date	Hour	Summary of Events and Information	Remarks and references to Appendices
	27 (contd)		Relief was complete at 7.10pm. On the right of the Battalion was the 19th Division	Srage
	28		Battalion in the Line, weather conditions very cold – Snow & frost prevailing. The chief work carried on was wiring the Battalion Front – Active Patrolling and Constructing Accomodation for the men. Deepening and widening the trenches. Enemy quiet and difficult to locate. Patrols went out as far as 700x and did not encounter any opposition. Isolated enemy Machine Gun positions were marked down.	Srage
	29		Battalion in the line. Conditions very cold & ground frozen hard – work of wiring & upkeep with general improvement to the trenches continued. Active Patrolling in white Patrol Suits carried on. Moon very bright. Inter Company relief took place "A" Coy was relieved by "C" on the Right & "B" by "D" on the left. A & B went back to the Support line.	Srage

2353 Wt. W2544/1454 700,000 5/15 D. D. & L. A.D.S.S./Forms/C. 2118.

(8)

Instructions regarding War Diaries and Intelligence Summaries are contained in F. S. Regs., Part II. and the Staff Manual respectively. Title pages will be prepared in manuscript.

WAR DIARY
or
INTELLIGENCE SUMMARY.
(Erase heading not required.)

Army Form C. 2118.

Place	Date	Hour	Summary of Events and Information	Remarks and references to Appendices
Line	29 (contd)		Parties collected salvage in Flesquières.	[illegible]
	30		Battalion in the Line.	
			At 6.40 am enemy put down a heavy barrage from the left of the BEETROOT FACTORY to the South. Right Company were subjected to a heavy fire of H.E. + gas shells. Casualties 10 O.R. in D + C Coys. It was afterwards ascertained that the enemy had attacked on the front of the 63rd Division on the right of the 19th Div in the neighbourhood of LA VACQUERIE + penetrated to the Support line.	
			Heavy gunfire from this direction about 2.30 pm.	[illegible]
"	31		About 12.30 am sounds of heavy firing were heard away to the NORTH.	
			2/Lt. S. LOWDEN with a patrol of 1 Sgt + 3 OR whilst trying to attack a hostile M.G. at L.13.a.60.45 encountered an enemy patrol of 15 men. Fire was opened + some hits were scored.	
			Work of wiring etc. carried on.	
			Inter Battalion Relief. The Battalion was relieved by the 7th EAST YORKSHIRE Regt. Relief was completed at 7.12 pm	[illegible]

Instructions regarding War Diaries and Intelligence Summaries are contained in F. S. Regs., Part II. and the Staff Manual respectively. Title pages will be prepared in manuscript.

WAR DIARY
or
INTELLIGENCE SUMMARY.
(Erase heading not required.)

Army Form C. 2118.

Place	Date	Hour	Summary of Events and Information	Remarks and references to Appendices
LINE. Relief	31st (contd)		The Battalion on relief complete moved back into Brigade RESERVE 2 Companies A + B going to the BILHELM CHAPEL WOOD SWITCH and 2 Coys "C" + "D" to the HINDENBURG LINE about K.34.a + b HQrs were at K.35.a.45 70. Total Casualties for 4 days in the Front System were 2/LT. W. PARKER and 3 OR attached 78th Field Coy RE were "gassed" with the Battalion 2 OR killed and 9 OR wounded	[illegible initials]
			P. R. Simner Lt Colonel Commanding 10th Bn West Yorkshire Regt. 2-1-18.	

2353 Wt. W2544/1454 700,000 5/15 D. D. & L. A.D.S.S./Forms/C. 2118.

Instructions regarding War Diaries and Intelligence Summaries are contained in F. S. Regs., Part II. and the Staff Manual respectively. Title pages will be prepared in manuscript.

WAR DIARY or INTELLIGENCE SUMMARY.

(Erase heading not required.)

Army Form C. 2118.

JANUARY 1918.

10th Bn WEST YORKSHIRE Regt

Place	Date	Hour	Summary of Events and Information	Remarks and references to Appendices
Ref Map MOEUVRES 1/20000.	1st		Battalion in Brigade Reserve. Relief by the 7th Bn EAST YORKSHIRE Regt the previous night. 'A' & 'B' Companies located in the BILHELM CHAPEL WOOD SWITCH in K.29.a & b. 'C' & 'D' Companies in the OLD HINDENBURG LINE in K.34.a & b, & K.35.a & b. HQrs were at K.35.a.50.75. Companies employed on cleaning up, and inspection repairs to boots etc.	[illegible]
	2nd		Battalion in Brigade Reserve. Work on the area occupied by Companies in improving accommodation was commenced. Monthly Audit Board was assembled. The Canteen was established near Bn HQrs for the benefit of the men. Weather conditions very cold & frosty.	[illegible]
	3rd		Battalion in Brigade Reserve. Work on the area continued — Parties from each Company went out to reconnoitre the most covered way up to the line. 2 OR. wounded.	[illegible]
	4th		Battalion in Brigade Reserve — Preparation for the relief of the RIGHT SECTOR of the RIGHT Brigade front.	[illegible]
		5.15pm	The Battalion moved off for the Relief of the 7th Bn EAST YORKSHIRE Regt. Relief complete was reported at 8.50 pm — 1 OR. Killed in action.	
	5th		Battalion in Front Line — Companies were disposed as per Sketch Map marked (A) attached — During the time the Battalion was in Reserve the Battalion in the line had side-slipped to the left about 400 yds, and the RIGHT of the Battalion and the Right boundary of the [illegible] were rested just to the right of the BEETROOT FACTORY	[illegible]

(A5092). Wt W12539/M1293 75,000 1/17. D. D. & L., Ltd. Forms/C.2118/14.

Army Form C. 2118.

WAR DIARY
or
INTELLIGENCE SUMMARY.
(Erase heading not required.)

Instructions regarding War Diaries and Intelligence Summaries are contained in F. S. Regs., Part II. and the Staff Manual respectively. Title pages will be prepared in manuscript.

Place	Date	Hour	Summary of Events and Information	Remarks and references to Appendices
	5th (contd)		The 47th Division were on the Right of the 17th Division —	
			Priority of work was wiring the Front – Patrolling – Improvement of Trenches	
			Strength of Battalion for the time was Officers 17 and 510. O.R. —	
			22 O.R. Joined the Battalion as Reinforcements — 1 O.R. Killed in action.	[illegible]
	6th		Warning order received of the impending Relief by the 141st Inf Brigade on the night 7th/8th January 1918	
			Inter-Company Relief carried out — "D" relieving "B" on the Right of the line and "A" relieving "C" on the left of the line – "B" & "C" Coys came back into Support —	
			The Right Support Company HQrs were burnt out. No lives lost, but considerable material damage was caused —	
			Work of wiring and improvement of Trenches continued —	
			1. O.R. wounded.	
	7th		Battalion in Front line – Relief – The Battalion was relieved partly by the 20th Bn LONDON. Regt. + partly by 18th Bn LONDON. Regt. of the 47th Division	[illegible]
			Relief complete was at 7.50pm —	
Ref Map 57c 1/40,000			On Relief the Battalion was destined for SAUNDERS. CAMP. O.4.c.3.8 about 10 miles march behind the line situated between BERTINCOURT + HAPLINCOURT.	
Ref Map MOEUVRES 1/20,000.			Owing to the hard weather conditions experienced in the line it was arranged to rest one night in the OLD BRITISH LINE in the neighbourhood of BUTLER'S CROSS. HQrs were at Q.3.b.1.1 and companies bivouaced near.	[illegible]

(A7092). Wt W12839/M1293 75,0.0. 1/17. D. D. & L., Ltd. Forms/C.2118/14.

Army Form C. 2118.

Instructions regarding War Diaries and Intelligence Summaries are contained in F. S. Regs., Part II. and the Staff Manual respectively. Title pages will be prepared in manuscript.

WAR DIARY
or
INTELLIGENCE SUMMARY.
(Erase heading not required.)

Place	Date	Hour	Summary of Events and Information	Remarks and references to Appendices
Ref 57c 1/40000.	8th		Battalion moved from BUTLER'S CROSS at 10.am, & proceeded by route march to SAUNDERS CAMP. ROUTE — PLANK ROAD – RUYAULCOURT – BERTINCOURT. A heavy blizzard was encountered on the march & the weather was very cold & snowy. Reached SAUNDERS CAMP about 2 pm. The Camp consisted of NISSEN HUTS and FRENCH HUTS for the men, accomodation was limited owing to the Camp being in the process of construction.	Hayes
"	9th		SAUNDERS CAMP — Inspections & general cleaning up – work on the Camp.	Hayes
" Ref Map MOEUVRES 1/20,000.	10th	12.5 pm	SAUNDERS CAMP. — Sudden orders received to be prepared to move forward at short notice as an attack was anticipated against the Divisional Front – All preparations made. Orders to move forward received 2.45 pm. The Battalion left Camp again at 3.25 pm & moved to Point of Assembly J.34.C.8.1. thence round J.36.d.9.9 – March delayed at start, reached area about 9 pm. Thence to area then accomodated in bivouacs & French shelters. Weather cold & rainy.	
	11th		Night passed without any hostile move by the enemy. Orders received to move back again – SAUNDERS CAMP was reached about 1 pm. Remainder of day spent in cleaning up & resting.	Hayes

(A7092) Wt W12839/M1293 750,000 1/17. D. D. & L., Ltd. Forms/C.2118/14.

4

Army Form C. 2118.

WAR DIARY
or
INTELLIGENCE SUMMARY.
(Erase heading not required.)

Instructions regarding War Diaries and Intelligence Summaries are contained in F. S. Regs., Part II. and the Staff Manual respectively. Title pages will be prepared in manuscript.

Place	Date	Hour	Summary of Events and Information	Remarks and references to Appendices
	12th		SAUNDER'S CAMP. — Parties sent forward to reconnoitre Left Battalion area of the RIGHT BRIGADE front preparatory to the relief of the 52nd Inf Bde. — Work on the Camp continued.	[signature]
Ref Map. MOEUVRES 1/20,000.	13th		SAUNDERS CAMP. Preparation for the Relief — Battalion moved from Camp at 3.15 pm to relief of 10th LANCASHIRE FUSILIERS in Brigade Support. 'A' + 'B' Companies were in LONDON SUPPORT. TR. (formerly TANK SUPPORT) 'C' + 'D' Companies were in LONDON. TR (formerly TANK TRENCH) HQrs K.21a.7.5. Work on improvement of Trenches and accomodation carried on.	
	14th		SUPPORT LINE. — Strength of the Battalion for this tour was 21 Officers 465. OR. Large Carrying Parties + working parties supplied daily for the Front line Battalions — 2 Companies and 1 officer + 50 OR were supplied daily for this work + carrying	[signature]
	15th		SUPPORT LINE — Work on Trenches — Same Carrying Parties supplied as for the 14th inst	[signature]
	16th		SUPPORT LINE. — Work on Support line — Parties supplied as for the 14th — 1 OR killed + 5. OR. wounded whilst out with Carrying Party	[signature]
	17th		Preparation for relief from SUPPORT to FRONT LINE. Battalion moved forward for Relief of Left Sector of Brigade Front at 5 pm and relieved 7th Bn EAST YORKSHIRE Regt, Relief was complete	[signature]

(A7092) Wt W12839/M1293 75,0.0. 1/17. D. D. & L., Ltd. Forms/C.2118/14.

5.

Instructions regarding War Diaries and Intelligence Summaries are contained in F. S. Regs., Part II. and the Staff Manual respectively. Title pages will be prepared in manuscript.

WAR DIARY
or
INTELLIGENCE SUMMARY.
(Erase heading not required.)

Army Form C. 2118.

Place	Date	Hour	Summary of Events and Information	Remarks and references to Appendices
	17th (contd)		at 8.50pm. H.Qrs were at K.15.d.9.5. — Dispositions as per attached Sketch Map marked (B).	[illegible]
	18th		FRONT LINE. (Left) Work on wiring the front & improvement to the trenches. About 6.25pm the 7th Bn Yorkshire Regt on our Right during a heavy enemy barrage of Field Guns & TM's sent up the S.O.S. It was afterwards ascertained that the enemy had raided two of their posts and captured two Lewis Rifles & made one OR prisoner. In spite of considerable number Shells falling on the right of the Battalion Front only 2.OR were wounded.	[illegible]
	19th		FRONT LINE Work on the line continued — Trenches in a very bad state a thaw having set in with rain. The enemy also attempted a raid about 12 midnight on our Posts on the right of the Bombing Stop. The Party about 12 in number were seen & met with a hot burst of Lewis Gun & Rifle fire. Bombs were also thrown. After throwing two bombs towards our Post, the enemy withdrew precipitately. Patrols sent out were unable to obtain any identification. Casualties 1.OR wounded.	[illegible]

(A7092) Wt W12839/M1295 75,000 1/17. D. D. & L., Ltd. Forms/C.2118/14.

6

Instructions regarding War Diaries and Intelligence Summaries are contained in F. S. Regs., Part II. and the Staff Manual respectively. Title pages will be prepared in manuscript.

WAR DIARY
or
INTELLIGENCE SUMMARY.
(Erase heading not required.)

Army Form C. 2118.

Place	Date	Hour	Summary of Events and Information	Remarks and references to Appendices
	19th (contd)		The following officers joined the Battalion 2/Lt. J. LAWRENCE, 2/Lt. C.W.S. SPENCER, 2/Lt. H.W. RAMSDEN, 2/Lt. H. WAINWRIGHT 2/Lt. B. REED —	Hayle
	20th		FRONT LINE. Work of wiring + improvement of trenches, and Patrolling continued — Suspected enemy relief caused great activity by L.G's + the M.G.C. — Casualties. 2 OR wounded during the day.	Hayle
Ref map MOEUVRES 1/20000	21st		Battalion Relieved in FRONT LINE by the 7th Bn EAST. YORKSHIRE Regt. — Relief Complete 7.50 pm on Relief Companies moved back to RESERVE — Companies were located in Trenches in OLD BRITISH FRONT LINE in K.32 Area — HQrs K.32.c.4.5.	Hayle
	22nd		RESERVE. "A" Company baths at J.36.b.9.4 — Two Companies working under R.E. building accomodation in SPOIL HEAP — Two Companies employed at night on wiring and Carrying for the two Battalions in the front line — Casualties on wiring party 2/Lt. W.K. NEWTON, and 4 OR wounded —	Hayle
	23rd		Baths for B, C, + D. Coys at J.36.b.9.4 — Companies employed on work, wiring, + Carrying as on the 22nd inst.	Hayle
	24th		Baths for any Details — Companies employed as on 22nd inst	Hayle
	25th		50th Infantry Bde relieved in the Line by 51st Inf Bde The 8th Bn SOUTH STAFFORDSHIRE Regt relieved the Battalion in RESERVE — Relief Complete 4.45 pm on Relief the Battalion marched to HERMIES to take over the DEFENCES from the 7th BORDER Regt H.Qrs were at J.23.d.6.0 and Companies were accomodated in shelters + dug-outs in the village ready to man the System of Defence.	Hayle
	26th		HERMIES Day spent in Cleaning up, and resting.	Hayle

(A7092). Wt. W12839/M1293. 750,000. /17. D. D. & L., Ltd. Forms/C.2118/14.

7.

Army Form C. 2118.

Instructions regarding War Diaries and Intelligence Summaries are contained in F. S. Regs., Part II. and the Staff Manual respectively. Title pages will be prepared in manuscript.

WAR DIARY
or
INTELLIGENCE SUMMARY.
(Erase heading not required.)

Place	Date	Hour	Summary of Events and Information	Remarks and references to Appendices
	27th	(SUNDAY)	HERMIES Two Companies employed in Parties of 1 officer + 50 OR. continuously in 8 hour shifts with AUSTRALIAN TUNNELING COMPANY in digging Dug-outs in the French System of Defences. — Two companies employed daily 2 officers + 150 OR. in two Parties working 4 hours each morning under 78th Field Company R.E. digging trenches + wiring the Defences of HERMIES — Voluntary Church Service in morning —	[illegible]
	28th		HERMIES — Battalion employed as on 27th inst — Baths for Batt HQrs + B Coy at J.36.b.9.4	[illegible]
	29th		HERMIES — Companies employed as on 27th inst — Baths for A + C Companies	[illegible]
	30th		HERMIES — Companies employed as on 27th inst — About 4.40 pm enemy sent a number of Gas Shells into the area occupied by Bn HQrs (ie Sunken Road J.23.d.6.0.) + D Coy. — Shelling continued until 6.10 pm. Casualties 10 OR. slightly gassed. Preparations for Relief of the Left sub-sector of the Left Brigade Sector. Reconnoitering Parties sent forward.	
	31st		HERMIES. Companies preparing for move up — The enemy again used gas shells on area J.23.d.6.0. — Shelling commenced at 3.50 pm and ceased at 4.10 pm — Concentration considerably more dense than on previous day — The Battalion moved from HERMIES at 6.25 pm and relieved the 10th Bn LANCASHIRE FUSILIERS in the Left Battalion Sector of the Left Brigade. The 7th YORKSHIRE Regt were on the RIGHT and the 1st BUFFS (E K Regt) on the LEFT (6th DIVISION.) Relief Complete was reported at 11.10 pm. The Relieved Battalion took over the Defences of HERMIES. Disposition of Companies as per attached Trace marked (C).	[illegible]
NEW YEAR'S HONOURS			The following Honours + awards were gained by the Battalion in the 1st January Gazette. Lt. Col. P.R. SIMNER D.S.O. Mentioned in Despatches 2/Lt. A.T. BROWN. MC. Awarded MILITARY CROSS a/R.S.M. TOSE DCM. Awarded D.C.M.	[illegible]

(A7092) Wt W12839/M1293 75,000 1/17. D. D. & L., Ltd. Forms/C.2118/14.

1-2-18.

P.R. Simner Lt Col
Commanding 10th Bn West Yorkshire Regt

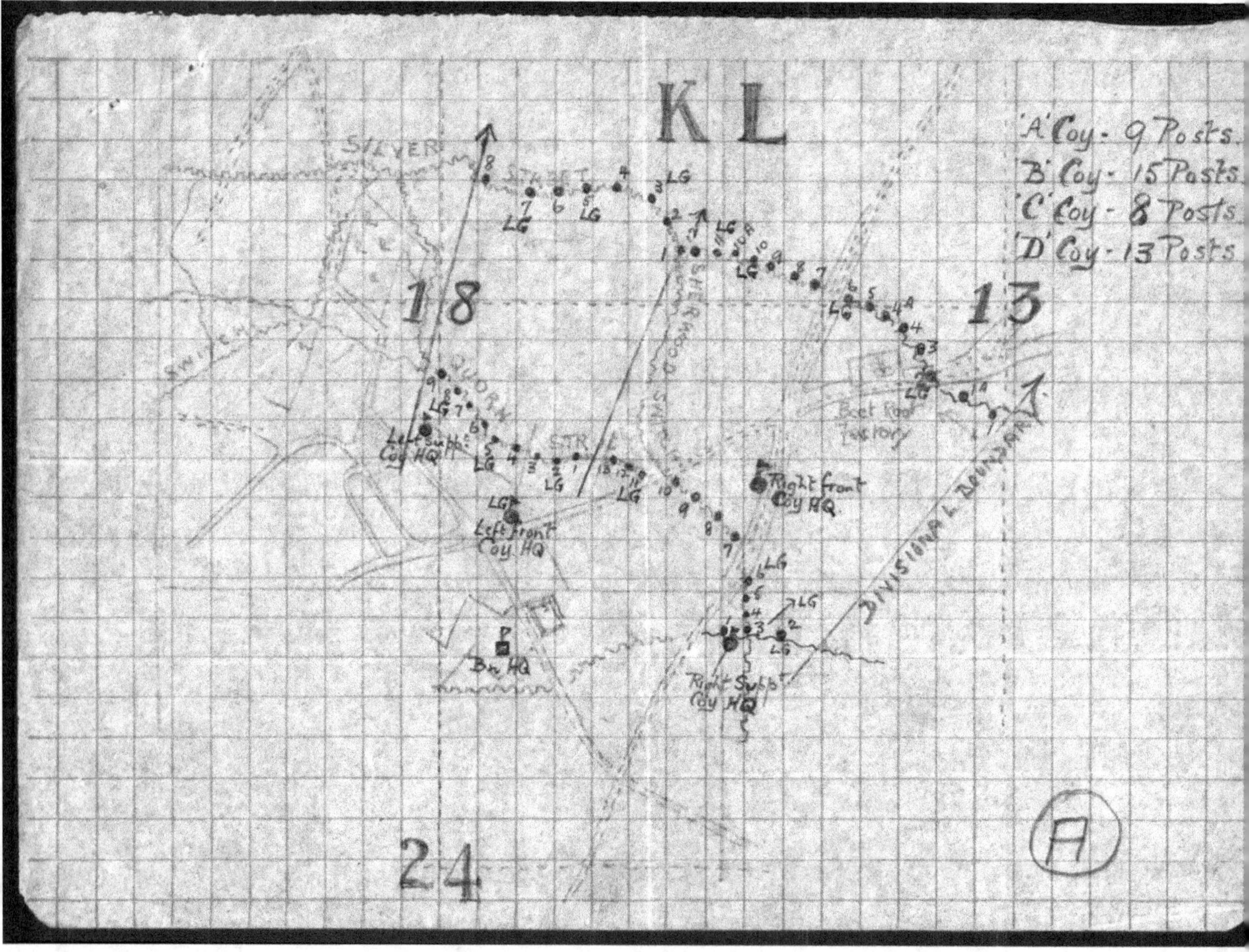

KL
'A' Coy - 9 Posts.
'B' Coy - 15 Posts.
'C' Coy - 8 Posts.
'D' Coy - 13 Posts.
18
13
24
SILVER
STREET
QUORN
Left Supp^t Coy HQ
Left front Coy HQ
Right front Coy HQ
Right Supp^t Coy HQ
Bn HQ
Beet Rot Factory
DIVISIONAL BOUNDARY
A

SKETCH · MAP · SHOWING · DISPOSITIONS · OF —
"HEDGE" — 21/1/18

REF. MAP, 'MŒUVRES' 1/20,000
and Aeroplane Photo.

B.S. = Bombing Stop
R.P. = Rifle Post
L.G. = Lewis Gun Post.
T = Tunnel
L = Latrine.

Bde. Boundary.

K

10

16

WHITEHALL

Bn. Hq.

HUGHES TRENCH

CAREY ST.

POST. OFFICE TRENCH

SHIP TRENCH

GEORGE ST.

SOAP TRENCH

SPIN ALLEY

OWEN SUPPORT

OWEN TRENCH

Of Supr. Coy.

Supr. Coy. Hq.

Sap for Supr. Coy.

Coy. Hq.

T.M.B.

A.A.

1 Platoon by day.

Scale of Yards.

yds. 100 50 0 100 200 300 400 500 yds.

B

Lewis Rifles
Coy H.2.
Batn H.2.
O.P.
Platoon Area
LEFT BDE. DISPOSITIONS.
DATE
TIME
SCALE: 1:10,000
SECRET
A Coy
B Coy
C Coy
D Coy
A Coy H.2
C Coy H.2
D Coy H.2
B Coy H.2.
LG Platoon
WESTON
SLAG AVENUE
BARN AVENUE
JERMYN STREET
KNIGHTSBRIDGE
SLOANE ST.
DRURY LANE
LONDON
LONDON TRENCH
SUPPORT
GEORGE STREET
BORLEE AVENUE
FAGAN AVENUE
FAGAN
BELL TRENCH
HUGHES TRENCH
EARLY TRENCH
STRAFE TRENCH
AVENUE
CANAL DU NORD
8
9
14
15
19
20
21

Instructions regarding War Diaries and Intelligence Summaries are contained in F. S. Regs., Part II. and the Staff Manual respectively. Title pages will be prepared in manuscript.

WAR DIARY
or
~~INTELLIGENCE SUMMARY.~~
(Erase heading not required.)

Army Form C. 2118.

Vol 26

Place	Date	Hour	Summary of Events and Information	Remarks and references to Appendices
			10th BN. WEST YORKSHIRE REGT.	
Ref. Map MOEUVRES 1/20,000	1st Feby 1918.		Battalion in the front line. A+B. Companies located in KELLET TRENCH, C+D Companies in BULLEN TRENCH, HUNT AVENUE, and ALBAN AVENUE, Bn. HQ at K8d.9.2. Work of wiring the front, improvement of the trenches and accomodation was commenced, also active patrolling was carried on from dusk to dawn.	See sketch map marked (A) attached MB
	2nd Feby.		Battalion in the front line. Work as on 1st Feby. continued with. Commencing on 2nd February rations were sent up to the front line from HERMIES by light railway, and this scheme proved very successful. 1 O.R. wounded in action. 2nd Lt E.L. TODD left for ENGLAND on duty, six months attachment.	MB
	3rd Feby		Battalion in front line. Work as on 1st February continued with. 2nd Lt H. WAINWRIGHT wounded.	MB
	4th Feby.		The Battalion was relieved in the LEFT BN. SECTOR of the Brigade front, by the 7th BN. EAST YORKSHIRE REGIMENT. Relief complete was reported at 8.30 pm. After relief the Battalion moved to positions in SUPPORT, vacated by the 7th BN EAST YORKSHIRE REGT., viz:- "A" Company in ALBAN AVENUE, "B" Company in FAGAN SUPPORT, "C" Company in HUNT AVENUE "D" Company in FAGAN TRENCH, Bn. HQ in LISCLOCHER LANE. Trench strength 17 officers, 381 O.R.	See sketch map marked (A) attached MB
	5th Feby		Battalion in SUPPORT. Work on the area occupied by Companies in clearing the trenches	MB

27 / 9 sheets

A5834 Wt. W4973/M687 750,000 8/16 D. D. & L. Ltd. Forms/C.2118/13.

Instructions regarding War Diaries and Intelligence Summaries are contained in F. S. Regs., Part II. and the Staff Manual respectively. Title pages will be prepared in manuscript.

WAR DIARY
or page 2
~~INTELLIGENCE SUMMARY~~.

(Erase heading not required.)

Army Form C. 2118.

Place	Date	Hour	Summary of Events and Information 10th BN WEST YORKSHIRE REGT	Remarks and references to Appendices
Ref Map MOEUVRES 1/20,000	5th February 1918. (Continued)		and improving accomodation commenced. In addition working parties were furnished by the Battalion for work under the 2nd AUSTRALIAN TUNNELLING Co. amounting to 1 Officer and 50. O.R. in reliefs. LT J.D. DAMS and 2/LT A.S. PENN and 64 O.R. joined the Battalion from the 18th BN. WEST YORKSHIRE REGT In addition to above working party 6 officers and 240 O.R. were furnished for work under the R.E.	AHB
	6th February 1918		Battalion in SUPPORT. Work and working parties as for 5th February.	AHB
	7th February 1918		Battalion in SUPPORT. Work and working parties as for 5th February. 4 O.R. wounded.	AHB
	8th February 1918		The Battalion relieved the 4th BN. EAST YORKSHIRE REGT in the front line. C and D Companies in the front line, A and B Companies in SUPPORT BN. H.Q. at K8d. 9.2 Relief complete was reported at 9.0 p.m. 2 O.R. wounded. LT G.T.E. HALL left for ENGLAND on duty, six months attachment.	See sketch map marked (A) attached AHB
	9th February 1918		Battalion in front line. Wiring and work in clearing the trenches and improving accomodation carried on, also active patrolling from dusk to dawn	AHB
	10th February 1918		Battalion in front line. Work and patrolling as for 9th February.	AHB

A5834 Wt. W4973/M687 750,000 8/16 D. D. & L. Ltd. Forms/C.2118/13.

Instructions regarding War Diaries and Intelligence Summaries are contained in F. S. Regs., Part II. and the Staff Manual respectively. Title pages will be prepared in manuscript.

WAR DIARY
or page 3
~~INTELLIGENCE SUMMARY~~.
(Erase heading not required.)

Army Form C. 2118.

Place	Date	Hour	Summary of Events and Information 10th Bn WEST YORKSHIRE REGT	Remarks and references to Appendices
	11th February 1918		Battalion in front line. Work and patrolling as for 9th February. 2nd Lt J.W. ARMITAGE from 18th Bn WEST YORKSHIRE REGT and 81 O.R. from the 5th RESERVE BN. WEST YORKSHIRE REGT joined the Battalion	MB
Ref. map. FRANCE Sheet 57C 1/40000	12th February 1918		The 50th Infantry Brigade was relieved by the 51st Infantry Brigade on nights 12/13th and 13/14th February 1918. The Battalion was relieved on the 12th February by the 7th Bn. LINCOLNSHIRE REGT in the left sector of the left Brigade front. Relief was reported complete at 9.45pm. After relief the Battalion moved into reserve at PHIPPS CAMP (O. 6c+d.) marching from the trenches to HERMIES and entraining there for PHIPPS CAMP. Lt J.R. KING joined the Battalion from the 18th Bn. WEST YORKSHIRE REGT 2 O.R. wounded.	MB
	13th February 1918		Battalion in PHIPPS CAMP The day was devoted to general cleaning up and inspection of all ammunition, arms, and equipment. The baths at HAPLINCOURT were allotted to "B" Company 2nd Lt W.P. ROBINSON evacuated to ENGLAND sick.	MB

A5834 Wt. W4973/M687 750,000 8/16 D. D. & L. Ltd. Forms/C.2118/13.

Instructions regarding War Diaries and Intelligence Summaries are contained in F. S. Regs., Part II. and the Staff Manual respectively. Title pages will be prepared in manuscript.

WAR DIARY

or ~~INTELLIGENCE SUMMARY~~. page 4

(Erase heading not required.)

Army Form C. 2118.

Place	Date	Hour	Summary of Events and Information 10th BN WEST YORKSHIRE REGT	Remarks and references to Appendices
	14th February 1918		The Battalion in PHIPPS CAMP. The Commanding Officer inspected all men of the draft from the 18th BN. WEST YORKSHIRE REGT Thorough inspection of all kit and equipment took place. Baths at HAPLINCOURT allotted to "A" "C" and "D" Companies. "A" and "D" Companies were required for night work under the 77th FIELD Co. RE and proceeded to HERMIES by motor lorries. One N.C.O and 26 men were detailed as a daily party for work on YTRES RE Dump.	[illegible]
	15th February 1918		Battalion in PHIPPS CAMP. The Commanding Officer inspected the draft from the 5th RESERVE BN. WEST YORKSHIRE REGT The Army Inspector of Armourers inspected the Lewis Rifles of all Companies and the rifles of "B" Company. Working party furnished by "C" Company, 3 officers and 100 O.R. Lt H. NEWTON left for ENGLAND on duty, 6 months attachment. 2nd Lt E. SMITH joined the Battalion from the 18th BN WEST YORKSHIRE REGT	[illegible]
	16th February 1918		Battalion in PHIPPS CAMP. The Brigade Gas N.C.O inspected the gas helmets and box respirators of the Battalion, and put all men through the gas chamber. O.C Companies lectured their men on Trench discipline. "B" and "C" Companies required for work in the line under the R.E and proceeded by Light railway to HERMIES.	[illegible]

A5834 Wt. W4973/M687 750,000 8/16 D. D. & L. Ltd. Forms/C.2118/13.

Instructions regarding War Diaries and Intelligence Summaries are contained in F. S. Regs., Part II. and the Staff Manual respectively. Title pages will be prepared in manuscript.

WAR DIARY
or page 5
~~INTELLIGENCE~~ ~~SUMMARY~~.
(Erase heading not required.)

Army Form C. 2118.

Place	Date	Hour	Summary of Events and Information 10th Bn WEST YORKSHIRE REGT	Remarks and references to Appendices
	17th February 1918.		Battalion in PHIPPS CAMP. The Battalion paraded for foot washing (French Treatment.) Divine Service for all denominations was held.	[initials]
	18th February 1918		Battalion in PHIPPS CAMP. Preparations made for moving to the forward area. Parties worked on the building of breastworks round the huts. The 50th Infantry Brigade relieved the 52nd Infantry Brigade in the right sector of the Divisional front on the nights 18/19th February and 19/20th February.	
Ref. Map MOEUVRES 1/20000			The Battalion relieved the 10th Bn LANCASHIRE FUSILIERS in Support on 18th February. "A" Company in LONDON TRENCH, "B" Company in LONDON SUPPORT and DRURY LANE. "C" and "D" Companies in the CHEETHAM SWITCH. Bn HQ at K 21 a. 7.5. in LONDON TRENCH. Relief complete was reported at 10.50pm. Trench strength 26 officers, 544 O.R.	See Sketch map marked (B) attached. [initials]
	19th February 1918.		"C" and "D" Companies moved from their positions in the CHEETHAM SWITCH to positions in K31 b and K32 a in the south bank of the CANAL DU NORD. The accomodation for "D" Company was almost completed and was carried on under RE supervision. No accomodation was available for "C" Company, and the preparation of shelters was at once commenced with the assistance of the R.E.	[initials]

A5834 Wt. W4973/M687 750,000 8/16 D. D. & L. Ltd. Forms/C.2118/13.

Instructions regarding War Diaries and Intelligence Summaries are contained in F. S. Regs., Part II. and the Staff Manual respectively. Title pages will be prepared in manuscript.

WAR DIARY

~~or~~ page 6

~~INTELLIGENCE SUMMARY~~.

(Erase heading not required.)

Army Form C. 2118.

Place	Date	Hour	Summary of Events and Information 10th Bn. WEST YORKSHIRE REGT	Remarks and references to Appendices
	19th February 1918 (Continued)		'A' and 'B' Companies carried on with the improving of the trenches, clearing and relaying duckboards etc. Carrying parties were furnished at night to the Battalion in the front line.	MG
	20th February 1918		Battalion in Support Work and carrying parties as for 19th February	MG
	21st February 1918		Battalion in Support Work and carrying parties as for 19th February	MG
	22nd February 1918		The Battalion relieved the 6th DORSETSHIRE REGT in the left sector of the Brigade front. Relief was reported complete at 9.10pm, Active patrolling took place until dawn.	See sketch map marked (B) attached MG
	23rd February 1918		Battalion in front line Work was carried on wiring the front where required, improving the trenches and accomodation with R.E. assistance. Active patrolling carried out from dusk to dawn. 1 O.R. wounded.	MG
	24th February 1918		Battalion in front line Work and patrolling as for 23rd February	MG

A5834 Wt. W4973/M687 750,000 8/16 D. D. & L. Ltd. Forms/C.2118/13.

Instructions regarding War Diaries and Intelligence Summaries are contained in F. S. Regs., Part II. and the Staff Manual respectively. Title pages will be prepared in manuscript.

WAR DIARY

~~or~~ Page 7

~~INTELLIGENCE SUMMARY.~~

(Erase heading not required.)

Army Form C. 2118.

Place	Date	Hour	Summary of Events and Information 10th Bn WEST YORKSHIRE REGT	Remarks and references to Appendices
	25th February 1918		Battalion in front line. Work as for 23rd February During the night two very good patrols were carried out, one with 2nd Lt DEAN as patrol leader, the second being led by 2/Lt BRAITHWAITE. In the latter, casualties were known to have been inflicted on an enemy patrol at close range, but a barrage of rifle grenades put down by the enemy made it impossible to secure an identification. The patrol then withdrew, 1 O.R. was killed and 2 O.R. wounded on this enterprise. 2 O.R. accidentally wounded	M.G.
	26th February 1918.		The Battalion was relieved by the 6th DORSETSHIRE REGT. Relief was reported complete at 10.15 pm. After relief the Battalion moved back to positions in support as occupied on 20th February	M.G.
	27th February 1918		Battalion in Support Work in improving the trenches carried on. Working parties under Brigade orders furnished amounting to 9 Officers and 261 O.R.	M.G.
	28th February 1918		Battalion in Support Work and working parties as for 27th February.	M.G.

P. R. Simner Lieut Col
Commanding 10th Bn West Yorkshire Regt.

A5834 Wt. W4973/M687 750,000 8/16 D. D. & L. Ltd. Forms/C.2118/13

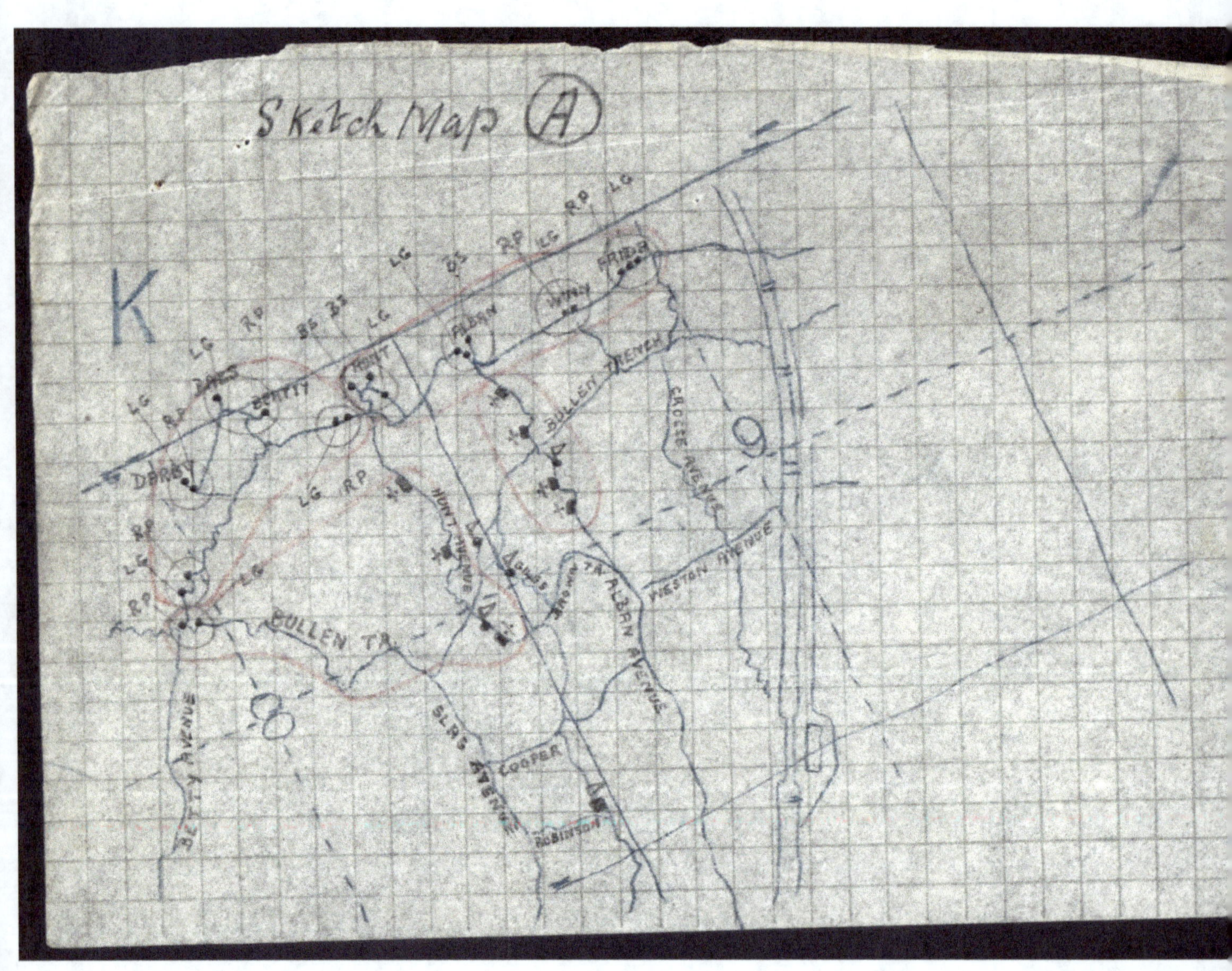
Sketch Map (A)
K
DERBY
HUNT
ALBAN
BULLEN TRENCH
BULLEN TR.
WESTON AVENUE
ALBAN AVENUE
HUNT AVENUE
BROWN TR.
COOPER
ROBINSON
BETTY AVENUE
LG
RP

Sketch Map
(A)
MAP. A.
HUGHES TRENCH
CAREY TRENCH
BULLEN TRENCH
TRENCH
BEATTY AVENUE
COOPER
WESTON TR.
RYDER
15
STREET
FAGAN TRENCH
FAGAN SUPPORT
FAGAN AVENUE
BORLAS AVENUE
GEORGE ST.
HUNT AVENUE
JERMYN ST
BELL TR.
LONDON
LONDON SUPPORT
DRURY LANE
SLAG AVENUE
O.B.L. AVENUE
8
9
14
19
20
21
SCALE 1/10,000
BL MAP No 3
22-4-18

Map (B)

RIGHT BDE. DISPOSITIONS.

DATE:............ TIME:............ SCALE: 1:10,000.

SECRET.

A Coy. plus 1 platoon from C Coy.

B Coy plus 1 L.G. team each from D Coy & C Coy.

D Coy less 1 L.G. team

C Coy less 1 platoon + 1 L.G. team

SHINGLER TRENCH

SHINGLER SUPPORT

DARWIN ALLEY

SNAKE

SWITCH

STREET

COLLINS

AVENUE

GEORGES

LONDON TRENCH

LONDON SUPPORT

STREET

JERMYN

KNIGHTSBRIDGE

SLOANE ST

DRURY LANE

BELL TRENCH

10

15

16

17

21

22

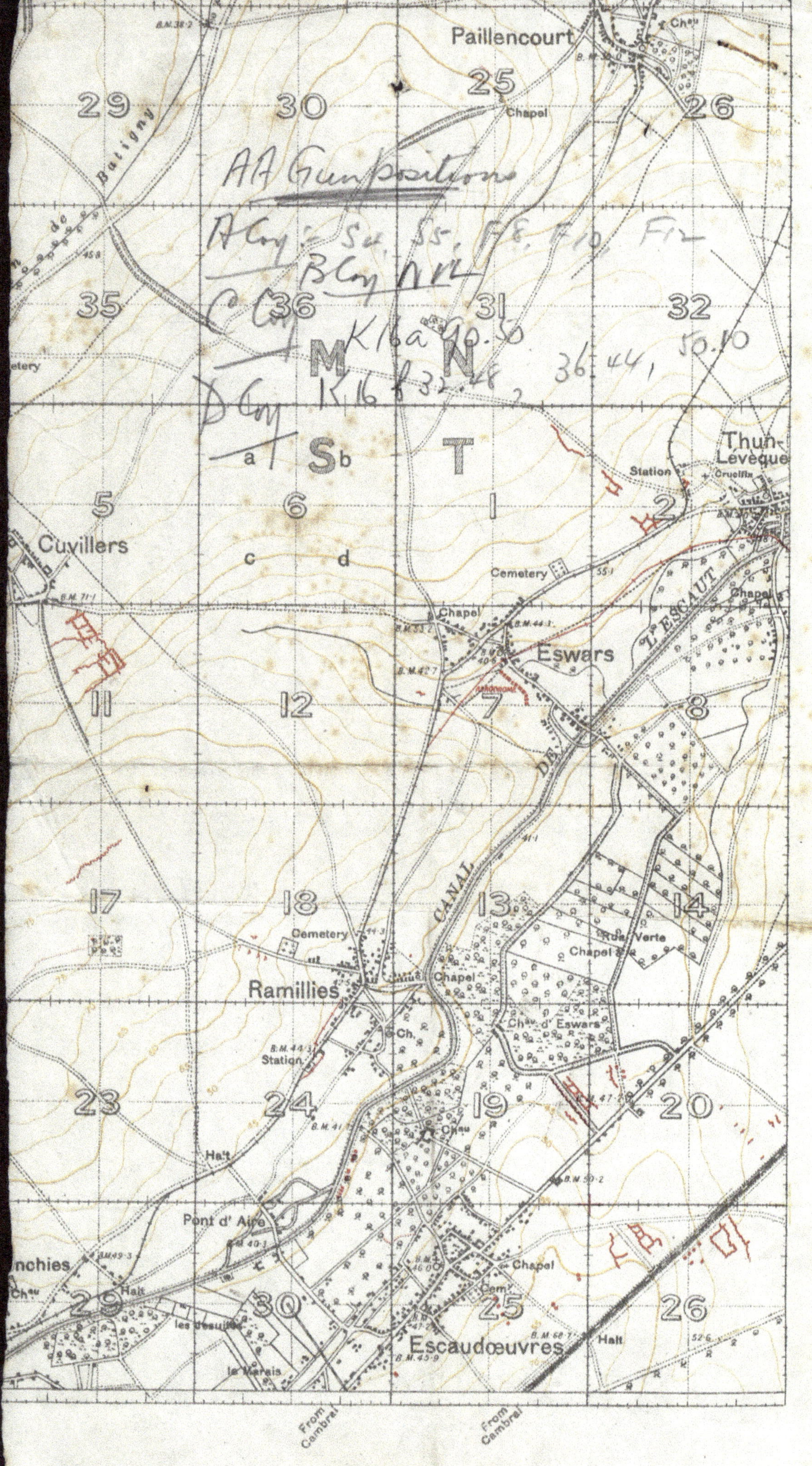

Paillencourt
Batigny
Cuvillers
Cemetery
Chapel
Eswars
L'ESCAUT
CANAL
DE
Thun-
Leveque
Station
Crucifix
Rue Verte
Ch^au d'Eswars
Ramillies
Ch.
Station
Halt
Pont d' Aire
les Marais
Escaudœuvres
Cem^y
From Cambrai
From Cambrai
AA Gun positions

50th Inf.Bde.
17th Div.

10th BATTN. THE WEST YORKSHIRE REGIMENT.

M A R C H

1 9 1 8

XVII

Feb
March
1918

10 West Yorks
Vol 9

H.E.

I 26

Instructions regarding War Diaries and Intelligence Summaries are contained in F. S. Regs., Part II. and the Staff Manual respectively. Title pages will be prepared in manuscript.

WAR DIARY
or
~~INTELLIGENCE SUMMARY~~.
(Erase heading not required.)

50/17

Army Form C. 2118.

10th (S) Battn WEST YORKSHIRE REGT.

Vol 27

Place	Date	Hour	Summary of Events and Information	Remarks and references to Appendices
K 21a London Trench	1/3/18		Battalion H. 2. The Battn was in Support. One Coy Drury Lane. One Coy London Support. Two Coys. Yorkshire Bank. Transport at BERTINCOURT.	
HEBBURN.	2/3/18		The Battn moved to HEBBURN. Two Coys HEBBURN. Two Coys Old British Line, K 32 c-d.	
			The Battn remained at HEBBURN from 2/3/18 to the 9/3/18. Ordinary parades and fatigues.	
ALBAN AV. K15a 4-8	9/3/18		On the night of the 9/3/18 the Battn moved up into FRONT LINE, astride the CANAL DU NORD. Two Coys in front line. Two Coys in close support. D Coy right front. B Coy right support. C Coy left front. A Coy left support. These dispositions remained until the night of the 13/3/18.	
do	13/3/18		Inter Coy relief. B Coy right front. D Coy right support. A Coy left front. C Coy left support.	
LISLOCHER TR. K 13d 8-3	14/3/18		The Battn moved into Support. B and D Coys FAGAN TR. A and C Coys GARFORTH Slag Heap.	
ALBAN AV. K 15a 4-8	15/3/18		The Battn relieved the 7th EAST YORKSHIRE REGT. in the front line. B Coy right front. D Coy right support. A Coy left front. C Coy left support.	
	20/3/18		Inter-company relief. D Coy right front. B Coy right support. C Coy left front. A Coy left support.	A.S.H.
	21/3/18	5 AM.	At 5 A.M. enemy opened heavy bombardment on whole Battn area. Trench Mortars on front line, and shells of all calibres on support and reserve lines. A large number of both Trench Mortars and shells contained gas.	
		10 AM	At about 10 AM the barrage was lifted from the front and support lines and the enemy advanced over the top from his Support line on the right Coy front immediately EAST of the CANAL DU NORD. No attack was attempted on the left Coy front. About three hundred of the enemy attacked on the right Coy front but were dealt with by rifle and M.G. fire, and	

A5834 Wt. W4973/M687 750,000 8/16 D. D. & L. Ltd. Forms/C.2118/13.

28 E
5 sheets

II.

Instructions regarding War Diaries and Intelligence Summaries are contained in F. S. Regs., Part II. and the Staff Manual respectively. Title pages will be prepared in manuscript.

WAR DIARY
or
~~INTELLIGENCE SUMMARY~~.
(Erase heading not required.)

Army Form C. 2118.

10th (S) Battn WEST YORKSHIRE REGT.

Place	Date	Hour	Summary of Events and Information	Remarks and references to Appendices
	21/3/18	10 A.M.	failed to reach our wire. On the immediate right the Lancashire Fusiliers evacuated their front line. The enemy got in the front line here and bombed along ~~the~~ it forcing our right front Coy to evacuate it for about two hundred yards. Temp. Sec. Lieut. H.W. Ramsden was slightly wounded but did not leave the line. Captain E J REYNOLDS (O.C. B Coy) was wounded but did not leave the Battn until the 22nd inst.	
		1 P.M.	At 1 p.m. a bombing party was formed, and the enemy was driven out of the whole of the 10th WEST YORKSHIRE REGTS front line, and also two hundred yards of the LANCASHIRE FUSILIERS front line where a bombing stop was made. During this operation Temp. Sec. Lieut. H. DEAN was killed. The situation for the remainder of the day was fairly quiet.	
	22/3/18	3.30 A.M.	At 3.30 A.M. on the 22nd the Battn was ordered to evacuate the front system of trenches and take up a position WEST of the CANAL DU NORD in K 25 and K 26. Battn H.Q. were in MAXWELL AV at K 25 d 50-90.	
MAXWELL AV. K 25 d 50-90.	23/3/18	3 P.M.	This position was taken up and held until 3 p.m. on the 23rd when a further withdrawal was ordered as the enemy had got through on both flanks. D Coy formed the Battn rear guard, and the position was evacuated without loss. The withdrawal was continued	
O 20 a		9 P.M.	through ROYAULCOURT - YTRES - BUS - ROCQUIGNY and the Battn formed up at night with the remainder of the 50th Brigade at O 20 a.	
BARASTRE	24/3/18	8 A.M.	The Battn moved up to a position S.E. of BARASTRE, but during the morning an order was	J.S.H.

Instructions regarding War Diaries and Intelligence Summaries are contained in F. S. Regs., Part II. and the Staff Manual respectively. Title pages will be prepared in manuscript.

Army Form C. 2118.

WAR DIARY
or
~~INTELLIGENCE SUMMARY~~.
(Erase heading not required.)

10th (S) Battn WEST YORKSHIRE REGT.

Place	Date	Hour	Summary of Events and Information	Remarks and references to Appendices
BARASTRE	24/3/18		received to withdraw through BEAULENCOURT to COURCELETTE. This order was cancelled shortly afterwards, but in the meantime about two Coys of the Battn had moved off and lost touch with the remainder of the Battn until the afternoon of the 26th, when ~~the remainder~~ this party of the Battn rejoined them at HENENCOURT. Temp Capt. P. HOWE. M.C. was the senior officer of this party in the 10th WEST YORKSHIRE REGT. The remainder of the Battn under Lt. Col. P.R. SIMNER. D.S.O.	
GUEUDECOURT		6 P.M.	received fresh orders and proceeded to GUEUDECOURT, which was reached at 6 P.M. During the day MAJOR R.E. COTTON, and Temp. Lt acting Capt. H.A.G. NEVILLE, M.C. were wounded and Temp. 2nd Lieut	
		9 P.M.	D. LYNCH was killed. The two Coys under Lt. Col. P.R. SIMNER, D.S.O. continued the withdrawal at 9 P.M.	
EAUCOURT L'ABBAYE	25/3/18	3 AM.	and at 3 A.M. on the 25th took up a position immediately to the EAST of EAUCOURT L'ABBAYE.	
		10 AM.	At 10 AM. the enemy attacked this position, using a large number of machine guns and at 11.30 A.M. part of the line ~~held~~ to the left of the Battn front broke. At 11.45 A.M. the line gave way on	
		11.45 AM	the right, and a few minutes afterwards the Battn was forced to withdraw being almost surrounded. During this engagement Lieut. Col. P.R. SIMNER, D.S.O. became missing believed prisoner; Capt. L.G. PETERS was taken prisoner; Temp. Lt F.A. SHURROCK missing believed wounded; Temp. Capt. D.W. HUNTER, D.S.O. (R.A.M.C.) missing believed killed; Lieut W.J. HARTNALL (S/R) wounded; Temp. Lieut S. LOWDEN wounded; The section of the Battn under Lt Col. P.R. SIMNER, D.S.O. was about ~~two~~ one hundred and fifty strong prior to this engagement, during which there were	A.B.H.

A5834 Wt. W4973/M687 750,000 8/16 D. D. & L. Ltd. Forms/C.2118/13.

IV.

Instructions regarding War Diaries and Intelligence Summaries are contained in F. S. Regs., Part II. and the Staff Manual respectively. Title pages will be prepared in manuscript.

WAR DIARY
or
~~INTELLIGENCE SUMMARY.~~
(*Erase heading not required.*)

Army Form C. 2118.

10th (S) Battn WEST YORKSHIRE REGT.

Place	Date	Hour	Summary of Events and Information	Remarks and references to Appendices
BEAUCOURT L'ABBAYE	25/3/18		about sixty casualties. During the further withdrawal which followed, this part got divided into two. One party consisting of one officer and twenty eight O.R. joined a party of seventy O.R of the 7th EAST YORKSHIRE REGT under Lt Col W.E. THOMAS, M.C. and a party of fifty O.R. and two officers of the 7th DORSETSHIRE REGT. and were attached to the 99th Infantry Brigade, 2nd Division, by order of the G.O.C. 50th Infantry Brigade. The party spent the night 25th/26th on the high ground immediately NORTH-WEST of BEAUCOURT. On the morning of the	
	26/3/18		26th this party formed the rearguard for the 2nd Division. The 2nd Div took up a position on the	
		8 AM.	old British front line immediately WEST of BEAUMONT-HAMEL, and at 8 AM. the party	
Q 16 a			withdrew through them and remained in reserve at Q16a. At midnight 26th/27th the party was relieved by NEW ZEALAND troops, and after spending the remainder of the night	
SENLIS	27/3/18		at MAILLY-MAILLY rejoined the 50th Infantry Brigade at SENLIS on the morning 27th. In the meantime the other party consisting of five officers and about thirty O.R. reached BEAUCOURT; spent the night on the high ground SOUTH WEST (Q17b), and on the afternoon of the 26th reached HENNENCOURT where it joined the two Coys. which had become separated from the Battn on the morning of the 24th. The Battn thus reformed, under the command	A.S.H.
HENNENCOURT	26/3/18	5 P.M.	of A/MAJOR W.A.K. HALL, left HENNENCOURT at 5 P.M. on the 26th and took up a position	

A5834 Wt. W4973/M687 750,000 8/16 D. D. & L. Ltd. Forms/C.2118/13.

Instructions regarding War Diaries and Intelligence Summaries are contained in F. S. Regs., Part II. and the Staff Manual respectively. Title pages will be prepared in manuscript.

WAR DIARY
or
~~INTELLIGENCE SUMMARY~~.
(*Erase heading not required.*)

Army Form C. 2118.

10th (S.) Battn WEST YORKSHIRE REGT.

Place	Date	Hour	Summary of Events and Information	Remarks and references to Appendices
SENLIS	26/3/18		on the high ground to the SOUTH of SENLIS. (V30 central to V18) On the morning of the	
	27/3/18		27th the Battn was joined by the party which had been attached to the 99th Bde, 2nd Division	
BOUZINCOURT		9 P.M.	The Battn was in support. At 9 P.M. the Battn relieved the 7th Norfolk Regt on the left	
	28/3/18	5 AM.	sector of the 5th Inf. Brigade front. (W15a)* Relief complete 5 A.M. 28/3/18.	
		12 NOON	At 12 NOON the enemy attacked on the Battn front, but were driven off by rifle and Lewis Gun fire. During the afternoon the Battn dug and occupied posts along the road in	
W15d	29/3/18	6 P.M.	W15d. Temp 2nd Lt J.C. BRAITHWAITE M.C. was wounded. At 6 P.M. on the 29th the posts in W15d were lost and the Battn had 15 casualties. An attack at W15a 5-9 on Lewis Gun posts was driven off. The Battn remained in the front line until the 31/3/18 when they	
	31/3/18	7.30 PM	were relieved at 7 P.M. by the 7th LINCOLNSHIRE REGT. The Battn went into reserve at	
HENNENCOURT			HENNENCOURT. On the 31st the following officers became casualties. Temp Capt A.N.L.CLARK wounded; Temp Lt A.R.FRETWELL wounded; S/R Temp 2nd Lt W.K.NEWTON Killed; Temp 2nd Lt E.CLOUGH wounded.	

W E Thomas Lieut. Col.
Commanding 10th S. West Yorkshire Regt.

A.S.H.

17th Division.
50th Infantry Brigade

WAR DIARY

10th BATTALION

THE WEST YORKSHIRE REGIMENT

APRIL 1918

I

Instructions regarding War Diaries and Intelligence Summaries are contained in F. S. Regs., Part II. and the Staff Manual respectively. Title pages will be prepared in manuscript.

WAR DIARY
or
INTELLIGENCE SUMMARY. 10th (S) Battn WEST YORKSHIRE REGT.

(Erase heading not required.)

Army Form C. 2118.

Vol 28

Place	Date	Hour	Summary of Events and Information	Remarks and references to Appendices
HENNENCOURT	1/4/18		REFERENCE MAP. 57D.SE	
	3/4/18		The Battn was in HENNENCOURT, in Divisional Reserve until the 3rd when it moved back	
PIERREGOT		10 AM	at 10 AM. to PIERREGOT, arriving at 1.30 P.M.	
PERNOIS	4/4/18	9 AM	At 9 AM. on the 4th the Battn left PIERREGOT and arrived at PERNOIS at 3 PM	
	5/4/18		On the 5th the Battn received a draft of 7 Officers and 174 O.R. Temp. Capt. A.A. ADAMS Temp Capt. H.F. LAWTON, Temp. D F. FIRTH, Temp 2nd Lt H. KNIGHT, M.C., Temp. 2nd Lt S. MOULSON, Temp. 2nd Lt M. DAYSH, Temp. 2nd Lt B. BAKER.	
MONTRELET	6/4/18	10 AM	On the 6th the Battn moved from PERNOIS at 10 AM. and arrived at MONTRELET at 1 P.M. Temp. 2nd Lt A.T. BROWN, M.C. was evacuated sick and went to England 11/4/18	
	7/4/18		On the 7th Lieut. A/Major C.E. WAITE was transferred to the Battn from the ROYAL WEST KENT REGT.	
	8/4/18		The Battn received a draft of 185 O.R. Temp. 2nd Lt J.C. BRAITHWAITE, M.C. who was wounded on 28th March 1918, rejoined the Battn.	
	10/4/18		The Battn received a draft of 79 O.R.	
RAINCHEVAL	11/4/18		On the 11th the Battn moved from MONTRELET to RAINCHEVAL.	
	12/4/18		The Battn left RAINCHEVAL and went under canvas in a small wood immediately	

W. Thomas

29 E. 5 Sheet

A5834 Wt. W4973/M687 750,000 8/16 D. D. & L. Ltd. Forms/C.2118/13.

II

Instructions regarding War Diaries and Intelligence Summaries are contained in F. S. Regs., Part II. and the Staff Manual respectively. Title pages will be prepared in manuscript.

WAR DIARY
or
INTELLIGENCE SUMMARY. 10th (S) Battn WEST YORKSHIRE REGT.

(Erase heading not required.)

Army Form C. 2118.

Place	Date	Hour	Summary of Events and Information	Remarks and references to Appendices
RAINCHEVAL	12/4/18		NORTH of RAINCHEVAL.	
ENGLEBELMER	14/4/18		On the 14th the Battn moved forward via FORCEVILLE to ENGLEBELMER and relieved the HOOD Battn 63rd Division in LEFT BRIGADE RESERVE. Battn H.2. were at Q19d 40-85 A and C Coys were in the village, and B and D Coys in bivouacs at Q26.	
	16/4/18		Inter-Company relief at 6·30 P.M.	
	17/4/18	8·30 PM	Battn relieved the 6th DORSETSHIRE REGT. in the front line, RIGHT BATTN. LEFT BRIGADE at 8·30 P.M. C Coy front line; A Coy support; B and D reserve. Battn H.2. were at Q28d 1-6, in MESNIL.	
MESNIL	19/4/18		On the 19th D Coy relieved C Coy in the front line.	
	20/4/18		On the 20th Temp. 2nd Lt. A.S. PENN was wounded.	
	21/4/18	5·P.M.	The Battn was to have been relieved in the front line by the 10th LANCASHIRE FUSILIERS, but at 5·P.M. the enemy put down a heavy barrage, principally T.Ms, on our front and support lines and also on those of the Battn on our right. (10th NOTTS. & DERBY	
		6·30 PM	REGT.) At 6·30 P.M. the enemy attacked from Q35b, and, after capturing the advanced posts of the 10th Battn NOTTS. & DERBY REGT moved NORTH and captured four of our advanced posts situated along the Railway (Q29d 4-5 to Q29d 4-0) which were garrisoned by one	

A5834 Wt. W4973/M687 750,000 8/16 D. D. & L. Ltd. Forms/C.2118/13.

[illegible signature]

III

Instructions regarding War Diaries and Intelligence Summaries are contained in F. S. Regs., Part II. and the Staff Manual respectively. Title pages will be prepared in manuscript.

WAR DIARY
or
INTELLIGENCE SUMMARY. 10th (S) Battn WEST YORKSHIRE REGT

(*Erase heading not required.*)

Army Form C. 2118.

Place	Date	Hour	Summary of Events and Information	Remarks and references to Appendices
MESNIL	21/4/18	6.30 PM	platoon of D Coy. The enemy then took up a position approximately from Q29d 4-5 to Q35b 3-7. During this attack enemy T.M. and M.G. fire was very severe.	
	22/4/18	4.30 AM	At 4.30 AM on the 22nd a counter-attack was launched in conjunction with the 10th Battn NOTTS. & DERBY REGT. to recover the lost posts. One and a half Coys of this Battn were used; one Coy. in front (A Coy) and two platoons in support (C Coy). Three of the four front platoons assembled on a line from Q29c 55-00 to Q29c 60-50, and the fourth moved down C.T. running into RAVINE at Q29c 8-8. The attack was preceded by a detailed artillery barrage which was very weak and ineffective. The advance of the 10th Battn NOTTS. & DERBY REGT. on the right was held up by a heavy T.M. barrage, and also enfilade M.G. fire, and they fell back to Q35b 1-7. This left the right flank of the 10th Battn WEST YORKSHIRE REGT unprotected, and they were obliged to withdraw.	
		9 AM.	At 9 AM. the line ran Q29c 2-3 to Q29c 5-0, and the 10th Battn NOTTS. & DERBY REGT. held from Q29c 5-0 to Q35b 1-7. The situation remained unchanged for the remainder of the day. CAPT. P. HOWE, M.C. "A" Coy was in command of the counter-attacking force of the	

A5834 Wt. W4973/M687 750,000 8/16 D. D. & L. Ltd. Forms/C.2118/13.

[illegible] Major

IV.

Army Form C. 2118.

WAR DIARY
or
INTELLIGENCE SUMMARY. 10th (S) Battn WEST YORKSHIRE REGT.

(Erase heading not required.)

Instructions regarding War Diaries and Intelligence Summaries are contained in F. S. Regs., Part II. and the Staff Manual respectively. Title pages will be prepared in manuscript.

Place	Date	Hour	Summary of Events and Information	Remarks and references to Appendices
MESNIL	22/4/18		10th Battn WEST YORKSHIRE REGT. During the whole of these operations the Battn had the following casualties. Lieut F.D. DAMS missing, (21-4-18) Temp Lieut J.R. KING Killed, (22-4-18) Temp. 2nd Lieut. S. MOULSON wounded, (22-4-18) Temp 2nd Lieut. M. DAYSH Killed, (23-4-18) and 77 O.R. Killed wounded and missing.	
	23/4/18		On the 23rd the 50th Infantry Brigade was relieved by the 52nd Infantry Brigade, and	
		9 P.M.	went into Divisional Reserve. The Battn was relieved at 9 P.M. by the 10th	
FORCEVILLE			LANCASHIRE FUSILIERS and marched into billets at FORCEVILLE.	
			CAPT. T.F.G. CARLESS (S/R) joined the Battn.	
	24/4/18		Temp. 2nd Lieut. H. APPLEYARD joined the Battn.	
	25/4/18		On the 25th Lieut. Col. G.K. BUTT took over the command of the Battn from Lieut Col. W.E. THOMAS, M.C. who became Second in Command and reverted to the rank of Major.	
			The undermentioned officers joined the Battn. Temp. 2nd Lieut R. CLEGG, Temp 2nd Lieut. J.M. COMPSTON, Temp 2nd Lieut T.M. BEEVERS, Temp. 2nd Lieut. E. COTTERILL, Temp. 2nd Lieut. H.S. THORNSBY.	
			A and B Coys moved out of FORCEVILLE and bivouaced at P27 a-b.	
	26/4/18	7 P.M.	On the 26th at 7 P.M. the Battn relieved the 6th DORSETSHIRE REGT. in the ENGLEBELMER-	

A5834 Wt. W4973/M687 750,000 8/16 D. D. & L. Ltd. Forms/C.2118/13.

V.

Army Form C. 2118.

Instructions regarding War Diaries and Intelligence Summaries are contained in F. S. Regs., Part II. and the Staff Manual respectively. Title pages will be prepared in manuscript.

WAR DIARY
or
INTELLIGENCE SUMMARY. 10th (S) Battn WEST YORKSHIRE REGT.

(Erase heading not required.)

Place	Date	Hour	Summary of Events and Information	Remarks and references to Appendices
ENGLEBELMER-MILLENCOURT LINE	26/4/18	7PM.	MILLENCOURT LINE and its vicinity. Battn H.2. were at P 30 c 8-2. A, B, and C Coys were bivouaced in P36 and Q31, and D Coy in Q 20a.	
	28/4/18		On the 28th Temp. 2nd Lieut. C. HOLMES joined the Battn.	
MESNIL	29/4/18	8.30PM	On the 29th the Battn relieved the 7th Battn BORDER REGT. at 8.30 P.M. in the LEFT SUB-SECTOR, RIGHT BRIGADE. A Coy left front. B Coy right front. C and D Coys in reserve. Battn. H.2. were at Q28 d 2-1. The line ran from Q35 c 3-8 to Q29 c 8-0. MAJOR W.E. THOMAS, M.C. left the Battn to become Second in Command of the 7th EAST YORKSHIRE REGT. MAJOR N. GIBSON, M.C. joined the Battn as Second in Command.	
	30/4/18		The Battn was in the line.	

G. H. Butt Lt Col.
Comdg
10th West Yorkshire Regt
2-5-1918

A5834 Wt. W4973/M687 750,000 8/16 D. D. & L. Ltd. Forms/C.2118/13.

Page 1

Instructions regarding War Diaries and Intelligence Summaries are contained in F. S. Regs., Part II. and the Staff Manual respectively. Title pages will be prepared in manuscript.

WAR DIARY for MAY – 1918
or
~~INTELLIGENCE SUMMARY.~~
(Erase heading not required.)

Army Form C. 2118.

10th (S) Bn West Yorkshire Regt

Vol 29

Place	Date	Hour	Summary of Events and Information	Remarks and references to Appendices
MESNIL	1-5-18		The Battalion was in the line in the left SUB-SECTOR RIGHT-BRIGADE	
"	2-5-18		disposition as follows – A Coy. LEFT FRONT	
	"		B Coy. RIGHT FRONT	
	"		C and D Coys RESERVE	
	2-5-18		Headquarters Q28 d 2.1	
MESNIL	3-5-18		The Battalion in the line. T/Capt. P. HOWE M.C. Wounded.	
	4-5-18		The Battalion was relieved in the front line and went into reserve at P.24a.	P.24a [illegible]
"	"		Owing to a re adjustment of the Brigade frontage and general dispositions	
	"		the Battalion was relieved as follows:	
and	"		B and part of A Coy were relieved by the 6th Dorsetshire Regt.	
	"		Remainder of A Coy by 10th Notts and Derbyshire Regt.	
	"		C Coy were relieved by 4th East Yorkshire Regt.	
	"		Owing to the new dispositions the accommodation vacated by D Coy in reserve	
	"		was not taken over.	
	"		A. B. and D Coys took over accommodation at P.24a C Coy at P.36 d.	
FORCEVILLE	4/5/18		Battalion Headquarters at FORCEVILLE Billet 43. C Coy was kept under	
			orders of the O.C. 4th East Yorkshire Regt. whilst at P.36d.	
	5/5/18		Battalion Headquarters moved to bank at P.24a.	P.24a

D. D. & L., London, E.C. (A8004) Wt W1771/M2031 750,000 5/17 Sch. 52 Forms/C2118/14

PAGE 2

Instructions regarding War Diaries and Intelligence Summaries are contained in F. S. Regs., Part II. and the Staff Manual respectively. Title pages will be prepared in manuscript.

WAR DIARY

or

~~INTELLIGENCE SUMMARY.~~

(Erase heading not required.)

6 MAY 1918

10th (S) West Yorkshire Regt.

Army Form C. 2118.

Place	Date	Hour	Summary of Events and Information	Remarks and references to Appendices
FORCEVILLE	6-5-18		The Battalion accommodated at P.24.a	P.24.a
	7-5-18			
LEALVILLERS	8-5-18		The 50th Infantry Brigade was relieved by the 190th Infantry Brigade.	O.O. attached (App. [illegible])
			The 10th S. W. Yorkshire Regt. was relieved by the Artists Rifles	
			The relief commenced at 11.0 AM for A B and D Coys and at dusk for C Coy.	
			A B and D Coys took over accommodation at LEALVILLERS vacated by 10th Lancashire	
			Fusiliers. C Coy on relief proceeded with the 7th East Yorkshire Regt to	
	8-5-18		billets in FORCEVILLE.	
ARQUEVES	9-5-18		A B and D Coys moved at 10.30 AM to ARQUEVES where they were joined at	O.O. attached (App. [illegible])
"			2.45 pm by C Coy. The whole battalion was accommodated in billets	
"			and tents in ARQUEVES.	
"	10-5-18		Battalion General Cleaning up and Training	
"	11-5-18		Battalion Training	
"	12-5-18			
"	13-5-18		T/Capt. A.F.G. ANDERSON rejoined the battalion from 6 months home service in England	
			and took over the duties of Adjutant from T/Capt. A.S. WILLIAMS M.C.	
"	14-5-18		T/Capt. A.S. WILLIAMS M.C. left the battalion to join the 7th East Yorkshire Regt	
"	15-5-18		The Battalion supplied a party of 200 ORs working strength to work on MAILLY	
			- ENGLEBELMER line under supervision of the 93rd Field Company R.E.	

D. D. & L., London, E.C.
(A8004) Wt. W1771/M2031 750,000 5/17 Sch. 52 Forms/C2118/14

PAGE 3

Instructions regarding War Diaries and Intelligence Summaries are contained in F. S. Regs., Part II. and the Staff Manual respectively. Title pages will be prepared in manuscript.

WAR DIARY for MAY. 1918

~~INTELLIGENCE SUMMARY.~~

(*Erase heading not required.*) 10th (S) Bn West Yorkshire Regt

Army Form C. 2118.

Place	Date	Hour	Summary of Events and Information	Remarks and references to Appendices
ARQUEVES	16/5/18		The 50th Infantry Brigade was inspected by the Corps Commander at 10.0 AM	
"	17/5/18		Battalion Training	
"	18/5/18		The Battalion supplied a party of 400 O.R. working strength to work in	
"			MAILLY - ENGLEBELMER area under supervision of the 93rd Field Company R.E.	
"	19-5-18		Battalion Training	
"	20-5-18		"	
"	21-5-18		The Battalion took part in a Brigade Tactical Scheme in the FORCEVILLE	
"			area. The following officers joined battalion:	
"			T/2/Lt W. A. HIRST	
"			" J. P. LAWSON	
"			" A. B. P. WOOD	
"			" J. KIRK	
"			" A. J. THOMAS	
"	22-5-18		The Army Commander inspected the Battalion in a tactical exercise on the range at T.5.b in the afternoon	
"	23-5-18		Brigade Tactical Scheme. 50th Infantry Brigade Horse and Transport Show in the afternoon in which the Battalion won the prize for the highest aggregate marks.	
"	24-5-18		Battalion Training.	
"	25-5-18		"	
"	26-5-18		The Battalion moved from ARQUEVES to ACHEUX WOOD and came tactical under	O.O. attached (App. 6)

D. D. & L., London, E.C. (A8004) Wt W1771/M2031 750,000 5/17 Sch. 52 Forms/C2118/14

PAGE II

Instructions regarding War Diaries and Intelligence Summaries are contained in F. S. Regs., Part II. and the Staff Manual respectively. Title pages will be prepared in manuscript.

WAR DIARY MAY– 1918

or

~~INTELLIGENCE SUMMARY.~~

(Erase heading not required.) 10th West Yorkshire Regt.

Army Form C. 2118.

Place	Date	Hour	Summary of Events and Information	Remarks and references to Appendices
ACHEUX WOOD.	26-5-18		of G. O. C. 17th Division. The 50th Infantry Brigade relieved the 35th Bde. in the left Sector. The Battalion moved up from ACHEUX WOOD at 10-0 P.M. and relieved the 9th Essex Regt. in the Right Sub-Sector.	O.O. attached (Appx. B.)
AUCHONVILLERS	"		Relief completed by 2-15 A.M.	
	27-5-18		The Battalion was in the line. Day quiet. Usual Artillery fire	
	28-5-18		– – do –	
	29-5-18		– – do –	
	30-5-18		1/2/Lt. T. W. BEEVERS and 4 O.R. wounded whilst bombing enemy sap.	
	31-5-18		50th Infantry Brigade relieved by 51st Infantry Brigade in the line. The relief of the Battalion by the 7th Lincolnshire Regt. commenced at 10-0 P.M.	O.O. attached (Appx. C)
			1-6-18 G. W. Butt Lieut. Col. Comdg. 10th West Yorkshire Regt.	

D. D. & L., London, E.C. (A8104) Wt W1771/M2031 750,000 5/17 Sch. 52 Forms/C2118/14

No 8.

Operation Order by SECRET.

Lt Col W. K. BUTT. App. 1.

4.5.18. Commanding 'HECTOR' Copy No. 2.

Ref Map Sheet 57 D. S.E. 1/40,000

1 The Brigade Front will be re-adjusted to night 4th/5th ~~April~~ May 1918.

The new Northern Brigade Boundary runs:-

Outpost Line – Q.35.a.95.80.
Main Line of Resistance – Q.35.a.20.75.
Support Line Q.34.b.80.80

The West Yorkshire Regt will be relieved as per attached table – Relief to commence at 9.0pm.

On completion of relief Companies will occupy accomodation as shewn in attached table and will be in RESERVE.

The portions of A. Coy which are at present N of the new Brigade Boundary will be relieved by the Lancashire Fusiliers and will close up to the Right, so that their Left flanks rest in the boundary. The posts of "A" Companies outpost line, will go into MAIN LINE of RESISTANCE when relieved, and will proceed out of line with remainder of 'A' Company. Guides for these portions will be stationed at extreme left flank at 8.10pm.

2 Guides. One guide per platoon and one for Coy H.Qrs will be stationed at extreme right flank of our line to guide Dorsetshire Regt in at 8.30pm. One Officer and two N.C.Os for Hd Qrs and one Officer and two N.C.Os per Company will assemble at B.H.Q at 2-0pm and will proceed to take over accomodation, stores etc, as under:-

A, B, and D. Coys will take over accomodation in banks at P.26 and P.27.

C. Company will take over from Sherwoods in Road at P.36 d.

3 Companies will march off independently when relieved. 200 yards will be maintained between platoons.

4 Trench stores Defence schemes and programmes of Work will be carefully handed over and receipts rendered to Orderly room by 10.0am 5th Inst

The Dorsetshire Regt will take over Trench stores of D Coy & Battn H.Qrs.

5 Officers mess kits, company cooking utensils and all water tins, whether full or empty, will be dumped at Ration dump by 8.0pm. The Transport Officer will arrange to collect and deliver to companies

6. Lewis Gun limbers will be stationed at Ration dump at 10.0 pm. Lewis guns + magazines will be loaded at this point and conveyed to new dispositions. Two L.G. N.C.O^s per company will march in rear of limbers and take charge of loading and unloading guns

7 Completion of relief will be reported to B.H.Q as per attached table.

8. Acknowledge.

A.S. Wellbourns
Capt.
A/Adjutant
Hector.

Company	Relieved by	Proceed to	Take over from	Completion of relief reported by CODE WORD
A PORTION REMAINDER	LANCS FUS DORSETS	Banks at P.26 and P.27	—	NEXT TUESDAY
B	DORSETS	— do —	—	— do —
C	1 Company E. YORKS	Road in P. 36. d.	SHERWOODS	THURSDAY AFTER NOON
D	—	Banks at P26 and P27	—	RATS.

No 9 Operation Order by SECRET
Lieut Col G. K. BUTT
7-5-18. Comdg 10th West Yorkshire Regt. Copy No 1.

REF MAP SHEET 57D 1/40.000

App. 2.

1. The 50th Infantry Brigade will be relieved in the line by the 190th Infantry Brigade on the night 8/9th May 1918.

The 10th West Yorkshire Regt will be relieved by the Artists Rifles. as follows:-

"A" Coy 10th West Yorkshire Regt relieved by "A" Coy Artists Rifles.
"B" " " " " " " "B" " "
"C" " " " " " " "D" " "
"D" " " " " " " "C" " "

Relief will commence at 11.0. am. for "A" "B" and "D" Companies and Battn Head Quarters and at dusk for "C" Company. On completion of relief the Battalion less one Company will march to LEALVILLERS via Cross Country track. Companies will march off independently. 200 yards interval will be maintained between platoons and 500 yards between Companies.

2. "C" Company 10th West Yorkshire Regt, when relieved will report relief complete to O.C. 7th East Yorkshire Regt and will proceed with that Unit to billets in FORCEVILLE, proceeding on following day to ARQUEVES, there rejoining their own Unit.

O.C "C" Company will get in touch with and act on the orders of O.C 7th East Yorkshire Regt as to relief and sending billeting parties to FORCEVILLE. Billets in ARQUEVES will be arranged from this Head Quarters.

3. GUIDES. O.C "C" Company will detail 1 guide per platoon and 1 for Coy Head Quarters to report to Battn Head Quarters at 10-0 am. tomorrow 8th inst.,

O.C's "A" "B" and "D" Companies will each detail 1 guide to report to Battn Head Quarters at 10.15 am. tomorrow 8th inst,

4. BILLETING PARTIES. One Officer and 2 N.C.O's per Company and one Officer and one N.C.O for Battn Head Quarters will assemble at Battn Head Quarters at 8.0 am. tomorrow. They will proceed to LEALVILLERS to take over billets occupied by the Lancashire Fusiliers.

Guides will be provided from these parties to meet Companies at Cross Roads O.23 b. 70.45 to guide Companies to their billets. The same parties will proceed to ARQUEVES on the 9th inst and report to Capt K.D. THIRSK, M.C., Town Majors Office at 9-0. am.

5. Lists of Trench Stores to be handed over will be rendered to Battn Head Quarters by 8-0 am tomorrow 8th inst.,

Certificates of cleanliness of vacated area will be obtained from relieving Unit and rendered to Battn Head Quarters by 5.0 pm 8th inst,

6. The Transport Officer will arrange to send Lewis Gun limbers to Company Head Quarters by 8-0 am tomorrow, 8th inst, Limbers will march in rear of Companies. The Transport Officer will also arrange to collect mobile reserve of tools at 8-0 am tomorrow, 8th inst,, Officers mess kits, valises and all water tins, whether full or empty will be dumped at "D" Company's Head Quarters by 9-0 am The Transport Officer will arrange to collect. The whole of the Transport will join the Battalion at LEALVILLERS on the morning of the 8th inst.,

7. DRESS Battle kit, Water bottles filled. Greatcoats will be rolled and carried over the haversack at the back The carrying of parcels and sandbags on the march is strictly forbidden.

8. The Intelligence Officer will hand over all Maps and Aeroplane photographs relative to this Sector and render receipts to Battn Head Quarters

9. O.C. Companies will report to Battn Head Quarters when their Companies are all in billets in LEALVILLERS.

10. ACKNOWLEDGE.

Copy No 1. War Diary
" 2. C.O.
" 3. O/c Coys "A"
" 4 " "B"
" 5 " "C"
" 6 " "D"
" 7 Q.M. and T.O.
" 8 O/c 7th E. YORKSHIRE REGT
" 9 R.S.M.
" 10 Retained

(Sd) A.S. WILLIAMS, Captain
A/Adjutant
10th West Yorkshire Regt

8.5.18. No. 10 Operation Order by SECRET.
Lt Col G.K. BUTT. Copy No 1.
Commanding 10th West Yorkshire Regt.
REF MAP. SHEET. 57/D. 1/40,000.

App. 3.

1. The Battalion less 1 Company will move to ARQUEVES, tomorrow 9th inst, via BELLE EGLISE.

2. STARTING POINT. O.17. d.00.00.

3. Companies will march off in the following order:-

H.Qrs
A. Coy
B. -
D. -

200 yards distance to be maintained between Companies. Head of column to pass starting point at 10.30 a m

4. DRESS. Battle Order. Water bottles filled. Great coats rolled and carried over haversack at the back.

5. Transport will march 200 yards in rear of last Company.

6. O/C. A Coy will detail 2 N.C.O.s to arrange billets for "C" Coy. They will proceed to ARQUEVES with the billeting party already detailed.

Officers i/c A B & D Companies billeting parties will arrange to have guides stationed at Cross Roads O.8.d.60.30 at 11.15 AM to guide Companies to their billets

Guides for C. Company to be stationed at same point at 2.45 PM.

7. Acknowledge.

(SD) A.S WILLIAMS. Capt
A/Adjutant
10th West Yorkshire Regt

2/Lt CWS Spencer.

IO

SECRET

No 14. West Yorkshire Regt Copy No 10

26-5-18. Operation Order. App. 4.

REFCE MAP 57d. 1/40,000.

1. The 50th Infantry Brigade will relieve the 35th Infantry Brigade in the left sector of the 12th Division Front on the night of the 26/27th May 1918.

2. The 50th Infantry Brigade will move to ACHEUX WOOD on 26th May and on arrival there will come under the tactical control of the G.O.C. 12th Division.

3 The West Yorkshire Regiment will move from ARQUEVES to ACHEUX WOOD (exact position will be notified later) on the morning of the 26th May.

Starting Point. — Road junction O.8.d.7.2.

Order of March. — H.Qrs, "A", "B", "C" & "D" Coys.

Time. — H.Qrs will pass the Starting Point at 10-10. a.m.

Route — LEALVILLERS – thence by track "C" to ACHEUX WOOD.

A party consisting of one Officer per Company & one N.C.O. from H.Qrs & one from each Company will reconnoitre this route tomorrow, 25th instant.

The party will report at Orderly Room at 9 am for instructions.

4. Administrative Instructions will be issued later

5. Advance Parties.

(a) A party consisting of 2/LIEUT. E COTTERILL and 5 runners (one from H.Qrs & one from each Company) will proceed to the right sub sector of the left sector of the line tomorrow, 25th instant & will report to the O.C. 9th Essex Regt and will remain there until after the relief.

Copy No. 10

West Yorkshire Regiment
Operation Order No 16

App. 6.

SECRET.

REFERENCE MAP. 57d 1/40.000

1. The West Yorkshire Regt will relieve the Essex Regt. in the right sub sector of the left sector of the Divisional line on the night of the 26th/27th May.

Dispositions — Front line 5 Platoons; Support line 7 Platoons; One Company in Reserve – distributed as follows:-

Front line — "C" Coy on the right – 3 platoons holding 3 platoon posts.
do. — "D" Coy on the left – 2 platoons holding 2 platoon posts.
Support line — The remaining platoon of "C" Coy on the right.
do — "B" Coy in the centre.
do — Two Platoons of "D" Coy on the left.
Reserve — "A" Company will occupy the trench (which at present forms the battle position of one of the Companies of the Cambridgeshire Regt) EAST of AUCHONVILLERS running from the communication trench at approximately Q.9.d.8.6 to Q.9.b.6.4.

2. Companies will proceed from ACHEUX WOOD, starting at 10-pm, by platoons at 200 yards interval in the order H.Qrs. "C" "D" "B" & "A" Companies.

Route via "C" track

Guides of the Essex Regt will be at the Church in MAILLY-MAILLET at 11-30pm to lead each Platoon to its position in the line.

3. Completion of reliefs will be notified to Battalion H.Qrs at AUCHONVILLERS STATION – Q.8.b.6.0. – by the following code phrases:-

"A" Coy — No thanks.
"B" Coy — One vacancy
"C" Coy — Four tins.
"D" Coy — Major Brown.

Relief to be completed by 2-30 am on 27th instant.

Copy No. 1 War Diary.
2 C.O.
3. Major Gibson MC.
4 O/C Coys. A
5 – B.
6 – C
7 – D
8 QM & TO
9. R.S.M
10 [illegible]

Sd. A.F.G. ANDERSON Capt
Adjutant
West Yorkshire Regiment

1st Yorkshire Regiment Second

No 1. Operation Order.

31.5.18.

Ref Map. 57d [illegible]

App. 7.

1 The Battalion will be relieved on the night of 31st May/1st June 1918 by the [illegible]

The Relief will commence [illegible]

(a) 'A' Coy will be relieved by 'A' Coy [illegible] Regt.
'B' " 'B' "
'C' " 'C' "
'D' " 'D' "

[illegible]

(b) Completion of relief will be notified to Battalion H.Q. by Companies as follows

'A' Coy	"	"One N.C.O"
'B'	"	"One more"
'C'	"	"Three Only"
'D'	"	"Five more"

(C) All stores, reserve water, and maps, and [illegible] documents relating to this sector will be handed over to the incoming Battalion & receipts forwarded to Bn H.Q. by 9 am 1st June

(d) All TOOLS - both Battalion property & [illegible] to the Brigade [illegible] will be handed at Bn HQrs and handed over to the Brigade Major by [illegible]. These must be [illegible] by [illegible] parties

(e) Companies will furnish one guide per Platoon for the incoming unit who will rendezvous at Bn HQrs at 7.30

II After relief the battalion will be moved to the PURPLE LINE and take over the positions now occupied by the Lincolnshire Regiment

(a) Companies will proceed independently on relief & will report arrival in the PURPLE line to Bn HQrs

A Coy will take over positions vacated by A Coy Lincolnshire Regt
B " B "
C C
D D

(b) Advance parties of one officer, one NCO and [illegible] runners per Company will reconnoitre their positions in the PURPLE LINE this afternoon and will take over stores from the Lincolnshire Regiment. The other [illegible] will return to [illegible]

[illegible] NCOs [illegible]

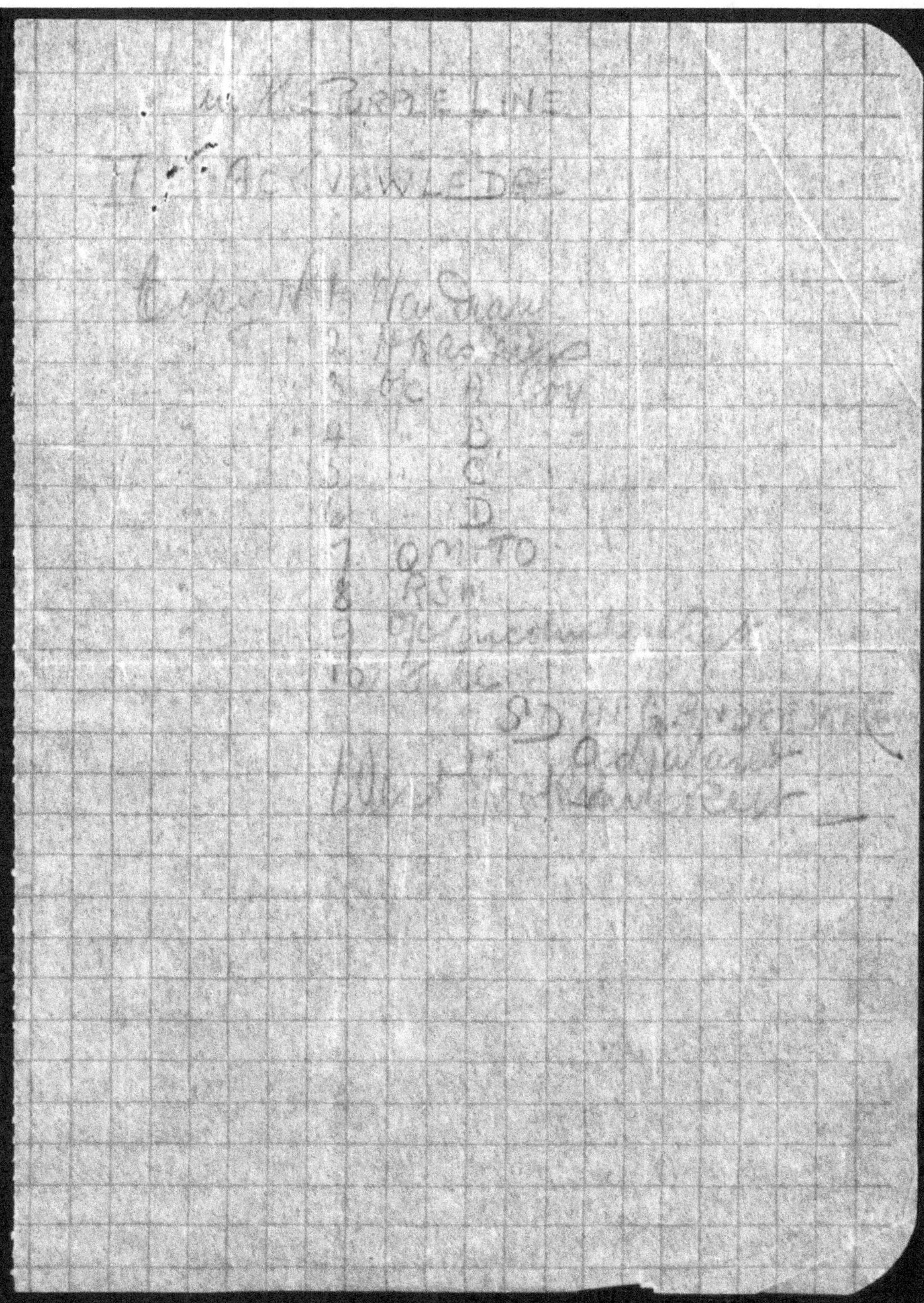

[illegible] PURPLE LINE

[illegible] ACKNOWLEDGE

Copy No 1 [illegible]
2 [illegible]
3 OC A Coy
4 B
5 C
6 D
7 QM TO
8 RSM
9 [illegible]
10 [illegible]

SD [illegible]
Adjutant
[illegible]

for War Diary

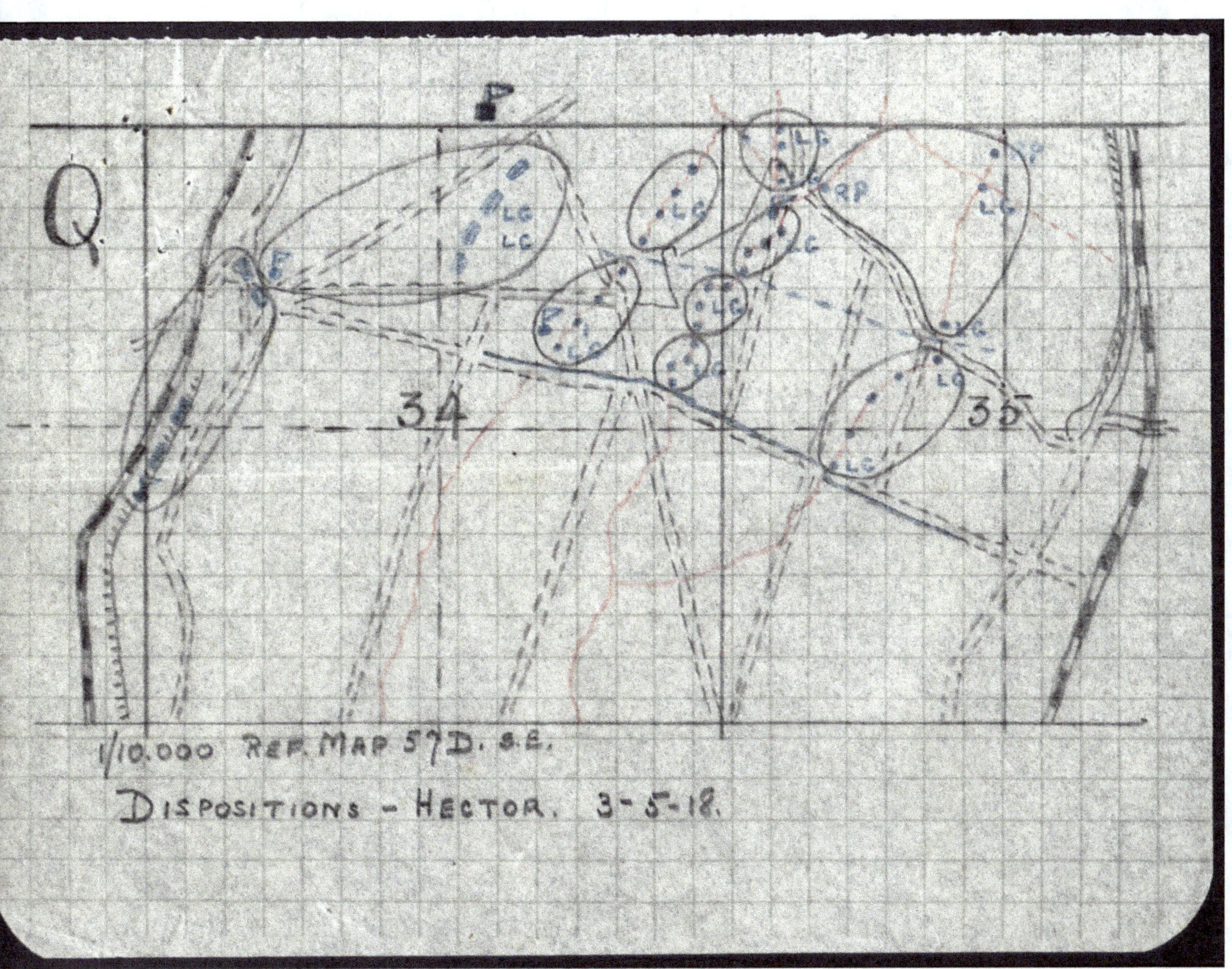
Q
P
F
LC
LC
RP
34
35
1/10.000 REF. MAP 57D. S.E.
DISPOSITIONS - HECTOR. 3-5-18.

Copy No 2 West Yorkshire Regiment SECRET

No 17 Operation Order 31 5 18

Ref Map. 57d. 1/40.000.

I The Battalion will be relieved on the night of 31st May/1st June 1918 by the Lincolnshire Regt.
The Relief will commence at 10 pm.

(a) "A" Coy will be relieved by "A" Coy Lincolnshire Regt
"B" " " " "B" " "
"C" " " " "C" " "
"D" " " " "D" " "
in the positions at present occupied.

(b) Completion of relief will be notified to Battalion HQrs by Companies as follows –
"A" Coy "One N.C.O."
"B" " "One more"
"C" " "Three only"
"D" " "Five more"

(c) All stores, reserve water, and maps, and "Special" documents relating to this sector will be handed over to the incoming Battalion and receipts forwarded to Bn HQrs by 5 am 1st June.

(d) All TOOLS – both Battalion property and those belonging to the Brigade will be dumped at Bn HQrs. and handed over to the Regtl Sergt Major by 5 pm to-day. These must be carried down by small parties.

(e) Companies will furnish one guide per Platoon for the incoming unit who will rendezvous at Bn HQrs at 7.30 pm.

II After relief the Battalion will proceed to the PURPLE LINE and take over the positions now occupied by the Lincolnshire Regiment

(a) Companies will proceed independently on relief and will report arrival in the PURPLE Line to Bn HQrs.
"A" Coy will take over positions vacated by "A" Coy Lincolnshire Regt
"B" " " " "B"
"C" " " " "C"
"D" " " " "D"

(b) Advance parties of one Officer, one NCO and one runner per Company will reconnoitre their positions in the PURPLE LINE this afternoon and will take over stores from the Lincolnshire Regt. The Officers and runners will return to guide their Company out on relief and the N.C.O.s will remain in the PURPLE, line.

Copy No 1		War Diary
"	" 2	HQrs Mess
"	" 3	O/C 'A' Coy
"	" 4	" B "
"	" 5	" 'C' "
"	" 6	" D "
"	" 7	QM + TO.
"	" 8	ASM
"	" 9	O/C Lincolnshire Regt.
"	" 10	File

A. F. A. Andrews
Capt.
Adjutant
West Yorkshire Regiment

10th West Yorkshire Regt

Page 1

June 1918

Army Form C. 2118.

WAR DIARY
or
~~INTELLIGENCE SUMMARY.~~
(Erase heading not required.)

Instructions regarding War Diaries and Intelligence Summaries are contained in F. S. Regs., Part II. and the Staff Manual respectively. Title pages will be prepared in manuscript.

Vol 30

Place	Date	Hour	Summary of Events and Information	Remarks and references to Appendices
MAILLY MAILLET	1/6/18		The battalion was relieved in the right sub sector of the left Brigade Sector of Divisional Front by 7th LINCOLNSHIRE Regt. Relief completed by 12.30 am. The battalion took up position in the Purple System E. of MAILLY-MAILLET.	Q.6.& 5.0. [illegible] Q.7.2.7.4
PURPLE SYSTEM	2/6/18		A working party of 200 was supplied to dig a cable trench from BEAUSSART to MAILLY-MAILLET.	
	3/6/18		2Lt P.H. HART joined the battalion. A working party of 200 was supplied to dig cable trench from BEAUSSART to MAILLY MAILLET.	
	4/6/18		The battalion supplied the same working party	
	5/6/18		Lt G.T.E. HALL joined battalion. The battalion supplied the same working party	
	6/6/18		The battalion supplied the same working party	
	7/6/18		Cable Trench completed.	
	8/6/18		The battalion was in reserve to the 7th EAST YORKSHIRE REGT and the 6th DORSETSHIRE REGT for the night raid on the enemy lines, and supplied two parties to escort the prisoners to BEAUSSART.	
	9/6/18		2Lt R.G. JONES & 2Lt B.J. HASEMANN joined battalion.	
ADVANCED FORWARD ZONE	10/6/18		The battalion relieved the 9th DUKE OF WELLINGTONS REGT in the right sector of the Divisional Front.	Q.5.[illegible] [illegible]

10th West Yorkshire Regt

Army Form C. 2118.

WAR DIARY
or
~~INTELLIGENCE SUMMARY.~~
(*Erase heading not required.*)

Instructions regarding War Diaries and Intelligence Summaries are contained in F. S. Regs., Part II. and the Staff Manual respectively. Title pages will be prepared in manuscript.

Page 2
June 1918.

Place	Date	Hour	Summary of Events and Information	Remarks and references to Appendices
ADVANCED FORWARD ZONE	11/6/18		Trenches. Relief complete 2.30 AM	
"	12/6/18		Battalion in the line	
"	13/6/18		Battalion in the line	
PURPLE SYSTEM	14/6/18		The battalion was relieved by the 7th EAST YORKSHIRE REGT in the line owing to	
"	and		re-distribution of the Brigade System and proceeded to the Right Sector of the	Q.13.b.2.8.
	15/6/18		Purple System. Relief complete 12 mid night.	O.O. No 19 & 20 attached
	16/6/18		Working party supplied for the front line	
	17/6/18		Working party supplied for the front line	
ADVANCED FORWARD ZONE	18/6/18		The battalion relieved the 7th EAST YORKSHIRE REGT in the Advanced Forward Zone of	
			right sector	Q.15.c.2.4
"	19/6/18		Battalion in line. Relief complete 1.0 am.	O.O. No 21 attached
"	20/6/18		Battalion in the line	
"	21/6/18		Battalion in the line	
"	22/6/18		Battalion in the line	
ACHEUX WOOD	23/6/18		The battalion was relieved by the HOOD battalion 63rd Division in the Advanced	Q.11.c.2.3
	"		Forward Zone of the right Sector and proceeded to ACHEUX WOOD. Relief	P.13.a Central
"			complete 1.30 am. Battalion in ACHEUX WOOD by 3.30 am.	O.O. No 22 attached.
ACHEUX WOOD	24/6/18		Battalion paraded 6.30 am and marched to RUBEMPRE, arriving 11.0 am	
			Total casualties during tour Killed 7. Died of Wounds 2. Wounded 45 Missing Nil	O.O. No 23 attached

D. D. & L., London, E.C.
(A8004) Wt W1771/M2031 750,000 5/17 Sch. 52 Forms/C2118/14

10th West Yorkshire Regt.

Army Form C. 2118.

Instructions regarding War Diaries and Intelligence Summaries are contained in F. S. Regs., Part II. and the Staff Manual respectively. Title pages will be prepared in manuscript.

Page 3.
June 1918

WAR DIARY
or
~~INTELLIGENCE SUMMARY.~~
(Erase heading not required.)

Place	Date	Hour	Summary of Events and Information	Remarks and references to Appendices
RUBEMPRE	25/6/18		Ceremonial parade by G.O.C. Brigade for presentation of medals.	WR
	26/6/18		Battalion training. T/Lt W.H. CLARK joined battalion.	WR
	27/6/18		Battalion training. A party of officers went forward to reconnoitre positions in the Brown and Purple System.	WR
	28/6/18		Battalion training. A party of officers went forward to reconnoitre positions in the Brown & Purple System.	WR
	29/6/18		Battalion Training. Major McGavin Greig & 2Lt E.G. Addington joined Battalion.	WR
RUBEMPRE	30/6/18		Sunday. Brigade Divine Service.	WR

G.H. Pott
Lieut Col.
Commanding 10th West Yorkshire Regiment

D. D. & L., London, E.C.
(A8004) Wt W1771/M2031 750,000 5/17 Sch. 52 Forms/C2118/14

24.6.16 Operation Order No 23. Secret

West Yorkshire Regiment.

Refce Map. 57D 1/40.000.

1 The Battalion will march to billets at RUBEMPRE today.

(a) Order of March. Band. Hdqrs.
A. B. C. and D Coys.

(b) Starting Point. P.14.C. 25. 95.

(c) Time 7-0 am.

(d) Route VARENNES road to "C" track. thence through O.24.C. 2.4; O.22. C. 0.4, O.19.C. 6.3. to O.35. central; HERISSART; & thence by road.

An interval of 200 yards between platoons will be observed as far as LEALVILLERS.

2 The strictest march discipline will be maintained throughout the march. No man will fall out without the written permission of an Officer.

3 The area occupied by the Battalion in ACHEUX WOOD must be cleaned up before starting.

SD A.F.G. ANDERSON Capt
Adjt
West Yorkshire Regiment

Battalion after posts have been taken over.
Each relieving patrol will be led out by an N.C.O of this Battalion from the post from which it starts.

(6) All dixies, cooking utensils & empty water tins will be brought to the Dump by 9.0 pm ready to be taken away by the Transport.

(7) LEWIS GUNS. The Transport Officer will arrange for limbers to be at the dumps to take away Lewis Guns and drums as follows:-
Battalion Dump 'B' & 'D' Coys & Hd Qrs
DORSET Dump 'A' & 'C' Coys.
Special care must be taken that no drums are left behind.

(8) FEET. Company & Platoon Commanders will exercise great care in the inspection of feet tomorrow in view of the possibility of a march the following day.

4. The Quartermaster will allot the area in ACHEUX WOOD P.14.a to Companies & Hd Qrs and will station guides at P.14.a 8.8 to guide the parties to their respective areas.

5. Company Commanders will report their arrival in ACHEUX WOOD to Bn. Hd Qrs.

6 ACKNOWLEDGE.

Copy No 1. War Diary
" 2. Hd Qrs Mess.
" 3. O/c Coys. A
" 4. " B
" 5. " C.
" 6. " D
" 7. QM & T.O.
" 8. O/c HOOD Batt.
" 9. R.S.M.
" 10. File.

(Sd) A.F.G. ANDERSON, Captain,
Adjutant,
West Yorkshire Regt.

Copy No.

Operation Order. No 18 SECRET

West Yorkshire Regiment 9th June 1918.

REFCE. MAP. 57d 1/40 000

I The 50th Inf. Brigade will relieve the 52nd Inf Brigade in the RIGHT Sector of the Divisional Front on the night 10th/11th June 1918.

Relief to be complete by 3.0 am 11th June.

II The Battalion will relieve the Duke of Wellington's Regiment in the right sub sector as follows.

"A" Coy on the right will relieve "D" Coy Duke of Wellingtons Regt
"B" " " left " " "A" " "
"C" " in Support " " "B" " "
"D" " in reserve " " "C" " "

(a) Companies will move off from present positions in the order - HQrs. "A", "B", "C" & "D" Coys at the following times :-

HQrs.	10-15 pm.
"A" Coy.	10 25 pm.
"B" "	10 35 pm
"C" "	10 45 pm.
"D" "	11- 10 pm.

(b). One guide for each Company HQrs and one for each Platoon will be waiting at Q.15.d. 4.4. (where the Communication trench crosses the railway) to guide parties to their new positions.

(c) Completion of relief will be notified to Battalion HQrs as follows :-

"A" Coy	"NO STOVES"
"B" "	"ALL DIXIES"
"C" "	"SMALL OVENS"
"D" "	"BENZINE CANS"

III Advance Parties from each Company Consisting of the Company Commanders, one runner, and one N.C.O. per Platoon will report at the HQrs of the Duke of Wellingtons Regt - Q.15.c.3.4. at the following times :-

"A" Coy.	10.0. am.
"B" "	10.30 am.
"C" "	11.0 am.
"D" "	11.30 am.

Company Commanders & messengers will return as soon as they have reconnoitred the new positions. The N.C.O's. will remain until the arrival of their Platoons.

(2) Sergt Hubbard & a proportion of signallers will proceed to the line at 1-30 pm to take over the signal Stations.

(3) 2Lt E.COTTERILL will proceed to the HQrs. of the Duke of Wellington's Regt at 2 pm and will take over all maps, Stores, intelligence papers & copies of the defence schemes. He will report to H

Adjutant for instructions before leaving.

IV Battalion HQrs will be established at Q15.C.3.4 to which all messages should be sent.

V ACKNOWLEDGE

Copy No 1. War Diary
" " 2 HQrs Mess
" " 3 O/C A Coy
" " 4 " B "
" " 5 " C "
" " 6 " D "
" " 7 " QM & TO
" " 8 " RSM
" " 9 " O/C Duke of Wellingtons Regt
" " 10 " File

A.F.G. Andrews
Capt
Adjutant
West Yorkshire Regiment

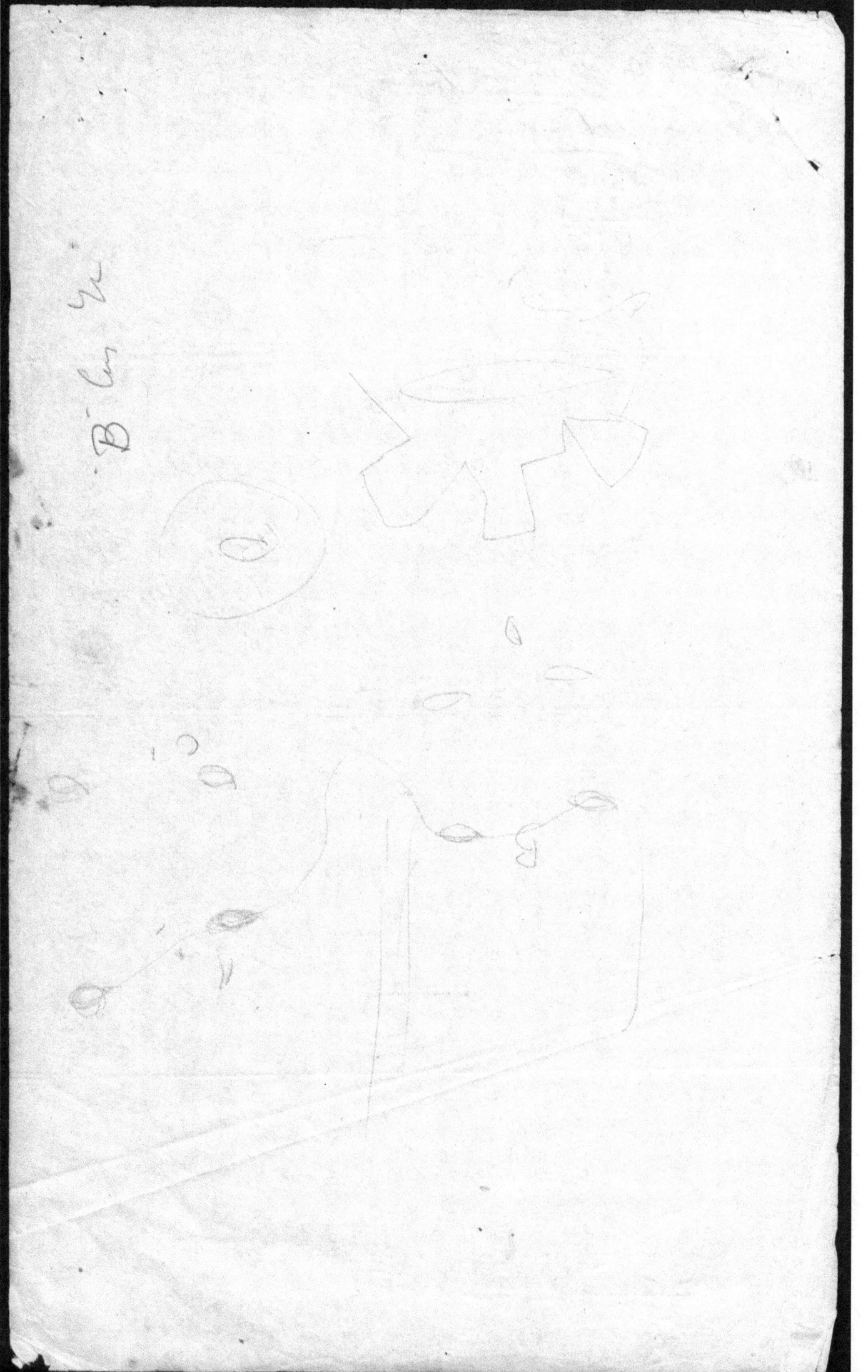

14.6.18 Secret

Copy No

Operation Order No 19.
West Yorkshire Regiment

Refce map attached.

I. Owing to a redistribution of the Brigade system the Battalion will be relieved by the East Yorkshire Regt in the advanced forward zone on the night of the 14th/15th June 1918 and will proceed to positions in the PURPLE SYSTEM in accordance with instructions to be issued later

II The relief will be carried out as follows:-

(a). One Platoon of A Coy at approximately Q.23. a. 4.9. (right front line post). will be relieved by one Platoon of D Coy East Yorkshire Regt.

One Platoon of 'A' Coy at approximately Q22. b. 7. 9. will be relieved by one platoon of D Coy East Yorkshire Regt.

The two Platoons of D Coy in approximately Q.16. d. 4. 2. and Q.16. d. 1. 2. will be relieved by two platoons of D Coy East Yorkshire Regt. i.e. 'D' Coy East Yorkshire Regt. will relieve 2 Platoons of 'A' Coy and 2 Platoons of D Coy of this Battalion.

The Coy H.Qrs at present occupied by 'A + D' Coys will be taken over by 'D' Coy East Yorkshire Regt.

(b) One Platoon of B Coy at approximately Q16. d. 6. 9. will be relieved by one Platoon of B Coy East Yorkshire Regt.

One Platoon of 'C' Coy at approximately Q.16 c. 4 3. will be relieved by one Platoon of B Coy East Yorkshire Regt.

One Platoon of C Coy at approximately Q16. c. 3. 5 will be relieved by one Platoon of 'B' Coy East Yorkshire Regt.

One Platoon of C Coy at approximately Q.16. c. 5. 8. will be relieved by one Platoon of B Coy East Yorkshire Regt. i.e. 'B' Coy East Yorkshire Regt will relieve one Platoon of B Coy & 3 Platoons of C Coy of this Battalion

The Coy HQrs at present occupied by C Coy will be taken over by 'B' Coy East Yorkshire Regt

(C) The remaining Platoons of A B C + D Coys will NOT be relieved but will proceed direct to the PURPLE SYSTEM under instructions to be issued later.

III GUIDES One guide from each Platoon and one from each Company HQrs which are being relieved will be at Q15. d 4 4 (where TRIGGER AVENUE crosses the railway) at 10-15 pm to meet the incoming parties & guide them to their posts.

IV STORES A & D Coys will hand over all trench stores, maps, documents & reserve water to D Coy East Yorkshire Regt.

'B' & C Coys will similarly hand over to B Coy East Yorkshire Regt.

All picks & shovels which are part of the Battalion mobilisation stores will be sent down to Bn HQrs by small parties in quiet periods during the day.

They must all be down by 10 pm.

V PATROLS The same patrols as ordered for last night will again be sent out tonight and will not be interfered with by the relief. These patrols will be withdrawn as soon as the two front Companies are definitely relieved.

VI Completion of relief will be notified to Battalion HQrs by the following phrases:-

'A' Coy – "One Sergeant"
'B' – "Two Corporals"
'C' – "Three Cooks"
'D' – "Four mules"

VII ACKNOWLEDGE

Sd A F G ANDERSON Capt
Adjutant
West Yorkshire Regiment

14.6.18.

Copy No

Operation Order No 20

Secret

West Yorkshire Regiment

Refce Disposition Map which will be issued later and which has been shewn to representatives of all Companies.

I

On relief by the East Yorkshire Regt. the Battalion will be disposed in the right sector of the PURPLE SYSTEM of defences as follows:-

Battalion HQrs.	Q.13.b. 2. 8.
'A' Company	Locality No 6.
'B' "	" No 4
'C' "	2 Platoons in Locality No 7 2 Platoons in Locality No 8
'D' "	3 Platoons in Locality No 9 1 Platoon in Locality No 5.

If sufficient accommodation is not available Company Commanders must select positions as near as possible to their localities in which to dispose their men until shelters can be prepared. Material for these has been indented for.

The localities however form the Battle positions in the event of attack and at least 50% of the personnel will be established in them normally

viz	No 6	2 Platoons.
	" 4	2 Platoons.
	" 7	1 Platoon
	" 8	1 Platoon
	" 9	1 Platoon.

These garrisons will maintain & hold the localities at all costs, the remaining 50% being available for counter attack.

Lewis Gun groups will be sited & disposed in depth & will be used to supplement & defend the localities.

Steps will be taken to see that the positions of the localities are not given away by undue movement in the vicinity.

II GUIDES. The officers & N.C.O^s who are reconnoitring the new positions this afternoon will return & guide their Companies on relief.

All Company Commanders will send an officer to Bn HQrs to report when their Companies have arrived & are in position

III STORES Companies will each send down an N.C.O to take over all stores in their new Company areas. These N.C.O^s will report to Capt K.S. RUDD at the new Battalion HQrs. Q.13.b.2.8. as soon as possible after 6pm

Copies of receipts rendered will be forwarded to Bn HQrs by 6 am tomorrow 15th instant

IV ACKNOWLEDGE

Sd A.F.G. AND[illegible] Capt.
Adjt West Yorkshire [illegible]

Copy No 1. Secret

Operation Order No 21
West Yorkshire Regiment

Refce Map 57D SE 1/20.000.

INTENTION

The Battalion will relieve the East Yorkshire Regt in the ADVANCED FORWARD ZONE of the Right Sector on the night 18/19th June.

INSTRUCTIONS.

1 Relief to be complete by 12 midnight

2. 'A' Coy West Yorkshire Regiment will relieve 'A' Coy East Yorks Regt
'B' " " " " " B " " "
'C' " " " " " 'C' " " "
D " " " " " D " " "

3 Companies will move off from present positions in the following order.

'A' Coy	at	9-40 pm.
'D'	"	9-50 pm
'C'	"	10-0 pm
B	"	10-10 pm
HQ	"	10-20 pm

4 ROUTE

'A' & 'C' Coys. via NEWBURY AVENUE
'D' & B " will move via TRIGGER AVENUE

5 GUIDES.

One guide per platoon and one for Coy HQ for 'A' & 'C' Coys will be at Cross-roads Q.9.C.4.2. at 9-30 pm

Guides on the same scale for 'B' & 'D' Coys will be at Q.15.C.3.4. at 9-30 pm

6. RELIEF

Completion of relief will be reported to HQ, code word being the name of the Company Commander concerned.

7 ADVANCE PARTIES consisting of one officer per Company and one N.C.O. per platoon will report to HQ East Yorkshire Regt at Q.15.C.3.4 at the following times.

'A' Coy	2 pm
'B' "	2.15 pm
'C' "	2.30 pm
'D' "	2.45 pm.

These parties will remain in the line until the arrival of their respective Companies.
Sgt Hubbard and a proportion of Signallers

will proceed to the ADVANCED FORWARD ZONE at 3pm to take over Signal stations.

The R.S.M. will also go forward at 3pm and take over Stores at Battn HQ.

8 MAPS. All maps, trench stores, defence schemes, and work policies will be taken over.

Duplicate receipts for all trench stores etc taken over, must reach Battn HQ by 6am 19inst

9 PROTECTIVE PATROLS will be sent out immediately the relief is complete.

10. AID POST at Q. 15. C. 2. 3.

11. RATION DUMP for 'A' + 'C' Coys. at Q. 9. C. 4. 2
for 'B' + 'D' " " Batt HQ (Q 15. C. 3. 4)

12. OFFICERS MESS KITS. will be dumped at Battn HQ by 9-30PM, whence they will be taken forward by the Transport.

13. ACKNOWLEDGE

17. 6. 18.

Copy No 1. War Diary
" " 2 HQ Mess.
" " 3 O/C 'A' Coy
" " 4 " B "
" " 5 " C "
" " 6 " D "
" " 7 Q.M + T.O
" " 8. O/C East Yorkshire Regt
" " 9 R.S.M.
" " 10 File

SD K. S. RUDD Capt
A/ Adjutant
West Yorkshire Regiment

Copy No 1

Operation Order No 22
West Yorkshire Regt

SECRET.
22.6.18.

REF MAP 57 D 1/40.000

1. The 17th Division is being relieved by the 63rd Division on the 22nd, 23rd and 24th June 1918.
The 189th Inf. Brigade will relieve the 50th Inf. Brigade on the night of 23rd/24th July 1918.

2 This Battalion will be relieved by the HOOD Battalion and will proceed after relief to ACHEUX WOOD - P.14.a Movement will be by platoons and the usual interval of 200 yards between platoons will be observed throughout.

3. DETAILS OF RELIEF.

(1) 'A' Coy will be relieved by 'A' Coy HOOD Battalion
'B' " " " 'B' " "
'C' " " " 'C' " "
'D' " " " 'D' " "

(2) Completion of Relief will be notified to Battn Hd Qrs by the following code phrases.

'A' Coy	MAYOR	JONES
'B' "	CAPT	DUKE
'C' "	LIEUT	OWENS
'D' "	SERGT	BROWN.

(3) STORES. All Stores, Trench Maps, Aeroplane photographs, Defence schemes, work policies, reserve water and S.O.S. rockets as enumerated in the Warning Order - No W.Y.F 163. issued this morning will be handed over to the advance parties of the HOOD Battalion at present in the line.
Receipts will be obtained & forwarded to Bn Hd Qrs by 6.0 pm tomorrow, 23rd June

(4) GUIDES. will be furnished for the HOOD Battalion as follows:-
One per platoon
One for each Coy Hd Qrs
Two for Bn Hd Qrs
These will parade at Bn Hd Qrs under 2/Lt J.P. LAWSON at 9.0 am tomorrow 23rd inst in order to proceed to ACHEUX and guide their respective parties to the line. 2/Lt LAWSON will report at Bn Hd Qrs at 8.30 a.m for instructions.

(5) PATROLS. Patrolling will not be interfered with by the relief - Protective patrols will be sent out as usual by the front line Companies and will be relieved by patrols of the HOOD

SECRET. **Operation Order No. 24** Copy No 1

West Yorkshire Regiment 24-6-18.

REF MAPS 57 D. S.E. / 57 D. S.W. } 1/20.000.

INFORMATION. While in the present area the 17th Division is the Right Supporting Division of the V Corps and as such will be prepared to:-

(a) Occupy the PURPLE SYSTEM within the Divisional Boundaries

(b) Occupy the BROWN SYSTEM within the Divisional Boundaries

(c) Counter attack to regain any part of the PURPLE SYSTEM and any other position on the V Corps front which may have been lost.

The 50th Infantry Brigade is the Left Brigade of the Division.
The 10th West Yorkshire Regt is the Right Battalion
The 7th East Yorkshire Regt is the Left Battalion
The 6th Dorsetshire Regt is the Reserve Battalion.
The Battalion is at one hour's notice to move from 12.0 midnight to 5.0 am. and at two hours notice during remainder of day and night.

INSTRUCTIONS.

1. "Take up Assembly Positions". On receipt of this message the Battalion will parade ready to pass the Starting Point T.14.a.70.30 at ZERO.
Route HERRISSART – TRACK "B" at T.4.c.5.2. – TRACK "B" North of TOUTENCOURT – U.2.a.30.40. – HARPONVILLE to Assembly Position at U.6.d.
Movement will be carried out by Companies at 200 yards interval.
Battalion will form up in Artillery Formation on reaching Assembly Position
Surplus Personnel will remain in billets at RUBEMPRE and await further orders
Transport. 1st Line Transport will assemble in the valley at U.3.a.
Baggage Wagons will rejoin No 2 Coy Train.

2nd Line Transport, in the case of a heavy attack necessitating the move of 2nd Line Transport, will on receipt of telegram "Rendezvous Transport", report to Col W. C. CROSSE, D.S.O. O.C. 17th Div Train at S.5.a 30.90.

2. In the event of the Division being ordered to occupy the PURPLE SYSTEM, the dispositions of the Battalion will be as follows:-

Battalion Boundaries (South). An EAST & WEST line through W.1.d.20.00.
(North). An EAST & WEST line through Q.31.c.60.50

Front	Right "A" Coy	W.1.d.20.00 to W.1.b.70.10.
	Left "B" "	W.1.b.70.10 to Q.31.c.60.50.
Support	Right "C" "	V.6.d.50.00 to V.6.b.70.10.
	Left "D" "	V.6.b.70.10 to P.36.d.20.50.

Batt H. Qrs. V.6.b.70.20.

The line will be held by posts which are to be prepared for all round defence; Companies distributed in depth, the two front Companies having two platoons in the front line and two platoons in close support.

1. M.G. Coy is attached to the Brigade

3. In the event of a counter attack on any portion of the PURPLE SYSTEM being ordered, further instructions will be communicated to O.C. Companies.

4. In the event of the Division being ordered to occupy the BROWN SYSTEM, the dispositions of the Battalion will be as follows

Battalion Boundaries (South). An EAST & WEST line through V.3.d.00.00.
(North). An EAST & WEST line through P.33a 40.10.

Front	Right "A" Coy.	V.3.d.00.00 to V.3.a.70.70.
	Left "B" "	V.3.a.70.70 to P.33a.40.10.

Support Right "C" Coy V.3.c.10.00. to V.3.a.10.50.
"D" " V.3.a.10.50 to P.33.a.10.20.

Batt H.Qrs. V.2.b.20.50.

1. M.G. Coy. is allotted to the Brigade.

5. "B" Coy. 3rd Tank Battalion now located in LEALVILLERS may operate with the supporting Division
All 3rd Batt. Tanks are painted with a White, Red, White Stripe 18" wide on the ends of both front horns. A similar mark is painted on the top of the turret. Tanks returning towards our lines will fly Red, White and Blue flags.

6. S.A.A. The following S.A.A. has been placed in the BROWN LINE
For M.G. 10 Boxes at each M.G. emplacement.
For Rifles 1 Box per 100 yards of front and additional dump of 50 Boxes per 1000 yds of front.

7. TOOLS. A reserve of 1000 shovels and 500 picks is maintained at the R.E. dump at VARENNES (O.30.b.50.50) for the use of troops occupying the BROWN SYSTEM.

(Sd) W. GIBSON, Major
10th West Yorkshire Regt

Copy No 1 War Diary
2 File
3 C.O.
4 O.C. "A" Coy
5 " "B" "
6 " "C" "
7 " "D" "
8 Q.M and T.O.
9. 50th Inf Bde.

2/Lt E. Cotterill
for War Diary

Instructions regarding War Diaries and Intelligence Summaries are contained in F. S. Regs., Part II. and the Staff Manual respectively. Title pages will be prepared in manuscript.

WAR DIARY
or
~~INTELLIGENCE SUMMARY.~~
(Erase heading not required.)

Army Form C. 2118.

10 W York R

S S 31

Place	Date	Hour	Summary of Events and Information	Remarks and references to Appendices
RUBEMPRE	1918. 1st JULY		Battalion training & Route march.	
"	2nd "		Battalion training & musketry competitions.	
"	3rd "		Company training & musketry.	
"	4th "		Battalion training – musketry on range.	
"	5th "		Company training – rapid wiring competitions, musketry on range.	
"	6th "		Battalion training – musketry on range, & wiring competitions.	
"	7th "		Sunday – Church Parade. Brigade Boxing Competition. Lieut. Col. G.K. BUTT evacuated to Hospital. Major W. GIBSON M.C. assumed command of the Battn.	
"	8th "		At midnight – 7th/8th, on receipt of a surprise warning, the 50th. Infantry Brigade moved to take up its position as LEFT Brigade of the RIGHT Supporting Division, V Corps. The Battalion moved by Cross Country Tracks to assembly position – U 6 d (Ref. map. 57 D SW), reaching this point at 4.30 a.m. On completion of the operation, the Battalion marched back to billets at RUBEMPRE.	G. G. No. 24.
"	9th "		Battalion training – Finals of wiring competitions & musketry on range. Battalion Sports.	
"	10th "		Owing to the 17th Division relieving the 12th Division in the RIGHT (AVELUY) Sector of the V Corps front, the 50th. Infantry Brigade moved forward to relieve the 37th. Infantry Brigade as Reserve Brigade to the RIGHT Division. The Battalion proceeded by march route to the encampment at V 8 d & V 14 b (Ref map 57 D SE) & relieved the 6th (S) Bn. R.W. KENT Regt.	G. G. No. 26
H.Q.	11th "		Company training – P.T., B.F. & musketry	
V 14 b 0.5	12th "		do – P.T., B.F. & musketry on range.	
(Ref map 57 D SE)	13th "		Sunday	

D. D. & L., London, E.C.
(A10266) W1 W5300/P713 750,000 2/18 Sch. 52 Forms/C2118/16

32 E
19 [illegible]

Instructions regarding War Diaries and Intelligence Summaries are contained in F. S. Regs., Part II. and the Staff Manual respectively. Title pages will be prepared in manuscript.

WAR DIARY ~~or~~ ~~INTELLIGENCE SUMMARY.~~

(*Erase heading not required.*)

10th West Yorkshire Regt. July 1918

Army Form C. 2118.

Copy No. 1 Page 2.

Place	Date	Hour	Summary of Events and Information	Remarks and references to Appendices
Bn. H.Q. V14b0.5 (Ref. map 57D S.E.)	1918 14th July		Battalion supplied a working party of 9 Officers & 400 O.R. on the defences of the PURPLE SYSTEM	
	15th "		Same working party again provided.	
	16th "		The 50th Inf. Brigade relieved the 52nd Inf. Brigade in the RIGHT sector of the Divisional front, the Battalion moving by cross country track to the PURPLE SYSTEM & relieving the 12th (S) Bn. MANCHESTER Regt. in Brigade Reserve.	G.O. No. 27
Bn. H.Q. V12c4.0 (Ref. map 57D S.E.)	17th "		Night working parties under R.E. supervision.	
	18th "		do	
	19th "		do	
	20th "		The Battalion (less "D" Coy) relieved the 6th (S) Bn. DORSETSHIRE Regt. (less "A" Coy) in the MAIN FORWARD ZONE. Bn. H.Q. established at W7b2.6 (Ref. map 57D S.E.)	G.O. No. 2[illegible]
Bn. H.Q. W7b2.6 (Ref. map 57D S.E.)	21st "		Night working parties under R.E. supervision	
	22nd "		do Lieut. Col. G.K. BUTT returned from Hospital & resumed command of the Battalion	
	23rd "		do	
	24th "		The Battalion relieved the 7th (S) Bn. EAST YORKSHIRE Regt. in the ADVANCED FORWARD ZONE & became front line battn. of the RIGHT Brigade. Bn. H.Q. established at W13a3.6 (Ref. map 57D S.E.)	G.O. No. 2[illegible]
Bn. H.Q. W13a3.6 (Ref. map 57D S.E.)	25th "		Battalion in the line — day quiet, enemy artillery fire normal.	
	26th		do do	
	27th "		The Battalion was relieved by the 6th (S) Bn. DORSETSHIRE Regt. in the ADVANCED FORWARD ZONE & moved into the MAIN FORWARD ZONE. Relief was complete at 5.55 p.m. Bn. H.Q. was established at W7b2.6 (Ref. map 57D S.E.) The Bn. was again relieved by the 7th (S) Bn. EAST YORKSHIRE Regt. in the MAIN FORWARD ZONE & moved into the PURPLE SYSTEM, becoming Reserve Bn. of the Brigade. Relief was complete at 10.50 p.m. Bn. H.Q. was established at V12c4.0 (Ref. map 57D S.E.)	G.O. No. 30
Bn. H.Q. V12c4.0 (Ref. map 57D S.E.)	28th "		Night & day working parties under R.E. supervision. Special training of "D" Coy for a proposed raid.	
	29th "		do do	
	30th		do do	
	31st "		do do	

G. K. Butt
Lt. Col.
Commdg. 10th West Yorks

D. D. & L., London, E.C.
(A10266) Wt.W5300/P713 750,000 2/18 Sch. 52 Forms/C2118/16

No 36
SECRET

West Yorkshire Regt
Operation Order

9.7.18.
Copy No 1

REF MAP 57 D 1/40.000.

1. The 17th Division is relieving the 12th Division in the Right (AVELUY) Sector of the Vth Corps Front on the 9/10th & 10/11th July 1918.
The 50th Infantry Brigade is relieving the 37th Infantry Brigade in Divisional Reserve on 10th July 1918.

2. This Battalion will relieve the 6th Bn Royal West Kents in the encampment at V.14. & 15. tomorrow, 10th July 1918. Relief to be completed by 5.30 pm. Battalion H.Qrs will be established at V.14. b.4.6.

3. The Battalion will move by march route as follows:-

Route "C" track to CONTAY - WARLOY road.

Starting Point T.14.d.2.4.

Order of March H.Qrs. "A", "B", "C" & "D" Coys.

Rendezvous. ARGYLL STREET SOUTH - the head of the column to be at the well outside Orderly Room.

Time. The column will be ready to move at 11.10. a.m. and will commence to pass the Starting Point at 11.30.a.m.

MOVEMENT. as far as V.22. will be by Companies at 300 yards interval - thence by Platoons at 300 yards interval. Similar intervals will be maintained between sections of Transport.

Guides. One per platoon, one per Coy H.Qrs and 2 for Bn H.Qrs will meet the Column at V.19.a.6.4.

Transport. Lewis Gun limbers & Ammunition mules will march behind their Companies. Cookers will proceed independently to the road at V.22 at 9.a.m. where C.Q.M. Sergts will see that hot tea is ready for the Battalion at about 1.30 pm. The remainder of the Transport will march independently behind the Battalion.

4. All billets must be left scrupulously clean.
A rear party consisting of 2 O.R's from each Company will report to Captain K. S. RUDD at Orderly Room at 10.45 a.m.

5. Packs will be stacked at the Q.M. Stores by 9. a.m. Great coats will be tied in bundles of 10 and stacked at the Q.M. Stores by 8 am ready to be taken forward by lorry.
Officers valises & mess boxes will be collected at 9.30 am

6. Company Commanders will report the arrival of their Companies to the new H.Qrs as early as possible.

(Sd) A. F. G. ANDERSON Capt
Adjutant
West Yorkshire Regt

Copy No 1 War Diary
" 2 C.O.
" 3 2nd in Command.
" 4 O/c Coys A
" 5 " B
" 6 " C
" 7 " D
" 8 Q.M.
" 9 T.O.
" 10 R.S.M.
" 11 Files.

SECRET

"GOZU"

Copy No.

No 27

Operation Order

16 = 7 = 18.

REFCE MAP 57 D. S.E. 1/20.000

1. The 50th Inf Brigade is relieving the 52nd Inf Brigade in the Right Sector of the Divisional Front on the night 16th/17th July, 1918

2. This Battalion will relieve the 12th Bn MANCHESTER Regt as Reserve Battalion of the Brigade, Companies relieving as follows:-

"A" Coy	will relieve	"A" Coy	12th Manchester Regt	
"B"	" "	"B"	"	"
"C"	" "	"C"	"	"
"D"	" "	"D"	"	"

Companies will march away from the present encampment in the order "A", "B", "C", "D" Coys & H Qrs by platoons at 300 yards interval Commencing at 10.0 pm

Route By track NORTH of SENLIS to the PURPLE SYSTEM

Guides at the rate of one for each Platoon, one for each Coy H Qrs and one for Batt H Qrs will meet the column on the track at V.11.c 85.6

Lewis Guns. One Lewis Gun limber for "A" & "B" Coys & one for "C" & "D" Coys will proceed with Coys as far as V.11.c 85.60 at which point Lewis guns & drums will be unloaded & carried to the new positions

Completion of relief will be notified to Batt H Qrs by messages giving the Company Commanders name

3. Defence Schemes, Work Policies, Sector Maps and Aeroplane Photos will be taken over and acted upon until further orders. Duplicates of receipts will be forwarded to Batt H Qrs by 9 am 17th instant

All Trench Stores, Soyers Stores, S.O.S rockets, Reserve Water & Tools will be taken over & carefully checked. Duplicates of receipts for these will also be forwarded to Orderly Room by 9.0 am 17th inst.

4 The present encampment must be left scrupulously clean and a certificate to this effect rendered to Orderly Room by Company Commanders before leaving

Greatcoats & Officers valises will be stacked at the side of the road near Bn H. Qrs by 9.0 pm ready to be conveyed to 'B' Echelon by the Transport

Officers mess Stores and Trench kits will be stacked at Bn H Qrs by 9.0 pm ready to be taken forward to the new positions.

All Mobilization Tools will be conveyed back to 'B' Echelon by the Transport

(Sd) A F G ANDERSON Capt

Adjutant

"GOZU"

SECRET. "GOZU" Copy No 2

No 28. Operation Order 20.7.18

1\. The Battalion (less "D" Coy) will relieve the Dorsetshire Regt (less one Coy) in the MAIN FORWARD ZONE on the night 20th/21st July 1918.
After relief, the Dorsetshire Regt (less one Coy) will take up the positions in the PURPLE SYSTEM which have been vacated by this Battalion.

2\. Companies will relieve Companies of the Dorsetshire Regt in the MAIN FORWARD ZONE as follows:-
"A" Coy will relieve "D" Coy Dorsetshire Regt in POST No 10.
"B" " " "C" " " " POSTS 9. 13 & 14
"C" " " "B" " " " 16 & 31.

3\. "D" Coy will take over from "C" Coy of this Battalion in POST No 30 in the PURPLE SYSTEM.
After completion of relief "D" Coy will be tactically under the command of O.C. Dorsetshire Regt.

4\. Companies of the Dorsetshire Regt are taking over positions in the PURPLE SYSTEM from our Companies as follows:-

5 STORES.

Companies will at once send advance parties to take over all Stores, Maps, Defence Schemes, Work Policies, S.O.S rockets & reserve water from the Companies of the East Yorkshire Regt which they are relieving.

The Dorsetshire Regt are sending similar parties to take over from Companies in the present positions. O.C. Coys will arrange for guards to be left over these stores until they are definitely taken over by the Dorsetshire Regt and receipts have been obtained. Duplicate copies of receipts will be forwarded to B. H.Qrs as quickly as possible.

6 Completion of Relief will be notified to B.H.Qrs as follows.

A. Coy — One Officer
B — Two Sanitary men
C — Three Cooks
D — Capt SMITH

(Sd) A.F.G. ANDERSON Capt
Adjutant
DONU

2/Lt H.W. Ramsden

SECRET "DONU" COPY No 1

No 29 OPERATION ORDER 24th JULY '18.

REF MAP 57 D
1/40.000

1. The Battalion will relieve the East Yorkshire Regt in the ADVANCED FORWARD ZONE today 24th July 1918.
The Worcestershire Regt will take over the MAIN FORWARD ZONE and the East Yorkshire Regt will move into the PURPLE SYSTEM.

2. "A" Coy of this Battalion will relieve
"C" Coy East Yorkshire Regt.
"B" Coy of this Battalion will relieve
"B" Coy East Yorkshire Regt.
"C" Coy of this Battalion will relieve
"A" Coy East Yorkshire Regt
"D" Coy of this Battalion will relieve
"D" Coy East Yorkshire Regt

3. "A" "B" & "C" Coys will commence relieving their respective Companies of the East Yorkshire Regt at 2 pm this afternoon
These Companies will not move more than one Platoon at a time.

"D" Coy will commence relieving "D" Coy of the East Yorkshire Regt at 10 pm tonight. H.QRS of this Battalion will be established at W.13. a 15.50 (present H.QRS of the East Yorkshire Regt at 3.0 pm

4. GUIDES.

1. The East Yorkshire Regt are providing guides for each platoon as follows:-
For A Coy at A Coys H.QRS at 2.0 pm
for "B" " "B" " " " "
For "C" " at W.8.c 7.6. (junction of KING STREET and SAUCHIEHALL RESERVE) at 2.0. pm
For "D" Coy at W.13.a 15.50 (new Battalion H.QRS) at 10 pm

2. After relief A, B & C Coys will send guides with the relieved Coys of the East Yorkshire Regt to conduct them to the positions which they have vacated in the MAIN FORWARD ZONE where these Coys of the East Yorkshire Regt are remaining until relieved by Coys of the Dorsetshire Regt tonight.
After relief "D" Coy will send guides with "D" Coy East Yorkshire Regt to conduct them to the positions vacated in POST 30.

"B" Coy Dorsetshire Regt from "B" Coy of this Battalion
"C" " " " "D" " " "
"D" " " " "A" " " "
"A" " " " are remaining in their present positions

5. Guides. Companies will at once send reliable guides from each platoon to reconnoitre the new positions. These will return and guide their platoons forward when relief commences.

The Dorsetshire Regt are similarly sending guides to reconnoitre the PURPLE SYSTEM who will return and guide their platoons on the completion of the relief.

6. Companies will commence moving forward independently to their new positions at 10.0.pm

7. Completion of relief will be communicated to Bn HQrs by messages giving the name of the Company Commander.

8. All Stores & Reserve Water in present positions will be handed over to the Dorsetshire Regt and duplicate lists forwarded to Bn HQrs as quickly as possible.

Stores and Water in the new positions will be taken over and duplicate lists forwarded to the new Battalion Hd Qrs by 6.0 am tomorrow 21st inst.

9. The Reserve Rations at present Battalion Hd Qrs will be taken forward by the Transport to the new Battalion Hd Qrs.

(Sd) A.F.G. ANDERSON Capt
Adjutant
"GOZU"

SECRET "DONU" Copy No

No 30 OPERATION ORDER 27th July 1918

REF MAP 57 D. SE
1/40 000.

1. The Battalion will be relieved by the Dorsetshire Regt in the ADVANCED FORWARD ZONE this afternoon 27th July 1918.
The East Yorkshire Regt is taking over the MAIN FORWARD ZONE and this Battalion will take over the PURPLE SYSTEM during the night 27/28th July 1918

2. Movement and reliefs by Battalions are being carried out as follows:-
   (a) Dorsetshire Regt will commence relieving this Battalion in the ADVANCED FORWARD ZONE at 2 pm, 27th July 1918.
   (b) This Battalion on relief will move to the localities in the MAIN FORWARD ZONE vacated by the Dorsetshire Regt and will remain there until relieved by the East Yorkshire Regt.
   (c) The East Yorkshire Regt will relieve this Battalion in the MAIN FORWARD ZONE at dusk relief to be complete by 10.0 pm.

2 (a) On relief by the East Yorkshire Regt this battalion will move to the PURPLE SYSTEM and will occupy the localities vacated by the East Yorkshire Regt.

3. Movements by Companies will be carried out as follows:-

(a) ADVANCED FORWARD ZONE.

'A' Coy will be relieved by 'D' Coy Dorsetshire Regt
'B' " " 'C' "
'C' " " 'B' "
'D' " " 'A' "

'B' & 'D' Coys Dorsetshire Regt will commence relieving at 2 pm.
'A' & 'C' Coys Dorsetshire Regt will commence relieving at 3 pm.

(b) MAIN FORWARD ZONE

(i) On relief by the Dorsetshire Regt Companies will proceed to localities in the MAIN FORWARD ZONE as follows:-

"A" Coy	Locality No 10	vacated by	'D' Coy.	Dorset Regt
'B' Coy	"	Nos 9, 13 & 14	" 'C' Coy	"
'C' Coy	"	Nos 16 & 31	" 'B' Coy	"
'D' Coy	"	Nos 6, 7 & 8.	" 'A' Coy	"

and will remain there until relieved
by Companies of the East Yorkshire Regt
(ii) 'A' Coy will be relieved by 'D' Coy East Yorkshire Regt

'B'	"	"	'B'	"
'C'	"	"	'A'	"
'D'	"	"	'C'	"

On relief by the East Yorkshire Regt, Companies will proceed to localities in the PURPLE SYSTEM as follows:-

'A' Coy	Localities 2 & 3.	vacated by 'C' Coy	East Yorkshire Regt
'B' Coy	" 32	" 'A' Coy	"
'C' Coy	" 30	" 'D' Coy	"
'D' Coy	" 4 & 5	" 'B' Coy	"

H. GUIDES. O.C. Coys will send one guide per platoon to report at the Coy H.Qrs of the relieving Coys of the Dorsetshire Regt before 2 pm.

On relief the Dorsetshire Regt are providing one guide per platoon to lead back our platoons to the localities vacated by them.

O.C. Coys will arrange to reconnoitre their positions in the PURPLE SYSTEM and will provide their own guides for their platoons

5. STORES.

Companies will at once send advance parties to take over all Stores, Maps, Defence Schemes, Work Policies, S.O.S. Rockets & Reserve Water from the Companies of the East Yorkshire Regt which they are relieving in the PURPLE SYSTEM.

Care must be taken to see that all the Reserve water has been properly turned over.

The Dorsetshire Regt are sending similar parties to take over from this Battalion in the ADVANCED FORWARD ZONE.

6. COMPLETION OF RELIEF.

(1) Completion of relief by Dorsetshire Regt will be notified to present Battalion Hd Qrs as follows.

"A" Coy One Officer "C" Coy Three Cooks
"B" Coy Two Sergeants "D" Coy Four runners

(2) Completion of relief by East Yorkshire Regt will be notified to Battalion Hd Qrs in MAIN FORWARD ZONE as follows:—

"A" Coy 50 Shovels C Coy 500 Sandbags
"B" Coy 100 Picks D Coy 40 Coils

(3) Companies will report arrival in PURPLE SYSTEM to the old Battalion H.Qrs by runner

ACKNOWLEDGE

(Sd) A.F.G. ANDERSON, Capt
Adjutant
DONW.

War Diary

50th Bde.
17th Div.

10th BATTALION,

WEST YORKSHIRE REGIMENT,

A U G U S T 1 9 1 8.

Army Form C. 2118.

10th (S) Bn. WEST YORKSHIRE REGIMENT

August 1918

WAR DIARY
or
INTELLIGENCE SUMMARY.

(Erase heading not required.)

Instructions regarding War Diaries and Intelligence Summaries are contained in F. S. Regs., Part II. and the Staff Manual respectively. Title pages will be prepared in manuscript.

Place	Date	Hour	Summary of Events and Information	Remarks and references to Appendices
	AUGUST			
Bn. H.Q. VIECH.O (Ref. Map 57D S.E.)	1		Night & day working parties	
		9.10 pm	D Coy carried out a very successful raid on the enemy [illegible] & sunken road in W15d (Ref. Map 57D S.E.) during the course of which 16 prisoners & 1 M.G. (light) were captured & 2 dugouts demolished. The prisoners taken included pioneers who were preparing dugouts for demolition prior to the enemy's retirement to the EAST of the river ANCRE, & very valuable information regarding this evacuation was gained. During this operation about 36 Germans were killed. There were no [illegible] in the raiding party. A message of congratulation was received by the Bn. from General Sir JULIAN BYNG, commanding the Third Army. Temp/Lieut. W.H. HIRST killed, Temp/2nd Lt. R.G. JONES wounded.	
	2		Night & day working parties	
	3		do	
	4		do	
	5		On the night of the 5th/6th the Bn., on being relieved by the [illegible] SOUTH WALES BORDERERS, proceeded by march route to HERISSART, staying at R26b7d (Ref. Map 57D S.E.) until 9.0 a.m. on the 6th.	
	6		Bn. arrived at HERISSART about 12 noon.	
HERISSART	7		Bn. Training & cleaning up.	
	8		Bn. Training. The 17th Division moved SOUTH at short notice to the Fourth Army [illegible]. The Bn. moved off at 1.30 pm by march route through CONTAY, BEAUCOURT, MONTIGNY, PONT NOYELLES, DAOURS to BOIS L'ABBAYE	
BOIS L'ABBAYE	9		On receipt of orders the Bn. moved off at [illegible] by march route to CORBIE	
CORBIE	10		Bn. awaiting orders.	
	11		do	
	12		The 17th Division relieved the 3rd Australian Division in the vicinity of PROYART, the [illegible] Inf. Bde. relieving the 10th Australian Bde. At [illegible] the Bn. moved off by [illegible] to PROYART relieving the 37th AUSTRALIAN Bn. & the 40th AUSTRALIAN Bn. ([illegible]) in the front line. Bn. H.Q. was established at R20a 7.4 (Ref. Map 62D S.E.)	

D. D. & L., London, E.C.
(A10266) Wt W5300/P713 750,000 2/18 Sch. 52 Forms/C2118/16

PAGE 2

Instructions regarding War Diaries and Intelligence Summaries are contained in F. S. Regs., Part II. and the Staff Manual respectively. Title pages will be prepared in manuscript.

10th (S) Bn WEST YORKSHIRE REGIMENT

WAR DIARY
or
~~INTELLIGENCE SUMMARY.~~

(*Erase heading not required.*)

August 1918

Army Form C. 2118.

Place	Date	Hour	Summary of Events and Information	Remarks and references to Appendices
Bn H.Q. R20a4.1 (Ref map 62DSE)	AUGUST 13		Bn in the line. Temp/2nd Lt. W.H. CLARK wounded. 'A' Coy on the LEFT front was relieved by a Coy of the 10th (S) Bn NOTTS & DERBY Regt & [illegible] the RIGHT relieved 'A' & 'B' Coys of the 7th (S) Bn EAST YORKSHIRE Regt & became RIGHT front Coy of the Bn. Lieut. Col. G.K. BUTT evacuated to hospital.	[illegible]
	14		Bn in the line.	[illegible]
	15		Dispositions changing from 2 Coys to 3 Coys in the front line, 'B' Coy moved up from reserve & became centre front Coy. Bn H.Q. moved to R19d1.4 (Ref map 62DSE)	[illegible]
Bn H.Q. R19d1.4 (Ref map 62DSE)	16		The 5th Australian Division relieved the 17th Division. The Bn was relieved by the 55th AUSTRALIAN Bn & on relief marched by cross country tracks to AUBIGNY staging at BOIS DEVAIRE.	[illegible]
AUBIGNY	17		Bn awaiting orders.	[illegible]
	18		The Bn moved off at 10.30 p.m. by march route to PUCHEVILLERS.	O.O. No. 3 [illegible]
PUCHEVILLERS	19		Bn Training. P.T. & Musketry.	[illegible]
	20		The Bn moved by march route to ARQUEVES.	O.O. No. 4
ARQUEVES	21		At 12 noon on receipt of orders the 50th Inf. Bde. moved by cross country tracks to MAILLY-MAILLET. The Bn occupied a portion of the PURPLE System in front of that village. Bn H.Q. established at Q7d (Ref map 57DSE)	[illegible]
Bn H.Q. Q7d (Ref map 57DSE)	22		Bn in the PURPLE System EAST of MAILLY-MAILLET awaiting orders to advance. The 10th (S) Bn WEST YORKSHIRE Regt, in support, relieved the 7th (S) Bn LEICESTER Regt in the old British front line & posts in Q16a & Q17 (Ref map 57DSE) on the WEST bank of the river ANCRE. Bn H.Q. established in Q16c (Ref map 57DSE)	[illegible]
Bn H.Q. Q16c (Ref map 57DSE)	23	5.30 pm	'A' Coy crossed the river ANCRE by the bridge at Q18d5.7 (Ref map 57DSE) & took over COMMON LANE in Q24 & R19 (Ref map 57DSE) from the 6th (S) Bn DORSET Regt.	[illegible]
		6.30 pm	'D' Coy crossed the river ANCRE via bridge at Q24a5.2 (Ref map 57DSE) & took over the southern half of COMMON LANE in Q24d & R19c (Ref map 57DSE)	

D. D. & L., London, E.C.
(A10266) Wt W5300/P713 750,000 2/18 Sch. 52 Forms/C2118/16

16th (S) Bn WEST YORKSHIRE Regt

WAR DIARY

or

~~INTELLIGENCE SUMMARY.~~

August 1918

(*Erase heading not required.*)

Army Form C. 2118.

Instructions regarding War Diaries and Intelligence Summaries are contained in F. S. Regs., Part II. and the Staff Manual respectively. Title pages will be prepared in manuscript.

Place	Date	Hour	Summary of Events and Information	Remarks and references to Appendices
Bn H.Q. – Q16c (Ref map 57D SE)	AUGUST 23 (cont)	7.30pm	"C" Coy crossed the river ANCRE & took up a position in rear of "D" Coy	H.K.
		7.30pm	"B" Coy do "A" Coy	
		10.15pm	Bn H.Q. moved the river ANCRE & were established at R19d3.9 in COMMON LANE (Ref map 57D SE)	
		11.50pm	Bn took up assembly position about 300 yards in front of COMMON LANE in R19c (Ref map 57D SE) for the attack on THIEPVAL RIDGE, "A" & "D" Coys in front line, with "B" & "C" Coys in support.	
Bn H.Q. – R19c (Ref map 57D SE)	24	1.0am	The Bn moved forward to attack THIEPVAL RIDGE.	H.K.
		1.55	First objective taken, prisoners commenced to come back. In contact with the 38th Division on the RIGHT	
		2.0	Bn H.Q. moved forward to R20c 0.1 (Ref map 57D SE)	
		3.20	Word was received that the LEFT front Coy had reached the final objective, & shortly afterwards the right front Coy reported having reached & consolidated their final objective.	
			The line at this period ran from R24c3.8 to R32b4.7 (Ref map 57D SE) – RED Line. The RIGHT flank was in the air for a distance of 2000 yards, & the LEFT flank unprotected except for 3 Platoons of the 6th (S) Bn DORSET Regt.	
			Some heavy fighting took place in the advance to the RED line, enemy M.G. teams holding out stubbornly. In nearly every case they were outflanked & then attacked from the rear. PRISONERS captured – 4 Officers & 240 O.R., also 18 M.Gs.	
			The big haul of prisoners was due to a great extent to the initiative of O/C "C" Coy, Temp/Sec Lt J.C. BRAITHWAITE M.C., who led his Coy through our barrage to a point in rear of the final objective. There he waited till the barrage lifted & then attacked the enemy in the rear whilst the other Coys made a frontal attack. This Coy alone captured 120 prisoners.	

D. D. & L., London, E.C.
(A10266) Wt W5300/P713 750,000 2/18 Sch. 52 Forms/C2118/16

10th (S) Bn WEST YORKSHIRE Regt.

WAR DIARY
or
INTELLIGENCE SUMMARY.

(*Erase heading not required.*)

August 1918

Army Form C. 2118.

Instructions regarding War Diaries and Intelligence Summaries are contained in F. S. Regs., Part II. and the Staff Manual respectively. Title pages will be prepared in manuscript.

Place	Date	Hour	Summary of Events and Information	Remarks and references to Appendices
Bn H.Q.–R.9.c (Ref map 57DSE)	Aug 24		The bold & skilful leading by Temp/Sec Lt. J.C. BRAITHWAITE M.C. ~~[illegible]~~ was beyond all praise. He possesses all the qualities of a leader together with instinct for seizing fleeting opportunities & taking full advantage of any enemy mistakes.	[illegible]
			O/C "D" Coy – Temp/Sec Lt. F. KIRK also led his Coy. with the greatest dash & determination. In a fight with a German Captain he was wounded three times before the latter would surrender. Many of the enemy fought the street fight, but the majority were glad to surrender.	
		9.0 a.m.	Advance resumed & by noon the ridge in R.29 R.34 (Ref map 57DSE) had been reached.	
		1.30 p.m.	In touch with 7th (S) Bn EAST YORKSHIRE Regt. on the LEFT & 38th Division on the RIGHT.	
		2.0 p.m.	Advance on POZIERES commenced.	
		4.0 p.m.	POZIERES taken.	
		4.30 p.m.	Enemy counter-attack on POZIERES well supported by artillery – driven off with heavy casualties to the enemy.	
		5.50 p.m.	Second enemy counter-attack with heavy artillery bombardment of all calibres & light Trench Mortars. By reason of this & heavy M.G. fire from both flanks, & also in view of the strength of the enemy & our open flanks, it was decided in conjunction with the 7th (S) Bn EAST YORKSHIRE Regt. to withdraw to a stronger line of trenches N.W. of POZIERES from X3 central to X3 b 7.5 (Ref map 57DSE). Bn H.Q. established at X3 b 6.4 (Ref map 57DSE).	
		11.0 p.m.	Enemy withdrew from POZIERES.	
			Lieut Col. W. GIBSON [illegible] M.C. wounded (at duty), Temp/Lt. F. FIRTH killed, Temp/Lt. E.G. ADDINGTON missing, Temp/Sec Lt. E. COTTERILL wounded, S/R Temp/Sec Lt. R. CLEGG wounded, Sec/Lt. T.H. GOULDING T.F. wounded, Temp/Sec Lt. J.A. RHODES (att. 50th Light T.M. Battery) killed, Temp/Sec Lt. A.S. THORNSBY killed, Temp/Sec Lt. A.T. THOMAS wounded.	
Bn H.Q.–X3b6.4 (Ref map 57DSE)	25	5.0 a.m.	52nd Inf Bde passed through the 50th Inf Bde which now became the Bde. in Divisional Reserve. The Bn ordered to follow 1000 yds in rear of the RIGHT flank of the 52nd Inf Bde & be prepared to protect the RIGHT flank of the Division.	[illegible]
		5.30 a.m.	Bn moved forward & at noon took up a position SOUTH of MARTINPUICH facing S.E. in S2 a 9.6 (Ref map 57CSW).	
		6.0 p.m.	Bn moved to a line facing EAST & S.E. in M33 c 7.5 2 b (Ref map 57CSW) in touch with the 12th (S) Bn MANCHESTER Regt. in front & the 38th Division on the RIGHT. Bn H.Q. established at M32 d 1.2 (Ref map 57CSW). S/R Temp/Sec Lt. A.G.P. WOOD died of wounds.	
Bn H.Q.–M32d1.2 (Ref map 57CSW)	26	10.0 a.m.	Commenced to advance in close support to the 12th (S) Bn MANCHESTER Regt. to a line facing EAST in N31 a 2.2 (Ref map 57CSW). Bn H.Q. established at M34 a 5.6 (Ref map 57CSW).	[illegible]
Bn H.Q.–M34a5.6 (Ref map 57CSW)	27	12.30 a.m.	Assembly position taken up prior to advance on FLERS.	[illegible]
		1.0	Advance commenced on FLERS [illegible] through the 12th (S) Bn MANCHESTER Regt.	
		2.0	Enemy [illegible] at N15 c 4.5 0 a (Ref map 57CSW). Fierce fighting in trenches WEST of FLERS until 4.0 a.m.	

D. D. & L., London, E.C.
(A10266) Wt W5300/P713 750,000 2/18 Sch. 52 Forms/C2118/16

PAGE 5

Instructions regarding War Diaries and Intelligence Summaries are contained in F. S. Regs., Part II. and the Staff Manual respectively. Title pages will be prepared in manuscript.

10th (S) Bn WEST YORKSHIRE REGIMENT

WAR DIARY
or
~~INTELLIGENCE SUMMARY.~~

(Erase heading not required.)

AUGUST 1918

Army Form C. 2118.

Place	Date	Hour	Summary of Events and Information	Remarks and references to Appendices
Bn H.Q. M34a5.6 (Ref map 57cSW)	AUGUST 27 (cont)	4.40am	Temp/Sec Lt F KIRK & 2 Platoons of "D" Coy pushed through FLERS under heavy fire, casualties very heavy – only the officer, 5 O.R. & 1 L.Gun reached their objective.	HWK
		5.0am	A & C Coys pushed through the village & established a line NORTH & SOUTH through N31 central (Ref map 57cSW)	
		6.30	Bn H.Q. established at M36 d 4.7 (Ref map 57cSW). The Medical Officer – Capt L TAYLOR (American Army att R.A.M.C.) went out & attended to the wounded under very heavy fire.	
		7.20 "	Strong enemy counter attack with heavy artillery bombardment & intense M.G. fire from high ground N.E. & S.E. of village.	
		7.30 "	Position in front of FLERS became untenable. Casualties heavy. "C" Coy lost the nos 1, 2 & 3 of all L.G. teams & all Guns. Coy withdrew to a position WEST of FLERS where a strong line was taken up from M36 b 4.2 to S 6 d 8.7 (Ref map 57cSW)	
		12 noon	Bn H.Q. moved to M35 d 9.8 (Ref map 57cSW). 4 German M.Gs [illegible] at this time [illegible] the front line. Temp/Sec Lt H BURKS killed, Temp/Sec Lt B J HASEMAN wounded.	
Bn H.Q. M35 d 9.8 (Ref map 57cSW)	28		Bn holding the same line	
	29		The 51st Inf Bde relieved the 50th Inf Bde & the Bn, on being relieved by the 10th (S) Bn NOTTS & DERBY R.F., marched to a rest area in M27 d (Ref map 57cSW). During the operations from the 22nd to the 29th – 450 PRISONERS, 32 M.G.s, 2 TRANSPORT WAGONS, 3 HORSES, & 3 T.M. stands were captured by the Bn.	
MARTINPUICH	30		Bn at rest. Owing to the 50th Inf Bde relieving the 52nd Inf Bde in SUPPORT, the Bn relieved the 9th (S) Bn DUKE OF WELLINGTON'S Regt. Bn H.Q. established at N25 c 8.6 (Ref map 57cSW)	
Bn H.Q. N25 c 8.6 (Ref map 57cSW)	31		Bn in SUPPORT in touch with the 52nd Inf Bde in front.	

C. Waite Major
Commanding 10th (S) Bn WEST YORKSHIRE R.

D. D. & L., London, E.C.
(A10266) Wt W5300/P713 750,000 2/18 Sch. 52 Forms/C2118/16

Instructions regarding War Diaries and Intelligence Summaries are contained in F. S. Regs., Part II. and the Staff Manual respectively. Title pages will be prepared in manuscript.

WAR DIARY
or
INTELLIGENCE SUMMARY.
(Erase heading not required.)

Army Form C. 2118.

Place	Date	Hour	Summary of Events and Information	Remarks and references to Appendices
[illegible] (Ref map 57c SW)	SEPT. 1	[illegible]	The Bn. moved forward to N.32 (Ref map 57c SW). Bn. H.Q. established at N.32 [illegible]	[illegible]
		8.10 pm	On receipt of orders the Bn. moved to [illegible] (Ref map 57c SW) – on high ground WEST of [illegible]	
		9.15 pm	Bn. H.Q. established at N.28c [illegible] (Ref map 57c SW)	
[illegible]	2	[illegible]	The Bn. moved forward to assembly positions facing S.E. along line O.[illegible] (Ref map 57c SW) for attack on ROCQUIGNY.	[illegible]
		[illegible]	Zero barrage commenced.	
		[illegible]	Bn. commenced to advance.	
		[illegible]	Leading Coys. reached [illegible] (Ref map 57c SW)	
		[illegible]	Final objective attained [illegible] EAST YORKSHIRE RGT. [illegible] (Ref map 57c SW)	
			PRISONERS captured [illegible] 24, MACHINE GUNS – 2	
[illegible]	3	[illegible]	[illegible] (Ref map 57c SW)	[illegible]
		[illegible]	[illegible]	
		[illegible]	[illegible]	
[illegible]	4	[illegible]	[illegible]	[illegible]

D. D. & L., London, E.C.
(A10266) Wt W5300/P713 750,000 2/18 Sch. 52 Forms/C2118/16

87

10th (S) Bn. West Yorkshire Regt.

PAGE 2

Army Form C. 2118.

Instructions regarding War Diaries and Intelligence Summaries are contained in F. S. Regs., Part II. and the Staff Manual respectively. Title pages will be prepared in manuscript.

WAR DIARY ~~or~~ ~~INTELLIGENCE SUMMARY.~~

(*Erase heading not required.*)

September 1918

Place	Date	Hour	Summary of Events and Information	Remarks and references to Appendices
Bn. H.Q. P2 b c 6.5 (Ref. map 57c SE)	SEPT. 5	3.0 am	The Bn. (less "A" Coy, which remained in [illegible]) on relief by the 10th (S) Bn. NOTTS & DERBY Regt. marched by cross-country tracks to area C29 a + C35 b (Ref. map 57c SW)	[illegible]
		11.0 am	Bn. H.Q. established at C29 b 5.3 (Ref. map 57c SW)	
		5.30 pm	"A" Coy rejoined the Bn.	
Bn. H.Q. C29 b 5.3 (Ref. map 57c SW)	6		Bn. [illegible] Coy [illegible] & [illegible]	[illegible]
	7	11.0 am	Owing to the 50th Inf. Bde moving forward to support the 52nd Inf. Bde, the Bn. moved to [illegible] P3 a (Ref. map 57c SE). Bn. H.Q. established in P34 c (Ref. map 57c SE)	[illegible]
Bn. H.Q. P34 a (Ref. map 57c SE)	8		Bn. in [illegible] at P34 (Ref. map 57c SE) as above	[illegible]
	9	12.0 mid-night	Bn. moved forward on receipt of orders.	[illegible]
		2.20 am	Bn. H.Q. established at P36 d 7.3 (Ref. map 57c SE)	
		12.15 pm	[illegible] resumed to a line [illegible] W3 a 4 c, W[illegible] (Ref. map 57c SE)	
		1.15	Bn. H.Q. established at Q32 d 2.4 (Ref. map 57c SE)	
		5.15 pm	The Bn. relieved the 12th (S) Bn. MANCHESTER Regt. in the FRONT LINE & became [illegible] FRONT Bn. of the Bde	
		4.75	Bn. H.Q. established at W4 a 05.50 (Ref. map 57c SE)	
Bn. H.Q. W4 a 05.50 (Ref. map 57c SE)	10		Day fairly quiet, [illegible] enemy shelling. Temp/2nd Lt. S. CORK wounded.	[illegible]
	11	8.30 pm	The Bn., on being relieved by the 7th (S) Bn. ROYAL WARWICK FUSILIERS, moved by cross-country tracks into ROCQUIGNY, staying at P33 b 7.2 (Ref. map 57c SE)	[illegible]
ROCQUIGNY	12	2.30 am	Bn. reached billets at ROCQUIGNY. M.G.s [illegible] between the 3rd & 12th — 1 Heavy, 3 Light	[illegible]
	13		Bn. at rest — Baths & Training of [illegible]. Reconnaissance of the line carried out by officers with a view to the impending attack	[illegible]
	14		As for the 13th.	
	15		do	[illegible]
	16	8.15 pm	On receipt of orders, the Bn. moved forward by cross-country tracks to W9 (Ref. map 57c SE) — FINS RIDGE.	[illegible]
			Bn. H.Q. established at W3 c 6.0 (Ref. map 57c SE)	
Bn. H.Q. W3 c 6.0 (Ref. map 57c SE)	17		[illegible] Assembly positions [illegible] for attack on GREEN LINE, & at dusk the Bn. moved into the assembly positions. Bn. H.Q. was established at W10 c 6.4.7 (Ref. map 57c SE)	[illegible]
Bn. H.Q. W10 c 6.4.7 (Ref. map 57c SE)	18	5.20 am	Zero. Bn. moved forward to the attack behind a creeping barrage. A, B & C Coys in FRONT LINE, D Coy in SUPPORT, going forward rapidly, first objective [illegible] on the [illegible] the 12th (S) Bn. MANCHESTER Regt. Pushing on, the Bn. [illegible] with little opposition & [illegible] the final objective in the GREEN LINE. Temp. Maj. (A/Lt. Col.) W. [illegible] M.C., [illegible] Temp/Major C. E. [illegible] [illegible]	[illegible]

D. D. & L., London, E.C.
(A10266) Wt W5300/P713 750,000 2/18 Sch. 52 Forms/C2118/16

10th (S) Bn. WEST YORKSHIRE REGT. PAGE 3

Army Form C. 2118.

WAR DIARY

or

~~INTELLIGENCE SUMMARY.~~

SEPT. 1918

(*Erase heading not required.*)

Instructions regarding War Diaries and Intelligence Summaries are contained in F. S. Regs., Part II. and the Staff Manual respectively. Title pages will be prepared in manuscript.

Place	Date	Hour	Summary of Events and Information	Remarks and references to Appendices
Bn. HQ – W10 b4.4 (Ref map 57c SE)	SEPT 18 (cont)		The objective was consolidated & the dugouts cleared. PRISONERS amounted to 4 Officers & 315 O.R. 11 M.G.s & 1 Trench mortar were captured. Bn. H.Q. established at W.5 d 1.3 (Ref. map 57c SE). Temp/Capt M.F. SMITH M.C. & Temp/Sec. Lt. E.A.W. FAULDER killed, Temp/Sec. Lt. P. REINOLDS missing, Temp/Sec. Lt. W. BOWER, Temp/Sec. Lt. F. KIRK, Temp/Sec. Lt. McKINNON wounded. Temp/[illegible] W. B. MARSH [illegible] wounded but remained at duty. Bn. H.Q. moved to W.5 d 6.2 (Ref map 57c SE).	[illegible]
Bn. H.Q. – W.5 d 6.2 (Ref map 57c SE)	19		At daybreak C & D Coys moved forward across X.1 & occupied GAUCHE ALLEY (Ref map 57c SE). Heavy shelling all day. At dusk "A" & "B" Coys relieved the 6th (S) Bn. DORSET Regt. [illegible] of the 51st Inf. Bde. in LANCASHIRE TRENCH & SOMME ALLEY (X.1 & 2 – Ref map 57c SE). C & D [illegible] up to [illegible] in SUPPORT SOMME ALLEY (X.1 & 2 – Ref map 57c SE). Bn. H.Q. established at X.7 a 4.4 (Ref map 57c SE).	[illegible]
Bn. H.Q. X.7 a 4.4 (Ref map 57c SE)	20		At dusk a patrol of "A" Coy [illegible] [illegible] 120 yards of LANCASHIRE TRENCH in X.2 (Ref map 57c SE) [illegible] [illegible] LANCASHIRE TRENCH [illegible] [illegible] LANCASHIRE TRENCH [illegible] Lt. (T.F.) Sec. Lt. [illegible] [illegible]	[illegible]
	21	1.35 am	[illegible] LANCASHIRE TRENCH [illegible] 200 yds of the [illegible] [illegible] 12 [illegible]	[illegible]
		5.30 & 11.35 am	Heavy shelling of LANCASHIRE TRENCH & SOMME ALLEY (X.1 & 2 – Ref map 57c SE).	
			At dusk Bn. [illegible] by 10th (S) Bn. NOTTS & DERBY Regt. & [illegible] W.9 [illegible] (Ref map 57c SE). Bn. H.Q. established at W.9 a 9.1 (Ref map 57c SE).	
Bn. H.Q. – W.9 a 9.1 (Ref map 57c SE)	22		Bn. resting.	[illegible]
	23	8.30 pm	do. Bn. moved off [illegible] 10th (S) Bn. LANCASHIRE FUSILIERS in the [illegible] sector of the Divisional front in Q.28 b, Q.29 c, Q.34 & Q.35 a & c (Ref map 57c SE). Bn. H.Q. established at W.4 a 6.7 (Ref map 57c SE).	[illegible] 6 G. Ho. 54
Bn. H.Q. – W.4 a 6.7 (Ref map 57c SE)	24		Bn. in the line, Situation quiet.	[illegible]
	25		do. do. [illegible] [illegible] the 21st Division [illegible] [illegible] 12th/13th (S) Bn. NORTHUMBERLAND FUSILIERS & [illegible]	6 G. Ho. 55

D. D. & L., London, E.C.
(A10266) Wt W5300/P713 750,000 2/18 Sch. 52 Forms/C2118/16

10th (S) Bn. WEST YORKSHIRE REGIMENT

PAGE 4

Army Form C. 2118.

Instructions regarding War Diaries and Intelligence Summaries are contained in F. S. Regs., Part II. and the Staff Manual respectively. Title pages will be prepared in manuscript.

WAR DIARY
or
~~INTELLIGENCE SUMMARY.~~

SEPTEMBER 1918

(*Erase heading not required.*)

Place	Date	Hour	Summary of Events and Information	Remarks and references to Appendices
Bn. H.Q. Whaby (Ref map 57c SE)	SEPT. 25 (cont.)		to rest billets near LE MESNIL-EN-ARROUAISE, staying at P33d 5.1 (Ref map 57c SE)	[illegible]
LE MESNIL-EN-ARROUAISE.	26		Bn resting & cleaning up	[illegible]
	27		Inspection of Coys by Commanding Officer – Baths – Examination of Lewis Guns & Rifles by the Armourer	[illegible]
	28		Inspection of the Bn. by the G.O.C. – 50th Inf Bde	[illegible]
	29		Sunday – Divine Service	[illegible]
	30		Bn Training – Training of Lewis Gunners to replace casualties	[illegible]
			The following decorations were gained by Officers, N.C.O.s & men of the Battalion during the month. –	
			12th. Military Cross to Temp/Capt. M.F. SMITH, & Temp/Sec Lt C.V.S. SPENCER	
			" Bar to Military Medal to 15597 C.S.M. A. McG. ANDERSON, M.M., 21715 Pte. T. McMAHON, M.M.	
			Military Medal to 11965 Pte C. MYNOTT, 235752 Pte W. STANCLIFFE, 10908 Sgt H. DACK, 51442 L/c R.J. SMITH, 18/390 Cpl J.A. BRINDLE, 16/157 L/c H. MARTIN	
			15th. Military Medal to 15170 Pte E.N. LLEWELLYN, 11546 Pte E. BARKER, 43276 Cpl J. DAKIN (att 50th I.T.M. Btty)	
			26th. Distinguished Service Order to Temp/Maj A/Lt Col W. GIBSON, M.C., Temp/Sec Lt J.C. BRAITHWAITE, M.C.	
			Distinguished Conduct Medal to 18536 Pte T. THOMPSON	
			Military Medal to 7601,28 Sgt. WHITE A.V., 43650 L/c NOBLE, H., 12/13948 Pte DOWNS A.H., 51796 Pte WIGHTON, [illegible]	

C.W. Waite Major

Commanding 10th (S) Bn. West Yorkshire Regt

A5834 Wt. W4973/M687 750,000 8/16 D. D. & L. Ltd. Forms/C.2118/13.

SECRET

Copy No.

OPERATION ORDER No. 35

Refce Map 57c SE. 1/20,000.

25-9-18.

WEST YORKSHIRE REGT.

Information The Battalion will be relieved in the line tonight by the 12th/13th/5th FUSILIERS, and on relief will move to LE MESNIL taking over accommodation previously occupied by units of the 62nd Infy Bde.

'A' Coy W. York. R. will be relieved by 'D' Coy 5th Fusiliers.

'B' Coy W. York. R. will be relieved by 'B' Coy 5th Fusiliers.

'C' Coy W. York. R. will be relieved by 'A' Coy 5th Fusiliers.

'D' Coy W. York. R. will be relieved by 'C' Coy 5th Fusiliers.

Instructions

1. Guides will reconnoitre the route from their Coys to the three cross roads Q 32 d 70.35 and will be prepared

to guide the incoming unit from this point.

One guide per platoon, one for Coy HdQrs and two for Battn HdQrs will be sent.

The guides will await the incoming Companies at this point, reporting to 2Lt H.W. RAMSDEN at 7 pm at Q 32 d 70.35.

2. On completion of relief Coys will move independently to P 33 d 5.1. where a hot meal will await them. The usual intervals between platoons will be observed. Guides from Cookers will meet Coys at V 6 a 2.6 and

[illegible] ~~3.~~ X ~~Stores~~. for billets will meet Coys at O 35 d 9.9.

3. Stores. All S.A.A, bombs, fireworks and trench stores will be handed over and receipts obtained.

These receipts will be forwarded to Battn HdQrs by 9 am tomorrow 26th.

4. <u>Dead Bodies</u>. Prior to relief all dead bodies lying in Coy areas will be buried. Graves will be marked, and locations and identification notified to Battn HdQrs.

5. <u>Lewis Gun Limbers</u> will await Coys at Road Junction Q 32 d 70.35 from 8-30 pm onwards.
Coy Commanders chargers will be at P33 d 5.1.

6. <u>Salvage</u> will be dumped at Bn HQ by 8 p.m.
Any Petrol tins that may be salved will be placed on the Lewis Gun limbers.

7. <u>Completion of Relief</u> will be notified to Bn HQ by code word — Name of Coy Commander concerned

8. ACKNOWLEDGE.

[illegible] Capt A/Adjt
10th West Yorkshire Regt

Copies to –

1 OC 'A' Coy
2. OC 'B' "
3 OC 'C' "
4 OC 'D' "
5 RSM
6 2/Lt H W RAMSDEN
7. O.C. 12th/13th/5th Fusiliers.
8 File
9 Spare

SECRET Operation Order No 34 Copy No 8

Map Ref:- 57c SE 1/20,000 23-9-18

West Yorkshire Regt

Information.

The Batt[n] will relieve the 10th Bn Lancashire Fusiliers in the left sub-sector of the left sector of the Divisional Front tonight 23rd/24th Sept.

'D' Co[y] W York R will relieve 'A' Co[y] 10th Lan. Fus.

'A' Co[y] W York R will relieve 'C' Co[y] 10th Lan. Fus

'C' Co[y] W York R will relieve 'B' Co[y] 10th Lan. Fus

'B' Co[y] W York R will relieve 'D' Co[y] 10th Lan. Fus.

Instructions

1. The Batt[n] will move off in the following order

'D' Coy

'B'

'C' Coy
'A' Coy
Bn. Hd Qrs.

2. The leading Coy will reach the [illegible] at W4 b 0.5 at 8.30pm where they will be met by 3 guides of the 10th Lan Fus.

The remaining Coys will move at ¼ hour intervals meeting their guides (3 per Coy) at the same spot.

Hd Qrs will move ¼ hour after A Coy and will proceed straight to their destination at W4 a 6.8

3 ~~Rations~~ will be dumped at Bn. HdQrs W4 a 6.8 at 10 pm.

Coys will provide their own ration parties.

4 ~~Stores~~ will be handed over and taken over in the usual way and receipts forwarded to Bn. Hd Qrs by 10 a.m. 24th inst.

5. <u>Disposition Maps</u> will be forwarded to B^n H.Q. by 4 a.m. 24th inst.

6. <u>Completion of Relief</u> will be notified to B^n H.Q. by runner.

Code word — Name of Coy Commander concerned.

7. ACKNOWLEDGE.

W.R[illegible] Capt A/Adjt
[illegible]

23.9.18

Issued at 11.45 p.m.

Copies to.

1 O.C. A Coy
2 O.C. B "
3 O.C. C "
4 O.C. D "
5 R.S.M.
6 T.O.
7 10th Lan. Fus.
8 File.

14

Vol 34

10th

West-Yorkshire Regt

35E.
11 sheets

15th Battn. P.W.O. the West Yorkshire Regt

SHEET 1

Army Form C. 2118.

WAR DIARY

or

~~INTELLIGENCE SUMMARY.~~

(*Erase heading not required.*)

Instructions regarding War Diaries and Intelligence Summaries are contained in F. S. Regs., Part II. and the Staff Manual respectively. Title pages will be prepared in manuscript.

October 1918

Place	Date	Hour	Summary of Events and Information	Remarks and references to Appendices
LE MESNIL-EN-ARROUISE	Oct 1st	0830 1200	Companies under Coy Commanders on Salvage Work	
"	" 2nd	0830 1230	Companies on Salvage Work + cleaning arms + equipment	
"	3rd	0900 to 1200	Baths for C + D Coy at LE MESNIL. Coys on salvage work	
"	4th	0900 to 1200	Baths for A + B Coys at LE MESNIL. Coys on Salvage work. Battn under 2 hrs notice to move	
"	" 5th	1130	Battn received orders to move to W4 + W5 SW of GOUZENCOURT	
GOUZENCOURT	5th	1730	Battn in position. BHQ established at W4d9.5	
"	6th		LT-COL W GIBSON DSO MC assumes command of battn on returning from leave	J.C. [illegible]
"	"		2/LT F KIRK 2/LT R CLEGG awarded MC. No20240 Sgt SCOTT J. A Coy 43313 Sgt DAMMS	
"	"		C Coy ~~Pte~~ 49352 Pte Hodgson H.D. D Coy awarded MM	
"	"	0900 1200	Officers all Coys reconnoitred forward crossings ST QUENTIN CANAL	
"	"	-	All Companies inspected by Commanding Officer	
"	7th	0900 1200	Further reconnaissance of forward area by Offrs + NCO's.	
			Coys training under Coy Cmdrs. SAA inspected by all Coys	

D. D. & L., London, E.C.
(A10266) Wt W5300/P713 750,000 2/18 Sch. 52 Forms/C2118/16

SHEET 2

Army Form C. 2118.

WAR DIARY
or
INTELLIGENCE SUMMARY.
(Erase heading not required.)

Instructions regarding War Diaries and Intelligence Summaries are contained in F. S. Regs., Part II. and the Staff Manual respectively. Title pages will be prepared in manuscript.

Place	Date	Hour	Summary of Events and Information	Remarks and references to Appendices
GOUZENCOURT	Oct 8	1100	Orders received to move to S4 Hindenburg Support Line E of HONNENCOURT	
		1130	Batt moved off	
		1730	Arrived in position BHQ at S4c95	
		2359	Orders received to position BHQ move battn to N32 NW of VILLERS OUTREAUX	
	Oct 9	0130	Batt moved off by cross country route to N32 Bde in support to 52nd Bde	
		0500	Bn arrived in position BHQ at N32c7550 E of MONTCOUVEY FARM	
		0800	Battn moved to V20a positions in front of GARD WOOD and SE of SELVIGNY. BHQ at SORVAL CHATEAU	
		2000	Bn moved to positions in O10c E of CHAULERY. BHQ at O9d4505	
	10	0130	Received orders to pass through 51st Bde and continue attack	
		0415	Battn moved to assembly positions	
		0510	Batt in assembly positions E of MONTIGNY on line O6c94 to O12b52	
		0520	ZERO Advanced commenced BHQ established at O6c8.3	
		0550	Reached 1st bound to J31d – P2a. No enemy resistance	
		0625		

D. D. & L., London, E.C.
(A10266) Wt W5300/P713 750,000 2/18 Sch. 52 Forms/C2118/16

SHEET 3

Army Form C. 2118.

WAR DIARY
or
INTELLIGENCE SUMMARY.
(Erase heading not required.)

Instructions regarding War Diaries and Intelligence Summaries are contained in F. S. Regs., Part II. and the Staff Manual respectively. Title pages will be prepared in manuscript.

Place	Date	Hour	Summary of Events and Information	Remarks and references to Appendices
	Oct 10	0625	Reached 2nd bound Rly J32b and J32c. No enemy resistance	
		0700	Reached 3rd bound J27 and J28c; came under enemy artillery fire	
			Captured two field guns	
		0720	Passed through INCHY	
		0740	Reached 4th Objective	
		0755	Reached 5th Objective. Battn dug in as ordered. Dispositions:- B Coy trenches in K13b. C Coy continued line across ravine J18b24. A Coy in support to B Coy 500 yds in rear	JO [illegible]
		1500	Orders received to attack NEUVILLY and high ground in K3 K4 + K10A	
		1645	Battn in assembly positions in K13. Front of 600 yds. B + C in front D + A in support. BHQ in ravine K7c92	
		1700	ZERO Batt moved forward to attack. Enemy encountered holding village in strength. Bridges across river blown up. Two left Coys definitely held up in village. Two right Coys forced crossing of river about K8b6000 in touch with one Coy SEAFORTH HIGHLANDERS of 33rd Div.	
		1900	Coy of SEAFORTHS withdrawn + later these two Coys were compelled to do so. The Battn established line along road from K7d38 to K14b86. BHQ at K13b44	
	Oct 11	1330	Orders received to establish crossing of river in K8d and K9c. and get in touch with reported post of the right div at K9c43	
		1700	B Coy + 3 Platoons C Coy moved forward towards river	

D. D. & L., London, E.C.
(A10266) Wt W5300/P713 750,000 2/18 Sch. 52 Forms/C2118/16

SHEET 4

Army Form C. 2118.

WAR DIARY
or
INTELLIGENCE SUMMARY.
(Erase heading not required.)

Instructions regarding War Diaries and Intelligence Summaries are contained in F. S. Regs., Part II. and the Staff Manual respectively. Title pages will be prepared in manuscript.

Place	Date	Hour	Summary of Events and Information	Remarks and references to Appendices
	Oct 11	1810	Advanced BHQ 100 yds W of river at K9c40	
		1815	Commanding officer + 2/Lt. P. HART reconnoitred river + crossed on tree trunk at K9c4510. "B" Coy were then led forward, + commenced crossing river at this point	
		2000	Two platoons 'C' Coy having crossed river, established a strong point at K8d99 flanking the village. "B" Coy crossed river + worked forward to Railway	
		2330	B Coy cleared all ground W of road through K9a C and d on a front of 700 yds. Three enemy posts were encountered 23 killed + two prisoners taken 2 belts of barbed wire fence found between this road + railway, and a further advance without artillery was impossible. Four platoon posts established on line of road K9a 1.3 to K9d 1.3. Protective Flanks formed at each end of this line. Three platoon posts established in support 100 yds E of river along line K8d99 to K9c71. Four bridges were constructed over river ~~on~~ this ~~point~~ line, by RE's + were completed before daylight.	JCL
	Oct 12	0310	9th Duke of Wellington R reached BHQ at K13b 44 and were given guides to assembly positions near road K14b and K15a and later 10th Lancs: Fus. were guided forward to their assembly positions immediately in rear of 9th D of W R	
		0500	ZERO 52 Bde moved forward to attack	
		0505	Heavy enemy barrage along road K14b and K15a. Attack of 52nd Infantry Brigade held up at this point	

D. D. & L., London, E.C.
(A10266) Wt W5300/P713 750,000 2/18 Sch. 52 Forms/C2118/16

SHEET 5

Army Form C. 2118.

Instructions regarding War Diaries and Intelligence Summaries are contained in F. S. Regs., Part II. and the Staff Manual respectively. Title pages will be prepared in manuscript.

WAR DIARY
or
INTELLIGENCE SUMMARY.
(Erase heading not required.)

Place	Date	Hour	Summary of Events and Information	Remarks and references to Appendices
INCHY	Oct 12	0900	Batt less 6 platoons in billets at INCHY	
MONTIGNY	14	1600	Batt less 6 platoons moved to billets at MONTIGNY	
	Oct 13	1030	"B" Coy + 2 platoons "C" Coy rejoined batt. at MONTIGNY	
			War Material Captured :- 2 Enemy Field Guns	
			Casualties :- Officers Killed :- Capt + Adjt. K.S. RUDD	
			" Wounded 2/LT H PRITCHARD 2/LT W.P. PEARSON	
			" B HARDAKER " A ALLINSON	
			" P de LACEY " W A COATES	
			A. SIMPKIN	
			Other Ranks Killed 16 Missing 27	
			" Wounded 125 Died of Wounds 1	
–		0900 1200	Inspection of deficiencies. Re-organisation of sections + platoons Lewis gunners + Signallers brought up to strength. Arms drill musketry &c	
MONTIGNY	14	0900 1230	P.T. Lewis Gun Training &c. Inspection of Bde by G.O.C.	
"	15.		58th Bde to relieve 5?th Bde in front system NEUVILLY sector	
		1600	Reconnoitring party 1 Offr + 2 OR per Coy left MONTIGNY	
		2045	Battn moved into position	
		2120	Relief complete BHQ established at J 24 a	JCS

D. D. & L., London, E.C.
(A10266) Wt W5300/P713 750,000 2/18 Sch. 52 Forms/C2118/15

SHEET 6

Army Form C. 2118.

WAR DIARY
or
INTELLIGENCE SUMMARY.
(*Erase heading not required.*)

Instructions regarding War Diaries and Intelligence Summaries are contained in F. S. Regs., Part II. and the Staff Manual respectively. Title pages will be prepared in manuscript.

Place	Date	Hour	Summary of Events and Information	Remarks and references to Appendices
NEUVILLY SECTOR	Oct 16		Battn in support. BHQ moved to J 02 b 65	
	-17		52nd Bde relieved 50th Bde	
		1700	B C + D Coy reliefs complete	
		2045	A Coy Relief complete	
			Billets in INCHY	
INCHY		2130	BHQ established at J 22 a 9025	
	-18	0900-1200	Baths in billets cleaning clothing + equipment Reorganisation of sections + platoons	JCE [initials]
	-19		Orders received for attack on NEUVILLY	
-		0900 1200	Training for attack + bombing practice.	
			Afternoon rest.	
-		1900	Battn left INCHY to take up positions for attack	
		2200	Battn arrived in position + relieved DUKE OF WELLINGTON R	
NEUVILLY		2330	Relief complete:- Positions:- A + D Coys E bank of river SELLE in K 1 d facing N.E	
			BHQ established at K 8 d 24	
SECTOR	20	0100	Patrol under 2/Lt E BARNES occupied the old mill + houses about K 9 c 57. Patrol under 2/Lt H BRYANT encountered enemy holding copse on E side of river in K 8 d and K 9 a 00. 2/LT BRYANT wounded + 8 casualties OR	

D. D. & L., London, E.C.
(A10266) Wt W5300/P713 750,000 2/18 Sch. 52 Forms/C2118/16

SHEET 7

Army Form C. 2118.

Instructions regarding War Diaries and Intelligence Summaries are contained in F. S. Regs., Part II. and the Staff Manual respectively. Title pages will be prepared in manuscript.

WAR DIARY
or
INTELLIGENCE SUMMARY.
(Erase heading not required.)

Place	Date	Hour	Summary of Events and Information	Remarks and references to Appendices
NEUVILLY	Oct 20	0200	ZERO. Barrage on enemy positions. DORSETS N. of village E. YORK R. S of village advanced to attack each closely followed by two Coys of W. YORK. i.e. A+D Coys North and B+C. South.	
-		0500	Village cleared + battn took up a position E of and along line of the Railway in K2d + K9a. BHQ established at K8A78	
		0600	Coys reorganised + commenced consolidation of their positions. Enemy shelled NEUVILLY + the valley intermittently throughout day mostly gas.	J. Ch[illegible]
	21.		Battn holding the line. E. YORK R + DORSETS, holding RED LINE from cross roads K2b to road junction K10a, were relieved by A C + D Coys who took over their positions. D Coy remained in support K8C00	
			War Material Captured :- Prisoners 84 Machine Guns 34 Trench Mortars 6 German T S Waggon 3 Horses 2	
			Casualties :- 2/LT R G JONES killed. 2LT H BRYANT 2/Lt L PEEL wounded Other Ranks killed 13 wounded 61 missing 7	
			5th Bde less 1 batn moved to INCHY. W. York R detailed to remain in	

D. D. & L., London, E.C.
(A10266) Wt W5300/P713 750,000 2/18 Sch. 52 Forms/C2118/16

SHEET 8

Army Form C. 2118.

Instructions regarding War Diaries and Intelligence Summaries are contained in F. S. Regs., Part II. and the Staff Manual respectively. Title pages will be prepared in manuscript.

WAR DIARY
or
INTELLIGENCE SUMMARY.
(Erase heading not required.)

Place	Date	Hour	Summary of Events and Information	Remarks and references to Appendices
NEUVILLY	Oct 22		Battn holding same line	
		1437	Battn ordered to withdraw to billets in INCHY at 1700 hrs	
		1700	Battn moved out to INCHY	
INCHY		1900	BHQ established in INCHY J22a 9055	
	-23	0800	Orders received for 17th Div. to follow up 21st Div. 50th Bde to move to AMERVAL	
		1135	Battn moved off from INCHY	
		1400	Battn arrived in position K4a	
		1600	Orders received for battn to move to billets in NEUVILLY	
NEUVILLY		1830	Battn in billets in NEUVILLY K8a. BHQ opposite church in K8a	
"	-24		Cleaning up billets, equipment rifles &c.	
	-25	0830 1230	P.T. Arms drill, close order drill, &c Specialists under specialist Offrs.	
			No 41830 Pte LUMBA awarded M.M.	
		1400	NCOs class under RSM Officers riding class under QM.	
	-26	0830	Bde received orders to move forward. Battn left NEUVILLY	
		1130	Battn halted at VENDIGIES for lunch.	
		1400	Battn in bivouacs on outskirts of POIX du NORD	
			BHQ established at 57B NE F2a 26	

D. D. & L., London, E.C.
(A10266) Wt W5300/P713 750,000 2/18 Sch. 52 Forms/C2118/16

SHEET 9

Army Form C. 2118.

Instructions regarding War Diaries and Intelligence Summaries are contained in F. S. Regs., Part II. and the Staff Manual respectively. Title pages will be prepared in manuscript.

WAR DIARY
or
INTELLIGENCE SUMMARY.

(Erase heading not required.)

Place	Date	Hour	Summary of Events and Information	Remarks and references to Appendices
POIX du NORD	Oct 26	1800	Companies moved to billets in POIX du NORD	
	-27		Coys cleaning up equipment &c	
		1930	All Coys of battn on working party under RE. to dig defensive system of trenches in 51a SE X 22d X 23c + X 29a.	
	-28	0200	Working party returned. Casualty 1 OR wounded.	
		0830 1200	Specialists training under specialist Officers	JCi
	29		Rifle inspection & close order drill. Burying horses & dead Germans	
	.	1200	50th Bde recd orders that they would be relieved by 62nd Inf Bde.	
		1600	Battn relieved by 12/13th N. Fus. & moved to NEUVILLY, occupying same billets which were vacated on 26th inst.	
			BHQ opposite Church in K8a.	
			13597 CSM. A McG ANDERSON MM D Coy awarded DCM	
			40126 Sgt A V. WHITE MM. D Coy - bar to MM	
			11965 L/c C MYNOTT MM A - bar to MM	
			Following were awarded MILITARY MEDAL:—	
			24339 Cpl S WHINCUP C Coy 52017 Pte T. BOOMSMA C Coy	
			39557 - W WAITE D - 79705 - H GREENHOW B -	
			42226 L/c J W. KILBURN D - 8346 - E TOWNSEND D - attd 50th Bde	
			27381 - W. TAYLOR attd LTMB	

D. D. & L., London, E.C.
(A10260) Wt W5300/P713 750,000 2/18 Sch. 52 Forms/C2118/16

SHEET 10

Army Form C. 2118.

WAR DIARY
or
INTELLIGENCE SUMMARY.
(Erase heading not required.)

Instructions regarding War Diaries and Intelligence Summaries are contained in F. S. Regs., Part II. and the Staff Manual respectively. Title pages will be prepared in manuscript.

Place	Date	Hour	Summary of Events and Information	Remarks and references to Appendices
NEUVILLY	Oct 30		Baths for all Coys in NEUVILLY	
		0830 1230	Inspection of rifle equipment &c Batn Drill	
		1400	NCO's class under RSM. Officers riding class under QM. Coys paid.	
–	31	0830 1230	PT. Musketry close order drill Batt Drill Specialists under specialist offrs	
		1400	NCOs class Officers riding class.	

W. Gibson Lt Col.
Comdg. 10th W. York R.

D. D. & L., London, E.C.
(A10266) Wt W5300/P713 750,000 2/18 Sch. 52 Forms/C2118/16

Vol 35

10th West Yorkshire R

86 E.
9 sheet

10th (S) Battn WEST YORKSHIRE REGT. SHEET 1

Army Form C. 2118.

WAR DIARY NOVEMBER ~~or~~ 1918 ~~INTELLIGENCE SUMMARY.~~

(Erase heading not required.)

Instructions regarding War Diaries and Intelligence Summaries are contained in F. S. Regs., Part II. and the Staff Manual respectively. Title pages will be prepared in manuscript.

Place	Date	Hour	Summary of Events and Information	Remarks and references to Appendices
NEUVILLY 34	NOV. 1st		Battn HQ at Sheet 57BNE K8a opposite church	[initials]
		0830 1230	Physical Training, Musketry & Battalion Drill	
		1400	NCOs Class under RSM. Lecture for all Officers on "Wood fighting" by C.O.	
"	2nd	0830	Inspection of arms & equipment. Orders received 50th Bde to relieve 64th Bde in VENDIGIES	[initials]
		1930	Battn left NEUVILLY	
VENDIGIES		2030	Battn in billets in VENDIGIES. BHQ established at 57BNE F7a77	[initials]
BHQ F7a77 (57BNE)	3rd	·	Training & preparing for next advance. Orders received for attack on FORÊT de NORMAL	[initials]
	4th	0130	Battn moved to preliminary assembly positions in Quarries in X20 (Ref 51ASE)	[initials]
			BHQ moved to F4b97 (Ref 57BNE)	
		0314	Movement complete	[initials]
		0700	All ranks had breakfast	[initials]
		0845	Battn moved forward to second assembly position X24c (Ref 51ASE)	
		0945	Battn moved to third assembly positions in S22d & S28b (Ref 51SW)	
BHQ S22d12		1200	Movement complete. BHQ established at Cross Rds S22d12 (Ref 51SW)	
			At ZERO 0530 hrs 52nd Bde had attacked & formed captured BLUE line. 51st Bde then passed through & captured second objective ie road running N & S through S17 S23 & S29 (Ref 51SW). Our third assembly positions was immediately WEST of this road	[initials]
		1230	Leading Companies A on right B on left moved forward in attack formation. B Coy in support C Coy in reserve. BHQ in position between support & reserve Coys	[initials]
		1259	Barrage came down 300 yds in front of Red line & commenced to move forward. Battn advanced keeping close to barrage.	
		1330	Battn reached N & S grid line S24a00 (Ref 51SW) S30a00. Advance continuing little or no resistance	[initials]

D. D. & L., London, E.C.
(A10266) Wt W5300/P713 750,000 2/18 Sch. 52 Forms/C2118/16

10TH (S) BATTN WEST YORKSHIRE REGT

SHEET 2

Army Form C. 2118.

WAR DIARY

NOVEMBER 1918

or

INTELLIGENCE SUMMARY.

(Erase heading not required.)

Instructions regarding War Diaries and Intelligence Summaries are contained in F. S. Regs., Part II. and the Staff Manual respectively. Title pages will be prepared in manuscript.

Place	Date	Hour	Summary of Events and Information	Remarks and references to Appendices
BHQ S24 a 00	Nov 4	1400	Battn reached edge of wood N of line running through S24 c 9.0 (Ref 51SW) MG fire from direction of T19 c 00 & from right flank	
		1414	D Coy reached INSTITUT FORESTIER S24 d 44 (Ref 51SW)	
		1440	INSTITUT FORESTIER cleared. Advance continuing. Considerable enemy opposition mainly from MG fire. LIASON POST established with 14TH WELSH R established at S29 b 8.8 (Ref 51SW)	
BHQ S24 d 04		1530	D Coy left flank reached S19 c 05 held up by MG fire from both flanks. A Coy reached S30 b 05 & were also held up by MG fire from LOCQUIGNOL. BHQ established at S 24 d 04. A Coy ordered to move NORTH round INSTITUT FORESTIER and then due EAST and to pass through D Coy who were much dis-organised. D Coy then to reform behind A Coy & follow in support. B Coy in support were moved forward & parallel to the LOCQUIGNOL ROAD to work S.E.	
		1700	B Coy reached line S30 b 44 to S24 a 70. A Coy encountered considerable enemy opposition	
		1710	Captain J.P. LAWSON (OC B Coy) and 2 O.R patrolled to within 200 yds of church. They killed two of the enemy whom they encountered but were fired upon by a MG just SOUTH of church. Two other enemy MG's were firing in a South Westerly direction	
		1800	A Coy on line T25 a 4.9 to T19 c 6.5 and D Coy reorganised in support. It was now dark. An Officers patrol under Capt C. ARCHER MC reached T19 c 9.5 BHQ at INSTITUT de FORESTIER	
BHQ INSTITUT FORESTIER				

D. D. & L., London, E.C. (A10266) Wt W5300/P713 750,000 2/18 Sch. 52 Forms/C2118/16

10TH (S) BATTN WEST YORKSHIRE REGT SHEET 3

Army Form C. 2118.

Instructions regarding War Diaries and Intelligence Summaries are contained in F. S. Regs., Part II. and the Staff Manual respectively. Title pages will be prepared in manuscript.

WAR DIARY
or
INTELLIGENCE SUMMARY.

(Erase heading not required.)

NOVEMBER 1918

Place	Date	Hour	Summary of Events and Information	Remarks and references to Appendices
INSTITUT FORESTIER	NOV 4	1945	Report of this patrol reached BHQ. It was then decided to attack village with artillery support ZERO to be at 2200 hours. At this stage Bde Major arrived at BHQ & stated that a definite line must be reported to Division before 2200hrs. The line was therefore reported as it stood & attack was cancelled. D Coy moved forward to fill gap between A Coy & DORSET R whose position on the left was uncertain at K19a 03 (Ref 57 SW)	[illegible]
		2300	Two patrols were sent out. 1) to reconnoitre village 2) to establish a post EAST of and covering cross roads T26 b 08	[illegible]
		2359	Report of patrols received 1) Village vacated by enemy 2) Post established WEST of cross roads strength 1 platoon in close touch with enemy post just EAST of cross roads	[illegible]
	NOV 5	0030	On these reports Bde ordered village to be held. C Coy from reserve moved forward & established two platoon posts SOUTH of village and one SE of it, with one platoon in support. C Coy obtained touch with WELSH R at T25 central	[illegible]
		0500	C Coy reported enemy retiring towards FOREST at T20 d & T26 b	[illegible]
		0630	B Coy ordered to move forward & establish three posts EAST of covering cross roads T26 b 08 with two platoons in support. All the objectives of the battalion was now held	[illegible]
		0645	Leading troops of 21st DIVISION passed cross roads T26 b 08	[illegible]
LOCQUIGNOL BHQ S24 d 32		0900	Battn withdrawn to billets and settled in LOCQUIGNOL BHQ established at S24 d 32	[illegible]

D. D. & L., London, E.C.
(A10266) Wt W5300/P713 750,000 2/18 Sch. 52 Forms/C2118/16

(18th(S) BATTN WEST YORKSHIRE REGT.) SHEET 2

Army Form C. 2118.

Instructions regarding War Diaries and Intelligence Summaries are contained in F. S. Regs., Part II. and the Staff Manual respectively. Title pages will be prepared in manuscript.

WAR DIARY or INTELLIGENCE SUMMARY.

NOVEMBER 1918

(Erase heading not required.)

Place	Date	Hour	Summary of Events and Information	Remarks and references to Appendices
LOCQUIGNOL BHQ S24d32	Nov 5		Prisoners captured - 10	
			Material " 1	
			MGs encountered estimated at 40	[initials]
			Casualties: Officers wounded 2/Lt C ARGILE	
			O.R. killed 20 wounded 35 missing 15	
	-6		Cleaning equipment rifles etc.	[initials]
	-7		Orders recd 17th div to relieve or pass through 21st div tonight	[initials]
		1130	Batt left LOCQUIGNOL	
AYMERIES		1600	Arrived at AYMERIES BHQ at cross roads U16a86 (Ref 51SW)	[initials]
		2100	Batt left AYMERIES	
BACHANT	Nov 8	0130	Batt arrived in BACHANT BHQ at V13c02 (Ref Sheet 51)	[initials]
		0430	Batt moved forward to take up position with remainder of Bde in support of 51st Bde	[initials]
BHQ V16d20		0530	Batt in support on outskirts of LIMONT FONTAINE BHQ at V16d20 (Ref Sheet 51)	[initials]
LIMONT FONTAINE V26a86	-9	0730	Village of LIMONT FONTAINE evacuated. Batt ordered to move into billets in village	[initials]
		0930	Batt in billets in LIMONT FONTAINE. BHQ at V26a86 opposite Church	[initials]
			Cleaning up equipment & salvage work	
	-10	1100	Divine service	[initials]
		1400	Sports	

D. D. & L., London, E.C.
(A10266) Wt W5300/P713 750,000 2/18 Sch. 52 Forms/C2118/16

16th (S) Bn. WEST YORKSHIRE REGT

SHEET 5

Army Form C. 2118.

Instructions regarding War Diaries and Intelligence Summaries are contained in F. S. Regs., Part II. and the Staff Manual respectively. Title pages will be prepared in manuscript.

WAR DIARY or INTELLIGENCE SUMMARY.

NOVEMBER 1918

(Erase heading not required.)

Place	Date	Hour	Summary of Events and Information	Remarks and references to Appendices
LIMONT FONTAINE	Nov 11	0830	News received that an armistice had been signed & that hostilities would cease at 1100 hours today. All ranks notified companies by Commanding Officer. As the enemy had been retiring there had been no firing for some time so there was no sudden cessation of hostilities at 1100 hours.	[illegible]
		0930	Battn left LIMONT FONTAINE from billets to march back	[illegible]
BERLAIMONT		1200	Battn arrived in BERLAIMONT & was billeted there for the night	[illegible]
	Nov 12	1030	Battn left BERLAIMONT	[illegible]
ENGLEFONTAINE		1430	Battn arrived in ENGLEFONTAINE BHQ at A20a02 (Ref Sheet 57)	[illegible]
			Battn billeted there for the night	[illegible]
	Nov 13	0930	Battn left ENGLEFONTAINE	[illegible]
BERTRY		1530	Battn arrived in BERTRY BHQ established at P14b37 (Ref Sheet 57B)	
BHQ P14b37			The whole brigade finally billeted in this area	
		1130	Foot inspection	[illegible]
	15	0900–1200	Coys under Coy commanders inspection reorganisation & fitting equipment	
			Arms drill etc & close order drill	
			BHQ reorganised as follows: Signallers 1 Sgt 18 OR Pioneers 1 Sgt 8 OR	[illegible]
			Regt Police 1 Sgt 1 L/Cpl & 6 OR	
		1400	Rugby & Association football. Two good grounds [illegible]	
	16	0900	Physical Training Coy inspections Close order drill Coy [illegible]	[illegible]
		1400	Football	
			Lieut Col. BRAITHWAITE DSO MC rejoined & resumed command [illegible] of D Coy.	[illegible]

D. D. & L., London, E.C.
(A10266) Wt W5300/P713 750,000 2/18 Sch. 52 Forms/C2118/16

10th (S) BATTN. WEST YORKSHIRE REGT. SHEET [illegible]

Instructions regarding War Diaries and Intelligence Summaries are contained in F. S. Regs., Part II. and the Staff Manual respectively. Title pages will be prepared in manuscript.

WAR DIARY

NOVEMBER or 1918

INTELLIGENCE SUMMARY.

(Erase heading not required.)

Army Form C. 2118.

Place	Date	Hour	Summary of Events and Information	Remarks and references to Appendices
BERTRY P14 b 3 7 (57B)	Nov 17	1000	Divine Services	
		1400	Sports	[illegible]
			Following awarded M.C. CAPT J.R. LAWSON 2T. P HART 2Lt E BARNES. DCM CSM PICKARD P C Cpl. [illegible]	
	-18	0900	Physical Training by Inspection. Saluting drill. Guard drill etc. Salvage work	
		1400	Sports	[illegible]
	-19	0900	P.T. Inspection S.B.R.s by Bde Gas NCO.	
		1400	Sports. Coys paid.	[illegible]
	-20	0900	Lecture to all Coys on Educational scheme for demobilisation by Battn. E.O.	
		1000	Route march. Coys complete, salvage work.	[illegible]
		1400	Sports	[illegible]
	-21	0900	P.T. Guard mounting. Arms drill. Battn. drill	
		1400	Sports	
	-22	0900	Baths in BERTRY allotted to Battn. All Coys bathed. P.T. by Coys	[illegible]
		1400	Inter platoon matches	
	-23	0900	P.T. Battn. drill	[illegible]
		1400	Sports	
	-24	1000	Divine Service	[illegible]
		1400	Football	
			CAPT J.C. BRAITHWAITE DSO MC proceeded to England to report to Ministry of Labour	[illegible]

D. D. & L., London, E.C.
(A10266) Wt W5300/P713 750,000 2/18 Sch. 52 Forms/C2118/16

10th Batt West Yorkshire Regiment

SHEET 7

Army Form C. 2118.

WAR DIARY or ~~INTELLIGENCE SUMMARY.~~

November 1918

(*Erase heading not required.*)

Instructions regarding War Diaries and Intelligence Summaries are contained in F. S. Regs., Part II. and the Staff Manual respectively. Title pages will be prepared in manuscript.

Place	Date	Hour	Summary of Events and Information	Remarks and references to Appendices
BERTRY	Nov 25	0900	Battn on salvage work	[initials]
		1400	Sports	
	26	0830	Coy Inspections	[initials]
		01100	50th Infantry Bde inspected by G-O-C 17th Division.	
		1400	Sports. Advance billeting party proceeded to HALLENCOURT. LT AHNEWTON i/c	
	27	0830	Morning devoted to cleaning equipment	[initials]
		1400	Sports	
	28	0830	Coy equipment inspected by Commanding Officer	[initials]
		1400	Sports	
	29	0700	Baths allotted to Battn in BERTRY. All Coys. bathed during the day	[initials]
		0830	Coy drill Inspections of platoons &c	
		1400	Sports.	
	30	0830	Battn route march	[initials]
		1400	Sport. Censorship restrictions relaxed. Names of places where the battn is may be mentioned in letters.	

D. D. & L., London, E.C.
(A10266) Wt W5300/P713 750,000 2/18 Sch. 52 Forms/C2118/16

10th (S) BATTN WEST YORKSHIRE REGT

SHEET 5

Army Form C. 2118.

Instructions regarding War Diaries and Intelligence Summaries are contained in F. S. Regs., Part II. and the Staff Manual respectively. Title pages will be prepared in manuscript.

WAR DIARY
NOVEMBER ~~or~~ 1918
INTELLIGENCE SUMMARY.

(Erase heading not required.)

Place	Date	Hour	Summary of Events and Information	Remarks and references to Appendices
			The following Officers quitted during the month	
	Nov 1		2/LT NR CASSON to 50th LTMB	
	- 4		- C ARGILE wounded	
	- 24		CAPT J.C BRAITHWAITE DSO MC to Ministry of Labour	[illegible]
	- 25		LT. P HART MC on leave	
	- 11		LT HAYWOOD leave	
	- 30		2/LT H APPLEYARD on leave	
			The following Officers joined during the month	
	Nov 1		LT P HART rejoined from 50th LTMB	[illegible]
	- 7		2/LT A WATSON joined	
	- 7		- G.F. WOODTHORPE	
	- 10		- S.L WILSON	
	- 22		LT. C HOLMES rejoined	
	- 22		- C ARGILE –	
	- 24		2/LT E INGHAM from course	
			The following were awarded decorations during the month	
	Nov 11		Military Medal:- 32948 Sgt HEAP CH	[illegible]
	- 17		Military Cross:- Capt J P LAWSON LIEUT P HART 2/LT E BARNES	
	- 17		Distinguished Conduct Medal:- 17/696 C.S.M PICKARD P. 76450 Pte WOLFENDON S	

W. Gibson. Lt Col.
Comdg 10th (S) Battn P.W.O. The West Yorkshire Regt.

D. D. & L., London, E.C.
(A10266) Wt W5300/P713 750,000 2/18 Sch. 52 Forms/C2118/16

10th (S) Bn P.W.O. (The West Yorkshire Regt)

Army Form C. 2118.

Instructions regarding War Diaries and Intelligence Summaries are contained in F. S. Regs., Part II. and the Staff Manual respectively. Title pages will be prepared in manuscript.

WAR DIARY
DECEMBER – 1918

~~INTELLIGENCE SUMMARY.~~
(Erase heading not required.)

SHEET 1

98 36

Place	Date 1918	Hour	Summary of Events and Information	Remarks and references to Appendices
BERTRY Sheet 57B	Dec 1	0845	Divine Services All denominations	
		1400	Afternoon Sports	
			52 OR miners sent to CAMBRAI to be sent to England	[initials] Sheet No 2
	-2	0900	P.T	
		1015	Battn parade Inspection of Coys By Commanding Officer	
		1400	Sports	[initials]
			35 OR Miners dispatched to CAMBRAI to be sent to England	
	-3	0730 -1600	Battalion on Salvage work in Brigade Area	
			Following awarded Military Cross T/2LT J. CHALMERS-PARK 2/LT A.J. LONG	[initials]
	-4	0900	Battalion proceeded to INCHY (Sheet 57B) 17th Division formed up on	
		1100	NEUVILLY-INCHY ROAD to be inspected by HM The KING.	[initials]
			The division was lined up informally in groups on each side of the road.	
			HM The KING accompanied by HRH The PRINCE OF WALES and HRH PRINCE GEORGE	O.O. 8/12/18
			walked slowly ~~through~~ down the road passed the Battalion. 57 J 30 6	
		1400	Sports	[initials]
			LT-COL W. GIBSON proceeded to England on Course of Instruction at School of Tactics CAMBERLEY	
			LT-COL E. JAMES D.S.O. M.C.,	
	-5	0900 1200	P.T. Platoon + Coy Inspections Close Order + Arms drill	[initials]
			Salvage Party completing work in area. Afternoon Sports	
	-6	0900 -1200	P.T. Platoon + Coy drill Coys at disposal of Coy Cmdrs.	[initials]
		1400	Sports	
			LT A.H. PHILLIPS and 2/LT H. WAINWRIGHT rejoined	

D. D. & L., London, E.C.
(A10266) Wt W5300/P713 750,000 2/18 Sch. 52 Forms/C2118/16

87E 5 sheets

Instructions regarding War Diaries and Intelligence Summaries are contained in F. S. Regs., Part II. and the Staff Manual respectively. Title pages will be prepared in manuscript.

WAR DIARY
DECEMBER 1918
INTELLIGENCE SUMMARY.
(Erase heading not required.)

Army Form C. 2118.

SHEET 2

Place	Date	Hour	Summary of Events and Information	Remarks and references to Appendices
BERTRY 57B	Dec 7	0900	P.T. Coys at disposal of Coy Cmdrs. Inspection of billets by Commanding Officer	
		1400	Sports	
	8		Orders received that 17th Divn would march to new area by stages taking 7 days.	[illegible]
	-8	0845	Battn left BERTRY & marched to MASIGNIERES (VAL. 1/100,000) via MONTIGNY - LIGNY EGNES CREVAUL. No men fell out.	[illegible]
MASIGNIERES VAL 1/100,000		1400	Battn arrived in MASIGNIERES. Billeted in Third Army HQ billets. 19 Kils.	
	-9	0900	Battn left MASIGNIERES & marched to HERMIES	[illegible]
HERMIES		1300	Arrived in HERMIES Battn billeted in tents. Weather wet & muddy.	
VAL. 1/100,000	-10	0900	Battn left HERMIES & proceeded via BEAUMETZ, CAMBRAI - BAPAUME RD to FAVRIEUL	[illegible]
FAVRIEUL LENS 1/100,000		1345	Arrived in FAVRIEUL Billeted in old trench defence system. Weather very wet & heavy rain most of the way.	
	-11	0845	Battn proceeded to ALBERT via BAPAUME - ALBERT RD.	[illegible]
ALBERT LENS 1/100,000		1400	Arrived in ALBERT Billeted in tents. Weather still wet & muddy	
	-12	0900	Battn proceeded to ALLONVILLE via ALBERT - AMIENS Rd & PONT NOYELLES.	[illegible]
ALLONVILLE Amiens 1/100,000		1430	Arrived in ALLONVILLE Very wet & severe march 2 men fell out but rejoined in billets. Billeted in Barns. Accommodation good.	
	-13	0900	Battn proceeded to PICQUIGNY via AMIENS DREUILLE & AILLY. Battn halted at DREUILLE for 30 mins. Hot tea served to men.	[illegible]
PICQUIGNY		1500	Arrived in PICQUIGNY. Billets good	
Amiens 1/100,000	-14	0930	Battn proceeded on march to new area via SOUES LE QUESNOY AIRAINES DREUILLE ALLERY to MERELESSART and CITERNE.	[illegible]
		1830	1 hours halt for dinner was made at LE QUESNOY	

D. D. & L., London, E.C.
(A10266) Wt W5300/P713 750,000 2/18 Sch. 52 Forms/C2118/16

Instructions regarding War Diaries and Intelligence Summaries are contained in F. S. Regs., Part II. and the Staff Manual respectively. Title pages will be prepared in manuscript.

WAR DIARY

DECEMBER or 1918 ~~INTELLIGENCE SUMMARY.~~

(Erase heading not required.)

Army Form C. 2118.

SHEET 3

Place	Date	Hour	Summary of Events and Information	Remarks and references to Appendices
MERELESSART	Dec 14	1630	Battn arrived in MERELESSART A + D Coys + BHQ established there.	
and		1700	B + C Coys ~~proceeded~~ arrived at CITERNE. Billets not good. Election Ballot Papers Received	JCl
CITERNE			During the whole of the march only 2 men had to be evacuated to Field Amb.	
(Dieppe 1/100,000	- 15		No parades. Battn rested in billets.	
BHQ at			CAPT. A.N. CLARK and 2/LT H. MILES rejoined. CAPT CLARK acting 2nd in command	JCl
MERELESSART	16	1410	Afternoon spent in Cleaning up	
			GRO 5585 published authority use of cameras	
	- 17	0900	P.T. Coys inspected in full marching order by Commanding Officer	JCl
			Audit board audited regimental accounts	
	- 18	0900	P.T. Coys at disposal of Coy Cmdrs. SBR's inspected.	
		1200	Bath at HALLENCOURT allotted to A + D Coys	
	- 19	0900	PT. Coys at disposal of Coy Cmdrs.	
			Hutting party under Lt C. HOLMES working on erecting huts for men.	
	- 20	0900	PT. Coys inspected by Commanding Officer	JCl
	- 21	0900	PT. Coys at disposal of Coy Cmdrs.	
	- 22	1000	Divine services all denominations	
		1400	Sports	
	- 23	0900	PT. Coys at disposal of Coy Cmdrs. NCO's + guards under RSM	
			Hutting parties completing arrangements for Xmas	

D. D. & L., London, E.C.
(A10266) Wt W5300/P713 750,000 2/18 Sch. 52 Forms/C2118/16

Instructions regarding War Diaries and Intelligence Summaries are contained in F. S. Regs., Part II. and the Staff Manual respectively. Title pages will be prepared in manuscript.

WAR DIARY
DECEMBER 1918
or
INTELLIGENCE SUMMARY.
(Erase heading not required.)

Army Form C. 2118.

SHEET 31

Place	Date	Hour	Summary of Events and Information	Remarks and references to Appendices
MERELESSART	Dec 24	0900	PT. Coys at disposal of Coy Commanders	
CITERNE			C Coy moved into huts in MERELESSART	
			Erection of extra huts completed for Xmas	JCI
	-25	10.00	Voluntary Services. Christmas Dinners under Coy arrangements. Good seating accommodation was provided which enabled all the men of a Coy to dine together. Rations were supplemented by Regimental purchases & by gifts of plum puddings from the 3rd (Res) Battalion of the Regiment at home.	
			The new recreation hut was open & there was a concert in the evening.	
	-26	0900	PT. Coys at disposal of Coy Cmdrs.	JCI
		1400	Sports. The weather has been persistently bad wet, & the grounds have been far too bad for games. Sports organised for New Years Day had to be cancelled.	
	-27	0900	PT. Coys at disposal of Coy Cmdrs.	
	-28	1045	Battn Route march.	
		1400	Sports	
	-29	1000	Divine Service All denominations. Sports	JCI
	-30	0900	PT. Coys under Coy Cmdrs.	
			First lot of Demobilizers & Pivotal men sent away. JCR.	
	-31	1030	Lecture to Bn by Major Monkton Div Education Officer "Place of History in Education"	
		1300	Baths at FORCEVILLE allotted to B & C Coy	

D. D. & L., London, E.C.
(A10266) Wt W5300/P713 750,000 2/18 Sch. 52 Forms/C2118/16

Instructions regarding War Diaries and Intelligence Summaries are contained in F. S. Regs., Part II. and the Staff Manual respectively. Title pages will be prepared in manuscript.

WAR DIARY

DECEMBER or 1918

~~INTELLIGENCE SUMMARY.~~

(Erase heading not required.)

Army Form C. 2118.

SHEET 5

Place	Date	Hour	Summary of Events and Information	Remarks and references to Appendices
			Officers quitting during the month	
	Dec 4		LT-COL W. GIBSON DSO M.C. to England on Course	[illegible]
			Officers joining during the month	
	Dec 4		LT-COL E. JAMES DSO MC from York & Lancs R Pioneer Battn 17 Div	
	Dec 4		LT. A.H. PHILLIPS rejoined from hospital	
	Dec 4		2/LT H. WAINWRIGHT rejoined from England	[illegible]
	Dec 14		Capt A.N.L. CLARK rejoined from	
	Dec 14		2/LT H.A. MILES rejoined from hospital	
	Dec 30		Major C.E. WAITE rejoined from Senior Officers Course ALDERSHOT	
			Military awards during the month	[illegible]
	Dec 1		Military Cross 2/LT. J. CHALMERS-PARK 2/LT. A.J. LONG	

C. Waite Major

Commanding 10th (S) Bn. "P.W.O." The West Yorkshire Regt.

D. D. & L., London, E.C.
(A10266) Wt W5300/P713 750,000 2/18 Sch. 52 Forms/C2118/16

17

Army Form C. 2118.

Instructions regarding War Diaries and Intelligence Summaries are contained in F. S. Regs., Part II. and the Staff Manual respectively. Title pages will be prepared in manuscript.

10th (S) Battalion P.W.O. "The West Yorkshire Regt"

WAR DIARY
January 1919
~~INTELLIGENCE SUMMARY.~~

(Erase heading not required.)

SHEET 1

Place	Date	Hour	Summary of Events and Information	Remarks and references to Appendices
	1919			
MERELESSART and CITERNE	JAN 1st		New Years Day. General holiday throughout the Division.	
BHQ at MERELESSART (Sheet 1/100000)		0900 1100	Baths at FORCEVILLE allotted to the battalion.	
		1400	Sports Inter-platoon Football Matches.	
	2nd	11.00	Lecture to the battn at CITERNE by Colonel E M BIRCH DSO Chief of Staff 17th Divn subject "The Achievements of the British Empire during the War"	
"		14.00	Football	
"	3rd	0900	Physical Training	
		11.00	Lecture to the Battn at CITERNE by Capt MONKTON Div Education Officer on "Citizenship"	
		14.00	Football.	
			~~[illegible]~~ Lt Col E JAMES DSO left the battalion to assume command of the 7th Bn Lincs Regt Major C E Waite assumed command of the battalion	
			Authority given for the Regimental censorship of letters to cease.	
			2 OR left the battalion for demobilization.	
	4	0900	Physical Training	
		10.00	Inspection of Billets at MERELESSART by commanding officer	
		14.00	Sports	

D. D. & L., London, E.C. (A7883) Wt. W6o7/M1672 350,000 1/17 Sch. 52a Forms/C2118/14

Army Form C. 2118.

Instructions regarding War Diaries and Intelligence Summaries are contained in F. S. Regs., Part II. and the Staff Manual respectively. Title pages will be prepared in manuscript.

10th (S) Battn PWO The West Yorkshire Regt

WAR DIARY

January 1919

or INTELLIGENCE SUMMARY.

(Erase heading not required.)

SHEET 2

Place	Date	Hour	Summary of Events and Information	Remarks and references to Appendices
MERZLESSART	1919			
CITERNE	JAN 4 (cnd)		Divnl Commander authorises Lieut (SR) PH. HART MC to wear badges of rank of Captain whilst commanding a company	[initials]
	5	09.00	Divine Services	[initials]
		14.00	Football	
	6	09.30	Physical Training Coys under Coy Cmdrs. Inspection of billets at CITERNE by Commanding Officer	[initials]
		14.00	Sports.	
	7	09.00	Physical Training	[initials]
		11.00	Lecture to the battn at CITERNE by Major WARNER 7th YORK + LANCASTER REGT subject 'a course of the War'	
			Baths at FORCEVILLE allotted to the battn all day	
		14.00	Football	
	8	09.00	Baths at FORCEVILLE allotted to Battn. Coys at disposal of Coy Commanders	[initials]
		14.00	Football	
			Div. Cmdr authorises Capt ANL CLARK to wear badge of rank of Major whilst acting as 2nd in command	

D. D. & L., London, E.C. (A7883) Wt. W603/M1672 350,000 4/17 Sch. 52a Forms C/2118/14

Army Form C. 2118.

Instructions regarding War Diaries and Intelligence Summaries are contained in F. S. Regs., Part II. and the Staff Manual respectively. Title pages will be prepared in manuscript.

18th (S) Battn PWO The West Yorkshire Regt
WAR DIARY or ~~INTELLIGENCE SUMMARY~~.
JANUARY 1919

(Erase heading not required.)

SHEET 3

Place	Date	Hour	Summary of Events and Information	Remarks and references to Appendices
MERELESSART		09.00		
CITERNE	JAN 9	11.00	Coys at disposal of Coy Cmdrs. Coys paid under Coy arrangements.	[initials]
	10	11.00	Lecture to the whole battalion on CITIZENSHIP by Capt W MONKTON	
		14.00	Football.	[initials]
			2/Lt F KELLEY + 41 OR left the battalion for Demobilization. Daily rate of	
			demobilization increased to 17,000 per diem.	
			Authority (Army Order 20 of 1919) given for 1914-15 medal to be worn by all ranks	[initials]
			entitled to wear it	
	11	0900	P.T. Coys at disposal of Coy Cmdrs	[initials]
		14.00	Football	
	12	0900	Divine Service	
		1400	Football	[initials]
			SRO 6003 authorizes NCOs + men when in mourning to wear band of black material	
			3¼" wide round left arm above the elbow	
	13	0900	P.T. Coy Drill.	
		14.00	~~Lecture [illegible] by Capt FLETCHER~~ Football	[initials]

D. D. & L., London, E.C. (A7833) Wt. W5o/M1672 350,000 4/17 Sch. 52a Forms C/2118/14

Army Form C. 2118.

Instructions regarding War Diaries and Intelligence Summaries are contained in F. S. Regs., Part II. and the Staff Manual respectively. Title pages will be prepared in manuscript.

10th (S) Battn The West Yorkshire Regt

WAR DIARY or INTELLIGENCE SUMMARY.

JANUARY 1919

(Erase heading not required.)

SHEET 4

Place	Date	Hour	Summary of Events and Information	Remarks and references to Appendices
MERELESSART – CITERNE	1919 JAN 14	10.15	Battalion Parade Battn drill ceremonial &c	JCL
		14.00	Football	
			Iron rations withdrawn from all ranks	
	15	10.30	~~Brigade~~ Battalion practice ceremonial parade	JCL
		14.00	Football	
	16	10.30	Brigade practice ceremonial parade	
		14.00	Football	JCL
	17	09.45	Battalion ceremonial drill	
		14.00	Football	JCL
	18	11.00	Brigade paraded on field adjoining the MERELESSART – CITERNE RD (Ref Hallencourt Special Sheet 1/40,000 F25 c2) for presentation of colours by Major-Gen P.R. ROBERTSON CB CMG Cmdg 17th Divn. The colours were consecrated by the Senior Chaplain of the Divn & presented to each battalion in turn by the G.O.C 17th Divn. Major ANL CLARK (2nd-in-Cmd) received the colours for the battalion & handed them to the senior subaltern Lt STE HALL. The Brigade marched passed the G.O.C in column & then formed up again in square when medal ribbons were presented to NCO's & men of the brigade	JCL

D. D. & L., London, E.C. (A7883) Wt. W593/M1672 350,000 4/17 Sch. 52a Forms C/2118/14

10th (S) Battn P.W.O. "The West Yorkshire Regt"

Instructions regarding War Diaries and Intelligence Summaries are contained in F. S. Regs., Part II, and the Staff Manual respectively. Title pages will be prepared in manuscript.

WAR DIARY or INTELLIGENCE SUMMARY.

JANUARY 1919

(Erase heading not required.)

Army Form C. 2118.

SHEET 5

Place	Date	Hour	Summary of Events and Information	Remarks and references to Appendices
MERELESSART + CITERNE	1919 JAN 18	contd	Battalions then marched passed (in close column of Coys) the colours. The battalion then marched back with the colours. A Coy escorted the colours which were placed in BHQ mess	
		14.30	Football match against the Australians	JCL
			LT C HOLMES 2/LT E INGHAM and 25 OR left the battn for demobilization	
			LT-COL W GIBSON DSO MC rejoined from School of Tactics Camberley & assumed cmd of the battn T/2LT J.CHALMERS-PARK to be T/Lieut (authority London Gazette 14/12/18)	
	19	11.00	Divine services	
MERELESSART		13.30	B Coy moved into billets in MERELESSART	JCL
	20	09.00	Baths at FORCEVILLE allotted to Battn.	
		14.00	Football	JCL
	21	10.30	Lecture to the battn by Major MUNDY subject "Colonisation from a practical point of view"	
		14.00	Football	JCL
	22	09.00	Physical Training Coy drill	
		14.00	Football	
			Civilian Advisory Board formed at Third Army HQ to assist officers & OR in choice of profession or occupation in civil life	JCL
			No 13069 Sgt LUND J W Transport Sgt awarded MSM	

D. D. & L., London, E.C. (A7893) Wt. W593/M1672 350,000 1/17 Sch. 52a Forms/C2118/14

10th (S) Battn P.W.O. The West Yorkshire Regt

Army Form C. 2118.

Instructions regarding War Diaries and Intelligence Summaries are contained in F. S. Regs., Part II. and the Staff Manual respectively. Title pages will be prepared in manuscript.

WAR DIARY or INTELLIGENCE SUMMARY.

JANUARY 1919

(Erase heading not required.)

SHEET 6

Place	Date	Hour	Summary of Events and Information	Remarks and references to Appendices
	1919			
MERELESSART	JAN 23	0930	Battn Route March	
		14.00	Football	[signature]
			Battalion cadre fixed. Photograph of all officers of the battn taken at MERELESSART	Bde A1017 31-12-18 [initials]
	24	0900	P.T. Coys at disposal of Coy Cmdrs	
		14.00	Football	[signature]
			LT A H PHILLIPS 2/LT H. APPLEYARD 2/LT H W RAMSDEN + 27 OR left battn for demobilization	
	25	0930	Battn Route March	
		10.00	Civilian Advisory Committee met at Bde HQ YONVILLE to interview officers	
		14.00	Football	[signature]
	26	10.00	Divine Service	
		14.00	Football	[signature]
			Lieut CR INGHAM + 19 OR left battn for demobilization	
			Inquiry bureau established in Recreation hut under supervision of Demobilization Officer to keep all ranks informed of the progress of demobilization + to give advice + assist individual cases.	

D. D. & L., London, E.C. (A7893) Wt. W803/M1672 350,000 1/17 Sch. 52a Forms/C/2118/14

10th (S) Bn Prince of Wales Own The West Yorkshire Regt

WAR DIARY or INTELLIGENCE SUMMARY.

JANUARY 1919

(Erase heading not required.)

Army Form C. 2118.

Instructions regarding War Diaries and Intelligence Summaries are contained in F. S. Regs., Part II. and the Staff Manual respectively. Title pages will be prepared in manuscript.

SHEET 7

Place	Date	Hour	Summary of Events and Information	Remarks and references to Appendices
	1919			
MERELESSART	JAN 27	0900	PT. Practice on Rifle range	
		14.00	Football	
	28	0900	PT. Close order drill	
		14.30	Bde boxing competition	
	29	0900	PT. Close order drill	
		14.00	Sports	
	30	0900	PT. Close order drill Coys paid out.	
		14.00	Football	
	31	0900	PT. Close order drill	
		14.00	Football	
			Capt + Adjt A T BROWN MC LT CARGILE +26 OR left Battn for demobilisation	

D. D. & L., London, E.C.
(A7883) Wt. W203/M1672 350,000 3/17 Sch. 52a Forms/C/2118/14

Army Form C. 2118.

Instructions regarding War Diaries and Intelligence Summaries are contained in F. S. Regs., Part II, and the Staff Manual respectively. Title pages will be prepared in manuscript.

10th (S) Battn P.W.O. West Yorkshire Regt

WAR DIARY
JANUARY 1919
or
INTELLIGENCE SUMMARY.

(Erase heading not required.)

SHEET 8

Place	Date	Hour	Summary of Events and Information	Remarks and references to Appendices
MERELESSART	1919		Officers quitting the battn during the month.	
	JAN 3		LT-COL E JAMES DSO MC to 7th Bn Lincs R.	
	10		2/LT. F.C KELLY to England for Demobilization	
	17		LT C. HOLMES " " " "	
			2/LT E. INGHAM " " " "	
	24		LT. A.H. PHILLIPS " " " "	
			2/LT. H APPLEYARD " " " "	
			2/LT H.W. RAMSDEN " " " "	
	31		CAPT + ADJT A.T BROWN MC " " " "	
			LT. C ARGILE " " " "	
	26		LT. C.R. INGHAM " " " "	
			Officers joining during the month	
	" 18		LT. COL W. GIBSON DSO MC rejoined from course.	
			Awards during the month:	
	" 22		13069 Sgt LUND J.W awarded MSM.	
			The following left the battn during the month for Demobilization	
			9 Officers 140 O.R.	
			H. Gibson Lieut-Colonel	
			Cmdg. 10th (S) Battn PWO (The West Yorkshire Regt)	

D. D. & L., London, E.C. (A7853) Wt. W593/M1672 350,000 1/17 Sch. 52a Forms/C/2118/14

Instructions regarding War Diaries and Intelligence Summaries are contained in F. S. Regs., Part II, and the Staff Manual respectively. Title pages will be prepared in manuscript.

The Prince of Wales Own West Yorkshire Regiment 10

WAR DIARY or INTELLIGENCE SUMMARY.

February 1919

(Erase heading not required.)

Army Form C. 2118.

SHEET 1.

Vol 38

Place	Date	Hour	Summary of Events and Information	Remarks and references to Appendices
	1919			
MERELESSART.				
	Feb. 1st	09.00 to 12.00	Physical Training. Companies at disposal of Company Commanders.	
		14.00	Sports.	
	– 2nd	11.30	Divine Services.	
		14.00	Sports.	
			LT. P. H. HART. appointed Adjt with rank of A/Capt. and pay and allowances of Lieut	
			CAPT. W. D. LANE and 19 O.R. left the battalion for demobilization	
			2/LT J. D. DAWSON. assumes command of "D" Company.	
	– 3rd.	09.00	Physical Training. Close Order Drill.	
			Kits of new draft inspected by Company Commanders.	
		14.00	Sports.	
	– 4th.	09.00	Physical Training Close Order Drill. Musketry	
		14.00	Sports.	
	– 5th.	09.00	Physical Training Close Order Drill.	
			Owing to decrease in numbers of Officers and N. C. Os. due to demobilization	
			Companys will work together as follows. – "A" + "C" and "B" + "D"	

D. D. & L., London, E.C. (A7883) Wt. W109/M1672 550,000 4/17 Sch. 52a Forms C/2118/14

39E 7 sheets

Instructions regarding War Diaries and Intelligence Summaries are contained in F. S. Regs., Part II. and the Staff Manual respectively. Title pages will be prepared in manuscript.

The Prince of Wales Own West Yorkshire Regiment

WAR DIARY

February 1919

~~INTELLIGENCE SUMMARY.~~

(Erase heading not required.)

Army Form C. 2118.

SHEET 2.

Place	Date	Hour	Summary of Events and Information	Remarks and references to Appendices
	1919.			
MERELESSART				
	Feb 5th	14:00	Sports.	
	– 6th	09:00	Companies inspected by Commanding Officer.	
		14:00	Recreation 14. O.R. left the battalion for demobilization	
	– 7th	09:00	Special programme of training arranged for all ranks liable for service in the Armies of Occupation as follows –: Lewis Gun classes arranged by Company Commanders: Signalling classes arranged by Signalling Officer: Physical Training for all ranks daily	
			2/LT J. H. GIBSON and 2/LT G. KINDER with 23. O.R. left the battalion for demobilization	
		14:00.	Sports.	
	– 8th	0900	Classes of instruction as arranged under their respective instructors. Those not actually attending classes of instruction at work on salvage in battalion billeting area.	
			14 O.R. left the battalion for demobilization	
		14:00.	Sports.	

D. D. & L., London, E.C. (A7883) Wt. W603/M1672 350,000 4/17 Sch. 52a Forms/C/2118/14

Instructions regarding War Diaries and Intelligence Summaries are contained in F. S. Regs., Part II. and the Staff Manual respectively. Title pages will be prepared in manuscript.

The Prince of Wales Own West Yorkshire Regiment.

WAR DIARY
February ~~or~~ 1919.
~~INTELLIGENCE SUMMARY.~~
(Erase heading not required.)

Army Form C. 2118.

SHEET 3.

Place	Date	Hour	Summary of Events and Information	Remarks and references to Appendices
	1919			
MERELESSART.				
	Feb. 9th	10.00.	Divine Services	
		14.00	Sports	
			12 O.R. left battalion for demobilization	
	-10th	09.00.	Classes of instruction under specialist instructors.	
			Battalion to find guards for supply trains. A and C Companies to detail 1 Officer. 16 N.C.Os and 64 men with full equipment + ammunition for the guard.	
		14.00	Recreation.	
	-11th	09.00.	Classes of instruction under specialist instructors	
		14.00	Sports.	
	-12th	09.00	Classes of instruction under specialist instructors	
		14.00	Sports.	
			19 O.R. left the battalion for demobilization	
	-13th	09.00.	Classes of instruction under specialist instructors	
		14.00	Sports. 11. O.R. left battalion for demobilization	

D. D. & L., London, E.C. (A7883) Wt. W2o3/M1672 350,000 4/17 Sch. 52a Forms C/2118/14

The Prince of Wales Own West Yorkshire Regiment

Army Form C. 2118.

Instructions regarding War Diaries and Intelligence Summaries are contained in F. S. Regs., Part II, and the Staff Manual respectively. Title pages will be prepared in manuscript.

WAR DIARY
February ~~or~~ 1919.
~~INTELLIGENCE~~ SUMMARY.
(Erase heading not required.)

SHEET 4.

Place	Date	Hour	Summary of Events and Information	Remarks and references to Appendices
	1919			
MERELESSART.				
	Feb. 14th.	09.00.	Classes of instruction as usual.	
		14.00	Sports.	
			Battalion detailed to find guards for supply trains. "B" and "D" Companies finding guards.	
			MAJOR. C.E. WAITE and 14 O.R. left battalion for demobilization	
	– 15th.	09.00.	Usual classes of instruction	[illegible]
		14.00	Sports.	
			17 O.R. left the battalion for demobilization	
	– 16th.	10.00.	Divine Services.	
		14.00.	Sports.	
	– 17th.	09.00.	Classes of instruction as arranged.	
		14.00	Sports.	
			Return of private telescopes & field glasses lent under Lord Roberts scheme, called for.	
			2/Lt. N. R. CASSON rejoined battalion from 50th L.T.M.B.	

D. D. & L., London, E.C.
(A7883) Wt. W803/M1672 350,000 2/17 Sch. 52a Forms C/2118/14

Army Form C. 2118.

Instructions regarding War Diaries and Intelligence Summaries are contained in F. S. Regs., Part II, and the Staff Manual respectively. Title pages will be prepared in manuscript.

The Prince of Wales Own West Yorkshire Regiment.

WAR DIARY or ~~INTELLIGENCE~~ SUMMARY.

February 1919.

(Erase heading not required.)

SHEET 5.

Place	Date	Hour	Summary of Events and Information	Remarks and references to Appendices
	1919			
MERELESSART.	Feb. 18th	09.00 – 12.00	Baths at FORCEVILLE allotted to battalion.	
			A and C Companies detailed to find guards for supply trains	
		14.00	Sports.	
	– 19th	09.00.	Classes of instruction as usual.	
		14.00	Sports	
	– 20th	09.00	Classes of instruction as usual.	
		14.00	Sports	
			Companies paid out.	
			Divisional Advisory Board met at Battalion H.Q to advise Officers and O.R. as to future employment. 34 O.R. left battalion for demobilization	
	– 21st	09.00 – 12.00.	Baths at FORCEVILLE allotted to battalion	
		14.00	Sports.	
			4 O.R. left battalion for demobilization	
	– 22nd	09.00	Classes of instruction as usual	
		14.00	Sports	
	– 23rd	10.00	Divine Services.	

D. D. & L., London, E.C. (A7883) Wt. W807/M1672 350,000 2/17 Sch. 52a Forms/C.2118/14

Instructions regarding War Diaries and Intelligence Summaries are contained in F. S. Regs., Part II. and the Staff Manual respectively. Title pages will be prepared in manuscript.

The Prince of Wales Own West Yorkshire Regiment.

WAR DIARY or INTELLIGENCE SUMMARY.

February 1919

(Erase heading not required.)

Army Form C. 2118.

SHEET 6

Place	Date	Hour	Summary of Events and Information	Remarks and references to Appendices
MERELESSART.	1919 Feb. 23rd	14:00	Sports	
	-24th	09:00	Kit inspection of all ranks under Company arrangements	
		14:00	Sports	
			Divisional Race Meeting held on the racecourse W of HANGEST (DIEPPE 1/100,000)	
	-25th	09:00	Classes of instruction as usual	
		14:00	Sports. Second day of Divisional Race Meeting.	
			In future the use of the phrase "In the field" will be discontinued in all official documents & the actual name of the place inserted instead.	[initials]
	-26th	09:00	P.T. & classes of instruction	
		11:00.	Lecture by G.O.C. 50th Infantry Brigade Subject :- "Causes of the War"	
		14:00	Sports.	
			2/LT J.A. HEDLEY & 12 O.R left battalion for demobilization	
	-27th	09:00.	Courses of instruction as usual.	
		14:00	Sports. No 13069 SGT. J. LUND awarded M.S.M. (Supp. to London Gazette 17.1.19)	
	-28th	09:00 to 15:00	Musketry practice for battalion at rifle range at ERUCOURT	

D. D. & L., London, E.C. (A7883) Wt. W593/M1672 350,000 4/17 Sch. 52a Forms C/2118/14

The Prince of Wales Own West Yorkshire Regiment

Army Form C. 2118.

Instructions regarding War Diaries and Intelligence Summaries are contained in F. S. Regs., Part II. and the Staff Manual respectively. Title pages will be prepared in manuscript.

WAR DIARY
February ~~or~~ 1919
INTELLIGENCE SUMMARY.
(*Erase heading not required.*)

SHEET 7

Place	Date	Hour	Summary of Events and Information	Remarks and references to Appendices
MERELESSART	1919		Officers quitting the battalion during the month.	
	Feb. 2nd		LT a/CAPT W.D. LANE — To England for demobilization	
	– 9th		2/LT. J.K. GIBSON — " " "	
			2/LT. G. KINDER — " " "	
	– 14th		MAJOR. C.E. WAITE. — " " "	
	– 26th		2/LT. J.A. HEDLEY. — " " "	
			Officers joining the battalion during the month.	
	– 17th		2/LT. N. R. CASSON — Rejoined from 50th L.T.M.B.	
			The following left the battalion for demobilization during the month	
			5 Officers and 193 OR	
			W. Gibson Lieut Col	

D. D. & L., London, E.C.
(A10266) Wt W3300/P713 750,000 2/18 Sch. 52 Forms/C2118/16

10th (S) Battn. IWO The West Yorkshire Regt

Instructions regarding War Diaries and Intelligence Summaries are contained in F. S. Regs., Part II. and the Staff Manual respectively. Title pages will be prepared in manuscript.

WAR DIARY
March 1st 1919
~~or~~ INTELLIGENCE SUMMARY.
(*Erase heading not required.*)

Army Form C. 2118.

SHEET 1

Vol 39

Place	Date	Hour	Summary of Events and Information	Remarks and references to Appendices
MERÉLESSART [illegible]	MARCH 1	0900	Coys under Coy Commanders. Reorganising of Platoons on a two platoon basis	
		1400	Sports	
	2	1000	Divine Service	
		1400	Sports	
	3	0900	Coys training as per programme. Range at FRUCOURT allotted to Battn.	
		1400	Sports	
	4	0900	Coys under Coy Cmdrs. Musketry & Arms Drill	
		1400	Sports	
	5	0900	Platoon training under Coy Cmdrs PT Musketry & Arms Drill	
		1400	Sports	
	6	0900	Coys under Coy Cmdrs. Coys Paid out	
		1400	Sports	
			LT-Col W Gibson DSO MC admitted to 46th CCS PONT REMY. Capt C ARCHER MC assumes command of battalion	
	7	0900	Coys under Coy Cmdrs Musketry. Range at FRUCOURT allotted to Battn.	
		1400	Sports	

D. D. & L., London, E.C. (A7883) Wt. W593/M1672 350,000 4/17 Sch. 52a Forms C/2118/14

410 E.

10th (S) Battn PWO (The West Yorkshire Regt)

WAR DIARY ~~or~~ INTELLIGENCE SUMMARY.

March 1919

(Erase heading not required.)

Army Form C. 2118.

SHEET 2

Instructions regarding War Diaries and Intelligence Summaries are contained in F. S. Regs., Part II. and the Staff Manual respectively. Title pages will be prepared in manuscript.

Place	Date	Hour	Summary of Events and Information	Remarks and references to Appendices
Méricourt	MARCH 8	0900	PT Coy drill & Arms drill	
		1400	Sports	
	9	1000	Divine Services	
		1400	Sports	
	10	0900	PT. Coys at disposal of Coy Cmdrs Kit inspection under Coy arrangements	
		1400	Sports	
	11	0900	Battalion detailed to furnish Train Guards for Supply Trains	
			Remainder of Coys under Coy Commanders	
		1400	Sports	
	12	0900	PT Platoon drill for those not on Train Guard	
		1400	Sports	
			4 OR left Battn for demobilization	
	13	0900	PT Arms drill &c. Coys paid out	
		1400	Sports	
	14	0900	Range at FRUCOURT allotted to Battalion	
		1400	Sports	

D. D. & L., London, E.C. (A.8851) Wt. W803/M1672 350,000 4/17 Sch. 52a Forms C.2118/14

Instructions regarding War Diaries and Intelligence Summaries are contained in F. S. Regs., Part II. and the Staff Manual respectively. Title pages will be prepared in manuscript.

10th (S) Battn PWO. The West Yorkshire Regt

WAR DIARY or INTELLIGENCE SUMMARY.

March 1919

(Erase heading not required.)

Army Form C. 2118.

SHEET 3

Place	Date	Hour	Summary of Events and Information	Remarks and references to Appendices
	MAR			
MERELESSART	15	0900	P.T. Coys under Coy Commanders.	
			Sports	
			2 OR left Battn for demobilization	
			Major ANL CLARK rejoined Battn from V Corps Concentration Camp & assumes command of the Battn	
	16	1000	Divine Service	
		1400	Sports	
	17	0900	P.T. Coys at disposal of Coy Commanders. Battn detailed to furnish Supply Train Guard	
		1400	Sports	
	18	0900	Coys under Coy Commanders	
		1400	Sports	
			5 OR left Battn for demobilization	
			Lt-Col W GIBSON DSO MC rejoined from hospital + assumes command of the Battn.	
	19	0900	Coys at disposal of Coy Commanders.	
		1400	Sports	
	20	0900	Battn detailed to furnish Supply Train Guards	
		1400	Sports	

D. D. & L., London, E.C. (A7883) Wt. W503/M1672 350,000 1/17 Sch. 52a Forms C/2118/14

Instructions regarding War Diaries and Intelligence Summaries are contained in F. S. Regs., Part II. and the Staff Manual respectively. Title pages will be prepared in manuscript.

Army Form C. 2118.

10th (S) Battn P.W.O. – The West Yorkshire Regt

WAR DIARY
or
~~INTELLIGENCE SUMMARY.~~

March 1919

(Erase heading not required.)

SHEET 4

Place	Date	Hour	Summary of Events and Information	Remarks and references to Appendices
	March			
MÉRÉLESSART	21	0900	P.T. Close order + Arms drill. Inspection by Coy Commanders	
		1400	Sports	
			2/LT H.A. MILES left battn for duty under Director Graves Registration MEAULTE	
	22	0900	P.T. Close order + Arms drill. Guard mounting.	
		1400	Sports	
	23	1000	~~Divine Service~~	
		~~1400~~	~~Sports~~	
			Authority given for Officers + OR to retain maps not marked SECRET if desired for sentimental reasons	
	24	0900	Baths at FORCEVILLE allotted to Battn. Kit Inspection under Coy arrangements	
		1400	Sports. Brig-Gen J.F. HOPE DSO left Brigade to join the Army of Occupation in command of Bde. Leave + demobilization suspended owing to threatened strikes in England	
	25	0900	P.T. Close order + Arms drill + Guard mounting	
		1400	Sports	
	26	0930	Battn route march	
		1400	Sports	

D. D. & L., London, E.C. (A7883) Wt. W593/M1672 350,000 4/17 Sch. 52a Forms/C2118/14

Instructions regarding War Diaries and Intelligence Summaries are contained in F. S. Regs., Part II. and the Staff Manual respectively. Title pages will be prepared in manuscript.

10th (S) Battn PWO The West Yorkshire Regt

Army Form C. 2118.

WAR DIARY or ~~INTELLIGENCE SUMMARY.~~

(Erase heading not required.)

March 1919

Sheet 5

Place	Date	Hour	Summary of Events and Information	Remarks and references to Appendices
MERELESSART	March			
	27	0830	PT Close order & Arms drill & Guard mounting	
		14.00	Sports	
	28		Battn received orders to move to HANGEST on the 29th inst.	
		0830	PT Close order & Arms drill	
		14.00	Sports	
	29th	0900	The Battalion left MERELESSART and proceeded by march route to HANGEST	
			(Amiens 17 1/100,000) via AIRAINES and SOUES.	
HANGEST		1310	Battalion arrived in HANGEST & settled in billets	
(Amiens 17)			Major ANC Clark remained in MERELESSART to settle civilian claims.	
1/100,000			Considerable trouble was experienced by excessive claims made by	
			civilians for damage. ~~[illegible]~~	
			Battalion organised as one company under Capt JP LAWSON MC.	
	30		Morning devoted to cleaning up of arms & equipment	
		14.00	Sports	
	31	0830	PT Inspection of Arms & equipment under Coy arrangements.	
		14.00	Sports	

D. D. & L. London, E.C. (A7833) Wt. W803/M1672 350,000 4/17 Sch. 52a Forms C/2118/14

10th (S) Batn PWO The West Yorkshire Regt.

Instructions regarding War Diaries and Intelligence Summaries are contained in F. S. Regs., Part II. and the Staff Manual respectively. Title pages will be prepared in manuscript.

WAR DIARY or ~~INTELLIGENCE SUMMARY.~~

March 1919

(Erase heading not required.)

Army Form C. 2118.

SHEET 6

Place	Date	Hour	Summary of Events and Information	Remarks and references to Appendices
	March			
			Officers quitting the battalion during the month	
	4		2/LT NR CASSON to hospital injured	
	6		LT-COL W GIBSON DSO MC to hospital sick	
	22		2/LT MILES to DRGR MEAULTE for duty	
			Officers joining during the month.	
	16		MAJOR ANL CLARK rejoined from V Corps Concentration Camp	
	18		LT-COL W GIBSON DSO MC rejoined from hospital	
	31		Honours & awards	
			Roumanian MEDAILLE BARBATIE SI CREDENTI	
			No 43231 Pte BARRAS T C Coy	
			DEMOBILIZATION	
			11 OR left Battn for demobilization.	
			W. Gibson. Lt Col	
Hangest 1-4-19			Comdg 10th (S) Batn PWO The West Yorkshire Regt	

D. D. & L., London, E.C. (A7853) Wt. W593/M1672 350,000 4/17 Sch. 52a Forms/C2118/14

Instructions regarding War Diaries and Intelligence Summaries are contained in F. S. Regs., Part II. and the Staff Manual respectively. Title pages will be prepared in manuscript.

Army Form C. 2118.

2 10th (S.) Bn. WEST YORKSHIRE REGIMENT

WAR DIARY or INTELLIGENCE SUMMARY.

April 1919

(Erase heading not required.)

Place	Date	Hour	Summary of Events and Information	Remarks and references to Appendices
HANGEST-SUR-SOMME (AMIENS 18).	April 1st		The Battalion was selected to send 1 Officer & 50 other ranks for duty in connection with PEACE Conference in PARIS.	
		09.30	Commanding Officer held an inspection of all other ranks eligible for the Army of Occupation & selected 60 to undergo training for this work. 2/Lt A. WATSON was selected for this duty.	
		14.00	Sports.	
			Extract from London Gazette "T/Major (A/Lt Col) W. GIBSON DSO M.C. to command 10th Battn West Yorkshire Regt and to be T/Lt Col (Dec 29/18) seniority 28th August 1918	
	2nd	09.00	Special Programme of training for Paris Party under 2/Lt Watson & the R.S.M.	
			Remainder P.T. & Route March.	
		14.00	Sports	
			Audit Board Audited Regimental Accounts.	
	3rd	09.00	Paris Party special programme of training	
			Remainder Physical Training, Arms, Saluting, Platoon Drill.	

A5834 Wt. W4973/M687 750,000 8/16 D. D. & L. Ltd. Forms/C.2118/13

10th (S) Batn West Yorkshire Regt

April 1919

Army Form C. 2118.

WAR DIARY
or
~~INTELLIGENCE SUMMARY.~~

(Erase heading not required.)

Instructions regarding War Diaries and Intelligence Summaries are contained in F. S. Regs., Part II. and the Staff Manual respectively. Title pages will be prepared in manuscript.

Place	Date	Hour	Summary of Events and Information	Remarks and references to Appendices
HANGEST	April 3rd	14.00	Sports.	
	4th	09.00	Baths at HANGEST allotted to Battalion.	
			Kit Inspection held A F 3321 completed for all ranks.	
	5th	09.00	Physical Training Arms Saluting & Platoon Drill.	
			Guard Party Special programme	
		14.00	Sports	
			Capt C ARCHER MC & 16 O Rs left Battn for demobilisation	
	6th	10.00	Divine Service	
		14.00	Sports	
	7th	09.00	Physical Training Arms Saluting & Platoon Drill	
		14.00	Sports	
	8th	09.00	Special Training for Guard Party	
		14.00	Sports	
			Capt J P LAWSON MC 2/Lt J D DAWSON 2/Lt A J LONG MC & 80 other ranks left Battn for duty with No [illegible] Prisoner of War Company ETAPLES, Lt (a/Capt) H NEWTON Lt G NICOLLS 2/Lt E BARNES MC & 80 other ranks left Battn for duty with No 160 Prisoner of War Company ETAPLES, (CANNES)	P.H.N.

A5834 Wt. W4973/M687 750,000 8/16 D. D. & L. Ltd. Forms/C.2118/13.

10th (S) Batt. West Yorkshire Regt. April 1919

Instructions regarding War Diaries and Intelligence Summaries are contained in F. S. Regs., Part II. and the Staff Manual respectively. Title pages will be prepared in manuscript.

WAR DIARY
or
INTELLIGENCE SUMMARY.
(Erase heading not required.)

Army Form C. 2118.

Place	Date April	Hour	Summary of Events and Information	Remarks and references to Appendices
LANGEST	9th	09.00	[illegible] Training for Peace Duty	
		14.00	Sports	
	10th	09.00	Baths allotted to Battalion	
		14.00	Sports	
	11th	09.00	Training for Peace Duty	
		11.00	Sports	
	12th	09.00	Programme of Training for Peace Duty	
		11.00	Sports	
			T/CAPT A N L CLARK & 16 other ranks left for demobilisation	
	13th	04.45	T/Lt A WATSON & 50 other ranks left for duty with PEACE CONFERENCE at PARIS	
		11.00	Sports	
	14th	09.00	All available: other ranks [illegible] [illegible] T/Lt H WAINWRIGHT [illegible]	
		14.00	Sports	

[illegible signature]

A5834 Wt. W4973/M687 750,000 8/16 D. D. & L. Ltd. Forms/C.2118/13.

Instructions regarding War Diaries and Intelligence Summaries are contained in F. S. Regs., Part II. and the Staff Manual respectively. Title pages will be prepared in manuscript.

10th (S) Batt. West Yorkshire Regt.

WAR DIARY
or
~~INTELLIGENCE SUMMARY.~~

April 1919.

(Erase heading not required.)

Army Form C. 2118.

Place	Date	Hour	Summary of Events and Information	Remarks and references to Appendices
HANGEST	April 15th		Battalion now reduced to CADRE A plus 4 Officers 71 other ranks awaiting instructions for duty with Army of Occupation. Information received that the Cadre will leave on the 18th inst & proceed to CADRE PARK LONCPRE. W YORK R E YORK & Brigade H.Q Cadre to proceed to England together to CATTERICK	
	16th	09.00	Coys at disposal of Coy Commander	
		14.00	Sports	
	17th		Coys making necessary preparations for move	
			All surplus to Cadre reported to DORSET R for duty	
			Lt J C PARK M.C.	
			2/Lt H WAINWRIGHT	
			2/Lt S L WILSON	
			2/Lt G F WOODTHORPE + 66 other ranks	
			Battalion now reduced to Cadre A & ready to move to England	

A5834 Wt. W4973/M687 750,000 8/16 D. D. & L. Ltd. Forms/C.2118/13

10th (S) Battn North Yorkshire Regt
April 1919

Army Form C. 2118.

Instructions regarding War Diaries and Intelligence Summaries are contained in F. S. Regs., Part II. and the Staff Manual respectively. Title pages will be prepared in manuscript.

WAR DIARY
or
INTELLIGENCE SUMMARY.
(Erase heading not required.)

Place	Date	Hour	Summary of Events and Information	Remarks and references to Appendices
	April			
HANGEST	18th	08.30	Cadre left for LONGPRE	
LONGPRE		10.00	Loading vehicles on train	
		15.30	Train departs for LE HAVRE	
LE HAVRE	19th	10.30	Arrived LE HAVRE reporting to No 1 Reception Camp.	
	20th	09.00	Despatched to No 1. Despatch Camp.	
	21st		Waiting at No 1. Despatch Camp	
	22nd	06.00	Loading Party for Ship	
	"	14.00	Left No. 1. Despatch Camp for embarkation	
	"	15.00	Embarked on U.S.A Ship NOPATIN	PHN

H. Gibson. Lt Col.
Comdg 10th (S) Battn N. Yorkshire Regt

A5834 Wt. W4973/M687 750,000 8/16 D. D. & L. Ltd. Forms/C.2118/13

Army Form C. 2118.

Instructions regarding War Diaries and Intelligence Summaries are contained in F. S. Regs, Part II. and the Staff Manual respectively. Title pages will be prepared in manuscript.

WAR DIARY
or
INTELLIGENCE SUMMARY.

(*Erase heading not required.*)

Place	Date	Hour	Summary of Events and Information	Remarks and references to Appendices

A5834 Wt. W4973/M687 750,000 8/16 D. D. & L. Ltd. Forms/C.2118/13.

www.ingramcontent.com/pod-product-compliance
Lightning Source LLC
Chambersburg PA
CBHW080815010526
44111CB00015B/2563
* 9 7 8 1 4 7 4 5 2 3 5 3 0 *